NEW DIRECTIONS IN ARCHAEOLOGY

Editors

Richard Bradley
Reader in Archaeology, University of Reading

Timothy Earle
*Associate Professor of Anthropology, University of California,
Los Angeles*

Ian Hodder
Lecturer in Archaeology, University of Cambridge

Colin Renfrew
Disney Professor of Archaeology, University of Cambridge

Jeremy Sabloff
Professor of Anthropology, University of New Mexico

Andrew Sherratt
*Assistant Keeper, Department of Antiquities, Ashmolean
Museum, Oxford*

QUANTIFYING DIVERSITY
IN ARCHAEOLOGY

QUANTIFYING DIVERSITY IN ARCHAEOLOGY

EDITED BY ROBERT D. LEONARD and
GEORGE T. JONES

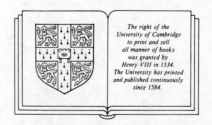

The right of the
University of Cambridge
to print and sell
all manner of books
was granted by
Henry VIII in 1534.
The University has printed
and published continuously
since 1584.

CAMBRIDGE UNIVERSITY PRESS

CAMBRIDGE

LONDON NEW YORK NEW ROCHELLE

MELBOURNE SYDNEY

Published by the Press Syndicate of the University of Cambridge
The Pitt Building, Trumpington Street, Cambridge CB2 1RP
32 East 57th Street, New York, NY 10022, USA
10 Stamford Road, Oakleigh, Melbourne 3166, Australia

First published 1989

Printed in Great Britain at the University Press, Cambridge

British Library cataloguing in publication data

Quantifying diversity in archaeology–
(New directions in archaeology).
1. Archaeology
I. Leonard, Robert D.   II. Jones, George T.
III. Series
930.1

Library of Congress cataloguing in publication data

Quantifying diversity in archaeology/edited by Robert D. Leonard and
George T. Jones
        p.   cm – (New directions in archaeology)
Bibliography.
Includes Index.
ISBN 0 521 35030 1
1. Archaeology – Methodology. 2. Material culture. I. Leonard.
Robert D. II. Jones, George Thomas. III. Series.
CC75.7.Q36 1989
930.1–dc19   88-12297   CIP

ISBN 0 521 35030 1

CONTENTS

CONTRIBUTORS

Bruce F. Ball, Archaeological Survey of Alberta, Edmonton, Alberta, Canada.

Charlotte Beck, Department of Anthropology, Hamilton College, Clinton, New York, U.S.A.

Peter T. Bobrowsky, Department of Geology, University of Alberta, Edmonton, Alberta, Canada.

Catherine M. Camerson, Department of Anthropology, University of Arizona, Tucson, Arizona, U.S.A.

Margaret W. Conkey, Department of Anthropology, University of California, Berkeley, California, U.S.A.

George L. Cowgill, Department of Anthropology, Brandeis University, Waltham, Massachusetts, U.S.A.

Robert C. Dunnell, Department of Anthropology, University of Washington, Seattle, Washington, U.S.A.

Donald K. Grayson, Department of Anthropology, University of Washington, Seattle, Washington, U.S.A.

George T. Jones, Department of Anthropology, Hamilton College, Clinton, New York, U.S.A.

Keith L. Kintigh, Department of Anthropology, Arizona State University, Tempe, Arizona, U.S.A.

Robert D. Leonard, Department of Anthropology, University of New Mexico, Albuquerque, New Mexico, U.S.A.

Prudence M. Rice, Department of Anthropology, University of Florida, Gainesville, Florida, U.S.A.

David Rindos, Department of Prehistory, Australian National University, Canberra, Australia.

Nan A. Rothschild, Barnard College, Columbia University, New York, New York, U.S.A.

Michael B. Schiffer, Department of Anthropology, University of Arizona, Tucson, Arizona, U.S.A.

Jan F. Simek, Department of Anthropology, University of Tennessee, Knoxville, Tennessee, U.S.A.

F.E. Smiley, Center for Archaeological Investigations, Southern Illinois University, Carbondale, Illinois, U.S.A.

David Hurst Thomas, Department of Anthropology, American Museum of Natural History, New York, New York, U.S.A.

PREFACE

The idea for this volume originated in the spring of 1983, in our discussions as to how most effectively to characterize archaeological variation and the statistical properties of archaeological assemblages. At that time, we were graduate students working on our dissertations in the Department of Anthropology at the University of Washington, Seattle. We had each amassed large data sets across which we wished to make valid statistical comparisons. Our training under Donald K. Grayson, whose research on faunal diversity is the basis for much current interest in this topic, had prepared us to be suspicious of straightforward comparisons of these data. At the same time, his work offered several directions that we thought could be profitably taken to make valid comparisons regarding assemblage diversity. In examining the contemporary archaeological literature we found that a number of archaeologists were beginning to show similar concerns regarding the valid measurement of archaeological diversity. Yet many other archaeologists had not yet given these issues full consideration. For this reason, and because no synthetic treatment was available, this volume was created to bring these issues to a broader audience of archaeologists.

We would like to thank Donald K. Grayson and Robert C. Dunnell for the encouragement they have offered throughout the history of this project. We would also like to acknowledge the past scholarly efforts of Donald K. Grayson in addressing the topic of archaeological diversity. The success of his efforts may be seen in that many, if not all, of the papers in this volume build on his research. Jeremy Sabloff and Timothy Earle, editors for the New Directions in Archaeology series, gave enthusiastic support for the volume, and its publication is due, in no small part, to their efforts. We thank Charlotte Beck, Margaret Conkey, and Trish Ruppe' for their timely advice and encouragement. Barbara Stark and Michael Jochim were kind enough to critique several papers in draft. We thank Peter Richards, Cambridge University Press, who expertly handled our inquiries and brought the volume to publication. We would also like to thank Margaret Deith of Cambridge University Press for her skillful copy editing. We are grateful to Thad Mantaro, Heidi Reed, and Jan Pieroni for bibliographic and editorial assistance. Finally, we acknowledge the authors who responded so well to our requests and the deadlines that we imposed upon them, and we thank them for their patience.

Robert D. Leonard
George T. Jones

The diversity concept

Chapter 1

The concept of diversity: an introduction

George T. Jones and Robert D. Leonard

The adoption of an evolutionary perspective on cultural change with an emphasis on empirical variability, its transmission and differential representation through time, marks a significant trend in modern archaeology (Dunnell 1980). It is quite common for archaeologists to examine how the archaeological record differs along gradients of various sorts, through time, for example, or across space. In this context, archaeologists devote considerable energy to describing and attempting to explain the patterns perceived. Virtually every model employed to achieve these ends has definite entailments for the distribution of artifacts among different classes on such gradients. This is the basic matter of diversity: how quantities of artifacts are distributed among classes.

While the adoption of an evolutionary perspective which focuses on variation and incorporates the concept of diversity in a rigorous manner is a relatively recent phenomenon, observations regarding variety, and thus diversity, have a long history. Indeed, such notions are fundamental, being basic to any discipline where phenomena are arrayed into a number of classes, and where those classes can have differing numbers of members. Of course, this is a common archaeological situation, and recognition of the great variety of material remains in archaeological settings was known in American archaeology well before the turn of the century. By 1919, the variety of material remains across the Americas was well enough characterized for W. H. Holmes (1919) to generalize about issues related to diversity, as regards a number of culture areas. Consider, for example, the following passages, beginning with a discussion of the Middle and Lower Mississippi Valley area (Holmes 1919: 107):

> As a result of the mineral riches of the area, the range of lithic artifacts is greater than in any other region north of the Valley of Mexico.

The North Andean–Pacific area (*ibid*: 135):

> It is noteworthy . . . that much diversity [regarding antiquities] is shown, especially in the more southern districts; a condition due partly, it would appear, to intrusive elements of race and culture as well as to isolation of communities by reason of the pronounced physical characteristics of the country.

The Middle Andean–Pacific area (*ibid*: 137):

> In no other area do the antiquities have so wide a range or tell so completely the story of the life and fate of the people. Above ground the more durable artifacts and works only are preserved, but in the depositories of the dead, especially in the arid districts, vast numbers of every conceivable product of handicraft are preserved almost unchanged.

And Primitive [sic] South America (*ibid*: 143):

> Stone implements and utensils of excellent make and considerable variety are widely distributed.

These passages exemplify that notions of diversity have had a long, albeit intuitive, formulation in archaeology. Likewise, it is apparent that archaeologists (Holmes at least) sought to characterize and explain diversity as a consequence of social and environmental conditions. It is through quantification that notions of diversity lost, for the most part, their intuitive component. The notions became measurable and, as such, gained access to assessments of validity and reliability. The passages also illustrate that issues of diversity are of concern in virtually all archaeological settings, although it often goes unrecognized even today.

Although diversity is a quite simple concept, there is some confusion surrounding its meaning. In part, this confusion arises from a rather substantial terminology which we will try to make clear, and through the concept's implicit beginnings. Moreover, the term 'diversity' has been employed as a synonym for variation, which it is not; diversity is a measure of variation. Specifically, diversity refers to the nature or degree of apportionment of a quantity to a set of well-defined categories (Patil and Taillie 1982). Thus, diversity is a referent for the structural properties of a population or sample made up of distinct categories. We can think of diversity as an average property, that is, a measure of variation composed as a single value.

Generally, diversity is rendered either as the number of categories represented in a sample or as the manner in which a quantity is distributed among those categories. These concepts are respectively termed richness (the number of classes), and evenness (the order of abundance values). Some confusion surrounds the fact that a number of familiar indices of diversity combine these components in a single measure. Peet (1975, following Good

[1953]) has chosen to term this dual concept of diversity as heterogeneity. However, others like Pielou (1975) refer to such statistics, which confound the number of classes and evenness, simply as diversity. An attempt to quantify evenness apart from richness is embodied in the notion of equitability. Measures of equitability assess evenness relative to some standard. Commonly, that standard is a theoretical distribution like a geometric or logseries distribution or a maximum possible value of heterogeneity for a given sample size and class number.

It is important to remember that indices of diversity constitute a powerful set of tools for characterizing the structure of populations and samples. When the measures employed to examine structure confound richness and evenness, it is always necessary at some level to break these measures down into the constituent components, to search for what may be a more parsimonious characterization. This is necessary because, unknown to the investigator, one or the other component (richness or evenness) may be the primary determinant of the value of the composite measure. Moreover, when two or more samples are compared, values of the composite measure across samples may be identical, yet the structure of richness and evenness may be extremely different. Such a characterization, while accurate, might lead to naive, or even erroneous, conclusions. It must also be considered an error when composite diversity indices formulated as information statistics (e.g., Shannon and Weaver 1949) are applied to values obtained as measures of information, rather than characterizations of population or sample structure, without the direct correspondence between artifact and information being known.

We do not want to give the mistaken impression that the concept of diversity and its many measures are equivalent, although the distinction often is not clear in the literature. As we shall see in the following papers, not all measures of diversity supply consistent information; all measures are not equally sensitive to different portions of class abundance curves. This does not mean that we should be pessimistic about the concept of diversity as a useful construct, because without the measure of diversity we actually have very little knowledge of our materials. This only means that we need to exercise selectivity in our choice of measure. Because there are these inconsistencies among measures, Patil and Taillie (1982) have suggested that we recognize an intrinsic diversity ordering that is independent of the indices in use. Such an order meets two criteria. First, with respect to richness, we say that the sample with the greatest number of classes represented is most diverse. Stated more formally, richness is increased as classes are successively added to a sample. Secondly, a maximally even distribution is most diverse. That is, diversity increases when abundance is transferred from one class to another, less abundant, class. Thus, we say that sample A is intrinsically more diverse than sample B if it contains more classes and has a more even distribution of class members.

In practice, the actual orders generated by diversity indices may depart from the intrinsic diversity order because samples are not necessarily comparable. This brings us to a number of requirements that must be met in order that comparisons of values of diversity may be made. Although these are detailed more fully in later papers, we will mention several here. First, the measurement of diversity rests on an unambiguous classification of the subject matter. This means that classes must be defined that are mutually exclusive, exhaustive, and composed at the same classificatory level. Secondly, if samples are being measured, they must be generated either randomly, or in some other manner be representative with respect to the gradients over which differences are evaluated. This means, for instance, that if the diversity of artifact samples from different microenvironments is compared, the samples must be a true reflection of the populations of artifacts from each zone. Because diversity, specifically richness, assumes a dependent relationship with sample size, several indices have been proposed as independent. Such indices make the further assumption that the relationship between sample size and richness remains constant over the samples compared. Other, measure-specific, assumptions also exist.

The reasons why archaeologists might be concerned with the measurement of diversity seem apparent enough, but let us discuss two general points. First, the structure of most archaeological data is such that it invites quantitative description. Diversity constitutes a measure of our perceptions of those data. The mathematical challenge in representing that perception as a single statistic has certainly led in part to the interest in diversity indices. We do not suggest that this is the sole reason or the most important reason for investigating diversity though it does account for the rather weighty mathematical underpinnings of the concept (e.g., Pielou 1975; Patil and Taillie 1982). For our purposes, concerns with the quantitative properties of diversity are rather sterile if not accompanied by an equal interest in diversity as a property of archaeological phenomena. Thus, we add a second reason for interest, which is that, by measuring archaeological diversity, we may provide the means to examine the nature of processes that govern the representation of different classes of phenomena in the archaeological record. Diversity studies then offer potential for resolving functional and processual relationships.

The authors of the following chapters take up both of these issues, variously exploring the statistical properties of diversity with respect to archaeological data and the place of diversity in models of archaeological explanation. We can all imagine that some of the inherent qualities of the archaeological record make study of the former issue critical, given the assumptions of diversity measures. It may be that, in coming to grips with diversity measured in an archaeological setting, we can offer a unique perspective on the general properties of diversity. On one point, the relationship between sample size and diversity, a number of chapters make such a contribution. This comes about because archaeologists deal with a very different set of phenomena than do biologists, in whose discipline most of the measures were developed. In biological applications, rarely can entire populations be censused but, most often, extreme precision regarding the context and size of samples taken can be maintained. In archaeological settings, however, we may deal with either complete populations, or samples of discrepant sizes. This situation is often, although not always, beyond the control of the investigator. Even in those instances where we have little doubt that we have a set of data that constitutes a population, this population may also be considered a sample in the context of human behaviour within a given time period and geographical expanse. Much of the potential of our contribution lies in addressing these issues.

While the following chapters address a large number of topics relating to diversity, we have by no means touched upon, let alone exhausted, the range of topics worthy of discussion. One issue only alluded to in the following pages, and of certain interest, centers on the classificatory units we employ, whether they are real or contrived, and how we should go about constructing them. Surely this point must bear on the meaning we assign to values of diversity.

We have just begun to explore the problem contexts in which this quantitative description of variation assumes significance. The research presented here joins a small, but growing, body of literature on the study of archaeological diversity. We think that it is safe to say that we are now at the stage of evaluating the progress of diversity as a useful archaeological construct.

Chapter 2

The theory and mechanics of ecological diversity in archaeology

Peter T. Bobrowsky and Bruce F. Ball

A perusal of recent literature indicates that *diversity* has become a popular concept in archaeological research, but observations like that made by Reid (1978:203) that '*Diversity* is what the diversity index measures' suggest a basic misunderstanding of the concept of diversity. There exist important differences in the application of the concept of diversity in archaeology, so that a formal examination of the concept is needed.

Perhaps the most elementary differentiation exists in its use in a qualitative sense (e.g., Binford 1982; Hayden 1981; Schiffer 1983) as opposed to its specific meaning in a quantitative analysis (e.g., Cannon 1983; Grayson 1984; Jones *et al.* 1983; Kintigh 1984a). Diversity is a well-defined and widely used concept in ecology. A variety of equations exists in ecological research to measure diversity; this is no less so in archaeology. Applications of the concept of diversity in archaeology, as well as the equations designed to measure diversity, abound. If everyone is measuring diversity with a different equation, either the term has multiple connotations or all equations are equivalent. The purpose of this study is to illustrate the complexity inherent in the concept of diversity and to demonstrate why a singular definition and measure is inadequate, misleading, and leads to inaccurate interpretation. In the following discussion we (1) reduce the concept of diversity into separate components known as richness, evenness, and heterogeneity; (2) examine the ecological characteristics of the three components; (3) provide and decompose equations which measure the characteristics of the components; (4) provide a historical review of the use of the concept in archaeology; and (5) examine the archaeological examples with regard to the formal ecological definitions.

Quantitative archaeology subsumes a broad range of activities, thus allowing archaeologists to count, measure, and weigh artifactual remains in a variety of ways. Nonetheless, one archaeologist recently concluded that the quantification and comparison of artifactual assemblages can be simplified to three basic forms. According to Cannon (1983:785), these three basic quantitative measures are: (1) absolute counts; (2) proportional frequency; and (3) diversity. All other measures may be interpreted as permutations and derivatives of the above. Following a review of the three types, Cannon concludes that diversity is the only reliable measure. This conclusion in itself warrants a detailed examination of diversity measures. Moreover, it can be shown that by definition both counts and proportions define aspects of diversity. If Cannon's thesis remains acceptable after our clarification, then all measures are in some manner related to diversity. In the discussion that follows, we support assertions and equations surrounding diversity with appropriate citation. However, we do not intend to provide an exhaustive review of the literature. Instead, we direct the interested to a treatise by Grassle *et al.* (1979) which contains over one thousand references on the subject of diversity.

Ecological concept of diversity

As generally understood, diversity describes complex interspecific interactions between and within communities under a variety of environmental conditions. By necessity, diversity description requires quantitative descriptors besides simple qualitative appraisal. As a natural consequence of this process, one witnesses the continued generation of new equations, each purportedly measuring diversity. Most of these new equations are simply modifications of existing equations; unfortunately they are also usually more complex, unmanageable, and probably unnecessary. Before adopting one or several such equations to describe diversity, one requires a clear understanding of what aspect of the interspecific interactions is actually being measured. In short, we suggest that a detailed decomposition of the concept and its associated viable measures will prove productive for archaeologists interested in its use.

The general concept of diversity embodies three distinct aspects or components: (1) richness; (2) evenness; and (3) heterogeneity. Following Hurlbert (1971:581), numerical *species richness* is defined as 'the number of species present in a collection containing a specified number of individuals'. Thus, in the biological usage, richness designates the variety of taxa, species, or types in an assemblage or community. Closely allied to species richness is areal species richness or *species density* which denotes 'the number of species present in a given area or volume of the environment' (Hurlbert 1971:581). Although allied, richness and density require distinction when quantitative appraisal is being attempted. In contrast, *species evenness* is considered to represent the absolute distribution of individuals across all species. Evenness attempts to describe the similarity in abundance of several species in the community. When evenness is compared to some given theoretical distribution, the resultant descriptors delimit *species equitability* (Lloyd and Ghelardi 1964). An unacceptable synonym of equitability is *relative diversity* (Sheldon 1969). The final component of diversity, termed *heterogeneity* (Peet 1974), reflects a dual concept in which richness and evenness are simultaneously measured. Heterogeneity is a measure that assesses the variability in both the numbers of species and the abundance of individual species with a single value.

Given the above definitions, general use of the term diversity is therefore equivocal unless distinctions are made as to which of the underlying characteristics is of concern. All three aspects uniquely describe different properties of community structure. Casual discussion and measurement of the properties of a community or assemblage invalidates resultant interpretations, whether ecological or archaeological. We suggest that the use of the general term *diversity* be abandoned in archaeological studies and be replaced with the threefold concept defined by ecologists.

Richness

The wealth or variety of species in a collection of individuals – *richness* – is an accessible property and provides a means by which differences or similarities in collections can be measured and compared. One of the simplest measures of richness favored by several researchers (e.g., MacArthur 1965; Williamson

1973) is the direct species count. With this approach, most community or population characteristics are ignored, and the observed variety of species in two or more assemblages is simply compared. A simple comparison of species counts ignores varying sample sizes. Since it is known that species richness is functionally dependent on sample size, simple species counts may be problematic. As evident in species area curves (Gleason 1922, 1925) and species individual curves (Odum *et al.* 1960), the number of types of species encountered in a collection increases asymptotically as the total area or number of individuals recovered increases. This asymptotic relationship and functional dependence has been confirmed by collector's curves for pollen (Duffield and King 1979), gastropods (Bobrowsky 1983) and benthic fauna (Sanders 1968). To circumvent this problem of sample-size dependence, one can compare collections containing equal numbers of individuals, or unequal samples of completely inventoried populations (see also Jones *et al.* 1983; Kintigh 1984a; and Grayson, Leonard *et al.*, Kintigh, and Schiffer in this volume in regards to sample-size considerations in archaeology). In practice it is difficult to obtain samples with the same number of individuals. Moreover, how many individuals constitute an adequate sample size? Palynologists prefer large but frequently unequal samples of 250 or more grains, thus assuming universal threshold points exist.

A more realistic alternative to the above dilemma is to assume that the relationship between species and individuals, or types and specimens, is constant and quantifiable within communities. The assumption appears valid as shown by the following measures of species richness which numerically describe a quantifiable relationship between species and individuals/area:

$$R_1 = (S - 1)/lnN \qquad \text{(Margalef 1958)} \qquad (1)$$

$$R_2 = S/\log N \qquad \text{(Odum } et\ al.\ 1960) \qquad (2)$$

$$R_3 = S/\sqrt{N} \qquad \text{(Menhinick 1964)} \qquad (3)$$

$$R_4 = S/\log A \qquad \text{(Gleason 1922)} \qquad (4)$$

$$\hat{S}_1 = \alpha ln(1 + N/\alpha) \qquad \text{(Fisher } et\ al.\ 1943) \qquad (5)$$

$$\hat{S}_2 = y_0 \tilde{\sigma}(2\pi)^{1/2} \qquad \text{(Preston 1948)} \qquad (6)$$

$$\hat{S}_3 = 2.07(N/m)^{0.262} \qquad \text{(Preston 1962)} \qquad (7)$$

$$\hat{S}_4 = 2.07(N/m)^{0.262} A^{0.262} \qquad \text{(MacArthur 1965)} \qquad (8)$$

$$\hat{S}_5 = kA^d \qquad \text{(Kilburn 1966)} \qquad (9)$$

$$\hat{S}_6 = aN/(1 + bN) \qquad \text{(de Caprariis } et\ al.\ 1976) \qquad (10)$$

$$\hat{S}_7 = \sum_{i=1}^{s} \left[1 - \frac{\dbinom{N - N_i}{n}}{\dbinom{N}{n}} \right] \qquad \text{(Hurlbert 1971)} \qquad (11)$$

where:

S	= the number of observed species,
N	= the number of individuals in a collection,

A = the area of the isolate or collection,

m = the number of individuals in the rarest species,

α = Fisher's slope constant,

y_0 = the number of species in the modal class interval,

$\tilde{\sigma}$ = the estimate of the standard deviation,

n = the number of individuals in a subsample,

N_i = the number of individuals in the ith species,

R = the constant of rate increment,

$\hat{S}$ = the number of expected or predicted species, and

k, d, a and b = empirically derived coefficients of regression.

All of the above equations have been reviewed previously (e.g., Buzas 1979; Fager 1972; May 1975; Peet 1974; Whittaker 1972). Given the results of research in mathematical ecology and the goals of archaeological quantification, we limit our discussion to three reliable measures of richness which may be profitably used by archaeologists.

Equation (6) describes what Preston (1948) calls the truncated lognormal distribution. This equation illustrates a method by which the number of species in a population can be determined from varyingly sized but randomly collected samples. In the derivation of the truncated lognormal distribution, one assumes that the distribution of the totally inventoried population is a complete lognormal distribution. The assumption is acceptable given the arguments of May (1981), who notes that most distributions, from GNP between nations to diatoms in a stream, are defined by lognormality. However, since most samples are incomplete representations of the sampled population, a portion of the lognormal distribution is absent, hence the truncated lognormal distribution. Application of the truncated lognormal distribution to various samples allows one to calculate the sample-specific degree of truncation (= the number of species missing in the sample but present in the population) and therefore permits the estimation of the total number of species (richness) in the population. Additionally, this distribution has a secondary advantage; namely, evenness can also be evaluated from the derived sample statistics (see later discussion).

The second measure of species richness we consider is that provided by de Caprariis and colleagues (1976, 1978, 1981). Their equation (10) is a rectangular hyperbola generated by simple regression of inversely transformed data. Following several of their algorithms, one notes that, not only can the maximum value of species richness be determined, but optimal sample sizes can be estimated for varying fractional deviations using the following:

$$\varepsilon = [1/(a/b)][(a/b) - an/(1 + bn)] \tag{12}$$

where ε is the expression of the fractional deviation at the limiting value a/b (ratio of regression coefficients) and sample size n. Having chosen an acceptable percentage error one solves for n as:

$$n = (1 - \varepsilon)/b\varepsilon \tag{13}$$

The final method of species richness estimation relates to the rarefaction technique of Sanders (1968). As originally proposed by Sanders, the technique is invalid (Fager 1972; Heck *et al.* 1975; Raup 1975; Simberloff 1972; Tipper 1979). Fortunately, a decomposition and proper revision of the method has been offered by Hurlbert (1971) and is provided as equation (11). A review of Hurlbert's family of measures by Smith and Grassle (1977) indicates that equation (11) applies to a finite population where sampling is without replacement. This expression is an adequate approximation of sampling from an infinite population as described by the following:

$$S(m) = \sum_{i=1}^{K} [1 - (1 - \pi_i)^m] \tag{14}$$

where π_i is the proportion of individuals in the ith species in a sample of size m. Further, it can be shown that when m equals two in equation (14) the function is related to Simpson's (1949) measure:

$$\lambda = \sum_{i=1}^{s} \pi_i^2 \tag{15}$$

where π_i is the proportion of individuals in the ith species (further discussion is provided under the topic of heterogeneity). An added advantage to equation (11) is that $\hat{S}_7$ has an unbiased minimum variance estimator (Smith and Grassle 1977).

In summary, each of the above three equations (6, 10 and 11) provides an estimate of species richness for differing sample sizes. Additionally, the truncated lognormal distribution can be examined for species evenness, the rectangular hyperbola with modification permits optimal sample-size calculations, while Hurlbert's measure allows for a variance estimate. Choice of particular species richness equations should vary between researchers depending on the secondary information required (cf. Bobrowsky 1983; May 1975; Wolda 1983).

Evenness

Knowledge of the species richness is indispensable to the study of diversity, but in itself fails to provide insight into particular underlying abundance distributions. In the analysis of any assemblage, one also requires knowledge of the frequency of representation of the contributing species. The basic question, whether all species are equally abundant, or certain species are more abundant than others, characterizes the necessity for measuring evenness.

According to Hurlbert (1971) and Peet (1974), most measures of evenness and equitability fall into one of two classes as defined by the equations:

$$E' = \Delta/\Delta_{max} \tag{16}$$

$$E = (\Delta - \Delta_{min})/(\Delta_{max} - \Delta_{min}) \tag{17}$$

where:

Δ = the observed value of the diversity parameter,

Δ_{max} = the maximum value attainable by the diversity parameter, and

Δ_{min} = the minimum value attainable by the diversity parameter.

We note that Pielou's (1975, 1977) popular measures:

$$J = H/H_{max} \tag{18}$$

and

$$J' = H'/H'_{max} \tag{19}$$

conform to equation (16) when H is Brillouin's index and H' is the Shannon and Weaver index (see discussion of heterogeneity below). Again, Δ in equation (16) may be replaced with Simpson's λ or any other measure as shown by Sheldon (1969) and Peet (1975). All of the above substitutions, H, H', and λ, apply equally well to Δ in equation (17). Similarly, Margalef's (1958) redundancy measure of evenness, given as:

$$R = (\Delta_{max} - \Delta)/(\Delta_{max} - \Delta_{min}), \tag{20}$$

derives its formulation from equation (17).

The evenness measures discussed thus far suffer from several inherent limitations. Briefly, these restrictions include a dependence on sample size, the species richness, and most importantly, the particular measure used in deriving Δ. Sheldon (1969) and others (Lieberson 1969; Peet 1974, 1975; Whittaker 1972) identify and address the difficulties surrounding evenness measures. Moreover, given the multiple problems associated with heterogeneity measures and their common use as Δ, the above expressions are considered unacceptable.

Although evenness remains an awkward property to measure, two methods appear to be the least problematic in regard to inherent limitations. The first of these is simply to plot the abundance of species in terms of their rank order from most abundant to least abundant, as suggested by Whittaker (1972). Abundance, as measured by the number of individuals or proportion of total, is plotted on the ordinate axis against the species sequence on the abscissa. The resultant curves and their slope values, commonly called importance values, have been successfully exploited by ecologists (e.g., Lamont *et al.* 1977; Odum *et al.* 1960; Whittaker 1972).

The second method of measuring evenness relates to the moments of the probability density function under study (i.e., mean and standard deviation). Thus, Fager (1972) suggests using the standard deviation of the number of individuals per species in the arithmetic frequency distribution, while Preston (1948, 1962) prefers the estimated standard deviation of the lognormal distribution. Both Whittaker (1972) and May (1981) recommend the variance or its associates as adequate measures of species evenness. In short, a simple estimate of the variance of the proportional abundance of species thus appears well suited for a comparison of the evenness between assemblages.

Heterogeneity

Heterogeneity and its family of measures attempt to simplify the complex relationship between the number of species present and their individual frequencies. The earliest approximation of heterogeneity is illustrated in Simpson's (1949) λ index, as given in equation (15). This expression (15) measures the probability that two individuals drawn at random, with replacement, are representative of the same species (Whittaker 1972). In the following expression, Simpson (1949) defines the probability of interspecific encounter when sampling is without replacement (finite samples):

$$H_1 = \sum_{i=1}^{s} n_i(n_i - 1)/N(N - 1) \tag{21}$$

where n_i is the number of individuals in the ith species and N is the total number of individuals; $N = \sum n$. It is evident that equation

(21) is a close approximation of equation (15). Since both λ and H_1 values vary inversely with the heterogeneity of the community, modifications to the equations have been suggested:

$$H_2 = 1 - \sum_{i-1}^{s} \pi_i^2 \quad \text{(Greenberg 1956; Lieberson 1969)} \tag{22}$$

$$H_3 = 1 \Big/ \sum_{i-1}^{s} \pi_i^2 \quad \text{(Williams 1964; Whittaker 1972)} \tag{23}$$

where π_i is the proportion of individuals in the ith species. Pielou (1977) notes that the best statistical approximation for the interspecific probability that two species are different in a finite sample is given by:

$$H_4 = 1 - \sum_{i-1}^{s} \{[n_i(n_i - 1)]/[N(N - 1)]\} \tag{24}$$

A second group of heterogeneity measures have been termed dubious indices by Hurlbert (1971). This group revolves around two fashionable measures that are 'linked by an ectoplasmic thread to information theory' (May 1981:218). As originally defined by Shannon and Weaver (1949), information for infinite populations can be expressed as:

$$H'_5 = -\sum_{i-1}^{s} p_i \log p_i \tag{25}$$

where p_i is the percentage of importance of the ith species. Commonly, H'_5 is estimated for finite populations by:

$$H'_6 = \sum_{i-1}^{s} (n_i/N) \log (n_i/N) \tag{26}$$

where n_i/N attempts to estimate p_i, as the proportion of individuals in the ith species of sample size N. Extensive criticism has been laid against the Shannon and Weaver index; most notably, the problem of sample-size dependence (Pielou 1975, 1977; Smith and Grassle 1977; Smith *et al.* 1979). In support of information theory, Pielou (1975) offers Brillouin's index for finite samples:

$$H'_7 = -\frac{1}{n} \log \frac{\pi (n_i!)}{(n_i!)} \tag{27}$$

where n_i is the number of individuals in the ith species in a finite sample n. This momentary reprieve for information theory was revoked following Peet's (1974, 1975) results of analysis on the inadequacy of the Brillouin and the Shannon and Weaver indices.

Given the analytical results of Peet (1974, 1975) concerning the inadequacies of the Brillouin and the Shannon and Weaver indices, coupled with the conclusions of Whittaker (1972), the group of fashionable measures appears suspect. Clearly, the use of a single value (i.e., heterogeneity) to describe diversity must be viewed with some caution, since, as emphasized by May (1981), a single value masks the different properties of richness and evenness. Indeed, the inherent difficulties of attempting to contend with two different properties with one value leads to the conclusion that use of the heterogeneity indices should be abandoned. However, with the acknowledgement that heterogeneity measures will continue to be employed, the expression given in equation (24) appears to be the least objectionable.

In our discussion of diversity we have identified and defined three related but distinct components: (1) richness; (2) evenness; and (3) heterogeneity. Richness is viewed as a measure of species variety and three viable methods are suggested to be most appropriate for its determination. The simple species count, also a measure of richness, is known to be biased, given a dependence on sample size (Peet 1974, 1975).

Evenness is viewed as a measure of the proportional abundances of individual taxa. There are two procedures which appear to be the most suitable descriptors of this property. Finally, the third component of diversity, termed heterogeneity, is shown to encompass both richness and evenness under a single value. One widely used example of a heterogeneity measure is the Shannon and Weaver index, also referred to as the information statistic. All heterogeneity measures are considered to be inappropriate at the present time for the purposes of archaeological research. Finally, we contend that the synonymous treatment of the terms 'diversity', 'richness', 'evenness', and 'heterogeneity' is equally unacceptable. In the discussion which follows we review the use of the concept of diversity in archaeological research. This review emphasizes past accomplishments in light of the preceding discussions.

The state of the art

As in most disciplines, archaeologists often profit by exploiting the methods and theories of others. Clearly, the need to interpret human behavior in time and space necessitates a rigorous and occasionally quantitative approach. It is not surprising, then, that attempts have been made toward the integration of diversity concepts into general archaeological thought. Accepting artifactual remains as a paramount source of data, one is in principle receptive to any attempt at recognizing theoretical and structural associations between and within artifact assemblages. In this way, a conceptual substitution of artifact types for species allows researchers to formally apply the concept of diversity to archaeology. In the previous section we briefly introduced and decomposed the concept of diversity as presently understood in ecology. Adopting the principles presented, we shall now review the state of the art. We confine our review to specific uses of the concept of diversity and intentionally ignore those many instances where components of the concept have been used but not identified under the rubric of diversity (e.g., Nance 1981; Tainter 1977b, 1978; Tainter and Cordy 1977).

One of the earliest attempts at integrating diversity into archaeological theory is that provided by Schiffer (1973). Schiffer (1973:114) proposed that *'when the frequency of access to the contents of a facility is either moderate or high, the amount of access volume increases as a function of increasing diversity of contents'* (italics original). To test this proposition Schiffer used the following equation:

$$D_v = \sum_{i=1}^{n} \left(\frac{A_i}{N} \right)^2 \qquad (28)$$

where D_v is the volume diversity, A_i is the number of items in the *i*th class and N is the total number of items. Since equation (28) is identical to Simpson's expression (15), the former is a measure of species richness. However, Schiffer defined his classes (= species?) as the uniform volume of 100 cm^3 and abundance as number of items per set volume. In other words, he has arbitrarily chosen a

sampling unit of 100 cm^3 and is therefore measuring the density per unit volume and not class richness as the equation would imply. By further regressing D_v on percentage access space, Schiffer creates a species area curve. Unfortunately, this results in redundancy since a change in class volume will alter the resultant D_v values but the correlation of D_v to access will remain as a collector's curve.

This example of the use of diversity in archaeology is important as it indicated the degree of sophistication which could be immediately exploited by the archaeological community at large. It is ironic that the earliest archaeological attempt should employ the earliest ecological equation known. Following Schiffer's brief but useful introduction to diversity, a number of years passed before the concept was again applied in archaeology.

Yellen's (1977) classic study on the !Kung owes much of its success to his conclusive results derived from a measurement of artifact diversity. Yellen proposed that

the longer an area is occupied, the greater the number of activities likely to occur and be repeated there. I guessed that nuclear areas and special activity areas could be distinguished on this basis and sought an index that could quantitatively measure the relative richness of any particular area within a site. I wanted *richness* to be based on two factors: the number of different kinds of remains present and the relative amount of each one. (1977:107)

As Yellen chose to measure both richness and evenness, he correctly opted for a heterogeneity (not richness) measure; in this case the Shannon and Weaver index (equation 25). Unfortunately, his data are defined as finite samples and because the Shannon and Weaver index is designed for infinite populations and is sample-size dependent, a different measure is required. Such finite samples require the use of Brillouin's equation (27), noting all along that all heterogeneity measures are affected by slight changes in richness and evenness so that the resultant values react erratically. A measure of either richness or evenness would be more appropriate. Another difficulty in this analysis is Yellen's tendency to treat bones, grass mats, and stones as taxonomically equivalent classes, and to include arbitrary 10 cm^2 areas as a species equivalent to discrete objects. We note as well that Yellen's periods of site occupation, which range between 5.87 and 6.98 days, may be problematic. Is this time period adequate to obtain a maximum value of community species richness for artifact assemblages? Would a longer period of occupation affect the taphonomy of the artifacts resulting in a balanced evenness value? Although Yellen produced one of the lengthiest examples of diversity application in archaeology, we feel that the final results should be re-evaluated in light of recently developed insights in the mathematics of diversity equations.

Dickens' (1980) study of ceramic assemblages in the South Appalachian ceramic province is unique, given his concern with time-transgressive changes in ceramic diversity. Briefly, he suggests that material traits will peak shortly after a period of 'increased interareal cultural exchange' (Dickens 1980:35). To test his 'Hopwellian interaction' hypothesis, Dickens used the following measure of ceramic diversity:

$$D_w = 1 - S \qquad (29)$$

where $S = \sum_i^n x_i^2$ and x_i is the proportion of individuals (specimens) in the ith species (= artifact type). Comparison with our previously defined measures indicates that equation (29) is equivalent to equation (22), which is a heterogeneity measure for the probability of interspecific encounter for infinite populations. Values obtained from this equation increase with increasing diversity, given the inverse effect of subtraction from the constant – one. As noted earlier, if heterogeneity values are thought to be acceptable, the more appropriate equation for Dickens' finite samples is given by equation (24). Nonetheless, we note several positive aspects in his study: (1) emphasis on strict chronologic control; (2) equivalency in species identification; that is, only ceramic artifacts were compared; and (3) his attempt to use samples with more than 500 specimens.

Coeval with Dickens' heterogeneity application on American ceramics, Conkey (1980) published an interesting European example employing Magdalenian bonework. Conkey's primary concern was to show that the site of Altamira differs considerably from other hypothesized dispersion sites in Cantabria. Following Yellen's earlier work, Conkey employed the Shannon and Weaver information statistic to meet the objective of testing an aggregation hypothesis. The underlying argument of her study is unique, that aggregation sites will display greater assemblage diversity than dispersal sites and in this way Conkey's study corollaries add considerably to the study of diversity. In short, she notes that group size, length of occupation, and extent of occupation will have important effects on the resultant observed or measured assemblage diversity. These factors should therefore be a part of all archaeological diversity interpretations.

In his study of archaeological sites near Patoka Lake, Indiana, Cook (1980) relies on Sanders' (1968) research to circumvent problems of sample-size dependency. Cook's attempt was novel; unfortunately the technique used is incorrect. As stated earlier, Sanders' (1968) original rarefaction methodology was revised into correct form in 1971 (Hurlbert 1971) and several times thereafter (Antia 1977; Fager 1972; Heck *et al.* 1975; Raup 1975; Simberloff 1972). Thus, if Cook had applied the proper algorithm (equation (11) above), the example would represent one of the best diversity applications to date.

In a comparison of two assemblages from sites located in the Birch Mountains of northern Alberta, Ives (1981) relies on a number of diversity equations. Ives notes that heterogeneity is composed of two parts: total number and evenness, and then uses the Shannon and Weaver index (equation 26) and the McIntosh index (equation 30) to measure heterogeneity.

$$D_{mc} = \frac{(N - \sqrt{\sum n_i^2})}{(N - \sqrt{N})} \qquad (30)$$

Quite correctly, Ives (1981) notes that equation (26) is more sensitive to changes in rare classes, while equation (30) is more sensitive to changes in the abundant classes. As a measure of evenness, Ives proposes use of the Kreb statistic given by:

$$E = \frac{H'}{H_{max}} \qquad (31)$$

which is equivalent to our earlier defined equation (16). Of particular interest in this study is the fact that Ives utilizes different measures to assess different characteristics of the assemblage populations rather than simply select a single measure. We consider this an appealing methodological approach given the variety of population characteristics that may be addressed and the variety of measures available that are suited to these characteristics.

Rice (1981) proposed to test a model of increasing craft specialization through time using ceramic data from the Mayan site of Barton Ramie, Belize. In formulating her test, Rice recognized two components to diversity: richness and evenness. To measure richness she employed the Shannon and Weaver index of heterogeneity given by equation (26) and then measured evenness using Pielou's equation (19). Her application of equation (26) does not require elaboration, as our earlier complaints to similar misapplication apply once again. Note, however, that reliance on equation (19) is also plagued with problems since this measure is subject to a dependence on sample size and richness. Unfortunately, Rice does not provide the resultant data of her richness (read heterogeneity) and evenness computations. Nonetheless, we suggest a visual assessment of her Figures 2 and 3 in relation to the number of sherds examined through the ceramic complexes (her Table 2). The obvious functional dependence (i.e., autocorrelation) of the Shannon and Weaver index and evenness values on sample size negates her final quantitative results and thus limits the validity of her interpretations.

We conclude our review of the first decade of archaeological uses of diversity with Jefferies (1982). Jefferies (1982) examined the relationship between debitage and site location for Woodland sites in northwestern Georgia, to understand the nature of prehistoric activity and adaptation. By assuming 'that the wider the range of activities carried out at a site, the greater the variety of tools required to perform the tasks' Jefferies (1982:114) chose to employ equation (29), and thus equation (22), as a measure of diversity. In certain ways the objectives and underlying premises of this study mimic parts of those provided by Yellen (1977) and Conkey (1980) if earlier diversity application analogues are sought. Still, Jefferies' study is important, given his reliance on debitage as a primary data source, rather than the commonly used ceramic source. In terms of constructive criticisms, use of equations (29) and (22) should be restricted to infinite populations; hence, equation (24) would have been more appropriate. However, this latter equation may also be considered inappropriate, given Jefferies' intention to measure variety; a richness measure is required and not a heterogeneity index. Finally, because the sample sizes used by Jefferies are unequal and range excessively from 136 to 603, the reliability of the resultant values is affected. This latter conclusion is supported by the results of Jones *et al.* (1983), Thomas (1983b) and our own brief review of sample-size dependency that follows.

Future diversity applications

It was not until 1983 that the use of diversity in archaeology was finally examined analytically. As the preceding review has attempted to show, applications of diversity in archaeology during the first decade were research-supportive; that is, archaeologists freely borrowed and applied existing mathematical equations related to diversity to answer specific research questions. Unfortunately, no one considered the concept and its family of measures worthy of being a research problem in archaeology.

The preceding discussions have explored the formal properties of diversity by emphasizing explicit definition of components and the viable measures which accompany these components. Similarly, the review of existing archaeological applications has sought to appraise those applications in light of the formal definitions. In the following discussion we (1) comment on recent archaeological diversity applications which signal future advances; (2) explore the practical limitations of applying the diversity concept; and (3) examine the relationship between artifact typology and species richness.

Given the inherent complexity of the concept of diversity, one usually prefers to emphasize the study of species richness (Whittaker 1972). By studying the number of species, one assumes that the species involved are tangible in the practical sense. If one equates artifact types or site types with the species concept, certain criteria must be met prior to analysis. First, diversity measurement 'requires a clear and unambiguous classification of the subject matter' (Peet 1974:286). In regard to archaeology, this reinforces the idea that researchers must be consistent in their identification of classes and application of typology. Next, the identification of individuals to a specific taxon assumes the individuals are in fact equal. Finally, the recognition of several taxa assumes each taxon is actually different (Peet 1974). For example, a Navajo utility sherd cannot be identified a second time as a Navajo painted sherd. Similarly, there must be an agreement as to what constitutes a kill site, a campsite, or a village. Thus, the initial typology employed by the archaeologist limits the extent of interassemblage analysis that can be carried out. Even more important is the methodology of interassemblage analysis. If diversity assessed for one site relies only on ceramics, this value may not be quantitatively compared to a diversity value from another site which includes lithics and faunal material. Finally, interassemblage diversity comparisons are compounded by simple sample-size constraints.

Using archaeological examples from site assemblages in the Steens Mountain area of southeastern Oregon, Jones et al. (1983) correctly demonstrated that simple artifact class richness is dependent upon sample size. Illustrating their argument graphically, these researchers convincingly showed that a high correlation exists in the bivariate relationship between number of tool classes and sample size for 81 sites.

Expanding on the above, we argue that artifactual assemblage interpretations are bounded by the theoretical and practical limits of typology. Figure 2.1 illustrates the *theoretical limits* of all typologies as described by Grayson (1978) and Jones et al. (1983). As one increases the number of artifact specimens (N) recovered

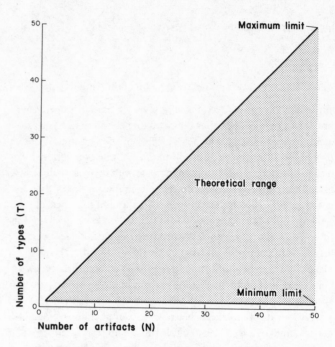

Fig. 2.1. Theoretical range for the number of artifact types (T) as a function of sample size or number of artifact specimens (N)

from a deposit, the concomitant behavior of the types represented by those specimens is restricted. The minimum limit line of Figure 2.1 implies that all specimens recovered will represent a single artifact type. Thus the ratio of types to specimens will be $1/N$. Conversely, the maximum limit line indicates that every new specimen retrieved will represent a new type, in which case the ratio of types to specimens is always one. The actual behavior of a typology within the theoretical range will reflect: (1) the excavation and analytical procedures of individual researchers; and (2) the underlying numerical structure of the assemblage under consideration.

In Figure 2.2 we illustrate the *practical limits* of three archaeological studies. By practical limits we mean the maximum number of types imposed on the assemblage by the researcher, given his or her choice of classification schemes. For example, range A in the figure applies to collections from the lower Chaco River in New Mexico (Reher 1977). Given the raw data in Reher's (1977) study, and the lithic typology adopted in that work, none of the sites examined could exceed a richness value of ten types. Ranges B and C in Figure 2.2 represent the practical limits of the Varangerfjord and Iversfjord (Bølviken et al. 1982) regions of Norway, respectively. Bølviken et al. (1982) employ differing lithic typologies in the two regions for which maximum richness values of 16 (Varangerfjord) and 35 (Iversfjord) cannot be exceeded by any one site. Individual collections for the three regions must fall within the particular circumscribed practical limits. The actual or observed behavior of collections can now be explored for all three regions.

Using the raw data of number of types and number of specimens for collections itemized in Reher (1977) and Bølviken et al. (1982), we generated collector's curves by regressing types on sample size. A natural logarithmic transformation of both variables

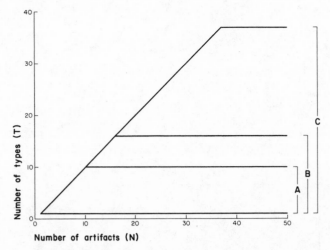

Fig. 2.2. Practical limits for the number of artifact types (T) as a function of sample size (N) for three study areas: (A) Chaco River, data from Reher (1977); (B) Varangerfjord, data from Bølviken *et al.* (1982); and (C) Iversfjord, data from Bølviken *et al.* (1982)

Table 2.1. *Summary statistics of natural logarithm transformation of the data from Chaco River, Varangerfjord, and Iversfjord. Raw data from Reher (1977) and Bølviken et al. (1982). Model 1 least squares regression performed on number of artifact types versus number of specimens.*

	Chaco River	Varangerfjord	Iversfjord
n	93	43	14
$\bar{x}$	3.703	2.416	3.991
α	0.389	0.468	0.831
β	0.244	0.439	0.434
S_{yx}	0.096	0.094	0.017
S_y^2	0.212	1.078	0.295
S_x^2	1.988	0.299	1.479
r	0.745	0.833	0.972
r^2	0.566	0.694	0.944
S.E.	0.310	0.306	0.133
N_{max}	991	141	284
T_{max}	10	16	37

n	is the number of assemblages or collections
$\bar{x}$	is the mean number of artifacts or sample size in natural logs
α	is the natural log intercept constant for the regression equations
β	is the natural log slope constant for the regression equations
S_{yx}	is the natural log standard deviation for y about x for the regression equations
S_y^2	is the natural log variance about y (artifact types $= T$) for the assemblages
S_x^2	is the natural log variance about x (number of artifacts $= N$) for the assemblages
r	is the coefficient of correlation for the regression equations
r^2	is the coefficient of determination for the regression equations
S.E.	is the natural log standard error for the regression equations
N_{max}	is the maximum number of artifacts (N) or sample size observed for the assemblages
T_{max}	is the theoretical maximum number of artifact types (T) for the assemblages

for all of the data and subsequent application of a Model I least squares regression generated three regression equations for which summary statistics are provided in Table 2.1. Respective curves for the three regression equations are shown in Figure 2.3 in the form of a $y = ax^b$ function whose variable axes remain arithmetic (not natural logarithmic). Note that all three examples show a good correlation between richness and sample size. Similarly, as expected, all three examples lie within their respective practical limits, indicating that different classification schemes result in different richness values. More importantly, however, is the behavior of the assemblages. Each curve mimics the collector's curves of ecologists discussed earlier and lacks a plateau or threshold point, indicating that maximum type representation has not been achieved. Discussion of richness variation between regions B and C would therefore be meaningless even though both are from Norway and both represent the expertise of the same researchers. In terms of sampling, the effect of differing sample size on the inherent richness values is also clear; there is no ideal sample size. These relationships are expected for most assemblages.

Given two hypothetical assemblages, one rich and the other poor in artifact types, several variables can be identified to be controlling the resultant richness character. This fact was implied by Thomas (1983b) in his innovative assessment of diversity applications for assemblages from Monitor Valley. We provide an idealized summary in Figure 2.4 which itemizes several factors affecting richness. The apparently richer assemblage may result from a larger sample size, biased collection favoring a variety of types, researcher error, reliance on a splitter typology, or from the fact that it does indeed represent a richer collection. An assemblage with low richness may occur as a result of small sample sizes, biased

collection favoring a monotony of types, researcher inexperience, reliance on a lumper typology, or simply a low richness character.

We offer no solution to the problems of researcher error and inexperience, since it is generally beyond the expectations of archaeologists to monitor each other's ability to identify artifacts. Similarly the splitter/lumper typologies cannot be readily resolved. Although we recognize the need for creating and adopting typologies suited for particular research questions, *discrepant typologies cannot be compared in the analysis of richness*, as shown in Figures 2.3 and 2.4. Moreover, if we consider the methodologies adopted by archaeologists in using diversity up to 1983, we would conclude

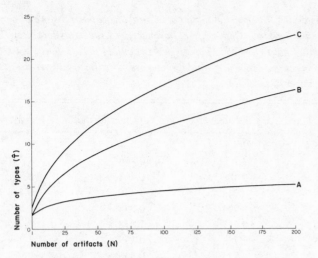

Fig. 2.3. Collector's curves defining the expected number of artifact types (*T*) as a function of sample size (*N*) for three study areas; coding same as Figure 2.2

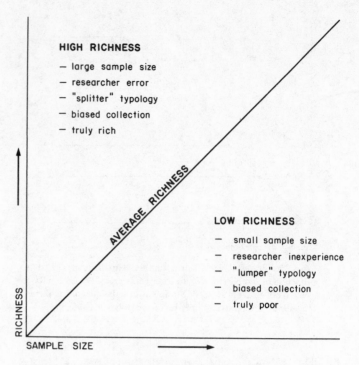

Fig. 2.4. Factors affecting high and low artifact richness values

that *discrepant sample sizes cannot be compared in the analysis of richness.* Fortunately, the efforts of Jones *et al.* (1983) and more recently Kintigh (1984a) offer solutions to the problem of variable sample sizes. Different sample sizes may also be accommodated using the methods outlined in our discussion of diversity. Specifically, we suggest use of equations (6), (10), and (11) for estimating species richness at varying sample sizes. The final compounding factor, biased sampling, can of course be eliminated by reliance on suitable random sampling procedures (Nance 1981, 1983). In short, the extent to which diversity analysis can be integrated into archaeological research depends on success in the following: comparable typologies, unbiased sampling, and comparable sample sizes. We consider the latter two factors to be no longer problematic, but the first aspect may require resolution on a case-by-case basis.

Summary

Since the early 1970s the concept of diversity has been increasingly employed in archaeological research. Diversity exists as a well-defined and discussed body of ecological method and theory. The concept of diversity and its family of measures assists in pattern recognition by describing relationships and interactions in what occasionally appears to be a disordered array of information and data. The intent of this study has been to outline the inherent complexity of the concept of diversity and the implication of its use in archaeology.

Diversity is shown to consist of three components termed richness, evenness, and heterogeneity. Richness defines the relative wealth or variety of species, while evenness describes the variability in the abundance of the species. Heterogeneity reflects a dual concept in which both richness and evenness are simultaneously assessed. All three components boast a suite of equations intended to measure respective characteristics of the components. Three

measures are considered suitable for archaeological research concerned with artifact richness. Similarly, two methodological approaches to the measurement of evenness are recognized as acceptable. Heterogeneity and its requisite measures are deemed to be of little value to archaeology. Several archaeological examples of diversity use are reviewed and the measures employed are equated to particular components and established equations. We suggest most studies to date lack an understanding of the application and thus the significance of the results. A further detailing of the methodological and theoretical limits and potentials of the diversity concept are integrated with general archaeological research. We conclude that diversity will play an increasingly successful role in archaeological studies as long as the misapplication of terminology, measures, and significance of the concept of diversity is avoided.

Acknowledgements

The authors acknowledge funding and logistic support from the Natural Sciences and Engineering Research Council of Canada, the Alberta Heritage Trust Fund and the Archaeological Survey of Alberta. Additionally, the following individuals were kind enough to provide us with references, unpublished papers and comments or both on an earlier draft, for which we are are most grateful: M. Conkey, D. Grayson, B. Hayden, J. Ives, G. Jones, K. Kintigh, R. Leonard, J. Reid, P. Rice, D. Rindos, N. Rothschild, M. Schiffer, J. Tainter and D.H. Thomas. Special thanks to Wendy Johnson and Kathy Miller.

Chapter 3

Diversity, variation and selection[1]

David Rindos

It is the use of mathematical methods for largely ceremonial purposes that I deplore and denounce as pernicious.

Berlinski 1976: ix

In recent years, diversity measures have become increasingly popular as analytical aids to the interpretation of the archaeological record. In this chapter, I seek briefly to describe some of the most popular indices for the measurement of diversity. I will give some consideration to the proper application of these measures, sketching out some of the conceptual and technical problems that must be considered in the choice of a specific index in a given situation. The application of a diversity measure to a data set implies that assumptions have been satisfied concerning its structure and the means by which it was recovered. Many of these problems also are discussed at length in the ecological literature and some are discussed in detail by others in this volume (e.g. Bobrowsky and Ball, Kintigh, Grayson). Hence, I will give special emphasis to a particular problem – the relationship between various evolutionary theories and measures of diversity. I will attempt to justify my belief that the rigorous utilization of a measure of diversity to anthropological and archaeological data presupposes acceptance of Darwinian processes to account for the structure found in the data.

Diversity measures are mathematical procedures that may be applied to any data set composed of individuals, or individual measurements, which can be allocated to classes. Since a tremendous number of data sets meets this simple criterion, one can appreciate both the strength and potential weakness of measures of diversity. The potential strength of diversity measurements is their wide applicability; their potential weakness lies in their tendency to make us believe we have an insight into the data when we merely have created a mathematical epiphenomenon.

Diversity indices measure the *form* data takes; they do not measure content or meaning: two collections of objects may differ in every conceivable manner *except* the number of classes and the number of individuals in each class. Under these conditions, the computation of *any* diversity statistic would produce exactly the same numerical result for both data sets. Likewise, since true diversity measures depend on two independent properties of the data set, class richness (number of classes) and evenness (proportion of individuals in each class), ambiguity is inevitable; a set with a low richness and high evenness may have the same measured diversity as another set with a high richness and a low evenness. Furthermore, differences in measurement will not be consistent between competing diversity measures: each index is particularly sensitive to differing components of diversity. Therefore, if we were to study a large number of data sets, their rank order in terms of diversity would not be the same for each index.

Since diversity statistics may be applied to any data set meeting the few requirements mentioned above – and this includes just about every anthropological and archaeological data set we might encounter – the reasons for using a diversity statistic should be made explicit. Good reasons should exist for believing that a diversity measure will tell the investigator something significant about the sample at hand. In being capable of measuring almost anything, diversity statistics may easily be abused and come to mean nothing. As the ecologist Pielou (1977:293) has put it:

> It should not be (but it is) necessary to emphasize that the object of calculating indices of diversity is to solve, not to create, problems. The indices are merely numbers, useful in some circumstances, but not in all. Much futile effort has been devoted to calculating diversity indices and then trying to explain the results as though the indices were worthy of study in their own right. Indices should be calculated for the light (not the shadow) they cast on genuine ecological problems.

Measurement of diversity is such a fascinating process that it may become an end in itself. To the scientist interested in deeper understanding of the data at hand, this is a pointless task – measures of diversity must provide means to answers for questions larger than 'What is the diversity of this sample?' As already noted, any sample composed of individuals capable of being allocated into classes may be subject to an analysis of diversity. But the analysis must be significant in terms of a larger question – anything short of this is simply numerology.

Creating the data

From a universe filled with potentially obtainable and measurable data, a working data set is extracted. This set contains nothing but objects – objects which are themselves subject to measurement. These discrete objects will be called 'individuals'. For the purpose of analysis of diversity, each of these individuals must be assigned to unique and mutually exclusive categories. Hence any analysis of diversity begins with three processes that are preconditions to that analysis. We define:

> d, our working data set. If we plan to use statistical inference, this set is seen as being representative of U, the broader set of interest. As will later be shown, certain measures of diversity are appropriate to a sampled data set while others are appropriate to an unsampled, or censused one. Rigor requires that these two types of data sets are not confused.
>
> n, the individuals $n_1, n_2, \ldots n_i$ existing in the set; that is, the total number of individuals (N) in the working data set d. In anthropological and archaeological studies the delimitation of individuals will often be problematic.
>
> c the classes $c_1, c_2, \ldots c_j$ into which individuals are apportioned; that is, the c_j subsets of d into which the N individuals are classified.

Note that these determinations must come before, and are entirely independent of, the analysis of diversity itself. Yet, decisions made during the establishment of d, n, and c also predetermine the results to be obtained from an analysis of diversity.

Numerous problems exist in the selection of d. A vast literature exists in both ecology and the new archaeology on problems encountered in the creation of a reliable sample. Since several of the papers in this volume touch on this issue (see Jones *et al.*; Dunnell, this volume), I shall give greater emphasis to the problems encountered in the delimitation of n and c.

First, the taxonomic level used for both n and c will have an obvious effect upon the results obtained from an analysis of diversity of any given data set. For example, given that c represents ceramic types, totally different numerical results may be obtained in a study of the diversity of ceramics from a given site (1) when n represents sherds or (2) when n represents pots. Depending upon method of excavation, preservation at the site, the internal characteristics of the data itself, and the aims of the analysis, different ways of defining n may be appropriate.

Secondly, the consistency of taxonomic levels must be assured before indices of diversity are used in a comparative manner – and many diversity indices will be used this way. They will be used to track changes in the diversity of samples over time or will be used to study the diversity of geographically separated samples. Under these conditions, classes must represent similar entities. An analogy from biology might be useful here: if the diversity of two communities were compared and in one case the classes represented species while in the other case the classes represented genera, any diversity measures obtained from the two samples would be incommensurable. The data would have to be reanalyzed to ensure that the classes in both cases were at a comparable taxonomic level before any meaningful comparison could be made.

Finally, the study of the diversity of a sample cannot be separated from the criteria used in the establishment of the classes themselves. The problems encountered in the establishment of a working taxonomic system in archaeological studies have been the subject of debate for some time (see Clarke 1968; Dunnell 1971; Rouse 1960, 1970; Spaulding 1953, 1960, 1974). Setting aside the multitude of practical problems that must be confronted in establishing a working taxonomic system and the inevitable difficulties to be met in implementing it, one matter should be clear – diversity indices are totally inappropriate to the analysis of a data set in which the classes are truly arbitrary. If diversity indices have been applied to a given data set, an implicit claim has been made that the classes recognized are accepted as natural ('real') rather then arbitrary (see Arnold 1971; Ford 1954; Spaulding 1953).

A moment's reflection will show why this must be the case: all indices of diversity include as a central factor the relative proportion of individuals in the different classes. An index of diversity will be meaningful *if* and *only if* the classes are seen as more than an arbitrary filing system for artifacts. If the classes are not a reflection of a patterning existing in nature (that is, if they are held to exist only in the mind of the investigator), then the index derived from the study of the patterning will be totally meaningless – an exercise in the study of the diversity of classifications existing solely in the mind of an archaeologist. This argument may be taken one step further: in most cases not only must the classes be recognized as real, they must also be seen as the results of natural processes that, over time, have generated the observable classes from an earlier situation in which the diversity was lower. I shall return to these issues at the end of this paper.

Measuring diversity

Diversity has a relatively clear intuitive meaning: the collection in which the individuals represent many types of classes is more diverse than a collection where the individuals represent only a few classes. Likewise (although with less intuitive certainty), if the same number of classes is present in two collections, the collection with a *similar* number of individuals in each of the classes is more diverse than the collection in which the classes have differing numbers of individuals. Any collection (regardless of whether it is regarded as a population in its own right or a representative sample from a larger population) may be described using two fundamental parameters:

S, a measure of the class *richness* of the population (the number of classes, c_j).
P, a measure of the relative abundances of individuals in each of the classes (the proportions created from comparison of the number of individuals, n_j, allocated to each of the c_j classes).

Note that, unlike S, which is a single number, P (unless defined differently) is a series of c_j numbers. P describes the *evenness* of the distribution of individuals into classes.

The two parameters S and P are included in all measures of diversity. As Pielou (1977:292) has noted: 'it should ... be emphasized that diversity, however defined, is a single statistic in which the number of species and the evenness are confounded.' And while a rigorous definition of diversity should not permit using either S or P by *themselves* as indicators of diversity, the tradition has grown up of using either of these statistics as indicators of the diversity of samples.

Since any mathematical procedure may be applied to a data set congruent with that procedure, and since numerous similar procedures are likely to be congruent but not necessarily equally appropriate to the data set, good reasons for the use of any specific mathematical procedure should be advanced. A reasonable rule of thumb exists for selection between competing procedures: use no procedure more powerful than the weakest link in the data permits. The choice of techniques for the analysis of diversity of a collection of objects is limited by the sampling procedure and the nature of the sample itself, which should be taken into account when the choice of a specific measure of diversity for describing the data is being made. The best measure is the one that does not overestimate nor make false claims concerning the reliability of the sample.

Many of the more sophisticated indices of diversity may be properly applied only if certain fairly rigorous conditions can be met. While the rules for the applicability of specific statistics to data sets are all too frequently honored only in the breach, the careful scholar will avoid 'rough and ready' approaches to statistical analysis and use the specific statistics best suited to the conditions at hand. Here S and P may become extremely useful in describing data sets under certain specified conditions.

Utilization of S, rather than a more complicated index (such as those described later in this paper), may be justified as the best summary statistic under certain conditions. Here, the only significant variable is the number of classes, since S is insensitive to the relative proportions of individuals allocated to each of the classes. Good reasons may exist for choosing to ignore the later parameter; one would be the belief that *any* number that might be produced for P would be unreliable, either for reasons of site formation or because of the nature of recovery. Another situation in which S might be deemed the best measure for describing diversity in the sample would be when two or more samples are being compared. In comparative studies it may be necessary to reduce the data set and drop P as a significant variable because the sampling and excavation procedures between sites or between temporal phases within a given site are judged to differ too much to permit reliable comparison. Nevertheless, the types and numbers of classes present under these conditions might still be judged significant.

Finally, the choice of a fundamentally metric statistic such as S can be dictated by purely philosophical considerations. Anthropology and archaeology have long considered the total number of classes present in a sample to be a (if not *the*) major index of social structure or of 'evolutionary stage.' From the point of view of systems theory and processual archaeology such quantitative measures are also of major significance (F. Plog 1974). S is a reasonable mathematical analogue to commonly used terms such as 'complexity' or 'specialization,' which, as generally understood, describe the total amount of differentiation present in a society (Seagraves 1982) but not among its sub-groups.

Our second statistic, P, the relative proportion of individuals in each of the classes, also varies with the number of classes in the sample, c_j, but not in a simple way. This statistic summarizes the distribution of individuals between classes. Here, the evenness of distribution will obviously be greatest when each class has exactly the same number of individuals. Any shift from this perfectly even distribution is defined as a decrease in diversity. Here maximal *evenness* is analogized to maximal diversity.

Note that intuitively it might as easily be claimed that the reciprocal measure, 'unevenness,' in which the number of individuals per class is extremely variable (that is when the set P has large variance), represents the conditions of maximal diversity. In all quantifications of terms such as diversity, the definition of the term must be made concise because the 'obvious' meaning of the terms is not necessarily obvious to all. As will be shown below, most indices of diversity have been derived from statistics in which the 'uncertainty' of a data set is seen as equivalent to its diversity. Here, uncertainty is determined by the probability of choosing an individual belonging to a specific class. Under these conditions, the greatest uncertainty that an individual picked at random will belong to a specific class occurs when all classes have the same number of individuals. It is in these terms that a data set with the *same* number of individuals in each class will be judged *most diverse*.

It should also be noted that measures of P which collapse the c_j observations into one term are inherently insensitive to the number of classes in the data set. The numerical value of P will be the same for all data sets with the same proportion of individuals in each of the classes, regardless of the number of classes in the various data sets. *P* may be operationalized in various ways, but since its insensitivity to the number of classes so goes against the intuitive meaning of diversity it has found little application to date in the archaeological literature.[2]

Sophisticated statistics

As already noted above, true indices of diversity combine in a single measure two different types of information – richness and evenness – present in the data set. Numerous ways exist to quantify either of these parameters. Likewise, these two components may be combined in several different ways to form the bases for different diversity indices. However, it is important to note that the various diversity indices do not respond to the parameters measured in the same manner. Two different measures of diversity applied to the same pair of data sets may produce conflicting interpretations of which set is more diverse (Peet 1974). Likewise, various measures of diversity show differing sensitivity to factors such as total size of the data set or variability in class sizes (Heltsche and Bitz 1979).

When we use any specific diversity index we are claiming, in effect, that our data fit specifiable preconditions for the use of that index. Among the most common of these are requirements for generating our data set *d* and its relationship to all potentially similar sets (*U*). As will be shown, certain statistics are useful with a censused population while others are appropriate to sampled data sets and hence statistical inference. The proper use of a given diversity statistic is dependent upon respecting the inherent limitations of that statistic. And since a large number of indices of diversity have been developed, no excuse exists for using, for example, a statistic that is defined only for an infinite population in a situation in which the data set is a small censused population. Other statistics *are* available for the analysis of such censused populations. It is pure nonsense to claim that an inappropriate statistic should be preferred to an appropriate one. One might claim[3] that any problems arising from the misapplication of a statistic in a case such as this are trivial or at least acceptable. Such an attitude trivializes mathematics, and, besides indicating sloppy thinking, in the final analysis provides uninterpretable results.

The Shannon measure of information content

A common and useful approach to the creation of mathematical models involves, first, the creation of a model appropriate to the most universal case (even if that case is unlikely to arise in reality) and, then, the development of a modification of the general model to make it more realistic. The well-known Shannon measure of information content provides a general algorithm that may be used in the creation of other measures of diversity.

Following Khinchin (1968), we know that, *given an indefinitely large* (for all intents and purposes, an infinite) population of individuals which can be arranged into classes without ambiguity, the probability that a randomly selected individual will belong to a given class c_j is p_j. As originally proposed by Shannon (Shannon and Weaver 1949), the classes stand for a specific number of discrete 'symbols' that occur in a 'code.' Here the probability of occurrence of the various symbols is $p_1, p_2, \ldots p_m$. The total uncertainty in the code may be expressed:

$$D_1 = -K\sum_j p_j \log p_j,$$

where *K* is a constant and *p*, as noted above, is the *probability* of encountering representatives of a specific symbol. In the utilization of this statistic, the units may be chosen with some freedom: *K* is arbitrary (although traditionally scaled as 1) and the natural logarithms (*e*), base 2 and base 10 are all utilized in determining D_1 in different contexts (Pielou 1977). Given these differences, some care must be exercised in comparing results obtained with this statistic (and related ones as well) to ensure that similar units have been employed.

Note well that the Shannon measure is strictly defined only for an effectively infinite population; the uncertainty expressed by D_1 is the uncertainty of a informational system or code; it does not measure the uncertainty of any particular message generated from the code (Goldman 1953). Hence, any attempt to approximate D_1 must be done by sampling a specific instance of the code and then inferring from the sample to the code.

Diversity from a sample

Consider now the case where a sample is taken from a large community. Here, the estimate of the diversity of the community is obtained from the sample by means of analogy to the Shannon statistic. We assume that the proportion of the individuals in the community in any given class n_j/N is the functional equivalent of the probabilities of occurrence, p_j, of the Shannon statistic. Hence by a simple substitution:

$$D_2 = -K\sum_j (n_j/N) \log (n_j/N),$$

where n_j indicates the number of individuals associated with each of the c_j classes and *N* indicates the total population.

Despite its intuitive appeal, this variant of the Shannon statistic is difficult to use properly. First, it is necessary to face the ever-present difficulties of sampling. This statistic is appropriate to a data set derived from a sample community. It is permissible to sample from a large community only if the boundaries of this community are *precisely* defined and the sample obtained from it is a *truly* random one. Everyone seems aware of this basic requirement for statistical inference (or at least should be). Nevertheless it seems a rather common belief that even if the boundaries of the larger community cannot be defined (as is frequently the case in archaeology), and even though a truly random sample has not been obtained, inappropriate statistical inference is better than no statistical inference at all.[4]

In passing, it might also be useful to note that archaeological data, even if it is drawn randomly, will seldom be composed of *independent* observations; our individual observations are inherently likely to be related to each other. This, of course, is no more than a consequence of the interdependence of the activities that produced the remains studied. Work areas, cooking areas, and other special-purpose areas will contain artifacts related to each other; the most dissimilar materials will likely be found in distant locales (some of which may never be sampled). In fact, it is likely that as the actual diversity within a site increases, any single small sampling unit of it will underestimate the total diversity by an increasingly greater amount. While this problem should be cause for concern, methods of compensating for the interdependence of the observations exist, and it is possible to estimate diversity even under these conditions (see the discussion in Pielou 1975).

Even if the practical problems associated with sampling can be overcome, the sampling version of the Shannon statistic remains problematic because it is inherently biased. If we use natural logarithms to scale D_2, the values obtained will consistently underestimate the true diversity of the collection by approximately

$$c_j*/X$$

(Basharin 1959) where c_j* is the true number of classes in the collection and X is the total number of observations. No way exists, in most cases, to correct for this inherent bias because c_j* is unknown.

Although the sampling version of the Shannon statistic has many practical problems associated with its use, conditions exist under which it may be applied to a data set. And if the preconditions for its use can be satisfied it is, of course, the best statistic to use. However, it must be remembered that D_2 is a quantity being estimated from a sample. Hence, it is subject to sampling error and any particular numerical estimate of D_2 that is published should be accompanied by an estimate of the sampling variance or the standard error.

The censused community

If we are not concerned with statistical inference to a larger community and are concerned only about the diversity of the data set at hand, a different measure of diversity must be used. One index appropriate to these conditions is Brillouin's (1962) function

$$D_3 = (1/N) \log \{N!/(n_1! \, n_2! \ldots n_j!)\}.$$

Here, $n_1, n_2 \ldots n_j$ represent the number of individuals associated with the classes $c_1, c_2 \ldots c_j$ and, as before, N is the total number of individuals in the data set.

This index of diversity differs in a fundamental way from the Shannon information measure in that it seeks to measure the diversity of a specific 'message' that has been generated from the 'code' and does not seek to measure the information content of the code itself. And, unlike the Shannon statistic as modified for sampled communities, the Brillouin function produces a result inherently free of sampling error. The reason for this is simple – all of the data is at hand and (barring errors in identification of individuals or errors in attribution to classes) the measure will entirely describe the diversity of the data set. In somewhat loose terms, the data at hand are treated as the universal set of interest: not only are the limits of the set of interest known, but also all of the data the set contains. Hence it is possible to describe the contents of the set in completely unambiguous terms.

One peculiarity of this statistic should be taken into account. It is very sensitive to the size of the collection. Two collections A and B may have the same number of classes

$$S_a = S_b$$

and the classes in both cases may have identical relative abundances

$$P_{a1} = P_{b1}, P_{a2} = P_{b2} \ldots P_{aj} = P_{bj}$$

but one collection may have a larger number of individuals than the other

$$N_a > N_b.$$

Under these conditions, the Brillouin function will give different values for D_3 such that

$$D_a > D_b.$$

If both collections are relatively large, the difference between D_a and D_b will be small. However, the smaller the two collections are, the more important this mathematical artifact will become. It is possible to see the size dependency of the Brillouin function as an advantage: it can be claimed that larger collections are inherently more diverse than small collections with a similar constitution. And, since we are relatively free to operationalize diversity as we choose, this may be acceptable to some. In any case, the bias of the measure to the size of the collections should be recognized.

Simpson's concentration index

Originally developed in 1949, Simpson's index of concentration measures the converse of diversity, 'concentration' (Simpson 1949). Consider a collection with N individuals arranged into c_j classes. If we select individuals from this collection, the probability that two individuals will belong to the same class will be a function of the proportions of the individuals in each of the classes. Concentration will be high when it is likely that a random drawing will yield two individuals belonging to the same class.

When it is used for a completely censused collection, the Simpson index takes the proportions of individuals from the various classes and uses them as the basis of an index of concentration:

$$C = \sum_j \{n_j(n_j - 1)\}/\{N(N - 1)\}.$$

Unlike our other indices of diversity, this same equation is also used for a sample community when statistical inference is desired.

The Simpson index may be used as an index of diversity rather than concentration by simply rescaling (Pielou 1975):

$$D_4 = -\log C.$$

Hierarchical diversity

In the discussion of classes presented above, mention was made of the problems that might arise if taxonomic level is not taken into account when the diversity of two or more data sets is being compared. All of the diversity measures considered to this point have been based upon the assumption of the existence of a simple, first-level, taxonomic scheme in which the individuals are arranged into mutually exclusive classes; no higher taxonomic nesting was assumed, nor would such a nesting affect the results obtained from applying any given measure of diversity to a specific data set. This seems a disadvantage because diversity intuitively includes some recognition of the *types* of classes present in the data set. A collection that includes highly dissimilar classes is more diverse than a collection with closely related classes. This would be true even if the number of individuals in each of the classes were comparable.

The creation of higher orders of taxonomic classification provides one way in which similarity of classes may be operationalized. In essence, taxonomic classifications provide a way to escape the problem mentioned at the beginning of this paper: indices of diversity measure only the form of the data set; they are insensitive to the content or meaning present in it. The recognition of higher orders in taxonomic classification permits the representation of certain types of *content* as *form*. Consider an ecological analogy. Two communities are studied. Both have similar numbers of species and the species have comparable numbers of individuals per unit area. However, in one case the species represent only a few genera while, in the other case, each species is a member of a different genus. Clearly the latter community is more diverse (in an intuitive sense) but the measures presented thus far would not be sensitive to the difference.

Consider the case in which a collection can be classified at two levels: the individuals can be apportioned to classes and these classes can be apportioned to super-classes. The total diversity of the collection may be seen as having two components: the diversity of the individuals as apportioned to classes and the diversity of the classes as apportioned to super-classes; or

$$D_{\text{total}} = D_{\text{classes}} + D_{\text{super-classes}}$$

How is the total diversity to be calculated? All discussion to this point has considered the calculation of the diversity of individuals arranged into classes. Hence the diversity of the classes is easily obtained. Calculating the diversity of the super-classes presents no problems. Merely treat the classes as the 'individuals' allocated to each of our super-classes, then perform a second analysis of diversity. The second analysis may be done using the same equation but with this difference – the calculation is done using as new inputs (1) the number of super-classes, S_k, as the equivalent of c_j, (2) the number of classes associated with each of the S_k super-classes, C_k, as the equivalent of n_j, and (3) the total number of classes in all super-classes, C, as the equivalent of N.

To illustrate this, consider the total diversity of a censused collection with two taxonomic levels as measured by the Brillouin function.

$$D_{\text{T}} = (1/N) \log \{N!/(n_1! n_2! \ldots n_j!)\}$$
$$+ (1/C) \log \{C!/(c_1! c_2! \ldots c_k!)\}$$

Again, the total diversity is equal to the sum of the diversity of the first level plus the diversity at the second level.

It is important to note that this process may be iterated as often as necessary for each and every taxonomic level recognized in a collection. If three or more levels of classification are recognized, the total diversity is merely the sum of the diversity at all levels. Hence for any classified collection, no matter what levels of classification are involved, the total diversity, D_{T}, is merely the sum of the diversities of all of the D_i levels recognized:

$$D_{\text{T}} = D_1 + D_2 + D_3 \ldots D_i.$$

Unfortunately, not all measures of diversity have the mathematical properties necessary to allow them to be treated in this manner. Among the indices considered in this paper, the Shannon index is the only one that is not hierarchically additive and hence may not be used for more than a single level of nesting. This should serve as fair warning, however, that the additive properties of an index of diversity should be explored before using the measure in an hierarchically additive fashion.

Discussion and implications

The discussion of hierarchical diversity just completed gives us an important insight into a subtle aspect of the application of diversity statistics. As has been continually stressed throughout this paper, it is possible to apply diversity indices to those – and *only* to those – data sets with a particular type of structure. Data sets amenable to an analysis of diversity have two peculiarities: first, the set may be described as comprising a collection of discrete classes, and, secondly, each individual observation may be attributed, unambiguously, to a particular class. If a hierarchical statistic is to be employed, one further criterion for applicability must be met: an inherent structure may be identified within which each class of individuals may be given its exclusive place within a hierarchical ranking of the several classes. Another way to view this is to note that within a hierarchical statistic we treat the classes as individuals attributable to higher levels of classification (cf. Hull 1976). Given these observations, the question must be asked: what process or processes create classes (and higher taxonomic levels)? That is, what creates the structure measured in a natural population by any diversity index. Numerous answers are possible to this question and I will discuss several. However, first we must dismiss two possibilities.

First, it is necessary to reject the notion that a diversity statistic may meaningfully be applied to situations in which the investigator believes the classes are totally arbitrary; where they have no 'reality' save in the mind of the observer and where the structure of the data is thus merely an artifact. This problem was discussed at length earlier and will not be considered further.

Secondly, no reasonable person would use a diversity statistic if he or she actually believed that it measured nothing of significance for the understanding of causation. Here, it would be held that the structure in the data to which the index responds, while the result of processes external to the observer, is, nevertheless, the result of totally stochastic processes. Therefore the ordering perceived in the data will give no insight into the *processes* that caused this ordering, that the pattern is a secondary result of the processes controlling the generation of variation. A study of diversity will gain no insight into these processes because they are *causally unconnected* to the form the data takes at any point in time. Form and pattern are connected only in the sense that pattern is a result of form, and meaning is removed from the observed patterns because both forms and patterns are merely accidental results of the history of the organisms under study.[5]

These two approaches, however, are alike in that no statement can be made concerning diversity and their objects of study. Other approaches do not make this assumption and therefore may utilize diversity in their analyses. In discussing the relationship between theories of change and diversity statistics, two contrasting types of approach will be considered. In the first type of approach, to be called here the 'historicist,' the appearance of new forms is emphasized (the appearance of new classes over time); diversity is accounted for by an internalistic process which governs both the form and content of diversity statistics. As we shall see, the historicists frequently emphasize the selective neutrality of character states in organisms. The reason why certain character states exist is unknowable *in theory* (as opposed to being unanswerable on the basis of limitations in the evidence itself). Changes in diversity become merely a reflection of the history of innovations in the entities under consideration.

In the second approach, emphasis is placed upon the relationship of existing forms to the environment. Here, diversity is controlled by an external parameter – usually, adaptative response to the environment. The aims of this school, to be called the 'functionalist,' are 'physiological' and functional, in contrast to the historicist school which emphasizes descriptive morphology. For functionalists, diversity should covary with environment. Common weaknesses of this school include environmental determinism and adaptationism (the assumption that all characteristics of organisms are adaptive and the confusion of evolved responses with the selective forces that created the observed traits). I will defend the premise that both of these approaches suffer from intellectual myopia and that Darwinian selectionism provides the best approach to account for, and explain, diversity difference in both time and space.

Historicist approach

In biology, the belief that change over time is mediated solely (or at least predominantly) by the appearance of new forms is known as mutationism (Simpson 1953); in anthropology a well-known school with a virtually identical 'explanatory' scheme is historical particularism (Rindos 1984). One necessary assumption for either of these schools is neutralism – the belief that traits of organisms have had little effect on individual survival and the differential spread of traits; that the evolutionary history of organisms is largely unconnected to the specifics of their morphology and behaviour. Given a neutralistic view of organic change, diversity statistics can have little inherent meaning because differences in diversity represent nothing more than correlative results of the differences in the history of the different collections.

Within a radical mutationistic or historical particularist interpretation of history, diversity statistics can serve as no more than summaries of changes in diversity over time. No particular insight into cause will be discerned by studying the types of changes to be found in the archaeological record. Instead, the Boasian mutationist will concentrate on the particulars to be found in the data itself as the only significant aspect of the record.

Within recent years a genetic equivalent of historical particularism has been advanced and defended (Kimura and Ohta 1971; King and Jukes 1969). Here, the claim is that much molecular variation is either adaptively neutral or that it represents adaptively indistinguishable solutions to similar problems. Hence, while selection may remove maladaptation, much of evolutionary change is the result of a historical 'drift' in the traits of organisms. The diversity seen in the record is a result of random processes that have acted through time.

Theories such as these cannot be rejected in their most general form (and indeed are represented in cultural phenomena such as the development of specific languages); however, they are not thereby given any definite support. Correlations between polymorphisms and environmental variation have tended to support a selectionist hypothesis, at least at the level of genetic response. Studies of correlative diversity have given us major insight into natural selection acting in a way few could have predicted (Ayala and Valentine 1979).

Mutationism is a lively school these days. In anthropology it is represented by Structuralism (Levi-Strauss 1963; Sahlins 1976), while in biology much of the work done by the advocates of punctuated equilibrium theory shows strong mutationistic tendencies. The emphases of these two approaches differ, however, in their treatment of temporality and hence their similarities are easily overlooked.

Within structuralism, time has been removed from the record (what Levi-Strauss calls '"mechanical" time, reversible and non-cumulative' 1963:286). Any structure which may be observed in the data is the result of a fixed set of laws which govern the production of and relationships between variants – the rules for the production of variation are 'hard-wired' into the species even if the working-out of these laws generates particulars in history. Within this tradition, diversity becomes a strange beast indeed. In one sense, it should remain constant over time. The method of generation of variation may permit the development of new forms, but, if properly analyzed, these forms will maintain a relationship to each other that should be recognizable by means of the (highly specific) structure they generate. On the other hand, the methodology of structuralism is similar to the procedures used in the creation of an index of diversity. Here, symbolic analysis generates an ordering of entities on the basis of their common origin in a similar generative structure. While much ado has been made about the 'mathematical' nature of the structuralist approach, much more could be done if practitioners would consider the possibility of using measures of symbolic diversity in their cultural analyses.

The punctuated equilibrium hypothesis (Eldredge and Gould 1972; Gould and Eldredge 1977) has been advanced as a specifically palaeontological theory. At first described as a simple extension of neo-Darwinism to the palaeontological record, it later became a reinterpretation of the theory itself. Here, major emphasis is placed upon the lack of connectivity between 'innovations' in morphology and immediate adaptive demands.[6] Invoking the founder principle first clearly expressed by Mayr (1942), advocates of this approach have gone way beyond the original implications of allopatric speciation (an extension clearly repudiated in Mayr 1982). Rather than seeing allopatry as one important way in which allelic change could be established in populations, they have extended the idea to the totality of evolutionary phylogeny. They hold that the 'gaps' seen in the fossil record are 'real,' that episodes of speciation are based upon macroevolutionary processes that differ in a fundamental manner from those generally witnessed during ecological time (S. Gould 1980), and that higher orders of taxa (genera, families, etc.) may evolve in one step rather than being the results of selective extinction and proliferation within lineages. Furthermore, the equilibrium established between speciation episodes is seen, by and large, as being independent of natual selection.

Here change in diversity receives a new meaning – major changes in diversity are the result of evolutionary 'catastrophes' instead of being explained as the result of gradual processes of origination and extinction. Natural selection may remove maladaptive forms, but it neither fashions major innovation nor maintains these innovations once they appear. Diversity is originated and maintained by internal processes; it is reduced by external processes.

Certain formal resemblances exist between punctuated equilibrium theory and historical particularism. In both, the maintenance of an equilibrium is not seen as a fact necessary to explain. Instead, emphasis is placed on the appearance of new types of variation. Mutations serve to increase diversity, then an equilibrium is established. After this time, the only events of importance are those that create new directions in evolutionary development. The connections between punctuated equilibrium theory and structuralism are less obvious (if for no other reason than that one is diachronic and the other synchronic). Yet both invoke an inherent dynamic as the process ultimately responsible for the generation of new patterns. Of far greater significance, however, is the antifunctionalism present in each of these essentially 'morphological' theories. As Sahlins (1976) makes clear, the total order and diversity present in culture could not be caused solely by the material relationships linking culture and nature. Likewise, punctuated equilibrium theory sees diversity as arising from basic changes in the internal, especially the regulatory, aspects of the organism. Both take structure and set it above function, especially function as related to the environment. Studies of diversity (as in historical particularism and mutationism) can only describe and can give precious little insight into explanation of the pattern.

Despite the difficulties presented by structured data, both particularist and structuralist positions may be integrated with the Darwinian paradigm by viewing such study as an example of the use of diversity as a means of understanding structured *variation*. Even in the extreme case of proven, neutral variation, this is not inconsistent with a selectionist position because Darwinism accepts that at least some 'neutral' characters exist – the undirected variation upon which selection acts. The problem arises in properly attributing the concept 'variation' – what forms are variants upon which selection might be acting, and what forms are the result of selection already having acted at earlier points in time?

Here we enter into an area that is as difficult in genetics as it is in anthropology. The debate is exemplified by the clash between the 'classical' and 'balance' schools in genetics (Lewontin 1974). The former holds that variation is generally limited in natural populations, while the latter holds that interactions within the genotype and between various phenotypes and a variable environment will result in large amounts of genetic variability.

Recent work examining the genetic polymorphism of natural populations has gone a long way in showing that diversity is, indeed, as high as the balance school would suspect. And while this goes a long way towards indicating that variability does exist, it cannot prove the stronger claim that, therefore, the variability is maintained by selection – the neutralism invoked by partisans of 'drift theory' mentioned above, while weakened by implication, has not thereby been disproven.

Cultural evolutionism in the sense of White (1959), Sahlins and Service (1960), or Carniero (1973) is a modification of mutationism that has a directional constraint added to the model, and it forms the intellectual bridge to functional approaches to the study of diversity. Here, an inherent 'tendency' towards 'increasing complexity' is posited to account for the origin of new variants. The data themselves are insufficient to account for the structure, but a structuring force admits itself in the Spencerian concept of 'progress' (see discussion in Rindos 1984, 1985). Here diversity statistics applied over time may be used as a test of the model because decreased diversity within a lineage would disprove the model (that is, unless 'devolution' – a tendency going against increases in complexity or differentiation – is permitted by theory).[7]

Functionalist approach

As Sahlins (1976) points out, anthropology has long maintained two very different traditions for understanding human culture. On the one hand historicists such as Boas and Levi-Strauss have sought the meaning of culture in meaning itself – the structural morphology of culture. On the other hand, Morgan, Marx, and Malinowski called for an analysis of culture rooted in praxis and in the interaction of humans and the environment (both cultural and ecological). This controversy, like many others that seem to haunt us at every turn in our study of man, is another of the bastard grandchildren of Descartes whose dualistic philosophy has long divided Western theorizing – body from soul and nature from nurture.

The basic premise of the functionalist school is that culture is rooted in the environment. Culture, perforce, may be seen as the fitting of human behavior to the contingencies of the natural world. Culture becomes 'Man's Adaptive Dimension' (Montagu 1968). And if culture adapts humans to the multitude of problems presented by the environment, it changes as a function of the changes in adaptive necessity.

Cultural ecology, the most important contemporary example of this approach, was first framed in a rigorous way in the work of Steward (1955), which made explicit the functionally adaptive nature of cultural change. Yet the fundamental premise had already been well developed in the functionalism of Malinowski and had separate roots in the adaptationist and transformational evolutionism of Spencer, Morgan, and Tylor (Dunnell 1980; Harris 1968; Sahlins 1976). The differences within this approach are vast, both in the conceptualization of culture itself and in the specific mechanisms held to be central to cultural change. Yet despite these differences, all representatives of this approach accept certain basic premises (Keesing 1974): (1) cultural systems relate human communities to their ecological settings; (2) cultural change is primarily a process of adaptation; (3) material parameters such as production, technology, and subsistence are of central importance in adaptation, hence, adaptation begins in and spreads from these spheres; and (4) ideational and cognitive aspects of culture are either unimportant (neutralism) or, if significant, are tied to adaptative realities such as population regulation or economic production.

The problems with this approach are many, but most reduce to the problem of adaptationism (Lewontin 1977; compare Sahlins 1976 on general problems of cultural ecology). Here change in systems becomes an idealistic model of transformational evolutionism leading to increased systemic adaptation (Dunnell 1980). Under a cultural–ecological perspective, differential change is the result of differential adaptations to changing environments. Changes in diversity therefore come to be viewed in a manner totally foreign to a Darwinian (although, ironically enough, they bear a close similarity to the position maintained by the historicist). Change is accomplished by *alternations of and responses by the cultural system as a whole rather than being the result of selective retention, elimination and proliferation of variations existing in the system at an earlier point in time*. In both the historicist and functional approaches, therefore, the generation of new variants is given priority; they differ only in that in the first case they are seen as largely unconstrained by the environment, while in the latter they are directed by the environment.

Within cultural ecology, adaptation is used to explain both the appearance of new traits and their maintenance during later periods in which the system is in equilibrium. Therefore, the cultural ecologist, while relying upon adaptive response (teleological behavior) for the origination of new variants, does maintain at least a negative selection for the maintenance of the system – the cost of maintaining a less than optimal response to the environment will prohibit the survival of maladaptive behaviors. This differs in a significant manner from the model proposed by the mutationist who holds both that the appearance of new mutations is unconnected to their initial adaptiveness, and also that their maintenance in the population is likewise unconnected to natural selection in a significant manner. The functionalist position is related to that held within a Darwinian model for the maintenance of equilibrium within culture.

In the field of evolutionary ecology, a clear functional approach is also employed. And it is from this field that functional anthropologists borrow their models. However, the role of diversity statistics in ecology has been largely based on the study of one particular, and peculiar, problem. Here, the most common rationale for studies of diversity has been the hypothetical relationship linking complexity (states of high diversity) to stability. Within the ecological literature, diversity statistics serve to measure the interaction of populations and environment. The hypothetical link between stable environments and increases in diversity is related to an ecological view in which environment – rather than interspecific competition – is held to be responsible for the structure of ecological communities. Conversely, stability might be induced by the numerous interactions present in a community, a condition closely identified with the pioneering work of Elton (1942, 1958). The problem being investigated was, essentially, the relative importance of ecological versus biotic parameters in the creation of observed patterns in the ecological record.

As applied, the concept of stability proved exceptionally complicated (Lewontin 1969; May 1974; Maynard Smith 1974; Pianka 1978), and it usually referred to a dynamic rather than a static equilibrium (see discussion in Rindos 1984). In recent years, the subject has fallen somewhat into disrepute, not so much because of the complexity of the arguments, but rather because of the confusion they have engendered. Furthermore, the empirical linking of stability and complexity (Connell 1978; Odum 1959) has been largely rejected in recent ecological studies in tropical environments (see the brief review in May 1981).

Darwinian evolution and middle-range theory

In biology as a whole, evolutionary theory provides the underlying rationale for the applicability of diversity statistics to observational data. The species concept permits the first-order attribution of individuals to species; further assignment of species to genera (and of genera to tribes, tribes to sub-families, etc.) is permitted by the knowledge that attribution to a given taxon is, ultimately, based upon similarities arising from commonality of descent. Because of the similarities existing between the data and the methods used to analyze them, diversity statistics can be used to cast some light on causal processes operational in the system under study. However, as we have just seen, the functional and evolutionary significance of diversity statistics will vary with the assumptions of the approach taken towards the data. A rigorous Darwinian approach to understanding diversity both in space and over time avoids the error of internalistic and externalistic approaches and, instead, attempts to integrate the best of both. Evolutionary explanation is never purely historical, which leads to the errors of mutationism and neutralism; neither is it inherently functional because this inevitably leads to the error of confusing evolved response with the evolutionary pressures that permitted the response to evolve.

Studies of diversity can play a major role in the Darwinian reformulation of the study of culture because of the close formal resemblance between the theory and the way in which diversity statistics are constructed. Raab and Goodyear (1984) have recently stressed the utility of 'middle-range' theories in the construction of a science of culture. They point out that the concept has been advanced as 'a strategy for integrating research problems and data into cumulative bodies of scientific knowledge in which theories of limited scope, arrayed at different levels of generality, could be subsumed under domains of increasingly general principles.' Furthermore, and of greatest significance, true middle-range theorizing must be 'part of a larger theory-building enterprise' (Raab and Goodyear 1984:255). Further, they convincingly make a case for an important contribution of middle-range theory to both theory and practice: the utilization of middle-range theories permits us to structure our data and hypotheses, our observations and models, into a coherent and functioning whole. By means of this process, we may avoid many of the problems traditionally encountered in the construction of general scientific models.

One outcome of middle-range theorizing can be the creation of a logical structure in which low-order working hypotheses tend to confirm or negate propositions in a middle stratum and the latter in turn reflect upon the validity of yet more generalized theories. From an inductive perspective, one can enter this hierarchy by means of . . . empirical findings. On the other hand, a series of testable propositions can be derived deductively from existing theories . . . [M]iddle-range theory is the critical *bridge* between theory and data that allows both kinds of operations to be effective. Debates about whether an inductive or deductive approach is 'best' are rendered pointless (Raab and Goodyear 1984:257).

Criticizing the current conceptualization of middle-range theory in archaeology, they note that middle-range theory is far more than the limited area to which it has been applied – the study of methodological issues of site formation processes. Of course, such studies are of great utility, especially in uncovering patterns and 'noise' in the data base; they present an opportunity to

understand the formation processes of the record and can eventually assign certain types of behavior securely to certain physical remains. . . At some point, however, behavioral scientists would like to know *why* the behaviors in question came to be. This constitutes a search for explanations of cultural behavior. . . The point here concerns the possible relationship between methodological adequacy . . . and true theory building. It would be a misunderstanding to think that the two are in some way incompatible. It seems more likely that little progress will be made toward archaeological explanation until both areas are considerably more advanced than at present. *Even more importantly, progress toward developing adequate forms of explanation depends upon a close integration of method and theory* (Raab and Goodyear 1984:263, emphasis added).

Here I would like to stress that Darwinian theory and studies of diversity provide a perfect example of that 'close integration of methods and theory' Raab and Goodyear are seeking. The structure of the data predicted by Darwinism and the type of structure needed for an analysis of diversity are equivalent – discrete entities that are arranged into a hierarchical structure. As Dunnell has put it, 'Evolution views change as a *selective* and not as a transformational process. Variability is conceived as discrete. Change is accomplished by alteration in the frequency of discrete variants rather than alterations in the form of a particular variant' (1980:38).

The relationship of this description of evolutionary change over time and in space to studies of diversity should be obvious. Variability is given an entirely different interpretation from what it would receive under a historicist or functionalist approach. Variability is not the problem to explain. Instead it becomes the way of approaching explanation. Under a historicist approach variabilty is seen as inherently limited and its production is seen as governing the direction evolution will take. Under a functionalist interpretation, variability is directed – its appearance is explained by the 'needs' of adaptation to a changing environment – and change is transformational and Spencerian.

To the Darwinist, variability is omnipresent. The appearance of a new trait, in and of itself, is neither particularly significant nor important. Sufficient variability exists within the system to provide evolutionary change with all of the 'raw material' it requires. However, the process does not end here. Instead, the second stage of the theory – natural selection – comes into play. Natural selection, working over time, alters the relative frequency of traits by means of differential survival and proliferation. Note that both survival and proliferation are invoked. Selection is not merely the 'weeding out' of maladaptation; it is also the 'positive selection' of advantageous traits by means of their relatively greater rate of increase. Hence, differences in the relative abundance of variant forms (whether 'merely' variation, or the consequence of long episodes of evolution) in space or over time become the *empirical basis on which the action of evolutionarily significant selective forces may be studied.* For the Darwinist, change in diversity *is* evolution.

Of course, this is not to claim that identifying changes in relative abundances explains anything. Explanation will be found in attempting to understand the selective forces themselves, what they were and how they functioned in bringing about observed change. We cannot blame Darwin for not having done our work for us. Natural selection theory provides explanation for only the most general case – the biological world as a whole – and therefore cannot provide specific answers for the specific processes that acted within a specific historical situation. That type of specificity may only be found in a study of the record itself.

Darwinian theory, like the object of its study, is hierarchically structured. Explanation within a Darwinian framework is, itself, hierarchically structured and imbedded in the specifics of the data set under consideration. To speak of biotic evolution as a whole, we base our explanations upon the common properties of the organisms under consideration. Here reproduction is the common denominator, and the concept of relative fitness as a generality may be used in explanations. This is because relative fitness is a deductive consequence of reproduction itself.[8] Note, however, that nothing has been said about any specific organism; to talk in more particular terms requires the introduction of knowledge about the traits of the organisms under consideration. Models therefore come to be modified in highly specific ways. For example, it is impossible to discuss intelligently the evolution of prokaryotes and eukaryotes using the same genetic models. Conjugation and sexual recombination have differing mechanisms and this results in significantly different evolutionary limitations and potentialities. The same will hold for discussions of genetic and cultural evolution. We must be sensitive to differences that arose during the evolution of a new inheritance system (Cavalli-Sforza and Feldman 1981; Rindos 1985, 1986). However, and this is of greatest importance, the understanding of the peculiarities inherent in cultural evolution are literally imbedded in the patterns it generates – Darwinian theory is a hierarchically nested set of theories, all of which specifically relate to the data at the appropriate level. Darwinian theory is imbedded in data while seeking to explain it.

This observation leads us to an important realization. The variations that are to be found in the cultural record provide us with all the data we need (albeit in different quantities and with differing expressions in the various parts of that record) to understand the functioning of cultural evolution itself. Changes in the relative abundances of various forms in the record cannot be understood by means of *pre propio hoc* hypotheses such as those invoked by the historicist or the functionalist schools. Instead we must seek to understand the forces that might account for the patterning we find in the data. *All* variation is significant because we cannot know, before the fact, the selective forces that might have brought about change. Hence, data receive a new input from theory. This cannot help but change the ways in which the data will come to be viewed.

To end with a simple example, the Darwinist cannot assume that changes in style are merely the incidental result of stochastic historical processes, that the particular changes observed in the data are unimportant in understanding the reasons behind the observed change. This is not to deny that we might find out that they are – genetic drift does seem to exist, but its interpretation is notably difficult. Neither can we assume that such changes are incidental to, but dragged along by, changes in important adaptive parameters not directly related to style. Again, they might be, but we will get nowhere by assuming our conclusion as a premise. Instead, we must look to the record and use that as the basis for hypothesis building.

Here is where careful and properly constructed studies of diversity become of great interest. The investigation of variation over time or in space will be facilitated by the interaction of data and theory. For example, in studying a seriation, 'outliers' become as important as 'dominant' variants. Much of stylistic change over time involves not only a relative change within major styles but also the 'random' production of forms that never show any florescence. Careful study of the total diversity of the sample may permit reconstruction of functional aspects of the record (time investment, functional morphology of shape and production, raw material constraints, etc.) as well as the interconnectiveness of the historical aspects of the record (design motifs, inheritance of patterns over time, etc.). These aspects taken together may then be the subject of an analysis that attempts to explain change over time as the result of the interaction of all of the factors within a multifaceted Darwinian model (see, especially, the discussion of CS_1 and CS_2 in Rindos 1985). Darwinian models attempt to integrate functional constraints and opportunities with an appreciation for the limitations and potentialities presented by the historical origin of new variants. Darwinism does not seek to overturn historicist and functional explanations, but rather attempts to unite them within a larger and more inclusive framework.

Notes

1. Sincere thanks go to the Center for Advanced Studies, The University of Illinois, Urbana, for a fellowship during the tenure of which this paper was drafted. There is no way for me properly to thank this institution, and its staff, for their kind and most important support during a critical time for my research.

2. For further discussions of evenness and for suggested measures of P see Pielou 1975, 1977, and Hurlbert 1971.

3. It is just this type of a cavalier attitude towards mathematics that provides much of the focus for Berlinski's (1976) scathing critique of the misapplication of mathematical procedures in the social sciences. Berlinski's volume should be read and pondered by anyone considering the use of mathematical aids to the analysis of anthropological data; it should be chained to the ankles of those who say 'Oh what's the difference anyway . . . the answer will be close enough.'

4. This unfortunate attitude is best answered by Thomas's 9th commandment of statistical anthropology (1976:467): 'COMMANDMENT IX. Thou shalt not take the assumptions of statistical models in vain. Honor these assumptions and hold them inviolate.'

5. This is directly related to the criticism that natural selection theory is a tautology, the 'poverty of historicism' criticized by Popper (1963) that leads to a 'metaphysical approach' (Popper 1974). In biology, this criticism directly leads to the erroneous claim that natural selection theory provides no testable explanations for change over time; that the whole theory is merely an elaboration of a tautology. Darwinian theory, in fact, does not suffer from this defect, a discussion that will not be of further concern to us in this context (see reviews in Caplan 1979; Rindos 1984; Ruse 1973, 1982).

6. The classic paper here is Raup *et al.* (1973) in which classes were generated by a random-number driven simulator. The resulting patterns closely resembled those found in the palaeontological record. Gould *et al.* (1977) performed a statistical comparison between generated and natural clades and confirmed the pattern of similarity between them. However, even if we subscribe to a view holding that the extinction of *species* is the result of processes that are random (i.e., we do not distinguish between species having different 'ancestral' species), we have not thereby demonstrated that the extinction of a given species was unrelated to selective forces acting upon the individuals that comprised the species. Stanley (1979) makes a similar argument, albeit to a vastly different end.

7. In which case abandonment of the whole approach is the only rational choice. We need not subscribe to a strict Popperian definition of science to ignore a theory which can explain any phenomenon – and its converse – by means of exactly the same explanation. This type of argument boils down to a useless and trivial statement: 'if events don't go one way, they go the other.'

8. Since genetic reproduction involves, at one level or another, a chemical process, and since such processes are inevitably subject to error, variants will appear over time in any population using such a system. If any of these variants give to their possessors any increase in relative fitness (that is, even a slight tendency to proliferate at a minutely higher rate), the generations of offspring related to the original possessor of the advantageous variant will come to dominate the population. This observation yields a most interesting implication. According to present models for the origin of the universe (the 'big bang' theory), the specific conditions for the laws of physical are established during the very first moments of the process. If conditions had been slightly different, the laws of physics that we would observe would likewise be different. However, given any possible universe in which an entity could exist such that it took in energy from the environment and made copies of itself (that is, reproduced), we could confidently claim from the argument just given that the law of natural selection would apply. Darwinism is a more general theory than any governing in physics. While this argument is only important as a heuristic, it does have the advantage of applying a dressing to the wound of 'physics envy' that seems all too frequently to bother scientists working in the natural sciences.

Components of diversity: richness, evenness, and factors influencing their assessment

Chapter 4

Sample size, significance, and measures of diversity

Keith W. Kintigh

Diversity is a concept that is used to discuss variability in the archaeological record. Application of the concept of diversity requires the specification of a measure of diversity and a sufficient understanding of the quantitative behavior of the measure to permit inferences concerning the archaeological record. This paper discusses simple measures of the two dimensions of diversity, richness, and evenness. These measures are applied using a method that attempts to deal explicitly with two methodological concerns: (1) the behavior of the measures with respect to sample size and, (2) the statistically aberrant distributions (see Diaconis and Efron 1983) that are typical in archaeological assemblages. The research presented here extends the formulation presented in an earlier *American Antiquity* article (Kintigh 1984a) through use of a broadened conception of diversity and through consideration of additional methodological and substantive topics.

The concept of diversity

Diversity has played an important role in archaeological interpretation (although it is sometimes discussed in terms of homogeneity or variability; Braun 1977; Conkey 1980; DeBoer and Moore 1982; Wallace 1983; Whallon 1968; Yellen 1977). Its utility, in part, derives from its robust ability to summarize a rather unspecific sort of variability in an archaeological assemblage (Cannon 1983). In general usage, diversity is a concept that is related to the number of classes of items present in an assemblage. In ecological terms, it is a function both of the number of classes

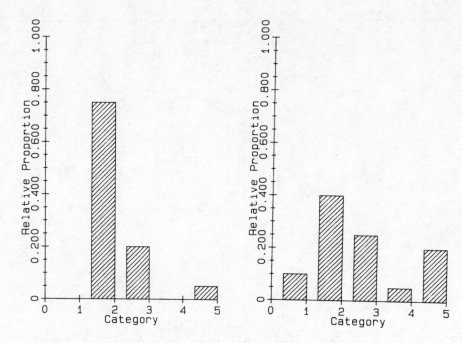

Fig. 4.1. Relative proportions of five tool types in two assemblages

present and of the evenness or uniformity of the distribution of relative abundances of the classes.

For example, let us assume that we have a stone-tool typology that includes five tool types, and two assemblages classified according to this typology (Figure 4.1). In the first, only three types are represented, sharing from 5% to 75% of the assemblage. In the second, all five types are represented with relative proportions from 5% to 40%. Clearly, one would say that the first assemblage is less diverse than the second.

Properties of diversity

As a way of moving toward a formal measure, several properties of diversity, as it is used in archaeology, may be listed. (1) Diversity is generally employed to discuss variation in a nominal variable, such as stone-tool type, design element, or ceramic type. (2) Diversity is typically a comparative property of distributions. That is, the interpretative concern is generally with the relative diversity of one assemblage when compared with another, not as an absolute property in which the magnitude itself is important. (3) Following the usage in mathematical ecology, diversity may be considered to have dimensions (Pielou 1977:292) of *richness*, the number of different classes present in the assemblage, and *evenness*, the uniformity of the distribution of relative proportions of the classes.

Although there exist measures of diversity that combine richness and evenness in a single statistic (Pielou 1977), in many cases measures of this sort appear to introduce unnecessary interpretive difficulties. Thus, I shall discuss separate measures of richness and evenness. As Pielou notes, 'diversity' is sometimes used synonymously with richness (e.g. Kintigh 1984a); however, for present purposes, these two dimensions are considered separately.

Richness

The *measure* of richness is the number of classes present in a collection. One problem in using this simple, intuitive measure arises when the effects of sample size on it are considered. In applications outside archaeology it is often possible to control sample size, so this is not an issue that has received much careful attention (see Smith and Grassle [1977] for a notable exception). In archaeology, sample sizes are generally imposed on us by the agents responsible for the archaeological record, and, unfortunately, they typically vary widely, often by a factor of 100 or more within specific problem domains.

With very small samples, the influence of sample size on richness is obvious; if you have only three items, you cannot have a richness less than one nor more than three, no matter how many categories have been defined. With larger samples, one suspects that with a sufficiently large collection there will be no appreciable sample-size effects, although it is not clear how large a sample is *sufficiently* large for this purpose.

The sample-size problem is illustrated by the plot, shown in Figure 4.2, of the total number of design elements recorded (abscissa) against the number of *different* design elements (the richness) found in five engraved bone collections (ordinate). (In this figure, the sample-size axis is plotted on a logarithmic scale, as it is for all plots presented here.) Of course, we must always be wary of measures that vary directly with sample size. This plot could not show a much clearer positive correlation between richness and sample size ($r_{xy} = 0.97$, $r_{\log(x)y} = 0.98$), indicating that, as a raw measure, richness is not satisfactory for comparing collections of different sizes. Although one might despair of obtaining *any* meaningful results because of the suspicious look of this plot, it is *possible* that, in fact, the site with the largest sample has the

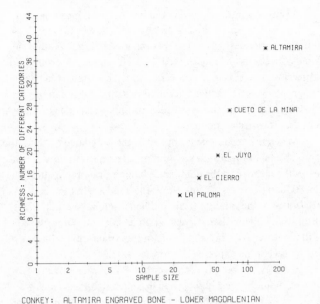

CONKEY: ALTAMIRA ENGRAVED BONE - LOWER MAGDALENIAN

Fig. 4.2. Plot of the number of different design elements (ordinate) against sample size (abscissa). Data reported by Conkey (1980).

greatest richness value, even if sample-size effects were removed.

Margaret Conkey has proposed an intriguing interpretation of the Lower Magdalenian sites plotted here, based in part on an analysis of diversity (Conkey 1980). She hypothesized that Altamira was an aggregation site for upper Paleolithic hunter–gatherers that exhibited an aggregation/dispersal settlement pattern. If Altamira were an aggregation site and if designs were to some extent micro-band specific, she argued that Altamira would have a greater diversity of design elements than the dispersal sites (the others), because elements representative of all micro-band groups should appear at the aggregation site.

The problem is that although Altamira obviously has the greatest richness of design elements, it also has by far the largest sample size. Thus, we need to know, *if sample-size effects were removed*, whether Altamira, with 152 design elements in total and 38 different elements represented, has a richness more than the other sites, such as Cueto de la Mina with 69 total elements and 27 different elements represented.

This example suggests that, in general, the question is not whether one assemblage has a greater richness than another, but whether one has a greater *relative* richness when the effects of sample size are removed. A related question is whether one assemblage has a *significantly* higher relative richness than another.

The model

One way to approach the problem of obtaining a relative richness measure is to develop, in some way, an *expectation* for richness that is based on the sample size. (See Jones *et al.* [1983] for an alternative, regression-based approach.) To accomplish this, I have proposed a simple model that can be used to generate the expected richness for a given sample size. This model provides a sort

of null hypothesis against which the actual data may be compared. The model provides a means of simulating the creation of an assemblage with a given sample size based on two simple assumptions:

Assumption 1. For a given typology of artifacts and a given cultural situation there is a culturally determined underlying frequency distribution. For example, it might be argued that the distribution of tool types for a time period in a region is the result of the stylistically and functionally determined repertoire of tools that has a probability distribution based on the frequency of the different activities performed and the use-life of the tools. The distribution of ceramic design elements might be the product of the popularity of the designs.

Assumption 2. A simulated archaeological assemblage can be created through a process of random selection of items of the different classes. To construct a simulated assemblage with a fixed number of objects, that number of objects is selected at random (with replacement) using the culturally determined probabilities for the classes.

The method

An expectation of the richness for a given sample size can be generated through construction of a large number of simulated assemblages at that sample size. While any one such simulated assemblage is only one probabilistic instantiation of the model, aggregating the information obtained from a large number of such simulations yields a statistical estimate of the richness for that sample size.

For example, consider selecting 70 items at random from the probability distribution of the 44 classes of design elements used by Conkey (Table 4.1). Given this distribution, it is not intuitively obvious how many different classes one would expect to find in a random selection of 70 items.

Figure 4.3 shows the results of simulating the construction of 500 random collections, each with 70 total elements. Each asterisk in the histogram represents six simulated assemblages, and its vertical position in the histogram indicates the richness obtained in that trial. It shows that two of the 500 simulated assemblages with sample size 70 had a richness of 19. That is, 19 different elements were found in two of the 500 trial assemblages (although in these two assemblages, the same 19 elements may *not* have been chosen). Near the middle of the distribution, 79 simulated collections had 26 different elements.

Choosing 500 simulated samples of size 70, we obtain richness values between 19 and 33, with a mean of 26.37. Therefore, our expectation of richness for a sample of size 70, using the probability distribution of the 44 elements, is this mean value, about 26.

A more complete evaluation can be done using a confidence interval of the expected richness. If we wanted to know in what range 80% of all random trials fell, we could create an interval using this histogram so that, at most, 10% of the trials are in the lower tail, and 10% are in the upper tail. Thus, at least 80% of the simulated assemblages are in the central interval, which is in-

Table 4.1. Probability distribution of Lower Magdalenian designs

Element number	Element percent	Element number	Element percent	Element number	Element percent
1	0.9	16	3.3	31	0.3
2	12.4	17	0.9	32	0.3
3	3.6	18	1.2	33	2.1
4	1.2	19	3.6	34	0.6
5	0.3	20	1.8	35	0.3
6	0.9	21	1.5	36	0.3
7	3.6	22	1.2	37	0.9
8	11.5	23	2.1	38	0.3
9	2.7	24	0.3	39	1.8
10	6.3	25	2.4	40	0.9
11	0.6	26	0.3	41	2.7
12	0.6	27	0.6	42	5.1
13	7.5	28	1.2	43	3.0
14	3.3	29	0.6	44	2.1
15	2.1	30	0.6		

dicated on the histogram by the arrows ('greater than' signs). (This is a slightly different method for drawing the band than the one presented in Kintigh [1984a].) In this example, at least 80% of the trials fall within the confidence interval. (Exactly 80% cannot usually be included because each trial must have an integral richness. Thus we must move in steps of richness values of 1.0.)

	Richness	No. of trials	% of trials	Cum % trials		Histogram * = 6 trials
	19	2	0.4	0.4		*
	20	1	0.2	0.6		*
	21	7	1.4	2.0		*
	22	17	3.4	5.4		***
>	23	31	6.2	11.6	>	*****
	24	52	10.4	22.0		*********
	25	72	14.4	36.4		************
+	26	79	15.8	52.2	+	**************
	27	67	13.4	65.6		***********
	28	74	14.8	80.4		************
>	29	54	10.8	91.2	>	*********
	30	27	5.4	96.6		*****
	31	12	2.4	99.0		**
	32	3	0.6	99.6		*
	33	2	0.4	100.0		*

Mean richness 26.37
Standard deviation 2.39
Confidence interval 0.80 (86% of trials w/i interval)

Fig. 4.3. Histogram of richness values from 500 simulated trials for a sample size of 70 using the probability distribution above

Using a computer program, this progress can be repeated for a range of sample sizes to gain expected (that is, mean) estimates of richness, given the random model. Five hundred simulated collections are constructed for each sample size from one to the maximum sample size that is relevant. The means and confidence intervals for richness at different sample sizes can be plotted along with actual richness values to get a visual idea of the effect of sample size on richness.

When this technique is applied to the Magdalenian data, the results shown in Figure 4.4 are obtained. Here, the middle line indicates the mean, and the confidence band is drawn to include at least 80% of the trials. Points above the band are in the upper 10% or less of the random trials and hence might be said to have substantially higher than expected richness. Points below the band are in the lower 10% or less of the random trials and might be said to have lower than expected richness.

Conkey's hypothesis implied that Altamira, as an aggregation site, would show a higher than expected richness. Thus, we see that this analysis is consistent with the interpretation. In addition, Conkey has reasons to believe that Cueto de la Mina might also have been an aggregation site, while she expects that the other sites were dispersal-type camps. Figure 4.4 demonstrates that Cueto de la Mina comes within the expected range and thus has a higher relative diversity than the sites that fall below the 80% interval, further supporting her interpretation.

Background frequency distribution

Thus far, I have glossed over one important question: How is the background distribution derived? For the purposes of the model, it is necessary to have an estimate of the proportionate dis-

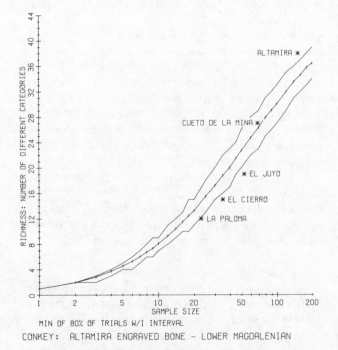

Fig. 4.4. Plot of the number of different design elements in engraved bones (ordinate) against sample size (abscissa) at five Lower Magdalenian sites. Data reported by Conkey (1980).

tribution of the classes in the population of all artifacts relevant to the collections considered. One way to get this is to use the total distribution from all available collections. Thus, the underlying distribution is formed by the sum of all assemblages that represent the cultural phenomenon being investigated. Clearly, using this method, the more representative our sample, the better should be the expectations produced by the model.

For the Magdalenian data I added up the *frequencies* of the 44 design elements from all sites to obtain their model probability distribution (given in Table 4.1). Although this seems to be satisfactory for many purposes, including the purposes of this discussion, other methods of obtaining this distribution might be suggested. In particular, independent data from those being analyzed might be used, or, in the context of a particular analysis, a theoretical distribution might be applicable.

Without going into detail, I should point out that using aggregated values derived from the data being analyzed does not generally lead to the problems of circularity one might expect. The worst case is probably one in which the frequencies in one collection numerically overwhelm all others. This is generally undesirable and has the effect of depressing the richness values. In this case, the method will be unable to separate the effects of sample size for the largest collection, and it will tend to show that collection within a random range.

Evenness

Evenness is more difficult to measure, although I think we all have an intuitive grasp of the term. Several measures of evenness have been discussed in the archaeological and ecological literature. The measure that I will use in my analysis is based on the information statistic (Shannon and Weaver 1949), using work by Zar (1974) and Pielou (1977). I will refer to it as H/H_{max}, although it sometimes termed J or V'. It produces a quantitative measure of the evenness of a distribution of classes.

The formula (Figure 4.5) for computing this measure on a single assemblage may appear formidable, but I will attempt to show that it behaves in an intuitive reasonable fashion. The salient aspects of this measure are:

(1) H/H_{max} varies from 0.0 where only one category is present, i.e., minimum evenness, to a maximum evenness of 1.0, where each category is present and is represented in equal proportions.

(2) As can be seen in the formula for H_{max} and the first formula for H, H/H_{max} is a relatively simple function of the number of categories, k, and the relative proportion of each category in the sample, p_i. (However, for the proportion, p_i, it is possible to substitute the frequency, f_i, of a category divided by the sample size, n, to obtain the second formula for H and the formula for J.)

(3) The measure cannot be applied to collections in which one or more classes are absent because the undefined term, log (0), is obtained during computation. This is obviously unsatisfactory for archaeological usage, in which classes are commonly absent. However, neither Pielou (1977) nor Zar (1974) mention this problem or propose a solution. Although the most

Definitions

$$f_i = \text{frequency of category i}$$
$$k = \text{number of categories}$$
$$n = \text{sample size}$$
$$p_i = \frac{f_i}{n}$$

Shannon–Weaver information function

$$H = -\sum_{i=1}^{k} p_i \log(p_i)$$

equivalently

$$H = \frac{n \log(n) - \sum_{i=1}^{k} f_i \log(f_i)}{n}$$

Maximum possible H for k categories

$$H_{max} = \log(k)$$

Evenness (Zar 1974; Pielou 1977)

$$J = \frac{H}{H_{max}}$$

Fig. 4.5. Computation of evenness

obvious remedy is to adjust the number of categories (k) to the number of categories *present* in that particular sample, use of this method leads to clearly undesirable behavior of the measure. The best solution appears to be to substitute 0.0 for any undefined term. This technique yields intuitively acceptable results and is used, where necessary, in all computations presented here.

Mathematical details aside, the evenness computation for the six distributions shown in Figure 4.6 suggests that H/H_{max} produces intuitively plausible results. In Figure 4.6a, a distribution with only one category has a minimum evenness of 0.0, and in Figure 4.6f, a distribution with an exactly uniform representation of each class leads to a maximum evenness of 1.0. The other distributions are in order of increasing evenness, an order that, I hope, agrees with an intuitive notion of evenness.

While H/H_{max} seems to be a satisfactory measure of evenness, there are still problems with sample size similar to those encountered with the richness measure. However, in contrast to richness, where the sample-size problems are rather obvious, the nature of the problem for evenness, is less clear, and, to my knowledge, it has not been dealt with in other than a summary fashion in the archaeological literature.

Consider the distribution of evenness values for different samples of ten types of ground stone collected from a set of sites in Arizona (Figure 4.7). There is a trend toward higher evenness values with larger samples, although it is not quite so clear-cut ($r_{xy} = 0.50$, $r_{\log(x)y} = 0.92$).

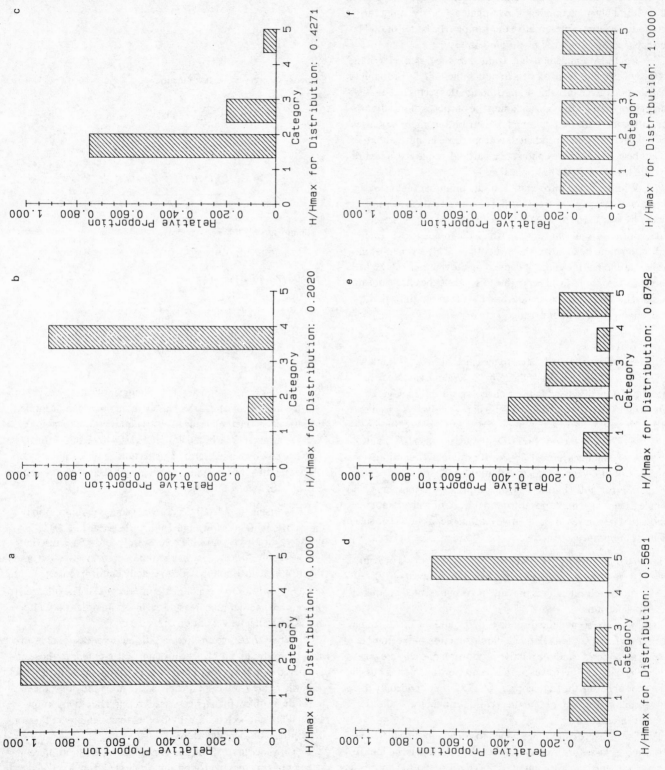

Fig. 4.6. Evenness (*H*/*H*max) of six distributions composed of one to five classes

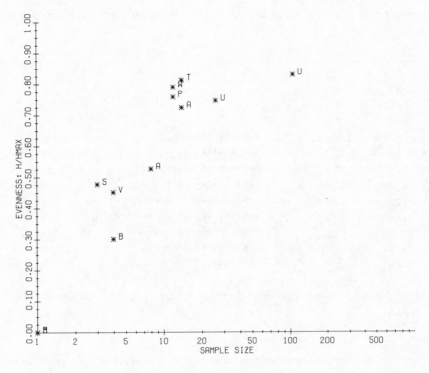

CHOLLA PROJECT: CHEVELON GROUND STONE DIVERSITY

Fig. 4.7. Plot of evenness (ordinate) against sample size (abscissa)   for 11 ground-stone assemblages

The solution I propose for this sample-size problem is the application of a Monte Carlo approach similar to the one used for richness. For a given sample size, a large number of simulated assemblages is constructed. However, rather than analyze the richness values obtained, the evenness measure is calculated for each simulated assemblage. Then, the distribution of evenness values in the simulated assemblages for a given sample size is used to calculate the mean (expected) evenness and its confidence interval.

The histogram in Figure 4.8 shows the results of 500 trials for a sample size of 30, using the probability distribution of the ground stone for all sites combined (Table 4.2). Here the mean evenness is 0.82, and the evenness values of 80% of the trials fall between about 0.725 and 0.875. Each asterisk represents three simulated collections and its vertical position shows its place in the distribution of evenness values.

Again, we can run these simulations for a range of sample sizes and plot the mean and confidence interval along with the archaeological data points. Using the ground-stone data, Figure 4.9 shows that *all* of the actual samples fall within the 80% confidence interval of the random model. I will return to an interpretation shortly, but the general conclusion is that the distribution of ground-stone types on sites is primarily a sample-size phenomenon.

Implications and applications

In the following sections, the proposed method is used to analyze diversity in a variety of collections from archaeological sites in Arizona.

The Cholla Project

The substantive analysis presented here uses material collected by the Cholla Project, directed by J. Jefferson Reid. The project involved investigation of archaeological sites along a 135-mile transmission-line corridor through central Arizona. The project recorded 248 sites and 84 artifact clusters, many of which appear to be analytically equivalent to sites. Cholla Project sites range in time mainly from about A.D. 900 until about A.D. 1350, from Pueblo II through Pueblo IV times. Sites investigated included surface scatters with no apparent architecture, scatters associated with one or more isolated rooms, occasional compounds associated with rooms, and substantial masonry pueblos.

In 1982, Reid published a five-volume report on the Cholla Project (Reid 1982). A major focus in his settlement study was the identification of site function. In dealing with this issue, Reid relied heavily on the evenness dimension of diversity (using H/H_{max} as a measure). His premise was that the longer the period a site was occupied each year, the more different kinds of activities would have taken place. Thus artifactual assemblages would reflect a longer annual occupation through a greater diversity of artifacts recovered. There was an explicit desire to view occupational intensity as a continuum indicated mainly by *artifacts* rather than use the usual habitation/limited activity dichotomy that is based almost exclusively on untested assumptions about the permanence of occupation at sites with *architecture*.

Because of the different cultural and natural environments involved, the project area was divided into three regions: the Chevelon, Q-Ranch, and Tonto–Roosevelt regions (of which only

Evenness	No. of trials	% of trials	Cum % trials	Histogram * = 3 trials
0.600	1	0.2	0.2	*
0.625	4	0.8	1.0	*
0.650	2	0.4	1.4	*
0.675	3	0.6	2.0	*
0.700	20	4.0	6.0	*******
> 0.725	31	6.2	12.2	> *********
0.750	55	11.0	23.2	*****************
0.775	59	11.8	35.0	******************
+ 0.800	89	17.8	52.8	+ *****************************
0.825	74	14.8	67.6	**********************
0.850	75	15.0	82.6	***********************
> 0.875	54	10.8	93.4	> *****************
0.900	23	4.6	98.0	********
0.925	10	2.0	100.0	***

Mean evenness	0.82
Standard deviation	0.06
Confidence interval	0.80

Fig. 4.8. Histogram of evenness values from 500 simulated trials for a sample size of 30 using the probability distribution above

Table 4.2. Probability distribution of Chevelon ground stone

Element no.	Proportion
1	6.8%
2	2.9%
3	3.9%
4	11.7%
5	9.7%
6	15.5%
7	1.5%
8	5.3%
9	25.7%
10	17.0%

the first two are of interest here). Systematic surface or excavated collections were obtained from 81 of the 249 Q-Ranch sites and artifact clusters. The Chevelon region had 14 sites recorded, of which 11 were collected or excavated.

When sites were collected, systematic surface collections were made. However, collections were not made at all sites, and excavations were conducted at only a few. The primary body of data deriving from the artifact identification consisted of counts of types within each of four material categories: ceramics, chipped-stone tools, other chipped-stone artifacts, and ground stone. Sample sizes of the individual collections varied tremendously. Ceramic samples on a single site range from zero to 7000; chipped-stone

tools from zero to 230; chipped-stone artifacts from zero to nearly 13,000, and ground stone from zero to about 100.

Ground-stone analysis
Let us now return to the ground stone from the Chevelon region that was used as an example in the discussion of the evenness measure. Ground stone was divided into ten classes for this analysis: basin, slab, trough, and indeterminate metates, unifacial and bifacial manos, modified unifacial and bifacial handstones, and unmodified unifacial and bifacial handstones.

Expectations If the sites that have ground stone present were functionally differentiated *and* if the morphologically distinguished ground-stone types were used for different activities, then there should be sites with *less than expected* evenness and richness for the ground-stone classes. A function-specific site should have a small number of functionally associated ground-stone categories well represented and other categories absent, which would lead to a lower evenness and richness than would be expected on the basis of sample size alone. For example, if at some sites bifacially worked manos were used with basin metates for grinding corn, but at different sites slab metates and unifacially worked manos were used for processing pinyon nuts, both types of sites should exhibit a low diversity of ground stone; even if there were many pieces of ground stone at the sites, we would expect only a small number of classes with an uneven distribution.

Results The most striking result of the diversity analysis of this material is that both the evenness and richness analyses show *all* collections falling within the 80% confidence interval produced

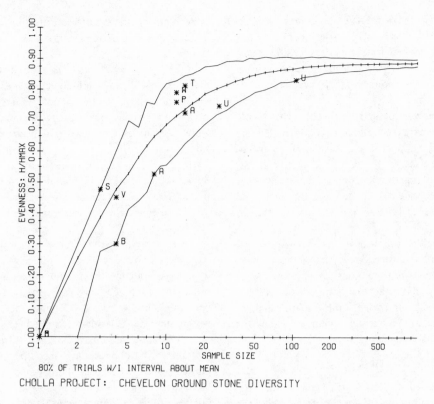

Fig. 4.9. Relationship between evenness (ordinate) and sample size (abscissa) with mean and confidence intervals plotted

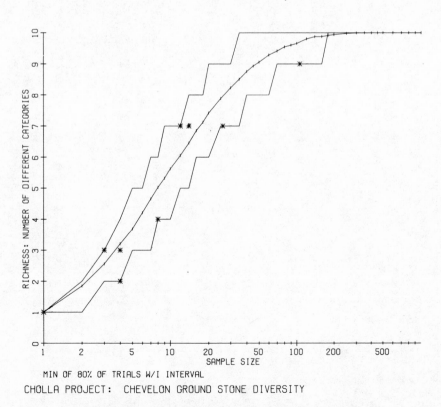

Fig. 4.10. Plot of richness (ordinate) against sample size (abscissa) with 80% confidence intervals for Chevelon ground-stone assemblages

by the model. In the plot of the richness against sample size (Figure 4.10), the confidence interval neatly encloses *all* of the actual data points, a fact that I think indicates that the very simple random model employed is, in some way, reflecting real processes. The evenness plot (Figure 4.9) shows an equally neat circumscription of the actual data points.

Contrary to the expectation that there would be sites with lower than expected diversity, the fit with the random model for both evenness and richness appears to indicate that the distribution of the ground-stone classes at these sites is a function of the sample size and the underlying distribution, and not much more. Stated roughly, whenever a site has ground stone, the whole repertoire tends to be represented within the limits imposed by the sample size.

This would suggest that sites with ground stone present were *not* strongly differentiated functionally, or that the ground-stone typology is not *functionally* significant despite *morphological* differences among the types. In either case, it may be that it is only the presence or absence of ground stone or the absolute numbers of ground stone items that are functionally significant, issues that are explicitly excluded by the diversity analysis.

Stone-tool analysis

An analysis of chipped-stone tools yields more positive results and provides some additional insights. Thirteen types of formal chipped-stone tools were identified and used in this analysis (although only 11 occurred in the Chevelon region). The 13 types are: scrapers, projectile points, perforators/drills, tabular knives, bifaces, notches, denticulates, truncations, multiple tools, varia, battered pieces, massive pieces, and axes.

Expectations As with the ground stone, sites with tool assemblages indicative of limited activities are predicted to show lower than expected richness and evenness. Long-term habitation sites where a wide variety of activities were performed should show an evenness above or within the expected range.

Results In the plot of *richness* against sample size, with an 80% confidence interval shown (Figure 4.11), one collection has higher than expected richness, several sites are within the confidence interval, and several sites show lower than expected richness.

The *evenness* plot (Figure 4.12) shows this pattern a little more clearly. We may tentatively interpret the sites below the 80% interval generated by the random model as conforming with our predictions for functionally differentiated sites. Those within the band might be interpreted as having longer annual occupations with more varied activities performed.

Of course, this interpretation requires a more careful examination, which can be accomplished through an analysis of the plotted points with respect to time and architectural complexity of the sites represented. The sites below the confidence interval are a mixture of Pueblo II and Pueblo III sites (basically, the only periods represented in the Chevelon sample), as are the sites within the interval, indicating that temporal differences are not producing this distribution.

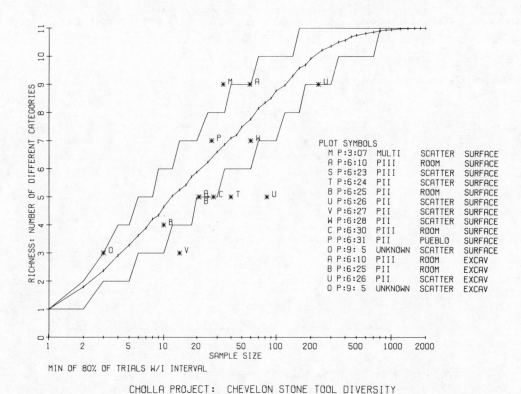

Fig. 4.11. Plot of richness (ordinate) against sample size (abscissa) with 80% confidence intervals for Chevelon chipped-stone tool assemblages

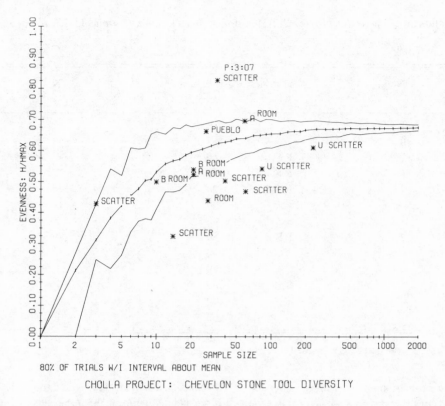

Fig. 4.12. Plot of evenness (ordinate) against sample size (abscissa) with 80% confidence intervals for Chevelon chipped-stone tool assemblages

More interestingly, examination of the architectural characteristics of the sites shows that, with one exception, the sites within the interval have masonry architecture (indicated as room or pueblo) and, with one exception, the sites below the band have no identifiable architectural remains (indicated as scatter). The single pueblo in this analysis shows both an evenness and richness near the top of the expected interval, indicating a relatively high diversity, which is not unexpected, given the architectural investment in the site.

Both surface and excavated samples were analyzed from three sites, labeled A, B, and U. In two of the three cases (B and U) the excavated and surface samples from the same site have approximately the same position relative to the confidence band, indicating similar evenness of the surface and excavated samples, when sample size is taken into account. In the third case (A), the excavated collection appears near the bottom of the interval while the surface collection from the same site appears at the top of the band. This site appears to be a multicomponent site, with the primary component a Pueblo III one. It is not surprising that the surface scatter representing multiple occupations shows a higher diversity (on both dimensions) than does the excavated collection resulting only from a single context from the Pueblo III occupation.

Finally, we may discuss AZ P:3:7(ASM), the site with above-expected richness and evenness. At this site more different types than would be expected at that sample size occur, and regionally rare types are more common than would be expected, given random choice from the regional distribution. This diversity is explained by the fact that P:3:7 is a deflated,

multicomponent site with components from the Archaic through the ceramic periods. The combination of assemblages from different (temporal components (and particularly the Archaic component) in this surface scatter results in a higher diversity than is expected from the regional distribution, which is primarily determined by the Pueblo II and Pueblo III materials.

Overall, this analysis shows an association of architecture with higher diversities of stone-tool assemblages, although it indicates that the relationship is not complete, and it has brought to our attention several non-conforming cases. Examination of the exceptions indicates that this method (like all others) will not interpret the archaeological remains, but it may point out loci for the fruitful application of expert knowledge by the archaeologist.

Comparison of relative evenness values This analysis illustrates the problems that could arise from comparing *absolute* evenness values rather than relative ones. If stone-tool collections were compared on the basis of their absolute evenness values, the higher relative diversity of sites with architectural remains was not observed. This can be seen in Figure 4.13a, a histogram constructed from the absolute evenness values. Here the site type of each collection is indicated by a P for a pueblo, R for a masonry room, and S for a scatter. In this histogram, the sites with architecture are pretty thoroughly mixed with those without architecture.

One way of obtaining a measure of evenness that is *relative* to the expectation would be to consider each collection's evenness

Figure 4.13. Evenness values (a) and percentiles (b) for Chevelon stone-tool collections. (P = pueblo, R = room, S = scatter)

	a				b		
Evenness value	N	Histogram		Evenness percentile*	N	Histogram	
0.30	1	S		0	6	R S S S S S	
0.35	0			5	0		
0.40	2	R S		10	0		
0.45	2	R S		15	2	R R	
0.50	4	R R S S		20	0		
0.55	0			30	0		
0.60	1	S		40	1	R	
0.65	2	P R		50	0		
0.70	0			60	0		
0.75	0			70	1	S	
0.80	1	S		80	1	P	
				90	1	R	
				100	1	S	

*Note that the percentile scale from 0 to 20 is expanded.

as a percentile relative to the distribution of evenness values derived from the simulated construction of assemblages at its sample size. Thus, a point well below a 90% confidence interval might be in the third percentile (or in the lower 3% of the trials), one just above the interval could be in the 95th percentile (in the upper 5%), and one at the median would be in the 50th percentile.

When this relative measure is applied to the same stone-tool data, the histogram in Figure 4.13b is obtained. With the exceptions noted in the discussion of the plot, sites with and without architecture are neatly separated in this histogram of evenness percentiles. This suggests that the evenness percentile at a given sample size may be a useful quantitative measure of relative evenness.

Conclusions

This analysis has proceeded rather inductively (although it could be applied in a more deductive framework) and has gone back and forth between two modes of discourse. In a *substantive* mode, the methods have been used to inform us to a significant degree about a particular set of data from the Cholla Project. In a *methodological* mode, I have used the analysis of the Cholla Project data to inform about the behavior of certain measures and techniques of analysis that I have proposed.

At this point let me summarize two of my conclusions. First, it appears that, under some circumstances, the simulation method I have proposed seems to illuminate and, in a weak sense, to *explain* a significant amount of the variation we observe. Secondly, because of the sample-size effects on both diversity measures I have used here, it seems essential to compare points by their positions *relative* to the expectation and to the confidence interval, not as absolute numbers.

It appears to me that diversity is a useful concept, particularly when one has a lot of variability and rather low-powered or noisy samples, such as the surface collections used here. Diversity provides a broad-range filter for data that helps point out the more interesting cases for further examination. I hope that this method has advanced our ability to use this important concept *within* the constraints imposed by the often intractable nature of our data.

Chapter 5

Formation processes of Broken K Pueblo: some hypotheses

Michael B. Schiffer

Introduction

This paper examines the formation processes of rooms at Broken K Pueblo (Hill 1970) in order to illuminate the many analyses and reanalyses of ceramics from that site that have taken place in the past two decades.

Broken K Pueblo is situated in the Hay Hollow Valley of east-central Arizona, and consists of about 95 masonry rooms arranged around a courtyard. Fifty-four rooms were excavated in 1963 under the direction of James N. Hill (Hill 1970; Martin *et al.* 1967). As is well known, Broken K was one of the most influential case studies of the New Archaeology, where theory and data seemingly meshed perfectly. Introductory textbooks of the 1970s proudly used Broken K to claim that social organization – even marital residence pattern – is archaeologically accessible. In that same decade, however, major critiques of Hill's work were published, some based on reanalyses of the data. Because of the problems identified by the critics, few archaeologists believe today that Hill successfully inferred uxorilocal residence. Nevertheless, Broken K continues to be of interest, if for no other reason than that Hill and his colleagues so profusely published the artifact data. Regardless of how one views Hill's inferences, there is no doubt that Broken K is one of the best excavated and most thoroughly reported large pueblo sites in the American Southwest.

Many critics of the Broken K study focused on the statistical and spatial characteristics of ceramic types and design elements, for it was factor analyses of these data sets that revealed the 'patterns' believed by Hill to be the predictable consequences of uxorilocal residence. Regrettably, other investigators – including Dumond (1977), Lischka (1975), and S. Plog (1978) – did not succeed in replicating those patterns. One obvious reason is that Hill and the critics used different analytical techniques as well as different criteria for determining the factor composition of rooms. A more revealing reason, argued by Dumond, is that these data sets contain *no* particularly strong patterns. This conclusion is not very attractive, but it may be correct.

One fundamental issue has lurked in the background throughout the reanalyses of broken K data: by what formation processes did those ceramic artifacts accumulate on room floors and infills? Although Plog (1978: 148–50) assigned a high priority to identifying the formation processes of Broken K, to this point the critics have paid no more than lip-service to formation processes. After all, no one has attempted to identify the formation processes of the Broken K deposits. One might expect such an analysis to shed some light on the causes of ceramic patterning – or its lack.

Insofar as gross cultural formation processes are concerned, Broken K presents a paradoxical picture. Some evidence indicates that Broken K held rich and highly patterned assemblages of Pompeii-like *de facto* refuse, whereas other lines of evidence suggest that Broken K underwent a gradual process of decline and abandonment, and so many room floors contain secondary refuse and little *de facto* refuse. Hill carried out the analyses *as if* he were treating Pompeii-like assemblages of *de facto* refuse. And, indeed, the artifact counts from floors used to distinguish room types are impressive (Hill 1970: 42). For example, habitation room floors contained a mean of more than two dozen non-ceramic artifacts. Moreover, the marked differences in floor artifacts between large and small rooms permitted Hill to distinguish room types having seemingly clear-cut functional differences. No one among the many Broken K critics has disputed the room function inferences; the floor assemblages evidently do behave like *de facto* refuse.

Yet, two aspects of Broken K stand in stark contrast to the Pompeii image projected by the high frequencies and strong patterning in the non-ceramic floor artifacts. First is the extreme paucity of restored ceramic vessels: only six are reported from all room floors, and a scant six more were found in room fills (Martin *et al.* 1967: 133, 136). Evidently, the ceramic assemblages in these 54 excavated rooms are highly depleted relative to systemic inventories (cf. Schiffer 1985). Second is the large number of rooms that Hill (1970:31) believes were used for refuse disposal after their initial use. Generally, as a result of lateral cycling, curate behavior, and scavenging during abandonment periods, one seldom finds much *de facto* refuse on the floors of trash-filled rooms (cf. Reid 1973; Schiffer 1976). That 19 of the 54 excavated rooms served as secondary refuse receptacles indicates a protracted period of settlement abandonment that is inconsistent with the large amounts of *de facto* refuse that are also claimed for the floors of those very same 19 rooms.

In order to reconcile these incompatible views on the nature of Broken K, one is tempted to draw the unhappy conclusion that much of the *de facto* refuse analyzed by Hill was actually secondary refuse that landed on the floor. Thus, Broken K is not much like Pompeii, and most of Hill's analyses are without substantial basis. Habitation-room floors contain many items because most trash-filled rooms were habitation rooms. However, without a detailed study of the formation processes of Broken K Pueblo, this resolution is arbitrary.

Despite the plethora of published Broken K data, information most relevant for inferring formation processes (cf. Schiffer 1983) was seldom provided. As a result, I devised a number of surrogate measures and applied these to the available ceramic data with varying degrees of success. The surprising finding of this study is that many potentially restorable ceramic vessels from Broken K rooms apparently were recorded as sherds. Various lines of evidence support this 'missed pot' hypothesis, and lead to the tentative conclusion that Broken K contained more *de facto* refuse and less secondary refuse than anyone – including Hill – has thought. The design-element patterns produced by the factor analyses are determined, not by marital residence behavior, but by the co-occurrence of design elements on pots – restored and potentially restorable. It is further concluded that the factor analyses of ceramic-type frequencies yield no interpretable patterns because the input data consist of variable mixes of 'orphan' sherds and sherds from restorable vessels. This study underscores the need to identify and take into account the formation processes of the archaeological record (cf. Schiffer 1975, 1976, 1983, 1985).

Trash-filled rooms?

Hill addressed some very basic questions about formation processes by furnishing lists of rooms that were built on trash and others that had been trash filled. Regrettably, his assignments of room to the latter class are problematic.

On the surface, Hill's (1970:31) claim that 19 of the 54 excavated rooms (35.2%) contained 'trash deposits above floors' seems neither high nor low. However, at the nearby and roughly contemporaneous Joint Site, only six of 24 rooms (25%) were used as dumps (Schiffer 1976: 130–1). Sherd counts for the fills of the Broken K dump rooms range from 67 to 1323, with a mean of 401 (Table 5.1). In contrast, fills of the six rooms used as dumps at the Joint Site contain a mean of 1518 sherds, with a range of 154–3396. It is possible that many Broken K rooms were used for only a small amount of dumping; it is also possible that the criteria used by Hill to designate trash-filled rooms were unreliable or were applied inconsistently.

Hill does not supply the criteria used to determine whether a room had been 'trash-filled.' However, in discussing excavation techniques, he describes a 'typical room':

> [It] was about 60 cm. deep and usually contained three natural levels, including the floors. Level A, from the surface to 40 cm. thick, contained windblown and water-washed brown humus and sand, fallen wall stones, and no trash. Level B, from 40 to 59 cm., contained water-washed red sand or clay, sometimes trash, and roof beams occasionally. The floor level. . . (Hill 1970:22)

Table 5.1. Sherd counts from fills of Broken K rooms labeled by Hill (1970:31) as 'trash-filled.' Data are from Martin *et al.* (1966).

Room number	Total fill sherds	Room function
1	1148	Habitation
4	1323	Habitation
5	163	Habitation
6	161	Kiva
7	432	Habitation
9	393	Storage
11	170	Habitation
29	447	Kiva
30	470	Habitation
31–33	124	Habitation
36	67	Storage
51	122	Storage
53	79	Habitation
61	77	Storage
62	723	Habitation
64	523	Habitation
69	965	Habitation
73	125	Habitation
78	103	Habitation
Total	7615	

Table 5.2. *Sherd counts from Level B of excavated rooms at Broken K Pueblo. Data are from Martin* et al. *(1966).*

Room	Sherds in Level B	Dump (in Hill's judgment)	Room	Sherds in Level B	Dump (in Hill's judgment)
1	425 (A and B mix)	Yes	39	68	
2	22		40	(no Level B)	
4	355	Yes	41	1	
5	46	Yes	43	(no Level B)	
6	37	Yes	44a	(no Level B)	
7	383	Yes	44b	(no Level B)	
8	(no Level B)		48	(no Level B)	
9	299	Yes	49	3	
11	90	Yes	51	81	Yes
19	12		53	4	Yes
20	115		54	23	
21	18		60	98	
22	3		61	38	Yes
23	14		62	361	Yes
24	63		64	347	Yes
25	6		65	(no Level B)	
27	5		67	3	
28	(no Level B)		68	36	
29	38	Yes	69	483	Yes
30	93	Yes	73	(no Level B)	Yes
31	89	Yes	74	15	
33	96	Yes	78	30	Yes
34	35		79	21	
35	(no Level B)		80	67	
36	26	Yes	82	75	
37	5		92	31	
38	7				

On the basis of this statement, one might expect dumps to be indicated by large numbers of sherds in Level B. A comparison of sherd counts in Level B for Hill's dump and non-dump rooms (Table 5.2) does reveal a large difference:

	mean	range
dumps	175	4–483
non-dumps	23	0–115

However, there is considerable overlap in the range of 25–100 sherds (nine dumps; eight non-dumps) and, regardless of where one draws the dividing line, at least one-half dozen rooms will be misclassified. Nonetheless, sherd counts in Level B seem to have been an important criterion for designating rooms as trash-filled. However, many rooms have Levels C, D, and X, and the origin of their contents is unexplained. Moreover, Level A sometimes has many sherds.

The definition of 'floor' provenience is also of interest in evaluating Hill's inferences about trash disposal. According to Hill (1970:22), 'The floor level was defined as including everything resting on the floor or clearly associated with it.' Martin *et al.* (1967:13) echo these criteria: 'Only cultural debris found directly on the floors of rooms were [sic] called "floor materials".' Although this definition is very strict, some have suggested that floor materials might have included artifacts from secondary refuse deposited after the room's abandonment. Phillips (1972:9), for example, argued that high counts of bone from Broken K floors 'are a function of trash dumping.' In support of this inference, Phillips computed the average number of bones from floors, for rooms with and without trash fill; the counts are 148.6 and 22.0, respectively. Dumond (1977:339) also noted that 'the presence of more than 55 mammal bones in rooms is quite predictably and positively associated with the presence of trash deposits above the floors.' Seemingly, Phillips and Dumond have furnished a basis for questioning the integrity and distinctiveness of the floor deposits in 'trash-filled' rooms. Regrettably, however, both investigators aggregated the data according to Hill's categories of

Table 5.3. Sherds and animal bone from 'trash-filled' rooms at Broken K Pueblo. Data are from Martin *et al.* (1966) and Hill (1970:111–2).

Room	Fill sherds	Fill bone	Floor bone
1	1148	38	117
4–5	1483	183	276
6-K	161	9	10
7	432	92	179
9	393	6	19
11	170	76	537
29	447	0	1
30	470	7	7
31–33	124	135	132
36	67	0	1
51	122	77	71
53	79	0	69
61	77	3	0
62	723	151	57
64	523	3	141
69	965	69	219
73	125	19	14
78	103	0	35

dump and non-dump rooms, and did not subject the rooms in either class to close scrutiny. When the data are examined in detail, the picture becomes more complex. For example, in 'trash-filled' rooms, the correlation between number of bones in fill and number of bones on floor (Table 5.3) is only 0.51 (Pearson's *r*). Moreover, although some 'trash-filled' rooms contained many bones, the fills of nine trash-filled rooms held fewer than ten bones. Even more surprising is the modest correlation between total fill sherds and fill bone in the 'trash-filled' rooms (Pearson's *r* = 0.51). Together, these observations suggest that Hill's 'trash-filled' rooms are a very heterogeneous group.

It is possible, of course, that rooms used as dumps had mixed fill and floor materials. Indeed, Hill (1970:22) acknowledges that floor and fill materials may have been mixed in rooms 1, 40, and 69. However, the narrow definition of floor provenience used by Hill results in another potentially serious anomaly: the inclusion of sherds from the same restorable vessel in both fill and floor proveniences (Schiffer 1976:136–7). In view of the overall low quantities of purported secondary refuse in the fills (relative to the Joint Site), the alternative hypothesis must be entertained that some of the ceramic material included in Level B (and other fill levels) and regarded by Hill as secondary refuse is actually *de facto* refuse.

Another line of evidence, based on the use of Reid's relative room abandonment measure (Reid 1973, 1978; Reid and Shimada 1982), also casts doubt on the secondary refuse hypothesis for some room fills. This measure rests on a generalized life history of pueblo rooms: use, abandonment, usable artifacts removed by curate behavior or scavenging, and use as a dump. If most rooms follow this sequence, then a scatter plot of rooms by fill-sherd density and floor-sherd density should provide clusters that are interpretable as gross abandonment classes. For example, early-abandoned rooms should have a high density of fill sherds (from secondary refuse) and a low density of floor sherds, indicating little *de facto* refuse; this pattern would be reversed for late-abandoned rooms. As noted elsewhere (Schiffer 1976:129–33), this simple model is complicated in practice by many factors, including differences in room use. However, as a springboard for considering gross formation processes, it has proved useful. Comparisons with the Joint Site should be instructive because its excavators employed the same strict definition of floor provenience used at Broken K.

A scatter plot of Broken K rooms by fill- and floor-sherd density is present in Figure 5.1; the latter is based on data in Table 5.4. Compared to the Joint Site, the Broken K scatter plot exhibits far less obvious clustering. The most interesting difference, however, is in the absolute values of fill density. The *highest* fill density

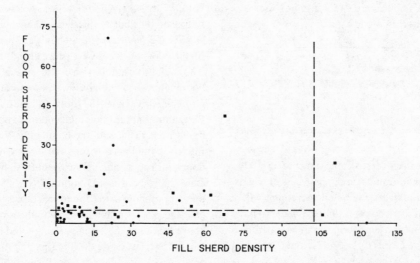

Fig. 5.1. Application of Reid's measure of relative room abandonment to Broken K ceramics. Square symbols refer to Hill's trash-filled rooms.

Table 5.4. *The application of Reid's relative room abandonment measure to Broken K. Data are from Martin et al. (1966) and Hill (1970:129).*

Room	Floor area	Fill-sherd density	Floor-sherd density	Room	Floor area	Fill-sherd density	Floor-sherd density
1	17.0	67.5	41.4	38	3.8	5.5	17.6
2	7.0	15.1	4.6	39	8.0*	123.5	0[+]
4–5	12.5	118.8	3.3	40	8.1	4.9	9.1
6	17.8	9.0	3.1	41	12.2	5.6	4.2
7	9.3	46.5	11.7	43	11.5	1.7	2.2
8	5.8	2.4	7.6	44a	7.5*	0.7	0.7
9	7.3	53.8	7.0	44b	4.0*	31.0	0[+]
11	13.2	12.9	12.1	48	4.5*	8.9	2.9
19	4.0*	12.5	1.5	49	4.1	1.7	10
20	9.8	33.1	2.8	51	5.9	20.7	3.4
21	9.2	9.2	6.8	53	8.0	9.9	22.1
22	2.5	3.1	0.3	54	5.5*	13.1	0
23	2.5*	2.7	0.3	60	6.2	20.3	29.8
24	7.3	12.1	21.5	61	6.0*	12.8	1.0
25	5.6*	4.3	1.6	62	11.7	61.8	11.4
27	4.8	56.0	3.5	64	33.5	15.6	14.8
28	7.3	22.2	0[+]	65	2.8	21.1	71.1
29	7.6	58.8	12.5	67	4.0	0.8	1.3
30	7.0	67.1	4.3	68	5.6	28.0	7.7
31	14.6	7.5	6.6	69	8.7	110.9	22.9
33	14.6	1.0	5.9	73	5.1	24.5	5.1
34	6.5	11.2	4.5	74	5.2	3.5	9.8
35	13.9	1.9	0[+]	78	10.5	9.8	4.7
36	5.5	4.8	6.9	79	10.4	2.7	5.6
37	13.9	0.8	3.8	80	8.6	18.8	18.5
				82	8.8	15.8	6.1
				92	11.2	9.0	13.1

* estimated from the site map (Hill 1970:9).
[+] assumed 0 floor sherds.

at Broken K, 123.5 sherds/m², falls on the low end of fill density for Joint Site dump rooms (28.0–522.5 sherds/m²; mean of 220). Moreover, some late-abandoned rooms at the Joint Site had relatively high fill-sherd densities. Room 31, for example, which contained at least four restorable pots on the floor, had a fill-sherd density of 111. That high density results from (1) refuse of unknown types, probably from the roof, and (2) sherds recorded in the fill but which belong to reconstructable vessels from the floor or roof.

Although the rooms Hill believes were used as dumps tend to cluster above a fill-sherd density of 40/m², such rooms can be found throughout the scatter plot (Figure 5.1). Relative to the Joint Site, few rooms ar Broken K provide unambiguous evidence that they were used as dumps. Indeed, many rooms are most like those at the Joint Site that yielded restored vessels and were abandoned late. A conservative interpretation of the scatter plot requires one to question the dumping inference for rooms 6, 11, 31, 33, 36, 53, 61, 64, and 78. In view of these comparisons with the Joint Site, a surprising interpretation of Broken K fills becomes

possible: many 'trash-filled' rooms were not used as dumps, but contain a variety of materials, possibly including *de facto* refuse. It should be noted that when I compiled the floor-sherd counts from Martin *et al.* (1966), I omitted features to ensure that sherds from subfloor features or the fill were not included in the counts. The result of this decision was in many cases to deflate the floor counts somewhat below Hill's (1970: 128–9) figures. Thus, the floor-sherd density figures in Table 5.4 are in reality too low, suggesting that there was even more *de facto* refuse in many rooms.

Another puzzling aspect of Hill's 'trash-filled' rooms is that they tend mostly to be habitation rooms (Table 5.1): 13 of 19 are habitation rooms, whereas only four are storage rooms. In contrast, the preference at the Joint Site was reversed: all six dumps were, in their previous use, storerooms (although one may have started out as a habitation room).

In evaluating Hill's secondary refuse interpretation it would be helpful to have some idea about sherd size. Generally, one would expect sherds in puebloan secondary refuse to be smaller *on the average* than those in *de facto* refuse. This comes about be-

Table 5.5. Sherd data from the fills of Broken K rooms. Data are from Martin *et al.* (1966).

Room	Total decorated	Total indeterm. decorated	Total textured	Total plainware	% Indet. decor tot. decor.	Room	Total decorated	Total indeterm. decorated	Total textured	Total plainware	% Indet. decor tot. decor.
1	694	298	406	48	42.9%	38	16	9	3	1	56.3
2	77	36	31	3	46.8	39	462	169	482	44	36.6
4	715	301	577	31	42.1	40	20	4	20	0	20.0
5	86	51	75	2	59.3	41	30	12	38	0	40.0
6	49	26	111	1	53.1	43	6	2	20	0	33.3
7	161	42	250	22	26.1	44a	4	3	1	0	75.0
8	8	5	6	0	62.5	44b	72	21	52	0	29.2
9	212	87	174	7	41.0	48	27	4	9	2	14.8
11[+]	47	20	121	2	42.5	49	1	0	6	0	–
19	25	5	25	0	20.0	51	111	23	21	0	20.7
20	164	72	162	6	43.9	53	45	14	32	2	31.1
21	32	4	27	0	12.5	54	58	6	14	0	10.3
22	13	2	10	0	15.4	60	23	4	96	8	17.4
23	12	7	6	2	58.3	61	41	16	30	6	39.0
24	61	14	17	0	22.9	62	374	116	329	19	31.0
25	20	3	4	0	15.0	64	112	24	396	18	21.4
27	156	33	101	12	21.2	65	16	7	16	1	43.8
28	108	33	33	2	30.6	67	2	0	1	0	–
29	214	67	205	28	31.3	68[+]	84	31	61	5	36.9
30	121	55	348	1	45.5	69	518	104	531	2	20.1
31	46	24	59	4	52.2	73	78	23	31	16	29.5
33	39	20	72	0	51.3	74	13	4	5	0	30.8
34	57	30	14	2	52.7	78	27	9	77	1	33.3
36	65	25	2	0	38.5	79	10	4	18	0	40.0
37	5	2	3	0	40.0	80	111	30	59	2	27.0
						82	21	6	117	1	28.6
						92	35	5	53	1	14.3

[+] Fill counts exclude 'roof' provenience.

cause *de facto* refuse vessels are usually broken into large sherds by the gradual collapse of walls and roofs, sometimes after a cushioning layer of windblown sand has accumulated. In contrast, breakage of a vessel during use is often quite violent, producing more fragmentation; moreover, the sherds from a vessel can be further reduced in size by trampling.

No direct information on sherd size or weight is available, so a surrogate measure was constructed. It is widely appreciated that small sherds are difficult to place into decorated types. Thus, the ratio of indeterminate decorated to identified decorated sherds in room fill can furnish a *crude* indication of average sherd size (Table 5.5). Table 5.6 presents the distribution of rooms in relation to this ratio. It can be seen that Hill's dump rooms are well distributed, and do not predominate where sherd sizes should be small. This surrogate measure is, of course, weak and certainly nondefinitive, but it can be helpful in isolating suspicious rooms – those that Hill believes were dumps, but which seem to have large sherds. Clearly, it is difficult to specify a non-arbitrary dividing line for this measure; I have chosen 30% indeterminate, a cut-off that is probably conservative. Trash-filled rooms falling below this percentage – 7, 51, 64, 69, and 73 – appear to have inordinately large sherds and should be considered likely candidates for containing *de facto* refuse vessels.

The 'missed pot' hypothesis

Another obvious line of evidence for evaluating the formation processes of Broken K rooms is restored pots (excluding miniatures), a listing of which is provided in Table 5.7. According to these data, only six vessels were found on 54 room floors. This contrasts markedly with the Joint Site, where at least 12 pots were found on the floors of only 24 excavated rooms. These are minimal figures because no concerted effort was made to restore pots from the Joint Site (Schiffer 1976:130). The dearth of obvious ceramic *de facto* refuse at Broken K is puzzling, especially when it is considered that Broken K was one of the latest, if not *the* latest, pueblo occupied in the Hay Hollow Valley, and there are no later sites nearby. Even if curate behavior were responsible for depleting the floor assemblages, one would expect some of the bulkier textured pots to have been left behind; but there are no restored textured pots.

Table 5.6. *Frequency distribution of rooms by the percentage of indeterminate decorated sherds in room fills at Broken K. Data are from Table 5.5.*

%	
0–5	
5–10	
10–15	21, 25*, 48*, 54, 92
15–20	19*, 22*, 40*, 60*
20–25	24, 27, 51, 64, 69
25–30	7, 44b, 73, 80, 82*
30–35	28, 29, 43*, 53, 62, 74*, 78
35–40	36, 37*, 39, 41, 61, 68, 79*
40–45	1, 4, 9, 11, 20, 65*
45–50	2, 30
50–55	6, 31, 33, 34
55–60	5, 23*, 38*
60–65	7, 8*
65–70	
70–75	44a*

* rooms with fewer than 25 decorated sherds
__ rooms designated 'trash-filled' by Hill

Table 5.7. *Restored ceramic vessels from Broken K rooms (Martin et al. 1967:133, 136)*

Room	Restored vessels
33	Snowflake B/W jar, Floor, pit 0 Snowflake B/W jar, Floor, pit 0
39	Snowflake B/W jar, fill, Level B (this vessel is very fragmentary)
41	Snowflake B/W jar, Floor, pit A (some sherds missing)
48	St. Johns Polychrome bowl, fill, Level A (some sherds missing)
53	St. Johns Polychrome bowl, Floor 1 (some sherds missing)
69	St. Johns Polychrome bowl, fill, Level B (very fragmentary) Pinto Polychrome bowl, Level B (some sherds missing) Snowflake B/W jar, Floor 1 and levels B and C; rim parts from Room 4, Level B (some sherds missing) Snowflake B/W jar, fill, 'east wall trench' (many sherds missing)
80	Snowflake B/W canteen, Floor 1 (some sherds missing)
92	Springerville Polychrome bowl, Floor (some sherds missing)

Probably the most conspicuous anomaly in the Broken K ceramic data is the vast number of floor sherds in rooms that Hill did *not* regard as dumps. Using Hill's counts, ten non-dump rooms contained 80 or more floor sherds (Hill 1970: 128–9), and only three of these (69, 80, and 92) yielded restored vessels. Clearly, these rooms (2, 21, 24, 40, 41-K, 60, 65, 80, 82, and 92) must be regarded as good prospects for having held restorable vessels that were 'missed.'[1] If floor and fill materials were well segregated, then some 'trash-filled' rooms having 80 or more sherds on their floors (1, 4–5, 7, 11, 29, 31–33, 53, 62, 64, 69, and 78) might also contain ceramic *de facto* refuse.

It is possible that the excavators of Broken K, like those of the Joint Site, did not strive to identify and reassemble restorable pots. When I was working for Paul Martin, he actively discouraged reassembly, arguing that it caused problems when the summer's finds were shipped to the Field Museum in Chicago. I do not know whether this policy prevailed at the time of the Broken K excavations; however, the documentation for Broken K contains several intriguing entries that bear on this question. In reference to 14 sherds of Snowflake B/W on Floor 1 of Room 92, Martin *et al.* (1966:186) state that they were 'part of ladle.' Two sherd groups in Room 51 also occasioned comment (Martin *et al.* 1966:122): 18 sherds of St. Johns Polychrome in Level B ('interior is distinctive and some fit') and 31 sherds of Snowflake B/W, Tularosa variety, in the fill ('all this Tularosa may add up to something, but I haven't played with it yet'). These notes suggest that the search for restorable pots was not systematic, thus additional restorable vessels might be present in Broken K rooms. Another factor that worked against reassembly of vessels was the refined provenience system in use at Broken K. Sherds from many bags would have to

be examined from each room to secure matches; indeed, many of the restored vessels are still fragmentary. For corrugated vessels, the refitting task would have been quite formidable.

Other lines of evidence may be examined in order to seek possible restorable pots that were not recorded as such in the field and laboratory.

Excess design elements in room fills and floors

One obvious place to look for missed pots is in the design-element tabulations from fills and floors. If many sherds from a single vessel are present in a unit, one might expect it to contain high counts of several different design elements. However, other processes could also be responsible for units that contain many occurrences of several design elements. For example, very common design elements, i.e., those occurring on many different vessels, could also form such clusters.

As Dumond (1977) has noted, the overall pattern is one of design elements thinly spread among rooms. Indeed, the most frequent entry by far is zero, and most design elements do not occur in most rooms! Moreover, 'design elements having fewer than 10 occurrences at the site' were not included in the tabular data (Hill 1970:131). Had they been, the spottiness of these distributions would have been even more striking. If one plots the frequency distribution of design-element occurrences in room fills (except zeros), an intriguing pattern emerges (Table 5.8). On the basis of

Table 5.8. The frequency distribution of design elements in Broken K room fills. Data are from Hill (1970:134–9).

Frequency of design elements	Number of occurrences	Total frequency	Relative frequency
0	(most are zero)		
1	447	447	24.45%
2	153	306	16.74
3	92	276	15.10
4	39	156	8.53
5	26	130	7.11
6	13	78	4.27
7	7	49	2.68
8	9	72	3.94
9	9	81	4.43
10	3	30	1.64
11	4	44	2.41
12	3	36	1.97
13	1	13	0.71
14	3	42	2.30
15	1	15	0.82
16			
17			
18			
19			
20			
21			
22	1	22	1.20
23			
24			
25			
26			
27			
28			
29			
30			
31	1	31	1.70
32			
33			

the steep fall-off of the first few values (1–4 design-element occurrences), one might expect to reach zero instances by ten occurrences, but such is not the case. Indeed, there are two occurrences of greater than 20 instances of the same design element in room fills. This distribution suggests that some process is leading to a number of very high values.

To investigate the nature of these higher values further, I returned to Hill's original tables (Hill 1970:130–9), seeking specific instances. If the frequency of a design element (in a room fill or floor) met either of the following two criteria, it was flagged as being suspicious:

Criterion 1:

The case included 25% or more of the total frequency of that design element among all rooms. For example, only 11 instances of design element 31 occur on the floors of all Broken K rooms. However, in Room 40 six examples of this design element were found, clearly exceeding the minimal 25%.

Criterion 2:

The case included 25% or more of the total of design elements in that provenience. For example, the floor of Room 7 contained 32 total design elements. Of these, nine were of design element 153, thus exceeding the 25% criterion.

The search was carried out on both room fills and room floors; Table 5.9 lists the resulting suspicious cases.

If a restorable vessel was not recognized because its sherds were divided up between floor and fill proveniences, then the *same* design element might occur in suspiciously high proportions in both the floor and fill of the same room. However, Table 5.9 furnishes no evidence of overlap. Even if one uses criteria much more generous than those described above for flagging cases, no appreciable overlap is found. Thus, if a restorable decorated pot was missed in a room, its sherds occurred mostly in fill or mostly on the floor. This result suggests a high degree of independence of fill and floor materials, at least with regard to decorated ceramics.

If Criteria 1 and 2 are capable of detecting potentially restorable vessels, then the proveniences that yielded the known restored vessels should be included among the suspicious cases. A comparison of the proveniences of the 12 known restored pots (Table 5.7) with the room fills and floors in Table 5.9 indicates, at best, an imperfect match: only five of the nine floors and fills containing restored pots or parts thereof appear to be listed among the suspicious cases. The failure of Criteria 1 and 2 to capture many of the known restored vessels in those rooms could result from incomplete or inconsistent recording of design elements on those vessels. In order to evaluate this hypothesis, I turned to the vessels themselves.

I examined the restored pots illustrated by Martin *et al.* (1967:127–37) and attempted to match the most frequently occurring design elements on each vessel with Hill's master list of design elements (Hill 1970:26–7). After each element was identified by number, I consulted the appendix where design elements are reported by provenience (Hill 1970:130–9). I looked up the provenience of each pot and sought tabulations of its design elements. When the design elements could not be matched, I looked for conspicuous numbers of design elements in the appropriate provenience, and attempted to make a reasonable *post hoc* match. Even if doubtful matches are included, the surprising result of this analysis is that the design elements from many restored vessels were not included in Hill's tabulations.

This finding accords with Hill's frequent statement that design elements on *sherds* were used in the analyses. However, no vessel was *recovered* intact, and most were composed of at least a half-dozen sherds. Thus, analytical consistency for Hill requires that the design elements on the sherds making up the restored vessels be recorded. Apparently, that was not done in many cases.

That many of the restored vessels were not included in the

Table 5.9. Rooms in which there is an excess of one or more design elements in fill or floor on the basis of Criteria 1 and 2. Fill data are from Hill (1970:134–9); floor data are from Hill (1970:130–3).

Room	Design element number	Meets Criterion 1	Meets Criterion 2	Room	Design element number	Meets Criterion 1	Meets Criterion 2
Fills					135	Yes	
1	89	Yes			136	Yes	
	173	Yes		73	131	Yes	
	175	Yes		80	141	Yes	
	176	Yes			165	Yes	
	178	Yes		Plaza-			
2	31		Yes	Kiva	30	Yes	
4–5	15	Yes			47	Yes	
	18	Yes			77–81	Yes	
	20	Yes			95	Yes	
	43	Yes			110	Yes	
	146	Yes			135	Yes	
	158R	Yes			158R	Yes	
	173	Yes			179	Yes	
20	156	Yes					
21	10	Yes	Yes	Floors			
24	141	Yes	Yes				
	135	Yes		2	82		Yes
27	164		Yes	6	127R		Yes
28	12	Yes			164		Yes
	108	Yes		7	153	Yes	Yes
29	41	Yes	Yes	8	50–51	Yes	
30	69	Yes		11	153		Yes
39	13	Yes		20	174		Yes
39K*	32	Yes		21	39	Yes	
	128R	Yes			156		Yes
51	140	Yes	Yes	30	146		Yes
53	164	Yes	Yes	33	45	Yes	
60	155	Yes	Yes		46	Yes	
62	99	Yes			146	Yes	
64	139	Yes			155	Yes	
65	29		Yes		158R	Yes	
69	7	Yes		37	39	Yes	Yes
	9	Yes		38	67		Yes
	45	Yes		40	31	Yes	
	46	Yes			67	Yes	
	49	Yes			169	Yes	
	77–81	Yes		64	110	Yes	
				80	148	Yes	

*Room 39-K is listed by Hill (1970:32–3) as unexcavated, and no sherds counts are furnished by Martin *et al.* (1966).

design-element tabulations raises one's confidence in Criteria 1 and 2. I now consider each of the suspicious cases.

Room 69 is interesting in that two restored vessels are reported by Martin *et al.* (1967:136) from the fill levels. Eight design elements occur in high frequencies by Criterion 1, and all but one corresponds to those in the two vessels illustrated by

Martin *et al.* (1967). Clearly, these procedures have some potential for also detecting restorable – but unrestored – vessels.

A cluster of five design-element types occurs in the fill of Room 1. However, two lines of evidence suggest that they do not indicate a restorable pot. First of all, because four of the elements are simple lines, instances of which occur in conjunction with other elements on many painted designs, they could easily derive from many vessels. Secondly, the design-element types are among the more abundant at the site. And, thirdly, the fill of room 1 contains 1148 sherds, which for a Broken K fill is a large number; it may well hold secondary refuse. These lines of evidence suggest that this combination of elements does not represent a restorable vessel.

Room 4–5 contained 1323 sherds – the largest total at the site. If this is a trash-filled room, as Hill believes, then this clustering of design elements may be a product of several large sherds or restorable vessels that were deposited as secondary refuse. Some of the elements could have co-occurred on designs. For example, element types 15 and 18, both of which are relatively rare at Broken K, could have been compatible on the same vessel. In short, some partly or completely restorable vessels may have been contained in the fill of room 4–5.

Other rooms provide additional cases of possible restorable vessels. Room 21 contains nine instances of design element 10, a type that has a total frequency at Broken K of 19. An equally compelling case is furnished by room 24, where the 11 instances of design element 141 represent more than half of its total occurrences. Room 27 has six examples of design element 164, a sizable cluster for a design that has a total frequency of only 30. Design elements 12 and 108 are both rare at the site but are found in excess in Room 28. Room 39 has a number of suggestive clusters of design elements, only one of which met a criterion for inclusion in the list of suspicious cases; clearly, its fill may contain some very large sherds or restorable vessels. It should be noted that design elements from the restored vessel from Level B of Room 39 do not appear to have been recorded. In Room 60 were found six instances of design element 155, a type that has a total frequency of only 20. Room 65 has a few small clusters of design elements, one of which was flagged because the fill contains only 14 design elements. A very strong case is provided by the abundance of rare elements 141 and 165 in the fill of Room 80. It is noteworthy that none of these rooms (21, 24, 27, 28, 39, 60, 65, and 80) is listed by Hill (1970:31) as being trash-filled.

In Hill's trash-filled rooms (in addition to Rooms 1 and 4–5), are found additional cases for restorable pots. Room 30 has several small clusters, which together are suggestive. In room 51 were found eight instances of design element 140; only 12 examples are found in all of Broken K. A cluster of nine instances of design element 164 occurred in Room 53. Room 62 contains a large number of small design-element clusters that did not meet either criterion; in addition, the seven instances of design element 99 are more than half of its total count. The fill of Room 64 contained a large number of small to moderate clusters. In Room 73 were found several small design-element clusters; seven samples of design element 131 occur in this room, almost half the site total. In short, even in the fills of rooms regarded by Hill as trash-filled there are many possible restorable pots.

Let us now turn to room floors. The number of suspicious cases overall is not great, owing in part to the paucity of floor design-element occurrences relative to those in fills. However, there are a few good candidates for restorable vessels. Room 33

Table 5.10. Design elements in room fills and floors at Broken K. Data are from Hill (1970:130–9).

Room	Floor		Fill	
	Number of different design elements	Total frequency of design elements	Number of different design elements	Total frequency of design elements
1	28	56	56	196
2	10	18	8	14
4–5	18	25	63	237
6	6	8	13	18
7	15	32	24	49
8	11	26	0	0
9	18	22	36	58
11	11	21	17	24
19	0	0	7	10
20	8	10	29	62
21	11	19	7	18
22	0	0	16	21
24	9	11	10	34
25	9	13	0	0
27	13	15	12	23
28	0	0	23	41
29	0	0	40	98
30	10	14	15	29
31–33	33	80	19	22
34	3	6	13	19
36	7	9	7	15
37	7	10	0	0
38	7	8	0	0
39	0	0	22	51
39K	0	0	31	80
40	19	53	8	11
41K	9	13	43	104
44	0	0	10	10
51	6	10	13	24
53	8	11	12	25
60	0	0	12	20
61	0	0	13	20
62	14	24	43	89
64	22	37	35	69
65	17	21	8	14
68	8	12	27	41
69	13	17	33	132
73	10	12	19	35
74	4	7	0	0
78	11	17	0	0
79	8	10	0	0
80	16	26	18	51
82	11	14	0	0
92	9	14	16	23

has a grouping of four design-element types, all of which could have come from a large jar of Snowflake B/W. It is of interest that Martin *et al.* (1967) report two large restored Snowflake B/W jars from the floor of this room; however, the group of four design elements is from neither restored pot. The likelihood that a third was present raises intriguing possibilities for the use of Room 33. Two large groupings of design elements, in Room 21 and 40, provide strong evidence of restorable vessels. The remaining rooms contain an excess of only one design element each, furnishing weaker evidence for restorable pots; perhaps they are merely large sherds. (Design element 148, in Room 80, is probably not from the restored pot on the floor.) Both strong and weak cases occur on floors of Hill's 'trash-filled' rooms. Table 5.9 seems to suggest that more than a few restorable (decorated) vessels in floor and fill contexts were recorded only as sherds.

Diversity of design elements

Another line of evidence that may be helpful in pinpointing missed pots is the diversity of design elements (Table 5.10). The present analysis deals with the property of diversity known as *richness*, the number of different types of entity in a unit (Kintigh 1984a). In general, richness is a function of sample size. In fills, especially, one might expect a close relationship between total number of design elements and the number of different elements (cf. Graves 1981). However, in rooms where restorable vessels – with their redundant design elements – contribute to the totals, the richness should be reduced relative to the sample size. In order to detect cases of reduced richness, Kintigh's (1984a) simulation technique was employed. Simulated samples of varying sizes were repeatedly drawn from the population of design elements. Thus, a distribution of richness values was generated for each sample size, making it possible to construct confidence intervals for richness.

When each unit (floor or fill) is plotted by sample size and richness in relation to the computer-generated confidence intervals, cases of excessive or reduced richness stand out.

Figure 5.2 is a plot of room fills against the richness confidence intervals. As anticipated, the general shape of this distribution follows closely that described by Kintigh (1984a): the more design elements are present, the more different kinds one finds. However, a large number of rooms exhibit significantly reduced richness; there is an appreciable overlap between these rooms and those flagged by Criteria 1 and 2.

The same exercise was repeated for design elements in floor assemblages (Figure 5.3), with very similar results. A great many rooms have low richness, and a small tier of rooms have very low richness. Again, many rooms pinpointed by Criteria 1 and 2 are also distinguished by low richness.

Clearly, the diversity analysis provides some additional support for the tentative conclusions of the 'excess' design-element analyses. Although the number of elements present (i.e., the sample size) is a reasonably good indicator of element richness, some process has caused many rooms to have significantly reduced richness.

Diversity of ceramic types

Another line of evidence, the diversity of ceramic types, supplies additional information about possible reconstructable vessels, especially the textured wares (Table 5.11). Figure 5.4 plots sherd count against type richness for room fills; Figure 5.5 presents a similar plot for room floors. Again, the overall shape of these distributions is quite expectable; type richness rises quite regularly with sherd counts. Even so, many rooms exhibit significantly reduced richness. In this analysis it is assumed that the sherds from a restorable vessel, comprising a local excess of that

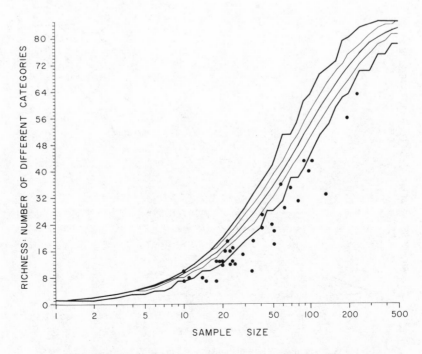

Fig. 5.2. Richness of ceramic design element in the fills of Broken K rooms

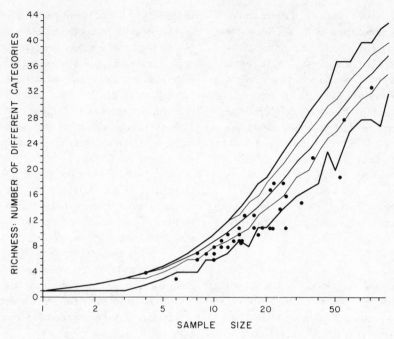

Fig. 5.3. Richness of ceramic design elements on room floors at Broken K

type, would depress the richness value for that provenience.[2] As a check on the reliability of the measure, I turn first to the proveniences of the known restored vessels (see Table 5.7).

Room 33 contains two Snowflake B/W jars (both Snowflake variety) in Floor Pit O. Although this room has a low richness of floor sherds (Figure 5.5), the excess is not caused by the two known vessels, but by St. Johns Polychrome (16 sherds, 18.6% vs 4.2% in the site as a whole – see Table 5.12) and Snowflake B/W, Carterville variety (31 sherds, 36.0% vs 6.5%). The known whole vessels do not contribute to the depressed richness because, in the

tabulation of floor-sherd counts, I did not include sherds in floor features. Room 39 contained a restored jar of Snowflake B/W, Snowflake variety in Level B. However, no sherds of this type are recorded in Level B (Martin *et al.* 1966:92), although a total of 67 are reported from levels C and D. The room has an unremarkable richness value which, together with the large number of sherds in the fill (988), the fragmentary condition of the whole vessel, and the lack of floor sherds, suggests this room may have been used as a dump – although Hill did not regard it as such.

Room 41 contained a jar of Snowflake B/W, Snowflake var-

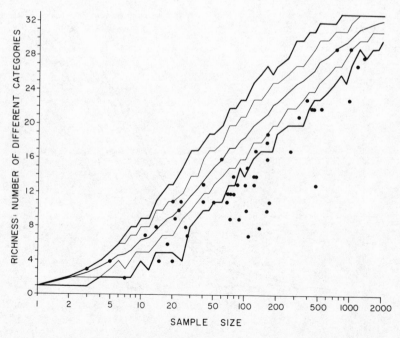

Fig. 5.4. Richness of ceramic types in the fills of Broken K rooms

Table 5.11. Ceramic types in room floors and fill at Broken K Pueblo. Data are from Martin *et al.* (1966). Indeterminate categories are included.

Room	Number of different types		Number of sherds		Room	Number of different types		Number of sherds	
	Fill	Floor	Fill	Floor		Fill	Floor	Fill	Floor
1	27	22	1148	704	39	29	0?	988	0?
2	15	7	106	32	40	13	17	40	111
4	28	11	1323	41	41	12	7	68	51
5	19	?	163	?	43	4	11	20	25
6	18	10	161	55	44a	4	2	5	5
7	22	12	432	109	44b	13	0?	124	0?
8	8	9	14	44	48	11	6	40	13
9	23	12	393	51	49	2	9	7	41
11	11	17	170	160	51	14	10	122	20
19	11	4	50	6	53	12	13	79	177
20	21	12	324	92	54	9	0	72	0
21	13	15	85	63	60	17	15	126	185
22	10	2	23	2	61	14	3	77	6
23	11	1	20	2	62	29	15	723	133
24	9	19	88	157	64	22	24	523	231
25	11	5	24	9	65	16	18	59	199
27	17	8	269	17	67	3	3	3	5
28	16	0?	162	0	68	19	11	157	43
29	22	8	447	95	69	23	16	965	199
30	13	12	470	50	73	14	11	125	26
31	7	17	109	97	74	6	14	18	51
33	8	10	107	86	78	10	14	103	49
34	12	6	73	29	79	7	13	28	58
35	8	0?	27	–	80	10	11	162	159
36	11	12	67	38	82	8	11	139	54
37	7	9	11	52	92	13	14	101	147
38	9	15	21	67					

iety, in Floor Pit A. This room has a reduced richness of floor sherds, but the cause is an excess of Brown Indented Corrugated (33 sherds; 64.7% vs 31.1%). Floor Pit A shows only one sherd of Snowflake B/W. Apparently, the sherds of this restored vessel were not tabulated by Martin *et al.* (1966:100).

Room 48 had a St. Johns Polychrome bowl in Level A, 13 sherds from which are counted in that provenience (Martin *et al.* 1966:116). The room fill has a reduced richness, and the restored vessel also shows up as a sizable local excess (13 sherds; 32.5% vs 4.2%).

Another St. Johns Polychrome bowl was found on the floor of Room 53. This room has a low richness, but the cause is an excess of Brown Indented Corrugated (127 sherds; 71.8% vs 31.1%) and a slight surplus of Snowflake B/W, Tularosa variety (12 sherds; 9.4% vs 2.5%). The seven sherds of St. Johns Polychrome in floor provenience is expectable for that sample. Although the richness measure failed to snare a known restored pot, it turned up other promising candidates.

Room 69, with a low richness value, has a pronounced ex-

cess of Snowflake B/W, Carterville variety. These sherds apparently come from the restored vessel noted and illustrated by Martin *et al.* (1967:133). However, the other B/W vessel from the fill of this room (Snowflake B/W, Hay Hollow variety) does *not* appear in the sherd totals – only one sherd of this type is reported from the entire room fill. Two other restored vessels reported by Martin *et al.* (1967) from this room are represented in the sherd counts. The Pinto Polychrome bowl does show up as an excess (seven sherds; 0.73% vs 0.25%), although the St. Johns Polychrome bowl does not. The provenience of the St. Johns bowl – only about two-thirds of which is present – is given at Level B, yet additional St. Johns sherds, perhaps from the same vessel, occur in other fill levels and on the floor. There is also a suggestive surplus of Brown Indented Corrugated (493 sherds, 51.1% vs 31.1%). Given the large number of restorable vessels recognized by the excavators and those indicated by the richness measure, it seems likely that this room contains a considerable amount of *de facto* refuse, not secondary refuse.

Room 80 provides another case. A Snowflake B/W, Carter-

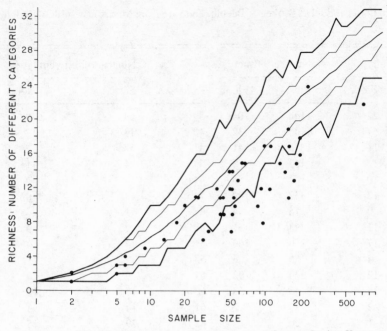

Fig. 5.5. Richness of ceramic types on room floors at Broken K

ville variety, canteen was recovered from the floor. Although 11 such sherds are numbered in the floor provenience, they did not contribute to the room's reduced floor type-richness. This vessel is incomplete; curiously, the fill levels in that room do disclose an excess of the type (35 sherds; 21.6% vs 6.5%). There is also a sur-plus of Snowflake B/W, Tularosa variety (23 sherds; 14.2% vs 2.5%) in the fill and an even greater excess on the floor (30 sherds; 18.9% vs 2.5%). I believe this room contains evidence for addi-tional restorable vessels, a conclusion that corroborates the same inference drawn above on the basis of design-element richness. However, this case again illustrates that the type-richness measure misses some vessels.

Finally, the floor of Room 92 yielded a Springerville Polychrome bowl. This room exhibits reduced floor type-richness attributable to an excess of Brown Indented Corrugated (73 sherds; 49.7% vs 31.1%) and Snowflake B/W, Tularosa variety (14 sherds; 9.5% vs 2.5%). The latter is thought to be 'part of a ladle' (Martin *et al.* 1966:186). Four sherds of Springerville Polychrome, noted as a 'mostly restorable bowl' (Martin *et al.* 1966:186), are recorded in a floor feature, suggesting that some restorable pots may be represented by only a few sherds, especially in floor con-text. This finding suggests that the type-richness measure fails to capture vessels that are not highly fragmented. Whether this technique can err in the other direction (indicate phantom restor-able vessels) cannot be known until the Broken K sherds them-selves are refitted in a test of the specific hypotheses presented here.

I have also considered several more rooms that exhibit reduced type richness in an effort to specify – as hypotheses – addi-tional restorable vessels that might be present in Broken K rooms.[3]

Discussion

The preceding analyses, taken one at a time, each point to the existence of possible restorable vessels in many rooms. Indeed, most of the rooms Hill regarded as trash-filled may contain *de facto* refuse vessels. Singly, none of these measures is apt to be very reliable, but together they point to some puzzling aspects of Broken K rooms, especially 'trash-filled' rooms, that can be acc-ommodated by the 'missed vessel' hypothesis.

In defense of the secondary refuse hypothesis for these rooms, one might argue that large sherds and restorable vessels can also occur in secondary refuse, leading to inordinate clusters of design elements and of particular types. This argument is not easily countered, and could very well be correct. Few investigators have ever bothered to assess the degree of reconstructability of vessels in pueblo room fills. In a study using materials from Awatovi, Burgh (1959) noted that sherds from the same vessel were widely disseminated. The many uses that puebloan peoples made of sherds also suggests that vessels fragments would follow different paths at different times to their final places of cultural deposition. (For an ethnographic description of some of these processes among the Hopi, see Stanislawski 1969.) Sherds had many prehistoric uses, including raw material for temper, scoops and scrapers, spindle whorls, chinking material, and 'gaming pieces.' Large sherds might have been especially prized for use in protecting new pots during firing. In addition, sherds in secondary refuse areas are sometimes quite small and damaged and may have been kicked around for some time in the activity area where breakage took place – or in provisional discard areas (Hayden and Cannon 1983), such as plazas or roofs, that may have been period-ically cleaned up. It is my guess that if the Completeness Index (Schiffer 1983) were calculated for vessels in puebloan secondary refuse areas, low mean values would result. However, until the requisite studies are carried out (on sherds from Broken K or other sites), one cannot rule out the possibility that the potentially restorable vessels occur as secondary refuse.

Table 5.12. The 25 most abundant pottery types at Broken K Pueblo. Data are from Martin *et al.* (1967:136–8).

	Sherd count	Relative frequency
Brown Indented Corrugated	8101	31.06%
Indeterminate B/W	3763	14.43
Snowflake B/W, Snowflake variety	2648	10.15
Snowflake B/W, Carterville var.	1682	6.45
St. Johns Polychrome	1099	4.21
Forestdale Plain	971	3.72
St. Johns B/R	878	3.37
McDonald Indented Corrugated	722	2.77
Indeterminate B/R	719	2.76
Show Low B/R	703	2.70
Snowflake B/W, Tularosa variety	646	2.48
Brown Plain Corrugated (jars)	600	2.30
Brown Indented Corrugated, smudged (bowls)	595	2.28
Brown Plain Corrugated, smudged (bowls)	456	1.75
Alma Plain	376	1.44
Patterned Corrugated (jars)	283	1.09
Gray Indented Corrugated, smudged (jars)	261	1.00
Snowflake B/W, Broken K variety	196	0.75
Forestdale Smudged	144	0.55
Snowflake B/W, Hay Hollow variety	115	0.44
Indeterminate Polychrome	81	0.31
McDonald Corrugated Plain (bowls)	74	0.28
Pinto Polychrome	65	0.25
Lino Gray	62	0.24
Indeterminate Red	52	0.20

The possible occurrence of restorable pots as *de facto* refuse in room fills is itself problematic. Nevertheless, I believe several modes of deposition can account for these vessels. First, as noted above, sherds from floor vessels – especially textured types – may have been recorded in fill proveniences. Secondly, pots may have been abandoned sometimes on roofs. After a roof collapsed, sherds from these vessels would be recovered in the fill. Thirdly, some pots may have been abandoned within rooms but above the floor, resting on shelves and other supports or suspended from walls and ceilings by netting or cordage. Indeed, many possibly restorable bowls of St. Johns Polychrome and B/R occurred in upper fill levels; I am tempted to propose that those vessels were hung from the ceiling. Fourthly, child's play and vandals might have removed vessels of *de facto* refuse from floors, redepositing them as sherds on the roof. Fifthly, and least likely, is the possibility that the vessels were deposited on second-story floors that went unrecognized. In short, several hypothesized modes of deposition can produce restorable vessels of *de facto* refuse in room fills.

Table 5.13. Frequency distributions of the five most common and five least common design elements in room fills at Broken K Pueblo. Data are from Hill (1970:134–9).

Number of design occurrences	Element frequencies									
	5 most common					5 least common				
	67	29	127R	127	175	43	47	130	151	162
0	22	19	20	24	23	36	35	35	34	33
1	6	9	5	8	8	5	6	5	7	8
2	4	4	5	1	4			1	1	1
3	6	3	5	4	4		1	1		
4	1	1	3	1	1					
5		2	1	1		1				
6	1	1	2	1						
7										
8		1	1							
9	1									
10										
11										
12	1				1					
13				1						
14		1		1						
–										
22					1					
Total frequency:	63	68	67	64	66	10	9	10	9	10

Factor analysis of design elements

The preceding discussions of Broken K ceramic data have laid a foundation for reconsidering the results of Hill's factor analyses of design elements in room floors and fills.

Since Hill's early use of factor analysis at Broken K, the technique has seen service in many archaeological studies. Its general properties are widely known and need not be recited here. However, brief discussion of the correlation coefficient frequently used in factor analysis, Pearson's *r*, is necessary in order to understand Hill's results.

One condition that should be met for the correct application of Pearson's *r* is that the variables being compared are distributed normally. This assumption is violated frequently in practice, and appreciable departures from normal distributions can be tolerated – if the data set is well understood. However, Hill does not present the frequency distributions of Broken K design elements; more surprisingly, neither do his critics. This was a mistake, for an appreciation of these distributions provides clues to understanding Hill's results. Graves (1981:58–9) examined some frequency distributions of Hay Hollow Valley design elements, demonstrating their considerable departure from normality. Table 5.13 presents frequency distributions of the five most common and five least common design elements in room fills; these examples adequately represent the distributions, and underscore the 'thinness' of the

Table 5.14. A comparison of Hill's design-element factors for room fills with predictions based on restored and potentially restorable vessels

Hill's Factors (Hill 1970:28)	Factor predictions (based on Table 5.9)
(1) 15, 17, 18, 20, 29, 43, 45R, 134, 146, 158R, 160, 161, 173	Room 4–5 15, 18, 20, 43, 146, 158R, 173 Room 65: 29
(2) 6, 89, 127, 130, 172, 173, 174 175, 176, 177, 178	Room 1 89, 173, 175, 176, 178
(3) 6, 17, 19, 22, 28, 30, 47, 77–81, 95, 110, 147, 158, 158R, 160, 179	Plaza–Kiva 30, 47, 77–81, 95, 110, 135, 158R, 179
(4) 7, 9–11, 45, 46, 49, 71, 77–81, 127, 135, 136, 147R, 160R	Room 69 7, 9, 45, 46, 49, 77–81, 135, 136, 139
(5) 32, 65, 128R, 133R, 159, 169	Room 39K: 32, 128R
(6) 115, 141, 151, 153, 165	Room 80: 141, 165
(7) 10, 156	Room 20: 156 Room 21: 10
(8) 12, 46R, 49R, 108	Room 28: 12, 108
(9) 41, 139, 159R	Room 29: 41 Room 64: 139

data (cf. Dumond 1977:344). The degree of skewness in these distributions is remarkable, replicating the distribution shapes found by Graves. The use of Pearson's r on variables distributed in this manner probably is inappropriate. However, most perplexing about the Broken K distributions is the presence of extreme high values.

Extreme values can have a profound effect on Pearson's r. High positive correlation coefficients can be achieved between otherwise unrelated variables if they both share one case that has extreme high values for both variables. This effect is exacerbated when there is a large number of paired zeros in the data matrix (Speth and Johnson 1976). The potential for co-occurring extreme values in the room-fill cases is great because of the previously demonstrated likelihood that anomalously high frequencies of design elements arise from (1) restorable pots or large pot fragments or (2) common, nondistinctive design elements that may derive from many different vessels, especially in deposits of secondary refuse. One might expect the higher values of Pearson's r, influenced by the co-occurrence of extreme element frequencies, to determine strongly the results of the factor analyses.

Table 5.9, because it comprises some anomalously high element frequencies, provides a convenient set of predictions for the outcome of Hill's room-fill factor analysis. If the present interpretation is correct, one would expect the factors to consist, in part, of the design elements that occur together in room fills in high frequencies. Table 5.14 displays a comparison between the

two sets of design-element variables. The reader may observe that there is a striking relationship between the predictions and the actual factors identified by Hill. For example, Room 69, which contained two restored vessels whose design elements were included in the tabulation, is clearly the basis of Factor 4. The co-occurring design elements in Room 1, which are commonly executed lines, probably represent many vessels and contribute importantly to Factor 2. Factor 3 is strongly influenced by the abundant design elements in Room 4–5, possibly resulting from large sherds, common elements, or restorable vessels. The probable restorable vessels in Rooms 28 and 80 contribute, respectively, to Factors 6 and 8. The co-occurring elements in the Plaza–Kiva are in large part responsible for the composition of Factor 3.

For several reasons, many design elements occur in Hill's factors that are absent in the predictions. First of all, many of these elements, for example 17, 19, and 22, have low sample sizes (20 or less) and their distributions lack extreme values. These elements can be viewed as 'riders,' because by chance they are correlated with some of the variables responsible for that factor. Secondly, the criteria identifying suspicious concentrations of an element were stringent, excluding some element occurrences that may indicate large sherds, restorable pots, or common elements. For example, if Criterion 1 were relaxed from 25 to 20%, element types 45R and 161 – which occur in Factor 1 – would be added to the predictions. In short, some design elements are present in Hill's factors because of random effects in small samples, whereas others are demonstrably related to the rooms and high-frequency elements that make up the predictions.

The above exercise indicates that there is a surprising amount of structure in the data matrix of design elements in room fills. This structure, represented by Hill's factors, can be readily accounted for by some relatively simple cultural formation processes, principally the deposition of abundant elements from many different vessels, large sherds, and restorable vessels.

Similar results were obtained from a detailed study of the floor data. However, because of overall lower sample sizes, there is a far less robust structure.

The first attempt to predict the composition of Hill's factor analysis of floor data was modeled after the fill analysis, using high-frequency design elements in Table 5.9. Although some matches were evident, the results were not at all convincing. I soon discovered that the predictions based on Table 5.9 failed to include the one case in Hill's input matrix (Hill 1970:130–3) that did have a large number of high-frequency occurrences: Burial 1 from Room 27, which was accompanied by eight decorated pots (Martin *et al.* 1967:129). Four of these vessels are illustrated and, with few exceptions, their design elements are tabulated by Hill. Thus, this case furnishes another control situation in which the effects of known whole vessels can be monitored. It is noteworthy that 12 different design elements are recorded for the burial pots, which occur in frequencies ranging from four to 11 – all high values for that data set.

In view of the design-element frequencies from known restored vessels in the burial, I reexamined the entire data set, pinpointing all design-element occurrences of four or more. The

Table 5.15. A comparison of Hill's design-element factors for room floors with predictions based on restored vessels, potentially restorable vessels, and large sherds.

Hill's Factors (Hill 1970:28)	Predictions
(1) 6, 45, 46, 50–51, 65, 82, 130, 133, 147R, 158, 169, 175	Burial 1: 6, 45, 46, 50–51, 65, 82, 130, 133, 147R, 169, 175
(2) 45, 134R, 135, 146, 155, 158	Room 33: 45, 46, 127R, 146, 155, 158R, 175
(3) 20, 29, 89, 127, 127R, 164, 174, 175, 176, 177	Room 1: 29, 127, 127R, 175
(4) 31, 67, 169	Room 40: 31, 67, 82, 169
(5) 95–99, 110, 159, 160	Room 64: 110
(6) 131, 134, 135, 148, 160R	Room 74: 160R, Room 80: 148
(7) 29, 84, 156	Room 8: 29, 50–51, 156
(8) 19, 84, 131	–
(9) 115, 131, 153	Room 11: 153
(10) 133R, 160	–
(11) 39	–
(12) 90–94	–
(13) 20	–

Table 5.16. The frequency distribution of pottery-type occurrences on the floors of Broken K rooms. Data are from Hill (1970:128–9); I have deleted the three proveniences not in pueblo rooms.

Number of sherds	Number of occurrences
1–3	173
4–7	86
8–10	35
11–15	23
16–20	18
21–25	13
26–30	7
31–40	10
41–50	3
51–60	3
61–70	4
71–80	2
81–90	1
91–100	
101–150	5
151–200	1
201–250	
251–300	
301–350	1

rooms meeting this criterion served as the basis for predicting the composition of Hill's factors (Table 5.15), and as can be seen, there is some degree of fit between the predictions and Hill's factors. It is of great interest that Factor 1 consists entirely of the design elements from the burial pots (see Hill 1970:80). A few other factors (2, 3, 4, 7) can be matched up reasonably well with design elements in rooms. Overall, this data matrix lacks much structure, and, as Dumond (1977) noted, some of the factors (e.g., 8, 9) are composed of design elements that are not mutually correlated. However, to the extent that there is structure in this data set, it seems to result from known restored vessels and likely restorable vessels.

Dumond (1977:344) failed utterly in his effort to replicate Hill's factors in the analysis of floor design elements. The reason is simple. Dumond converted the design-element frequency data to a presence–absence matrix, thereby eliminating the only source of structure in the data: the few high-frequency occurrences. In any event, it is doubtful that meaningful social information can be extracted from this data matrix by factor analysis.

A consideration of orphan sherds at Broken K

Before turning to Hill's last factor analysis, that of pottery types on room floors, it is necessary to evaluate in some detail the likely formation processes of all sherds on room floors. In virtually every provenience at Broken K (and probably all other ceramic sites) one finds 'orphan' sherds, those *not* belonging to restorable vessels from that unit. For example, the floor of Room 69 contained one sherd of McDonald Indented Corrugated (Martin *et al.* 1966:157), and two sherds of that type were also found in the fill. Needless to say, together these three sherds do not constitute a strong case for a restorable vessel. Although similar orphan sherds are found in all levels of Broken K rooms, their identification as such is not always so straightforward.

Let us first examine the overall frequency distribution of pottery-type occurrences on room floors (Table 5.16). The apparent multimodality of this distribution is mostly an artifact of changes in the interval size used to group the frequencies. However, as in the design-element distribution, one does find a number of occurrences that seem quite high in relation to the overall distribution. One interpretation of this pattern is that the floor-sherd assemblages were formed by at least two independently varying processes: (1) those responsible for orphan sherds and (2) *de facto* refuse deposition of restorable vessels. Because of variability in vessel size, shape, and breakage patterns, one cannot draw a hard-and-fast line in the distribution between restorable vessels and orphan sherds. However, when the number of sherds of a simple pottery type on a room floor exceeds 20, one may entertain the hypothesis that some goodly portion of a vessel, maybe all of it, is present. It is easy to account for the majority of potentially restorable vessels or pot fragments as *de facto* refuse, but the orphan sherds are much more problematic. A number of hypotheses can explain the presence of orphan sherds in floor provenience (Table 5.17). Regrettably, the additional information needed to distin-

Table 5.17. A provisional framework for generating hypotheses to account for orphan sherds on pueblo room floors. Based on Schiffer (1976, 1983, 1985).

1. Culturally deposited on the floor
   a. Sherds in storage awaiting reuse (as in temper), deposited as *de facto* refuse.
   b. Primary refuse (the last few sherds of a vessel broken in that room).
   c. Materials incorporated into plaster used to refurbish floor.
   d. Sherds used for other purposes (e.g., gaming piece, scoop, collectible), deposited as *de facto* refuse.
   e. Sherds deposited or disturbed by child's play and vandalism.
   f. Sherds awaiting transport to a dump as provisional refuse (cf. Hayden and Cannon 1983). Restorable vessels–broken in systemic context–may be also present in provisional refuse.
2. Culturally deposited in nonfloor context
   a. Chinking from wall material, brought into floor contact by deterioration of wall.
   b. Sherds from secondary refuse deposited after the room was abandoned. Sherds may have fallen directly on floor or could have been moved there by rodent activity.
   c. Sherds deposited as part of roof construction or maintenance. The occasional burned room indicates that mud was laid upon the roof beams. The earth to make roof plaster may have been quarried from areas where sherds had been previously deposited. Melting or collapse of the roof can bring such sherds into floor contact.
   d. Sherds deposited as primary, secondary, or *de facto* refuse on the roof. At Broken K, the investigators identified several roof levels containing sherds. Analyses in the present paper indicate that much more material may have been deposited on the roofs.
   e. Subfloor materials moved upward by disturbance processes.

Table 5.18. The distribution of plainware sherds in fills and floors of Broken K rooms. Data are from Martin *et al.* (1966).

Room	Plainware sherds on floors	Plainware sherds in fills	Room	Plainware sherds on floors	Plainware sherds in fills
1	35	48	38	0	1
2	0	3	39	0	44
4	5	31	40	0	0
5	0	2	41	0	0
6	0	1	43	10	0
7	2	22	44a	0	0
8	0	0	44b	0	0
9	1	7	48	9	2
11	7	2	49	7	0
19	0	0	51	3	0
20	0	6	53	3	2
21	2	0	54	0	0
22	0	0	60	9	8
23	0	2	61	0	6
24	13	0	62	9	19
25	0	0	64	13	18
27	0	12	65	10	1
28	0	2	67	0	0
29	2	28	68	0	5
30	0	1	69	1	2
31	23	4	73	5	16
33	2	0	74	1	0
34	0	2	78	3	1
35	0	0	79	0	0
36	21	0	80	1	2
37	16	1	82	0	1
			92	2	1

guish the factors at work in specific instances – the traces of formation processes (Schiffer 1983) – is not available. However, a few cases can illustrate the process of explaining the occurrence of orphan sherds.

Broken K was not the first settlement to occupy that spot in the Hay Hollow Valley. Not only were earlier pithouses found beneath Broken K rooms, but plainware sherds, possibly centuries old when the pueblo was founded, are relatively abundant *within* Broken K rooms. Indeed, Forestdale Plain, at 3.72% of the assemblage, is the fifth most abundant pottery type (Table 5.12); and Alma Plain comprises 1.44% of the assemblage. Referring to these early sherds, Martin *et al.* (1967:138) claim that 'All the plain pottery types came from pit houses, the floors of which were about 2 m. below the present surface. These earlier houses were beneath rooms 33, 48, and 41-kiva.' Unfortunately, this statement is in error, for many plainware sherds occur on room floors and in

fills (Table 5.18). The plainware counts have two striking features. The first is the very unusual frequency distributions; although zeros are abundant and low frequencies (1–5) common, there is an unexpected number of high counts in both floors and fills. Secondly, by inspection one can observe that there is no pronounced relationship between fill and floor sherd counts. There is no simple explanation for the highly clustered distribution of plainware sherds. Some hypotheses, mostly based on various disturbance and reclamation processes, will be considered.

The most obvious – and palatable – hypothesis is that these plainware sherds were moved upward into the pueblo by rodent activity or other disturbance processes from the pithouses. However, if that were the cause, one would expect the plainware sherds to occur in high frequencies in those rooms known to overlie the pithouses: 33, 48, and 41-Kiva. A glance at Table 5.18 discloses, to the contrary, that rooms 33 and 48 do not contain excessive numbers of plainware sherds. (The pithouse Kiva, 41-K, almost certainly was trash-filled, and is not strictly comparable to the pueblo rooms.) However, there is a tendency for rooms containing large numbers of plainware sherds to cluster spatially (e.g., 62, 64, and 65; 36, 37). Such clusters might be expected if sherds were moved upward from (undiscovered) pithouses or refuse areas beneath those rooms. However, spatial clustering could also occur if adjacent rooms were built at one time with floor and roof plaster quarried from areas having a high concentration of plainware sherds. Such a process could also account for most of the remaining plainware sherds.

Another hypothesis is that the plainware sherds were *de facto* refuse from collections made by the inhabitants of these rooms. This process cannot as easily account for all plainware occurrences, but some may have been deposited in this way. I shall elaborate the collecting hypothesis below with reference to Pinto Polychrome.

Finally, the inhabitants of Broken K may have manufactured plainware vessels or obtained them by trade. Thus, some of the sherd clusters may represent restorable vessels deposited as *de facto* refuse.

At present, none of these hypotheses can be entirely ruled out. It is likely that some combination of processes is responsible for the plainware sherds.

The distribution of Pinto Polychrome is also intriguing, as 21 sherds of this type are spread among the floors of ten rooms (Hill 1970:128). Yet, the total of Pinto Polychrome in all of Broken K is only 65 sherds (Martin *et al.* 1967:137). The latter number seems far too small to accommodate the hypothesis of primary refuse for the sherds on room floors. It is possible, of course, that when a vessel of Pinto Polychrome broke anywhere in Broken K, most of its sherds were gathered up and disposed of in a few special locations, which were not excavated.

Another hypothesis that needs to be seriously considered is that the Pinto Polychrome sherds were actually *de facto* refuse. This implies that the inhabitants of Broken K for some reason made use of Pinto Polychrome *sherds*. The process responsible for sherd procurement may have been trade; more likely the people of Broken K collected these sherds. Martin *et al.* (1967) have already documented the collection of Archaic and pre-pueblo points by the inhabitants of Broken K; they also may have been sherd collectors.

Several corrugated types also appear on room floors, almost exclusively as orphan sherds. It is well known that many corrugated 'types' lack logical consistency when applied to sherds. For example, a single corrugated vessel can yield sherds of both 'Brown Indented Corrugated' *and* 'Brown Plain Corrugated.' Thus, many of the orphan sherds of rare corrugated types may actually be from the restorable vessels of the more common corrugated types in the same room. Regrettably, this hypothesis cannot be tested, because the corrugated sherds were not saved (Martin *et al.* 1967:127).

There are two rare types of Snowflake B/W, Broken K variety and Hay Hollow variety, that are found on room floors only as orphan sherds. Despite their names, little evidence indicates that these types were made in the Hay Hollow Valley, much less at Broken K. It is possible that sherds of these types were collected and thus represent *de facto* refuse. Another hypothesis is that the

orphan sherds of these types were preferentially saved for reuse and stored on room floors, but were abandoned as *de facto* refuse. A final hypothesis is that a single vessel of Snowflake B/W can yield sherds of several different varieties. In short, a number of hypotheses can account for the orphan sherds of rare B/W pottery types on room floors, but none at present is strongly supported.

In explaining the distributions of orphan sherds (and other artifacts) at prehistoric pueblos, we may have to abandon the model, derived from the modern Hopi, that ancient puebloans were always meticulous housekeepers (cf. Stanislawski 1973). Many pueblos, including Broken K, contain sherds on room floors and on the roof that most likely were primary or secondary refuse. Moreover, refuse may have accumulated in some activity areas, such as plazas and roofs, as provisional refuse. Such locations may have been cleaned periodically, but for a time would have made sherds (and other refuse) accessible to disturbance and reclamation processes and to child's play, contributing to the further disorganization of sherds from individual vessels. Moreover, during the pueblo's abandonment period, housekeeping practices may have been suspended (cf. Stevenson 1982), especially in extramural areas like roofs (Schiffer 1985). These possibilities need to be carefully evaluated, using the many traces of formation processes (Schiffer 1983), as data from new pueblo excavations are analyzed.

Hill's factor analysis of type-frequency data from floors

That room-floor assemblages consist of varying mixes of orphan sherds and sherds from restorable vessels has important implications for understanding Hill's factor analysis of pottery types on room floors. Hill used the type-clusters that resulted from this analysis as a basis for establishing a variety of inferences. Two attempts have been made to replicate this analysis, neither of which was especially successful. The lack of behaviorally meaningful patterns in these analyses is entirely predictable from a knowledge of the probable formation processes of pottery type-frequencies on room floors.

Using a different type of factor analysis from that of Hill, Lischka (1975) obtained a different factor solution. In consultation with Hill, Lischka (1975:225) learned that Hill's analysis was actually based on a different input matrix than the data presented in Appendix 6 (Hill 1970:128–9). Thus, the divergent results probably stem from differences in both techniques and input data. However, Lischka (1975:226) concluded that 'The low reliability coefficients of the BC TRY factors and the generally low communalities exhibited by the pottery types do not permit us to place much confidence in either analysis as the test of a hypothesis.' He also underscored some apparently meaningful associations and suggested the potential for further work.

Dumond (1977) also reanalyzed the type-frequency data in Hill's Appendix 6, despite Lischka's demonstration that it was not the actual input matrix, and failed to replicate Hill's factor solution. His most important finding is that the types within each of Hill's clusters are only weakly correlated with one another. Dumond makes a general point well worth heeding: unless the types that make up a factor are correlated with one another – a state of affairs that factor analysis does not guarantee – one cannot claim, as did Hill, that the types are related in systemic context.

Both Lischka and Dumond have shown that the type-frequency data from room floors at Broken K are not strongly structured. This is a disconcerting result that makes no sense behaviorally: at the household level, there had to be strong groupings of vessel types, especially those used for cooking and serving food. In order to understand why expectable systemic patterns are not evident in Hill's factor analysis, one must assess the formation processes of the input matrix: sherd counts (or percentages) on room floors. On the basis of preceding discussions, one can begin with the proposition that the sherds in each floor assemblage probably result from different and independent formation processes. Treating all room-floor data as equivalent, as does factor analysis, leads to a situation in which variability caused by formation processes overwhelms any that might be caused by the behavioral and organizational phenomena that Hill sought. The result is a set of factors that faithfully monitors neither formation processes nor the behaviors of interest. I now examine a number of these formation processes in greater detail, beginning with the processes responsible for orphan sherds.

Because many processes – cultural and noncultural – can bring sherds into floor contact (see Table 5.17), orphan sherds are apt to have heterogeneous origins. Even if most orphan sherds were primary refuse, it is doubtful that factor analysis of them could disclose any behaviorally meaningful patterns. This is easily shown by a brief consideration of the causes of sherd frequency variability in primary refuse.

The sherd frequency of a pottery type as primary refuse in an activity area, such as pueblo room, has five principal determinants: (1) breakage rate, which is influenced by the number of vessels in use and uselife (Schiffer 1976), (2) vessel properties (e.g., shape, size, and mechanical strength) and manner of breakage, which contribute to the frequency distribution of sherd size, (3) the last clean-up and the abandonment of the activity area (some were abandoned clean, others dirty) and (5) intensity of trampling. Clearly, even within a single community like Broken K, these somewhat independent factors will vary among activity areas *for the same vessel type*. The predictable result of these causal factors is the creation of highly variable type-frequency counts in primary refuse.

This discussion leads to the following tentative conclusions about primary refuse sherds in activity areas:

1. In a *large* deposit of primary refuse sherds, the variety of pottery types may approach the variety used in that activity area.
2. The relative frequencies of pottery types in use are not directly mirrored in the relative frequencies of sherd types in primary refuse.
3. The presence of a pottery type in primary refuse – even as one sherd – indicates the use of that type in the activity area.
4. The absence of a pottery type in primary refuse does not indicate the absence of that type in the past, unless such absence repeatedly recurs in *large* samples of primary refuse.

In view of these discussions, it should be apparent that factor analysis of primary refuse sherd counts holds little promise for yielding behaviorally meaningful patterns. The nature of primary refuse is such that behavioral information can probably be extracted by more straightforward means. For example, one can divide up activity areas on the basis of architectural attributes, as did Hill, and then aggregate and compare the primary refuse for each type of activity area (cf. Schiffer 1975). Regrettably, we cannot know which Broken K orphan sherds are actually primary refuse without examining the traces of formation processes on the sherds themselves (cf. Schiffer 1983).

In addition to the orphan sherds, not all of which are apt to be primary refuse, Broken K room floors contain sherds from missed restorable vessels as *de facto* refuse. Under conditions of a true Pompeii-like abandonment, restored vessel (not sherd) counts from rooms might comprise a data matrix that could yield behaviorally meaningful patterns when factor analyzed. However, at Broken K, *de facto* refuse vessels seem to have been present on floors, in rooms, and on roofs. Thus, factor analysis of floor vessels alone will be misleading because they comprise only part of the *de facto* refuse assemblage from any household. Moreover, although Broken K probably contained many restorable vessels as *de facto* refuse, the abandonment was not catastrophic. Clearly, many rooms – perhaps most – fell short of complete systemic inventories, probably as a result of curate behavior, scavenging, vandalism, and other 'depletion' processes (Schiffer 1985). Under these conditions, multivariate analysis of restored and restorable floor-vessel counts (if they could be approximated) would not be an appropriate strategy. Again, given the variable completeness of the *de facto* refuse assemblage, more is to be learned by applying simple techniques of comparison, where presences are stressed and absences are weighted only if there is a recurrent pattern not easily explained by another formation process.

These discussions have now brought us to the point of appreciating why Hill's set of type-frequency data contains so little structure: each provenience holds the summed products of different and independently varying formation processes. For example, some room floors consist entirely of orphan sherds; others may have as many as a half-dozen restorable vessels in addition to varying numbers of orphan sherds. When such heterogeneous samples are treated as equivalent and factor analyzed, the result can only be specious 'patterns' that are but statistical artifacts. In the 1960s, of course, no one knew better.

I believe the type-frequency data can provide meaningful information on vessel-use patterns. To extract that information will require the use of analytic techniques that are appropriate for assemblages formed by the processes identified so far. As further work is pursued on the Broken K ceramics — especially on the collections themselves – we can expect to obtain well-founded inferences about other behavioral and organizational aspects of the Broken K community.

Discussion
That Broken K Pueblo contained much more *de facto* refuse and much less secondary refuse than Hill believed has implications

for inferences about Broken K's occupational history. If relatively few rooms were trash-filled, it suggests that Broken K was a robust community just prior to its abandonment; otherwise, a period of slow decline (i.e., several years or more) would have resulted in a much greater accumulation of trash in rooms, as the latter were gradually abandoned and used as dumps.

More significantly, the possible scarcity of secondary refuse in the room blocks hints at an overall short occupation of the pueblo, since no substantial middens were found in extramural areas. As Hill (1970:22) notes, 'No true midden area was located outside the main portion of the pueblo.' Two test trenches and a number of 'exploratory holes' provided the basis for this claim, a claim that is well founded. From 1968 to 1971 I visited Broken K annually, and was able to observe the profiles of and backdirt from the many potholes dug in extramural areas. Overall, these potholes revealed a very low density of materials that did not extend to great depths. However, pothunters did find the Broken K cemetery that eluded Hill. It was located just to the north of the pueblo. Judging by the area covered with human bone fragments on the surface, the cemetery was not very large; it is doubtful that more than several dozen interments had been present. These data also suggest that Broken K had a short existence.

The tentative conclusion that Broken K was not occupied for very long – perhaps less than 50 years – finally resolves a major puzzle: Why, overall, did Broken K yield so few sherds? Martin *et al.* (1967:132) first framed the question:

> Although Broken K Pueblo is larger (by over 50%) than Carter Ranch site... about 30% fewer sherds were recovered from the former. (Broken K Pueblo, about 26,000 sherds; Carter Ranch Pueblo, about 34,000)... No adequate explanation for this discrepancy is at hand.

Although Martin *et al.* (1967:133) do suggest a 'shorter occupation' as one hypothesis, that hypothesis was not apparently accepted; the published dates for Broken K allot it – like Carter Ranch – an occupation span in excess of a century: A.D. 1150–1280 (Martin *et al.* 1967:144), 1150—1280 or 1300 (Hill 1970:8). Hill (1970:8) avoids making occupation-span comparisons with the Carter Ranch site, arguing only that Broken K was not occupied for as long as the 460 years suggested by the radiocarbon dates. In support of his version of 'a relatively short occupation,' Hill (1970:8) notes:

> Although the architectural evidence shows at least two major periods of construction, there was remarkably little remodeling. In addition, the later parts of the pueblo were constructed with the same type of masonry as the earlier portions had been, and the stylistic attributes of room features are virtually homogeneous throughout the pueblo.
>
> The paucity of midden material may also be indicative of short occupation. Very few rooms at Broken K contained dense trash deposits, and no general midden area was discovered.

Why these pertinent observations did not cause Hill to contract Broken K's occupation span relative to the Carter Ranch site –

where indications of a lengthier occupation *are* present – is not known.

The Joint Site, although its occupation span is not well dated, provides another reference point. On the basis of tree-ring and radiocarbon dates, I estimated the Joint Site occupation span at A.D. 1220–1270 (Schiffer 1976:149). This figure is highly provisional, yet I regard it even today as reasonable. Like Carter Ranch – and in contrast to Broken K – the Joint Site had many extramural middens and evidence for remodeling; moreover, in just the fills and floors of the 24 excavated rooms was recovered a total of 19,899 sherds (Schiffer 1976:130). In short, relative to Carter Ranch and the Joint Site, Broken K seems to have been occupied briefly. This conclusion appears to account for the relative paucity of sherds at Broken K.

Conclusion

The preceding analyses have led to several interrelated hypotheses regarding the formation processes of Broken K Pueblo. Clearly, many rooms that Hill believes were used for trash disposal furnish no compelling evidence of dumping behavior; indeed, some of the fill material may be *de facto* refuse. Thus, Broken K – while not exactly a Pompeii – could have contained relatively large numbers of restorable ceramic vessels (as *de facto* refuse) that were not recorded as such during excavation and analysis.

The hypothesized 'missed pots,' as well as the vessels restored by the excavators, determine to a large extent the patterns in Hill's factor analysis of design elements in room fills and, to a lesser extent, those in the room floor analysis. Moreover, that pottery type counts on room floors consist of independently varying components – orphan sherds and sherds from restorable vessels – furnishes an explanation as to why Hill's type-frequency factor analysis lacks behaviorally meaningful patterns. Although the formation processes of Broken K ceramic artifacts are still imperfectly known, the hypotheses advanced in this paper can play a heuristic role in orienting future treatments of Broken K data. It is clear that any new analyses of this important data set must be founded on a better understanding of Broken K's formation processes than is available today.

The present study of Broken K Pueblo is not without implications for other intrasite analyses. Indeed, the following statements are offered as general advice.

1. As Sullivan (1978) emphasizes, processes of archaeological recovery and analysis introduce variability into the archaeological record. Some restorable vessels from Broken K (and the Joint Site) were reported as whole vessels, whereas others were reported only as sherds. I am certain that this practice is far from unusual.

2. Artifacts recorded in a single provenience from within a structure may have been deposited by different formation processes (Schiffer 1976:133–8). For example, a host of processes could have been responsible for the artifacts found on the floor of a room, including primary refuse and *de facto* refuse deposition (for an extended treatment of this problem see Schiffer 1985).

3. Artifacts recorded in different proveniences in a structure could have been deposited by the same formation process (Schiffer 1976:133–8). For example, artifacts of *de facto* refuse – even sherds from the same pot – could be recorded in floor and fill proveniences.

4. Generally, regardless of provenience, the formation processes of restorable vessels, vessel fragments, and orphan sherds are quite different. Such ceramic artifacts must be segregated early on during the process of analysis.

5. After one has made the initial segregation, the next analytic task is to identify the specific formation processes of the various artifacts and deposits (Schiffer 1983), taking into account (3) and (4) above. By identifying formation processes (that is, inferring that they occurred), the investigator is able to pinpoint areas of research potential and to select (or devise) appropriate analytic techniques (Schiffer 1983).

6. The use of pattern-discovery analytic techniques on artifacts and deposits of unknown formation processes will seldom yield behaviorally meaningful results. That is so because the statistical patterns reflect varying mixes of effects produced by formation processes and by the past behaviors of interest.[4]

Notes

1. In the category 'restorable vessels' I also include vessel fragments that have been reused, such as the base of a jar that was recycled into a bowl. In addition, puebloan rooms also sometimes contain pot fragments or large sherds, perhaps as provisional refuse (Hayden and Cannon 1983) or as material awaiting reuse (cf. Stanslawski 1969). Because the techniques applied in this paper cannot distinguish among these possibilities, the generic 'restorable vessel' should be understood as simply designating a range of ceramic phenomena that leads to sherds with *relatively* high completeness indices (cf. Schiffer 1983).

2. Strictly speaking, of course, an excess of a type does cause the richness of a unit to be depressed. However, when one type is in abundance, the total sample size – and thus richness – of all other sherds is necessarily reduced. In effect, a type in great abundance increases the sample size without causing a corresponding increase in richness.

3. Additional restorable vessels that might be present in Broken K rooms on the basis of reduced pottery type richness in fills and floors.

Room fills with reduced type richness:
Room 30 contains evidence of restorable vessels. The reduction in diversity is caused primarily by 213 sherds of Gray Indented Corrugated that are confined to the level called 'Fill Just Above Floor' (Martin *et al.* 1966:68). These sherds comprise 45.2% of all fill sherds, yet this type makes up only 1% of all Broken K sherds (see Table 5.12). Hill regards this room as having been used as a dump, but only 471 sherds were contained in the fill; moreover, more than 300 sherds were found between the purported dump (Level B) and the floor. These data strongly suggest that one or more restorable pots was deposited in this room.

Another case, somewhat weaker, is provided by Room 31. The reduced diversity seems to be the result of an excess of St. Johns Polychrome (19 sherds; 13.3% vs 4.2% in the site) and Brown Indented Corrugated (77 sherds; 48.3% vs 31.1%). However, only three redware design elements (all different) are reported from the fill, suggesting that the 19 sherds did not come from the same vessel. A more disconcerting possibility is that the design elements from these sherds were not recorded. In order unambiguously to assign a sherd to the type 'St. Johns Polychrome,' one must find a sufficient

amount of the black painted design (usually on the interior) to distinguish it from the other White Mountain Redwares and at least some white paint (usually on the exterior) to separate it from St. Johns B/R. If enough painting was present on these sherds to permit their type identification, then it should have been possible to record their design elements. In any event Room 31 retains the possibility of containing restorable vessels.

Room 11 has a considerable excess of Brown Indented Corrugated (120 sherds; 70.6 vs 31.1%) in Levels A and B. In addition, the room is one of the very few that contains a roof provenience, and among its 21 sherds are ten Brown Indented Corrugated. These data suggest that a restorable corrugated vessel was once on the roof.

Room 82 has a vast excess of Brown Indented Corrugated (116 sherds; 83.5% vs 31.1%), furnishing strong evidence for a restorable corrugated vessel.

Room 27, also a convincing case, has its richness reduced by many sherds of St. Johns Polychrome (90 sherds; 33.5% vs 4.2% in the site) occurring in Level A. It is likely that one or more St. Johns Polychrome bowls was deposited as *de facto* refuse. That only five redware design elements are reported for the fill of this room points to a recurring inconsistency in design-element recording. If the underrecording of design elements was widespread, then the previous search for excess design elements probably fell short of identifying all missed pots.

A similar instance is furnished by Room 24, which contains a sizable excess of Snowflake B/W, Tularosa variety (29 sherds; 33.0% vs 2.5%). These sherds occur in levels A and B, and three sherds are found on the floor. Design elements from this possible vessel apparently were recorded; the room was previously identified by Criteria 1 and 2.

Room 78 has suggestive evidence for a Brown Indented Corrugated vessel (65 sherds; 63.1% vs 31.1%); because these sherds occur in Levels A and B in a ratio of about two to one, this vessel may have rested on the roof.

Room 64 has many fill sherds, as well as more than 200 on the floor. An appreciable excess of Brown Indented Corrugated is found in Level B (279 sherds; 63.6% vs 31.1%), and other sherds of this type are found in Level C (49) and on the floor (87). The great excess of Brown Indented Corrugated may indicate more than one restorable vessel.

Room 20 provides another strong case. There are 92 sherds on the floor and 324 in the fill. Level B contained 13 sherds of Pinedale Polychrome, and four more of this type were found on the floor; these 17 sherds represent 81% of all Pinedale Polychrome reported from Broken K. Clearly, those sherds argue for a restorable vessel. In that same room, floor and fill, are many sherds of the more common types, suggesting that these, too, could have been reassembled into pots.

Room floors with reduced type richness:
Room 7 contains slight excesses of Brown Indented Corrugated (53 sherds; 48.6% vs 31.1%) and Snowflake B/W, Carterville variety (13 sherds; 11.9% vs 6.5%). These figures hint at restorable vessels.

On the floor of Room 29 is a great surplus of Brown Indented Corrugated (74 sherds; 77.9% vs 31.1%), suggesting one or two restorable vessels.

Another strong case for one or more corrugated vessels is furnished by Room 60, where Brown Indented Corrugated is in considerable excess (115 sherds; 62.2% vs 31.1%).

4. I am deeply indebted to Keith Kintigh for applying his diversity simulation method to the Broken K ceramic data. He also provided helpful comments on earlier versions of the paper, as did Randall H. McGuire, David Braun, and the editors of this volume. In many cases I pondered the advice of these sympathetic colleagues but decided, reluctantly, against making changes. N.S.F. Grant No. BNS-83-10609 contributed to the support of this research. An abridged version of this paper was read at the 49th Annual Meeting of the Society for American Archaeology, Portland.

Chapter 6

Structure and diversity in intrasite spatial analysis

By Jan F. Simek

Intrasite spatial analysis in archaeology has traditionally focused on variability in the content of material accumulations over a site surface (e.g., Carr 1984; Hodder and Okell 1978). Typically, this variation is analyzed and interpreted with reference to causal models stressing specific prehistoric human activities (Schiffer 1976). As described by Schiffer (*ibid.*) and others, the Activity Model conceives of activities as functionally, spatially, and temporally discrete tasks usually involving the use of a few tools (e.g., Binford and Binford 1966). It is assumed that activities will be reflected in the archaeological record as Activity Sets, made up of the Tool Kit involved in a task and located in an Activity Area where it was used (Schiffer 1976: 45–6). Because of this (often implicit) activity emphasis, archaeologists have concentrated their analytic efforts on detecting associations or co-occurrences among artifact classes over space (e.g., Dacey 1973).

I argue that interpretation of spatial accumulations in terms of specific behavioral events is warranted only when the distribution *structure* – the global or site-wide arrangement of artifacts and relations among artifact classes – indicates that activity areas may be preserved in the deposit. In fact, such areas may not have been present in the past, may not have contributed to the spatial organization of archaeological materials in the record, and/or may not have survived into the present (e.g., Binford 1983b; Yellen 1977). In short, there is no a priori reason to believe that a distribution will display structure produced by specific past activities. Thus, it is necessary to examine the structure of a distribution to show that activity areas may be present *before* devoting resources and energy to analyzing such areas.

If such areas are preserved in a distribution, the activity model implies that certain structural characteristics will be present. In general terms, activities comprise local processes; they occur within delimited spaces. Thus, the presence of activity areas will *not* be reflected by patterning in artifact class co-occurrences over the entire site surface, i.e., on a global scale. (This expectation would seem to raise questions concerning the utility of traditional approaches to spatial association in archaeology that depend on global measures yet interpret results in terms of activities.) When activity areas are reflected in a distribution, there should be clusters of materials at the activity locations, and cluster contents should reflect the activities performed. It follows that clusters reflecting different activities should have different contents, and any single cluster should be composed primarily of the few tools used at that place. Thus, the content of individual activity clusters should have low *diversity* relative to the overall site assemblage composition. In the context of spatial analysis, this means they will contain a few of the tool classes present on the site, reflecting the limited nature of the local activity, viz. the sum total of activities performed at the site during occupation. (A more general analytic definition of diversity will be discussed shortly.) At the same time, the presence of activity areas should result in clusters that are *heterogeneous* on a global scale, i.e., are different from each other in content, again assuming the functionally discrete and local character of activities. In this paper, I propose that assessments of spatial diversity and heterogeneity are important first steps in spatial analysis and provide the kind of information that may warrant the search for activity areas in specific cases. In the pages that follow, I will examine several methods for assessing these structural characteristics. Data from the Upper Paleolithic rockshelter site Le Flageolet I (Dordogne, France) (Rigaud 1969, 1982) will provide a case study for comparing techniques.

Background

Beginning with the earliest studies of archaeological spatial data, a primary goal of intrasite analysis has been the recognition of prehistoric activity sets, conceived as sets of objects used together in specific tasks (e.g., Dacey 1973; Freeman 1978; Hodder and Okell 1978; and see Hodder and Orton 1976 for a general discussion of methods). Moreover, the conventional view is that when activity sets are identified (by class co-occurrence), their spatial locations are the activity areas where they were used (e.g., Cahen and Keeley 1980).

Methods for defining activity sets and, by extension, activity areas usually involve some measure of artifact-class co-occurrence. Measures of co-occurrence (i.e., association) are employed because, under the traditional model, activities involve the use of tool kits; these kits are considered existential – they were the 'real' material units of past human action. Because the artifact classes used in an activity set formed a behavioral unit, it is assumed that they also constituted a depositional set and will therefore be found together in the archaeological record. Measures for co-occurrence are used to define sets of classes which are then interpreted rather directly: when a statistically significant relationship is found, a functional set of classes is inferred.

This approach to spatial analysis in archaeology is, perhaps, best articulated by proponents of the 'Behavioral Archaeology' (Schiffer 1976). In this view, the underlying cause of spatial patterning in archaeological sites is past human activity (conceived as defined above). Even when it is allowed that various factors may complicate the functional/spatial relation (e.g., refuse disposal, multiple use for a single tool), the traditional activity model sees them as 'transformations' or 'distortions' of the presumed systemic structure (Schiffer 1972, 1976; but see Binford 1981). These distortions can be eliminated if the proper analytic methods are used (e.g., Carr 1981, 1984) and/or if the site was excavated correctly (Schiffer 1983). Using measures of artifact class co-occurrence, the activity sets that make up a distribution can ultimately be identified:

> If an activity set contributes refuse differentially to two or more secondary refuse areas, different total quantities of various elements are produced which have the useful property of being proportional to one another among the secondary refuse areas. Elements of the activity set should be identifiable by their mutual correlations among the secondary refuse locations. (Schiffer 1976: 68)

This view suffers from some important presumptive biases. One such assumption is that the functional and spatial dimensions

of tool technology overlap. In other words, tool classes are used together in space when they are part of the same functional process. The activity approach also requires that artifact deposition overlap with the dimensions of function and space; artifacts used together were also deposited together. To admit that interclass co-occurrence may be complicated by the deposition of distinct activity sets in a single location (e.g., Schiffer 1976: 68–9) is not to deny the presumed spatial relation of these critical dimensions. In fact, the traditional view insists that such relations *will* exist even when transformations have obscured them or when they involve 'polythetic' or 'fuzzy' activity sets (Carr 1981, 1984). Thus, defining activity sets can become a complicated problem, but it is a technical rather than theoretical one (Carr 1984; Graham 1980; Schiffer 1983).

Recently, the behavioral approach to spatial analysis has been called into question by empirical work in a variety of realms (cf. Binford 1983b). It is becoming increasingly apparent that a variety of processes contributes to the formation of archaeological spatial distributions (Leroi-Gourhan and Brezillon 1972; Rigaud 1978; Schiffer this volume). Past human activities *may* be among these processes. However, many observed formation processes have little to do with specific activities (Binford 1978b, 1983; Yellen 1977). The number of social groups present during an occupation, cycles of redundant site use, and duration of occupation may all contribute significantly to the nature and form of material accumulations over a site surface. Moreover, the formation of accumulations during the occupation of a place may have nothing at all to do with the activities performed there; artifact co-occurrence may be determined as much by stochastic processes (e.g., dropping, breakage, loss of tools) as by the performance of specific activities (Ammerman and Feldman 1974). Analytically extracting activity sets from distributions influenced by random effects of unknown magnitude is surely a misguided strategy.

At the very least, the traditional approach to analyzing archaeological spatial distributions, with its fundamental reliance on artifact-class co-occurrence as the basis for inferring activity sets, must be reevaluated in light of recent research. New theoretical and empirical work has shown that this view is too simple. In fact, a multitude of factors and processes may affect artifact class co-occurrence, and specific human activities need not be among them. Thus, before an archaeological distribution is analyzed in terms of activity sets, it must be demonstrated that they may be present and are reflected by spatial patterns and patterns of interclass co-occurrence.

Content diversity in artifact distributions

According to the activity model, activity sets comprise a few artifact classes that are spatially associated within a limited number of discrete material accumulations corresponding to their use locations. In other words, certain artifact classes are associated in some places while other classes are concentrated in other accumulations. These assumptions are held to be valid 'all other things being equal' (untransformed in Schiffer's terms [1972; 1976]).

Using these characteristics, the effects of activity sets on the spatial structure of a distribution can be anticipated. When activity patterning is present, the content of material accumulations will be heterogeneous over the whole distribution and, in addition, individual, activity-specific accumulations will have a relatively lower diversity of artifact classes (see above). In other words, patterns of artifact class co-occurrence will be local. High content diversity within and homogeneity among accumulations violate the activity model's expectation. These characteristics indicate a global pattern of inter-class association. Because the activity model assumes that activities are discrete local events, global co-occurrences among classes suggest that a different set of causal processes may have contributed to the formation of the distribution under study. In short, either activities are not of the nature defined by the model, or activities are not reflected at all in the deposits under study.

The concept of diversity used here follows Zar's definition (1974: 35): diversity simply characterizes the distribution of observations (here, objects or artifacts) among categories (here, artifact classes). Diversity has two basic components, (i) the number of classes represented in an accumulation relative to the number possible (class richness), and (ii) the frequency distribution of objects in the classes present (evenness). In archaeological spatial analysis, accumulations dominated by a few classes (the condition expected under the activity model) have low diversity; when no specific classes dominate a local assemblage, accumulations have high diversity.

A variety of methods is available for measuring diversity (e.g., Pielou 1966, 1969), ranging from simple characterizations of richness to more complicated indices derived from information theory. Perhaps the most immediately appealing measure is class richness, expressed as the number of artifact classes present in an assemblage or accumulation (e.g., Jones *et al.* 1983; Kintigh 1984a; various papers in this volume). Class richness is a rather simple measure of diversity (since it fails to consider the way classes are filled), but richness does account for one basic dimension involved in the concept. Information theory has stimulated the development of more complex indices that do attempt to account for variation in frequencies among classes (e.g., Shannon 1948). Some of these measures combine the number of classes present in a given category with the way the classes are filled, measuring the evenness of the diversity distribution.

While methods are available for characterizing diversity within a set of observations, sample-size effects must be controlled before observed variation can be reliably assessed. This is because a certain range of values is expected even when assemblages were created by random processes. For example, an accumulation of three artifacts can have a minimum richness value of one and a maximum of three, even if there are many more artifact classes present at a site. Thus, the effects of varying sample sizes on specific measures must be assessed. In short, accumulations must be defined as more or less rich or even in content than probable, given the number of classes present and the size of individual concentrations.

With these considerations in mind, I turn now to illustrations of how diversity and heterogeneity might be measured to determine whether activity patterning is present within an archae-

ological distribution. Specifically, the utility of class richness and the *J* index of evenness (referred to as *V* by Pielou 1966) will be examined. In addition, the use of correlation matrices to examine heterogeneity among accumulations will be discussed. Several techniques for assessing the effects of sample sizes will be employed in these examples, including a regression-based approach (Jones *et al.* 1983) and a technique using Monte Carlo simulations (Kintigh 1984a). Before turning to these analyses, however, I shall present a brief outline of how spatial accumulations are defined for Le Flageolet I Couche V, since these will provide the basis for subsequent studies.

Spatial analysis of Le Flageolet I Couche V
The archaeological level designated Couche V at Le Flageolet I is a vertically thin but very rich Upper Perigordian layer (Ri-

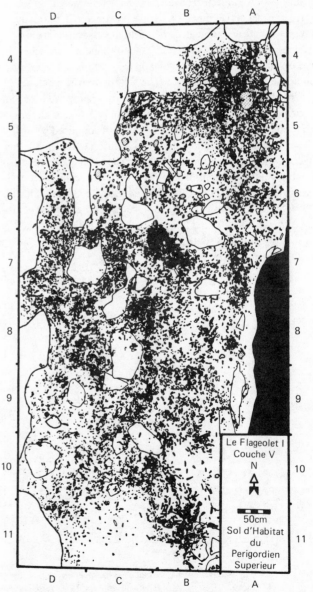

Fig. 6.1. Plan map of the Couche V artifact distribution (courtesy of J-Ph. Rigaud)

Table 6.1. *Artifact classes used for spatial analysis of Couche V. Listed are the traditional type numbers included in each class, the number of artifacts in a class, and the percentage of the total assemblage made up of each (N = 506). Repeated type numbers are compound tools.*

Class	Types	N	% Total
Burins	18, 19, 22, 30–46	256	50.8
Endscrapers	1–18	43	8.5
Retouched	61–63	43	8.5
Bladelets	77, 84–95	36	7.1
Notched	72–74	29	5.7
Truncations	19, 53–60	28	5.5

gaud 1982). All objects recovered from the level were mapped in three dimensions (Figure 6.1). Of specific concern in the analyses presented here are retouched chert artifacts classified into six general groups: burins, endscrapers, miscellaneous retouched pieces, bladelets, notched pieces, and truncations. These groups compose nearly 90% of the Couche V stone-tool assemblage; burins alone make up over 50% of the entire retouched tool component. The six classes contain only a small portion of all the material catalogued from Couche V (which also contained bone debris, fire-cracked rock, and debitage in addition to tools), but they will serve in the illustrations to follow. The site and various other analyses of the materials from it have been discussed in detail elsewhere (e.g., Laville *et al.* 1980; Rigaud 1969, 1978, 1982; Simek 1984; Simek and Leslie 1983). Table 6.1 gives the number of artifacts from Couche V that fall into each of the six classes, and Figure 6.2 presents these data as a histogram for the level assemblage.

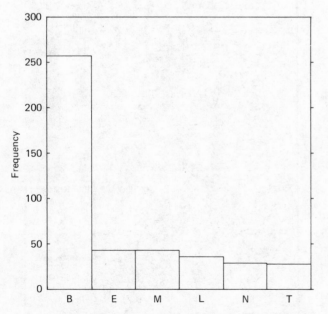

Fig. 6.2. Histogram of six artifact class frequencies for Le Flageolet I Couche V. B = burins; E = endscrapers; M = miscellaneous retouched pieces; L = bladelets; N = notched pieces; T = truncations.

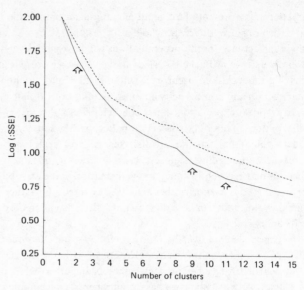

Fig. 6.3. Plot of log (%SSE) against cluster solution for Le Flageolet I Couche V. Solid line represents actual data; broken line represents random data; arrows point to inflections indicating optimal solution levels.

Horizontal coordinates (x and y) for all materials grouped in the six classes were entered into k-means cluster analysis for initial spatial pattern recognition (Ammerman *et al.* 1983; Kintigh and Ammerman 1982; Larick 1983; Simek 1984; Simek and Larick 1983). Cluster solutions defined during the run relate to material accumulations regardless of the specific classes involved, since all 435 artifacts were combined into a single point distribution. Cluster solutions were produced for the distribution from one to 15 cluster configurations, and the accompanying log (%SSE) statistics were used to identify optimal clustering levels. Figure 6.3 shows log (%SSE) plotted against the k-means clustering levels.

Inflections in the log (%SSE) plot, while not strong, suggest that the Couche V distribution is well-described by two-cluster, nine-cluster, and 11-cluster configurations. Figure 6.4 shows a map of the 'medium scale' or nine-cluster solution for the distribution. Similar maps could be produced for the two- and 11-cluster patterns; however, because of space constraints, only this medium-scale solution is illustrated. Clusters solutions can also be described in terms of cluster content. Tables 6.2, 6.3 and 6.4 give artifact class frequencies and overall accumulation sizes for the two-, nine-, and 11-cluster patterns, respectively. These three tables characterize accumulation content at three optimal spatial pattern scales for the Couche V surface. Only the medium-scale solution, nine clusters, will be discussed in detail below. However, the analyses described were also carried out on the low-scale (two-cluster) and high-scale (11-cluster) patterns. The results of these studies will be incorporated into following discussions where appropriate. The nine-accumulation pattern defined by k-means analysis will be used to show how diversity and heterogeneity over space can be assessed.

Regression in measuring archaeological diversity
At first glance, accounting for the effects of sample size on

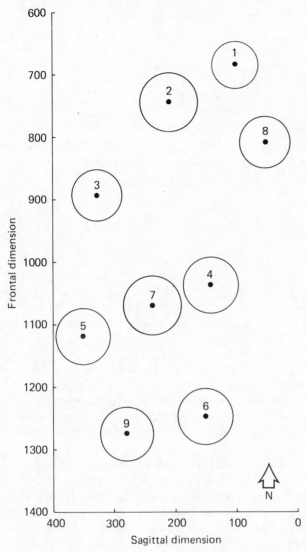

Fig. 6.4. Map of nine-cluster solution for Le Flageolet I Couche V. Clusters are numbered as on Table 6.3.

Table 6.3. *Matrix of artifact class frequencies for Couche V nine-cluster K-means solution*

Class	Cluster number								
	1	2	3	4	5	6	7	8	9
Burins	47	25	38	45	22	20	14	24	20
Endscrapers	3	5	7	5	3	2	9	2	7
Retouched	4	6	7	5	1	4	5	9	2
Bladelets	5	4	0	4	12	2	3	3	3
Notches	2	5	6	6	1	0	3	4	2
Truncations	6	1	4	2	3	4	3	2	3
Total	67	47	62	67	42	32	37	44	37

class richness and evenness values would appear to be a simple problem. Both measures can be defined as dependent variables, with sample size modelled as an independent variable. Regression analysis of the relation between each dependent variable and accumulation size defines its strength and form, and those accumulations that have measures independent of sample size can be identified by examination of regression residuals. This regression approach was successfully applied by Jones *et al.* (1983) to assemblage data from the Steens Mountain area of southeastern Oregon. Importantly, Jones and his colleagues show that, in cases where there are a few abundant classes and a few rare ones, a function of the form $Y = aX^b$ characterizes the relation between sample size and class richness (*ibid.*: 58). This equation is linear in log–log form. Because this situation holds for the artifact class distribution from Couche V, variables in the present analysis were log-arithmically transformed prior to regression.

The regression method is illustrated for the Couche V data using the nine-cluster solution defined during *k*-means analysis. Following Jones *et al.* (1983), the class richness of each cluster was determined, based on how many of the six artifact classes are present (see Table 6.3 above). The log of richness for each accumulation was regressed against the log of accumulation sample

Table 6.2. *Matrix of artifact class frequencies for Couche V two-cluster K-means solution*

Class	Cluster number	
	1	2
Burins	107	149
Endscrapers	13	30
Retouched	22	21
Bladelets	13	23
Notched	14	15
Truncations	9	19
Total	178	257

Table 6.4. *Matrix of artifact class frequencies for Couche V 11-cluster K-means solution*

Class	Cluster number										
	1	2	3	4	5	6	7	8	9	10	11
Burins	47	27	34	20	23	10	13	24	20	18	20
Endscrapers	3	4	2	3	4	1	7	2	5	5	7
Retouched	4	5	2	1	6	1	4	9	5	4	2
Bladelets	5	0	3	11	4	0	2	3	3	2	3
Notches	2	4	2	1	5	0	4	4	3	2	2
Truncations	6	3	3	3	1	3	1	2	0	3	3
Total	67	43	46	39	43	15	31	44	36	34	37

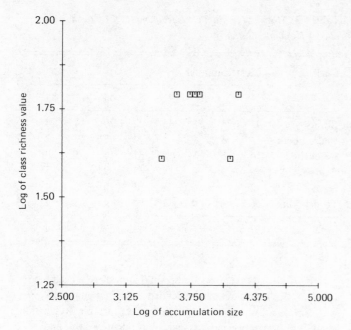

Fig. 6.5. Plot of class richness versus sample size when nine clusters are defined. Several points mark multiple cluster locations.

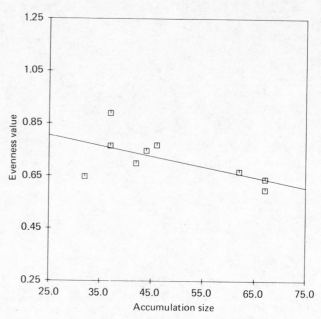

Fig. 6.6. Plot of regression solution for J versus sample size when nine clusters are defined.

size using the least-squares method. Figure 6.5 shows the plotted relation between class richness and sample size for the nine accumulations. No pattern is indicated, and the corresponding r value for the relation is an insignificant .09.

The results of this analysis highlight the dependence of regression on the classification scheme employed when discrete category variables are being treated. For Couche V, the number of classes potentially present in an accumulation is very small (i.e., six) and results in corresponding limits to the potential length of the regression line. In fact, the line is a short segment bounded at the lower end by zero and at the upper end by six (or more generally by the number of possible classes); in other words, the closed data array tightly limits the range of potential class richness. Such constraints have not seemed important in other applications where there are many 'potential' classes to fill and few filled in most specific cases (e.g., Grayson 1984; Jones *et al.* 1983). However, there clearly are constraints on the regression model when predicted Y values (the number of classes present in a sample of stipulated size) approach Ymax, the number of potential classes (Cowgill, personal communication). Use of the method should probably be restricted to cases, like those just cited, where the classification is much larger than the richness for any individual observation.

Lack of success in the preceding analysis might also relate to the fact that richness is a discrete variable. For this reason, a second regression analysis was performed using the J index of evenness (Zar 1974). J is a ratio value and in this case expresses accumulation evenness in terms of how the six artifact classes are filled at a given sample size (using Shannon's H) relative to the maximum potential evenness for the distribution (Hmax). Figure 6.6 shows the relation between the two variables as a scattergram on which the best fit regression line is plotted ($Y = .90535 + - .00399X$). Note that the relationship is nega-

tive ($r = - .60805, p > .05$), suggesting that accumulations become less even as sample size increases. None of the cases has a J value defined as a two standard deviation outlier by regression residuals. Here, regression analysis indicates that evenness values for the nine accumulations may be at least partly influenced by sample size.

Still, the regression line defined for J accounts for only about 37% of the extant variation. Since the J statistic measures the evenness of accumulation content, this difference suggests some independent variation in the proportional representation of classes among the nine accumulations. However, the regression analyses performed here are not designed to identify that variation.

The 'painless approach' to measuring archaeological diversity

Kintigh (1984a; this volume) recently proposed another approach to assessing sample-size effects using Monte Carlo techniques. In this method, the relation between sample size and richness/evenness measures is examined by using simulated random distributions of known structure. Simulated distributions provide expected values for the indices of interest at specified sample sizes and are generated by repeated sampling trials from a model probability distribution. Using the results of many trials, observed values can be compared to random expected values, and the probability of observing a particular richness or evenness at a given sample size can be determined. The model proportions employed in the simulations can be generated from theory or from empirical population parameters. Kintigh's program implementation produces easily interpreted graphic depictions of simulation results and shows how the observed values compare to the random pattern. (For a complete description of the method, the reader is referred to Kintigh's original presentation.)

The nine clusters from Couche V were analyzed using Kin-

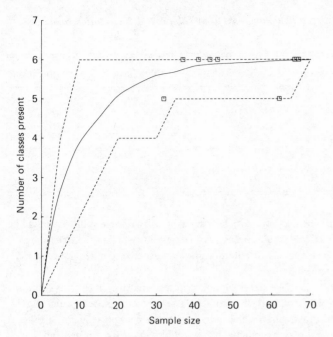

Fig. 6.7. Plot of simulation solution for class richness versus sample size when nine clusters are defined. Solid line indicates simulated random values; broken lines indicate 95% confidence range for random values; boxes locate actual data cases.

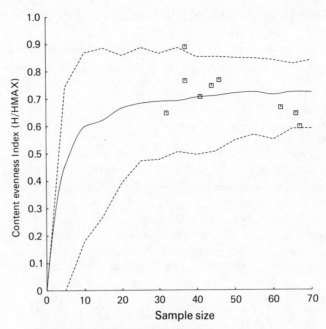

Fig. 6.8. Plot of simulated solution for *J* versus sample size when nine clusters are defined. Solid line indicates simulated random values; broken lines indicate 95% confidence range for random values; boxes locate actual data cases.

tigh's method. The model employed in random simulations represents the known proportions of the entire Couche V assemblage comprising each of the six artifact classes (Table 6.1 above). This probability distribution was sampled 300 times at a variety of sample sizes from one to 70 artifacts. In addition, Kintigh's program implementation performs sampling trials at each of the observed sample sizes (i.e., for each of the accumulations defined here; see Table 6.3).

Two separate simulation analyses were carried out. The first assesses the effects of sample size on class richness values for the clusters, given the underlying frequency distribution for the assemblage. Figure 6.7 shows the results of this analysis. As all Couche V accumulations lie within the 95% confidence range of random richness, none of the nine clusters is significantly richer than those of comparable size produced by random sampling.

The second analysis assesses the effects of sample size on the *J* measure of evenness. Figure 6.8 shows the results of this second run. Here, a single cluster, number 7 in Table 6.3, is significantly more even than would be expected from chance. This cluster, located in the center of the occupied area (Figure 6.4), has a class richness value of six. Of particular importance in producing the high *J* value are the paucity of burins and relatively large numbers of other classes. In short, the classes are filled more evenly than is likely, given the overall pattern at the site. Other Couche V accumulations are no more even than the simulated random distributions for their sizes.

Kintigh's simulation method seems somewhat more applicable to the Couche V data than the regression approach applied earlier. Because the technique employs the underlying class frequency distribution for the assemblage, the richness and evenness

of clusters are assessed in terms of what *ought* to be represented in an accumulation if sampling effects are the only influences on content. This assessment is also independent of the number of classes involved. In short, the relationships of interest can be analyzed within any empirically based constraints. There are fewer limitations on the form of the data and the nature of their measurement scale here than seems to be the case for regression.

Measuring heterogeneity over a site surface

To this point, neither diversity analysis warrants a search for activity patterning in Couche V. However, the methods applied up to now consider the individual clusters and do not make comparisons between them for heterogeneity over space. Such a step is necessary if the kinds of local association predicted by the activity model are to be identified.

Accumulation heterogeneity is a relative variable that characterizes an entire distribution of clusters. It must therefore be measured by comparison between distinct sets of accumulations. Because the problem of concern here is variation within a single distribution, how can a measure of heterogeneity for Couche V be produced?

From the general concepts discussed in the introduction to this paper, it is clear that accumulation heterogeneity is most easily measured by assessing cluster content on a global scale. When many artifact classes are distributed in similar ways among all clusters, the accumulations are homogeneous. When little global patterning is apparent, artifact class relations may be local in nature, and the search for activity sets is warranted. One obvious way to perform this assessment is correlation analysis among clusters; clusters with high correlation coefficients are 'more similar' than clusters with low values. However, results

Table 6.5. *Matrix of Kendall's* tau *statistics for Couche V artifact class associations computed from Table 6.2. All correlation values are significant at p < .05.*

Class	Burins	Endscrapers	Retouched	Bladelets	Notches	Truncations
Burins						
Endscrapers	1.0					
Retouched	−1.0	−1.0				
Bladelets	1.0	1.0	−1.0			
Notches	1.0	1.0	−1.0	1.0		
Truncations	1.0	1.0	−1.0	1.0	1.0	

from such an approach suffer from equifinality; similarity defined in this way might be due to a variety of causes (including activity-set presence). In fact, this approach may be more appropriate for examining local processes when they are indicated than for investigating global structure in accumulation contents, since only individual clusters are being compared.

A second approach to this problem (the one proposed here) also involves the use of correlation, but examines the distribution of classes among clusters. Here, artifact classes are the variables. Significant *positive* correlation between classes indicates that they are distributed in similar fashion among *all* the accumulations, i.e., patterned relationships exist between classes on a global level. A matrix in which many artifact classes are intercorrelated implies that the classes have similar patterns over the whole distribution, and the structure of inter-class relationships is homogeneous. Conversely, few significant positive correlations in the matrix indicate that patterning is *not* global but may be local for most classes and that the structure of the distribution is heterogeneous. A basic problem lies in defining how many global relations constitute a 'homogeneous' pattern and how few represent a 'heterogeneous' structure. It is here that heterogeneity can best be measured in comparative terms, relative to another distribution.

In the present case, it is a single distribution, Couche V, that is of interest. Fortunately, k-means analysis provides a series of pattern descriptions for that distribution that can be compared *across scales of spatial resolution*. In addition to the nine-cluster pattern that has been the focus in preceding analyses, a coarse-pattern scale (two clusters) and a fine-scale configuration (11 clusters) are identified as optimal solutions for the spatial data. Com-

paring accumulation heterogeneity across these solutions might be precisely what is necessary to determine whether the structure of the Couche V distribution should be analyzed in terms of activity patterning.

As the activity model predicts small, discrete areas containing a few associated artifact classes, the finer pattern scales should be those within which activity structuring is present. The artifact assemblages predicted by the activity model are limited and mutually exclusive. If activity sets are present, then the accumulations defined at fine scales of spatial resolution should be heterogeneous. Accumulations at coarse scales should be homogeneous, since large-scale units will represent mixtures of activity sets.

When heterogeneity at a single clustering solution scale is being measured, the effects of both varying sample sizes and relations among individual artifact classes must be taken into account. To satisfy both of these requirements, Kendall's *tau* statistic for nonparametric correlation is computed among the artifact classes within each solution scale (e.g., Blalock 1972). Table 6.5 shows the *tau* matrix for two clusters; Table 6.6 is the matrix for nine clusters; and Table 6.7 gives the *tau* values for 11 clusters.

As was discussed earlier in this paper, inter-class correlations can result from a variety of causes. More importantly, correlations like those in Table 6.5, calculated between only two cases (clusters), can display only perfect positive or negative coefficients. For these reasons, the actual relationships defined by individual coefficients will not be discussed. However, it is the *structure* of these matrices and how structure changes between accumulation patterns that are of concern here. For Table 6.5, nearly all artifact classes have their highest frequency values in cluster 1 and their

Table 6.6. *Matrix of Kendall's* tau *statistics for Couche V artifact class associations computed from Table 6.3. Significant correlations (p < .05) are underscored.*

Class	Burins	Endscrapes	Retouched	Bladelets	Notches	Truncations
Burins						
Endscrapers	−0.1494					
Retouched	0.0870	0.0606				
Bladelets	0.2689	−0.2188	−0.3638			
Notches	0.4348	0.3638	0.5882	−0.2136		
Truncations	0.0000	−0.0318	−0.2772	−0.2540	−0.4004	

Table 6.7. *Matrix of Kendall's* tau *statistics for Couche V artifact class associations computed from Table 6.3. Significant correlations* $(p < .05)$ *are underscored.*

Class	Burins	Endscrapes	Retouched	Bladelets	Notches	Truncations
Burins						
Endscrapers	− 0.2942					
Retouched	0.2774	0.0808				
Bladelets	0.3843	− 0.0619	− 0.0208			
Notches	0.1840	0.2711	0.8004	− 0.0645		
Truncations	0.2887	− 0.2717	− 0.3889	0.0234	− 0.4958	

second values in cluster 2. This basic structure is reflected in the proportion of inter-class correlations that are + 1.0. Although the individual class relations can only be positive or negative, the proportion of the matrix comprising positive values can vary. It is this proportion that will be of interest here.

It should be evident from simple inspection that rather dramatic changes occur between levels of spatial resolution in the number of inter-class correlations. When two clusters are con-

sidered, the rank values for five of the six classes match in both clusters. At the nine-cluster level, two coefficients are positive and significant (between notched and retouched pieces and between burins and notches). Only the first pair of classes has a significant positive relation at the 11-cluster scale.

Differences in heterogeneity among the three pattern scales can be illustrated by computing the percentage of each table taken up by significant, positive values. Figure 6.9 shows these percentages plotted against the scale of spatial resolution for Couche V and three other Upper Paleolithic levels (see Simek 1984). Note that large spatial accumulations are homogeneous and that small accumulation patterns are heterogeneous for three of the levels; all three are from Le Flageolet I. The heterogeneity profile for the fourth archaeological level is different, with around 40% of all artifact classes intercorrelated across all spatial scales. This plot was generated for the open-air Magdalenian site at Pincevent 36 (Leroi-Gourhan and Brezillon 1972; Simek 1984; Simek and Larick 1983). The excavators interpreted the Pincevent deposits as a series of rich secondary dump zones that mixed refuse from a variety of specific activities. The fact that these deposits are homogeneous over different scales of spatial refinement would support this inference. The Le Flageolet I distributions, however, display the kind of accumulation heterogeneity at fine-pattern scales that might warrant further investigation of possible activity patterning.

Summary and discussion

Three different techniques have been used to analyze archaeological spatial distributions in order to determine whether a search for activity patterning can be warranted. All three techniques assess variation in the contents of material accumulations in terms of structure rather than activity-set definition. Two of the techniques, the regression approach and Kintigh's simulation method, explicitly examine individual spatial accumulations to determine whether they are more or less diverse in content than expected, given their sample sizes. In each of these methods, two separate measures, richness and J, were used together to characterize components of diversity. The third technique compares the heterogeneity of accumulations across scales of spatial refinement to determine whether and at what level of resolution local activity patterning might be present.

The results of these analyses vary in their utility. Class rich-

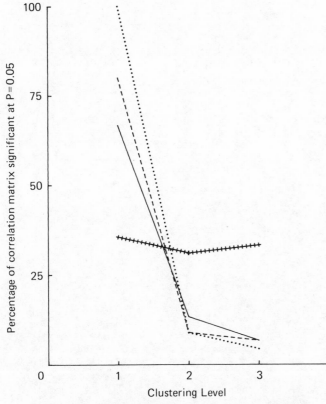

Fig. 6.9. Heterogeneity plots (cluster level versus % significant positive correlations) for four Upper Paleolithic distributions. Solid line is Le Flageolet I Couche V; dotted line is Le Flageolet I Couche VIII-1; broken line is Le Flageolet I Couche VIII-2; hashed line is Pincevent Section 36. Low-, medium-, and high-scale solutions for Pincevent are three, six, and nine clusters. For Le Flageolet I Couche VIII-1: twom nine and 11. For Couche VIII-2: two, eight and 12.

ness does not seem sensitive enough to content variation in the present case where only a few classes are defined. The J index of evenness would seem to be a more useful measure here, since it takes into account the proportional representation of classes in a location.

In comparing methods for assessing sample-size effects, the simulation technique would seem to be preferable to regression in this particular analysis, since it is unclear whether the assumptions of the regression model are being met by the Couche V data. Because the simulation method accounts for varying prior probabilities of class inclusion by determining random expectations based on a specific model, the number of potential classes does not seem to be an important influence on the method's efficacy.

To assess accumulation heterogeneity over the Couche V surface, a technique that examines patterns of global artifact class co-occurrence is proposed. By plotting the structure of inter-class correlation matrices over a series of spatial resolution levels, heterogeneity in accumulation content is demonstrated for Couche V (and for two other levels from the Le Flageolet I rockshelter) when spatial units are small. This pattern conforms to that predicted by the activity model and suggests that a search for activity patterning in Couche V may be possible. At another Paleolithic site, Pincevent Section 36, a different profile suggests that activity patterning may not be present in the site's accumulations and that other explanations should be tested.

In conclusion, the presumptive search for activity patterning in archaeological distributions has serious problems. Such patterning may not be present (e.g., at Pincevent), and inferences of activity structuring in the absence of warranting analyses are dangerous. It would seem possible, using examinations of spatial diversity and heterogeneity, to determine if and when activity patterning should be sought or other causal factors should be investigated. Such preliminary analyses are critical if spatial archaeology is to advance beyond the realm of speculative reconstruction.

Acknowledgments

I owe the greatest debt of gratitude to J-Ph. Rigaud for access to the superb data from his Le Flageolet I excavations. I must also thank K. Kintigh for freely making his simulation program available and for contributing constructive comments on an earlier draft of the paper. I also acknowledge the aid of G. Cowgill, R. C. Dunnell, D. K. Grayson, G. T. Jones, and R. Leonard, who read and criticized previous drafts of the manuscript. The final product is, of course, my own responsibility. Finally, I especially thank the L. S. B. Leakey Foundation for generously providing research funding for the Couche V spatial analysis.

Chapter 7

Measures of diversity and expedient lithic technologies

George T. Jones, Charlotte Beck and
Donald K. Grayson

In the past ten years or so, the scope of archaeological settlement study has expanded its focus to include entire landscapes as well as the distribution of sites. Thomas' work (1971, 1975) anticipated this direction with his focus on 'nonsite archaeology.' With our increased awareness of the importance of technological organization, artifact and spatial reuse, and geomorphic processes, we have gained a more sophisticated understanding of the complexities of this record.

As the spatial perspective has expanded, so too has insight into the complex interaction of processes that contribute to patterning at regional and finer areal scales. Particularly through ethnoarchaeological research (e.g., Binford 1977, 1978b, 1980, 1982, 1983a, b; Gifford 1978; Gould 1980; Yellen 1977), we have grown increasingly aware of the fact that a number of factors influence archaeological patterning, not the least of which are locality reuse and technological organization. As a result, we may question to what degree patterns of varying artifact density over a landscape parallel activity differentiation in space. In this paper, we consider the argument that, under conditions of technological expediency and high residual mobility, variations in the density of artifacts and tool diversity across a landscape are attributable to the differential distribution of manufacturing and use activities. Using data from the Steens Mountain area of southeastern Oregon, we explore ways of measuring formal variability in clustered and dispersed archaeological manifestations as a means to characterize land use more fully.

Technological expediency, context of tool discard, and spatial artifact variation

Binford (1977, 1979) suggests that technological organization can be viewed as a continuum, running between cases that center on the production of highly modified tools and those cases of complete expediency. At the latter extreme, production costs associated with individual tools are low; production is often situationally defined (Binford 1979). Because of their low costs and often short use-lives, expedient tools are expected to be produced and typically discarded in the context of their use. If, for the moment, we assume the accuracy of this characterization, and thus that expedient tools are not subject to the same constraints as curated artifacts, then to some extent an archaeological record of expedient tools in its distribution and density character is a fair reflection of the distribution of activities over a landscape (barring extensive reuse of the same locality). If these notions about spatial behavior are indeed accurate, then we should expect highly variable patterns of artifact density across space, and, importantly, we should anticipate that low-density phenomena do occur and do reflect aspects of land use that most likely differ from those at specific loci. Moreover, as several authors have suggested (e.g., Binford 1980, 1983a, b; Foley 1981a, 1981b; Isaac 1981), neither clustered nor dispersed artifact phenomena arrive in their spatial contexts as a consequence of random processes. Foley (1981a) points out that, although some human activities may be confined preferentially to settlements or to areas just beyond them, many activities do not have such tightly constrained spatial contexts. Out of these observations we might argue for a simple land-use model that associates artifact density with activity variation across space. In this case, the spatial distribution of foraging or energy-extraction activities will be conformant with low-density scatters of artifacts within the so-called foraging radius, while more centralized or localized activities will conform in space to dense artifact scatters, assuming that the rate of artifact discard across space holds a commensurate relationship with the level of activity in that landscape.

Although this portrayal of spatial use may be quite simplistic, and the archaeological referents not quite so easily determined, such an activity model lies at the center of many characterizations of hunter–gatherer land use. Yet, while such models have some currency, few attempts have been made to examine the entire range of archaeological distributions (i.e., 'offsite' as well as site) in order to evaluate whether such models of spatial behavior have applicability to archaeological situations. If human foragers actually utilize specific locales and the areas beyond them in this manner, and certainly ethnoarchaeological research points in this direction (e.g., Gould 1980), how might these be differentiated in an archaeological setting? What expectations have we for the spatial and functional patterning of archaeological phenomena?

If, for the moment, we employ a simple distinction between domestic, maintenance, and extractive activities (Binford and Binford 1966), we might have certain expectations concerning the functional and spatial character of artifacts across a landscape. Isolated events pertaining to domestic and maintenance activities or even composites of these events are generally thought to be localized in nature, and certainly such maintenance activities as lithic tool production can create considerable amounts of debris. Such patterns of focal use are contrasted with extractive activities that represent wide-ranging events and create dispersed artifact patterns of much lower density. Hence, in any landscape, we can reasonably expect to distinguish minimally between clustered and dispersed phenomena. Beyond this, functional correlates of density are anticipated. To draw again upon the above activity characterizations, a smaller range of functions is expected to be associated with extractive activities occurring beyond a residential base than the variety that comprises domestic and maintenance activities. Obviously, this relationship need not be universal. Quarry assemblages, which often consist of great quantities of debris but low functional diversity, lie outside this general expectation. For the most part, however, the variety of classes and the proportionality among those classes can be expected to decrease along a gradient between dense, highly clustered manifestations and more dispersed or isolated phenomena (see Thomas 1983b; this volume).

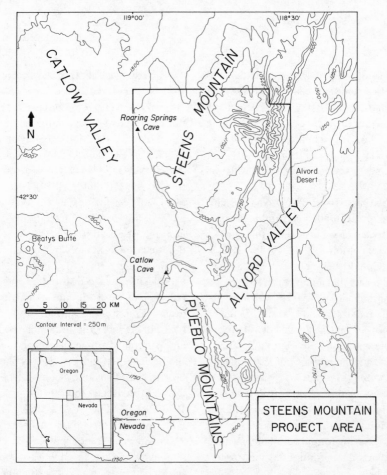

Fig. 7.1. Location of the Steens Mountain Project area

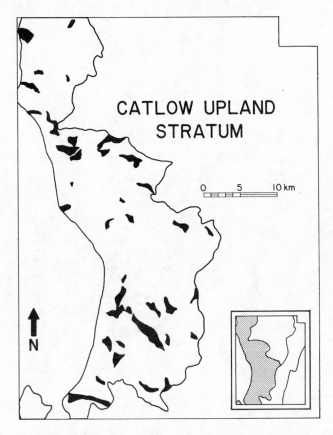

Fig. 7.2. Catlow Upland Survey units

The Steens Mountain data base

The data used here were collected by the Steens Mountain Prehistory Project in southeastern Oregon (Figure 7.1). [For a summary of this project and its goals, see Aikens *et al.* 1982.] The present analysis focuses on the data from one sampling stratum, the Catlow Upland, selected from among the four principal strata because it contains the largest number of survey units as well as the greatest number of sites, and thus has the greatest potential for yielding clear distinctions between site and offsite manifestations (Figure 7.2). The data were collected by means of systematic surface survey. All artifacts encountered by surveyors spaced at 15-meter intervals were collected and located on scaled enlargements of USGS topographic maps. When artifact densities were too great to allow for accurate recording of artifact locations on the enlarged maps, these dense scatters of artifacts, termed 'sites,' were mapped and collected by crews using plane table and alidade or tape and compass.

In all, 40 Catlow Upland sample units, covering 621.4 km², were surveyed. Fifty-one high-density sites were recorded, and of these, 41 were mapped and collected. Some 36,412 artifacts were recovered and analyzed from this sampling stratum. Ninety-two % of the objects came from sites; the remaining artifacts came from lower density, or 'offsite,' areas.

Description and analysis of these artifacts included identification with both technological and functional classifications. The former is based on general morphological and material criteria,

and produces categories comparable to others used in the Great Basin. The functional classification is based on macroscopic use-wear (e.g., Dunnell and Campbell 1977). Chronological controls were established using projectile point seriation and typological cross-dating.

Technological variability in site and offsite samples

The Steens Mountain samples are the product of a largely expedient technology, consisting primarily of flaked stone artifacts that may have served many generalized functions. In contrast to the abundance of utilized flakes, prepared tools or retouched artifacts are rare components of most assemblages. Retouched artifacts comprise only 3.7% of the entire Catlow Upland assemblage, and many of these artifacts appear to represent manufacturing failures. Although this sample group as a whole contains a preponderance of utilized flakes, many individual samples represent accumulations of debris resulting primarily from lithic reduction activities rather than the products of tool use and discard. By examining technological attributes it is possible to distinguish between these activities.

In our earlier discussion, we suggested that, because certain activities, such as domestic or maintenance activities, produce different artifactual patterns than procurement activities, we might expect differences in technological diversity between site and offsite areas. For example, if tool production was carried out predominantly at sites, then those artifacts deposited outside of the context of manufacture in offsite space would occur there as a result of tool use and discard or, less frequently, as incidental loss. Thus, since a major source of lithic artifacts at sites is manufacturing debris, flake artifacts would be expected to represent a larger

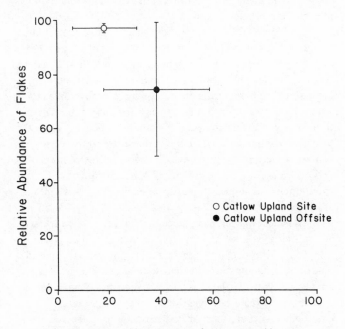

Fig. 7.3. Relative abundance of flakes and relative abundance of worn artifacts as an average for all site and offsite samples in the Catlow Upland. Bars represent one standard deviation.

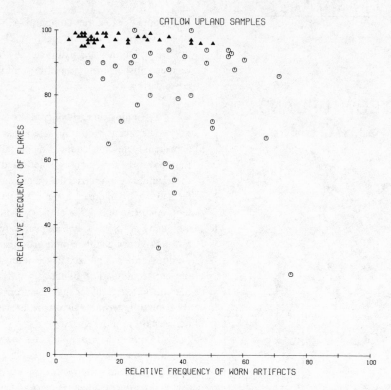

Fig. 7.4. Distribution of individual site (triangles) and offsite (circles) samples

proportion in site assemblages than in offsite assemblages. Also, the average size of site flakes would be smaller than those in offsite contexts, and a smaller proportion of these flakes would show evidence of use.

In Figure 7.3 the relative abundances of flake artifacts are plotted against the relative frequency of worn artifacts as a means of comparing site and offsite assemblages in the Catlow Upland. As this plot illustrates, with respect to these variables, site samples are markedly different from offsite samples. Moreover, the variances about the stratum centroids (shown as one standard deviation) are especially narrow for site samples, particularly along the *Y*-axis, flake abundance. In contrast, the offsite sample clearly contains widely divergent sample members. The distribution of individual samples is shown in Figure 7.4. In comparison to the distribution of site samples, the scatter of offsite samples is considerable.

It is clear that site samples contain far fewer worn artifacts as a proportion of the total artifact assemblage than do offsite samples. At the same time, prepared tools, particularly projectile points, often comprise a large share of the worn implements among samples of the latter group. The positions of most samples with respect to these variables thus follow our expectations if, to a large degree, sites are accumulated manufacturing debris and offsite samples are the consequences of artifact deposition following use.

If sites do represent a major focus of lithic reduction, flake sizes should be smaller in these contexts than in offsite areas. If

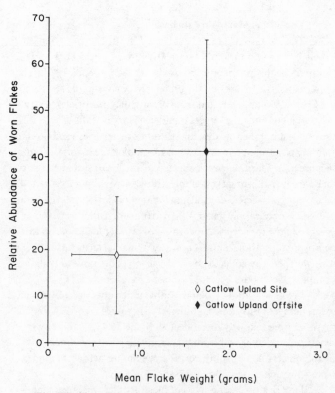

Fig. 7.5. Mean flake weight and relative abundance of worn flakes as an average for all site and offsite samples in the Catlow Upland. Bars represent one standard deviation.

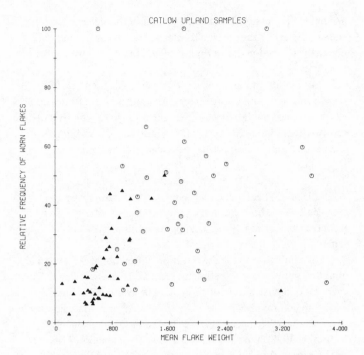

Fig. 7.6. Distribution of individual site (triangles) and offsite (circles) samples

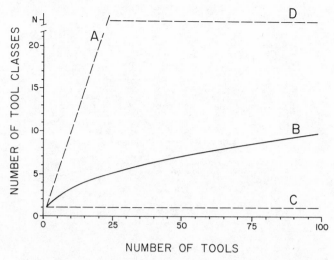

Fig. 7.7. Relationship between class richness and sample size. Line A represents a sample in which each artifact is unique; line C represents a sample in which each artifact belongs to the same class. Line B displays the general form of the usual relationships between these variables. Line D indicates the limit imposed on class richness by a typology with finite limits.

this is the case and much of the flake debris is detrital in character, a smaller proportion of those flakes would be expected to exhibit traces of wear. Mean flake weight (used as a surrogate for flake size) and the percentage of worn flakes are aligned on the *X*- and *Y*-axis respectively in Figures 7.5 and 7.6. The points in Figure 7.5 again represent the stratum means computed from individual site and offsite samples. Figure 7.6 shows the distribution of individual samples. Quite clearly, these distributions mirror the differences expressed in the relationship discussed above. Moreover, the ranges of variation are proportionate to those recognized earlier.

These results are fully compatible with the conclusion that the use of site and offsite space differed. Offsite areas appear to represent predominantly zones of tool use and discard, while sites probably encompass a more complex overlaying of events combining both tool-using and manufacturing activities. Taking this a step further, then, given these suggested differences in the range of activities practiced on- and offsite, what are the expectations in terms of functional diversity for each of these areas? First, if sites represent a more complex set of activities, functional diversity should be greater in these areas than in offsite areas. And secondly, since site and offsite use differed in terms of the set of activities practiced, functional composition of site and offsite assemblages would also be expected to differ.

Functional diversity

The notion of diversity has been used most often by archaeologists in an intuitive sense, to suggest a greater or lesser variety of classes rather than specifically to denote variation in the number of classes present and their relative abundances among a set of artifact assemblages. These characteristics of archaeological distributions have respectively been termed rich-

ness and evenness. There is little dispute about how richness is most appropriately measured; the same cannot be said, however, of evenness.

Richness is simply the number of classes or categories represented in a sample. Class richness is a simple and intuitively appealing measure, and, provided we recognize its sensitivity to sample-size effects (Jones *et al.* 1983; see also Grayson 1984), it can be a powerful expression of archaeological variability. The relationship between class richness and sample size is bounded at the lower end by populations containing only a single class and, at the upper end, by populations in which each artifact is unique (Figure 7.7). Further constraining this relationship is an upper limit on class richness that may reach, but not exceed, the number of classes constituting a typology with finite limits. In practice this limit obviously varies considerably, from the most general morphological typologies containing only a few classes, to multidimensional paradigms with thousands of potential classes. In the same sense, the largest and smallest assemblages among a group of samples form another set of limits (Figure 7.7).

We have shown elsewhere, using regression to compare samples of very different sizes from the Steens Mountain area, how class richness varies in a statistically predictable manner within these boundaries (Jones *et al.* 1983; see also Beck 1984; Jones 1984). Applying this approach in the present situation, we expect the relationship between class richness and sample size of homogeneous tool populations, once logarithmically transformed, to be strongly linear. Unless divergent artifact populations are sampled, cases of highly deviant character, represented graphically as extreme residual outliers, are not expected. If, on the other hand, site and offsite samples differ from one another in terms of the relative levels of class richness, they should assume different arrangements of points, with significantly different regression slopes.

When site and offsite samples from the Catlow Upland are

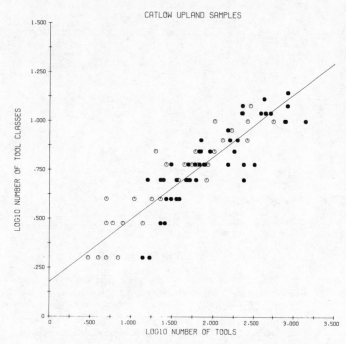

Fig. 7.8. Relationship between class richness and sample size among all Catlow Upland samples. Solid circles represent site samples; open circles represent offsite samples.

around the regression line. Even if similar in character to the off-site samples, site samples would be expected to lie predominantly above the regression line in Figure 7.9 if, in fact, they were more diverse.

When site and offsite samples are examined separately, there is no significant improvement in sample group variance in either case, nor do the slopes of the regression lines differ significantly when compared statistically. Again, visual inspection of these scatterplots fails to reveal any clear patterns in the distributions of either site (Figure 7.9a) or offsite residuals (Figure 7.9b). Thus, we conclude that, except for differences in the sizes of the assemblages that comprise each sample group, with respect to sample richness, both site and offsite samples have been drawn from the same or nearly identical populations in the Catlow Upland.

We now turn to the examination of functional class relative abundance, or evenness, between site and offsite assemblages. The evenness of a distribution of classes can be evaluated in several ways, but commonly a single index of diversity is used. A number of indices have been proposed (see Pielou 1975; Simpson 1949; Whittaker 1972). We have chosen to describe evenness (J) as the ratio between the Shannon–Weaver index (H') and the logarithm of class richness (Pielou 1975), in which the common logarithm of richness is equal to H' for a perfectly evenly distributed sample. Thus, a value approaching 1.0 for this ratio indicates that all classes are represented in nearly equal proportions in a sample, while lower values reflect increasingly less even class abundance structures. Unfortunately, this index cannot distinguish between samples that contain many classes, but are very unevenly distributed, and cases in which there are few classes, but each occurs in similar proportions. Because such a distinction may be important, we have created two evenness indices using different estimates of class

plotted together with respect to these variables, the relationship is in fact strongly linear (Figure 7.8). In this example, a correlation coefficient of 0.90 ($p < .01$), corresponding to an explained variance of 80%, indicates that a large amount of the variation in class richness among these samples may be statistically accounted for by sample size. Inspection of the scatterplot shows that members of both site and offsite sample groups are well distributed

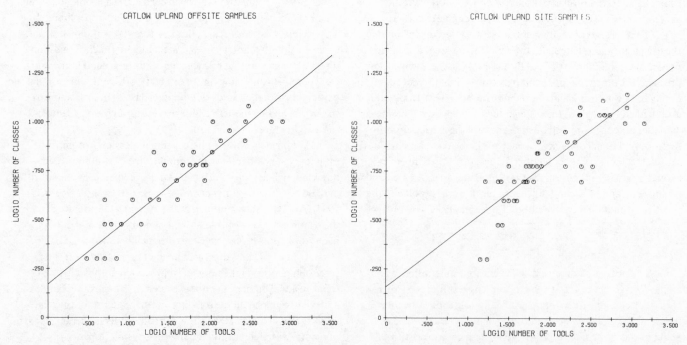

Fig. 7.9. Relationship between class richness and sample size among (a) all offsite samples and (b) all site samples

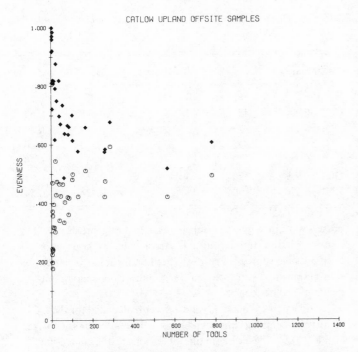

Fig. 7.10. Relationship between evenness and sample size among all Catlow Upland offsite samples. Circles represent J_2 evenness; diamonds represent J_1 evenness.

richness. In the first (J_1), richness represents the maximum number of classes (17) possible under the classificatory scheme in use. The second index (J_2) employs the logarithm of the actual richness of the sample under consideration as the denominator.

While the Shannon–Weaver statistic is relatively independent of sample size (Whittaker 1972), class richness and its log-

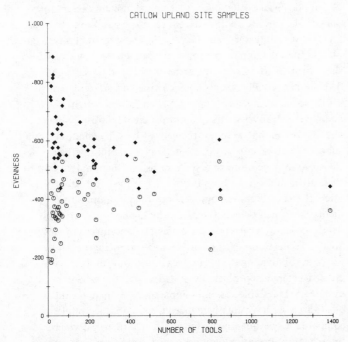

Fig. 7.11. Relationship between evenness and sample size among all Catlow Upland site samples. Circles represent J_2 evenness; diamonds represent J_1 evenness.

arithm are not. Thus, archaeological samples of different sizes, although drawn from the same artifact population and of nearly identical structure, may not yield equivalent evenness values. Figures 7.10 and 7.11 illustrate how sample size constrains both computed measures of evenness (see Kintigh, this volume). In each plot the upper distribution of points (diamonds) represents evenness calculated using the logarithm of the sample richness as the denominator (J_2), while the lower distribution (circles) employs the logarithm of 17 (J_1). If every sample is of equivalent class structure, each should assume a paired distribution of points aligned horizontally on these graphs. Instead, the scatter of points deviates quite sharply at small sample sizes, but this is quite easily explained. Among the cases of the lower distribution, most are small samples and have a very low evenness value, strictly as a consequence of having so many unfilled classes. This is particularly true of those samples having fewer than 17 tools, the minimum number of tools necessary in order to fill each class. The reverse is the case among samples of the upper distribution since the denominator in this equation is always small for cases with small sample sizes. We can further illustrate the effects of sample size by examining at what sample size these indices stabilize with respect to each other. When the absolute differences between the two values obtained for each sample are aligned against sample size (Figure 7.12), we note that the indices begin to stabilize only after samples reach about 150 tools. An even more conservative estimate places this point at about 400 tools, a size that far exceeds most of the samples from the Steens Mountain Project area.

Beyond differences related to sample-size variation, however, site and offsite samples assume largely overlapping patterns of evenness. On average, site evenness values are slightly lower, indicating somewhat lower proportionality among constituent classes. However, both groups of samples reflect low levels of diversity. Assemblages are dominated by one or a small number of tool classes and include a variable number of rarer categories. On the whole, class evenness appears to differ only slightly between site and offsite samples.

Thus far in our examination of technological and functional variation between site and offsite samples, we have detected some unexpected patterns, given our preliminary expectations. First, offsite samples appear to exhibit greater technological variability than do site samples. Further, across all offsite samples we sense relatively greater technological variability than among site samples, which are really quite similar to one another. With regard to functional diversity, offsite samples as a group are perceptibly more diverse than site samples, but only barely so, and they are considerably more uniform in relation to each other. Site samples, on the other hand, though technologically uniform, vary more widely among cases as to functional class abundance. On the whole, however, functional variability between clustered and dispersed phenomena is not nearly as great as our simple model of spatial use anticipates. Although we expect that the differential apportionment of activities in space will create distinctive functional patterning beyond simple density gradients, we find, at best, only slight confirmation of this prediction. In fact, archaeological theory offers few predictions as to the precise behavior

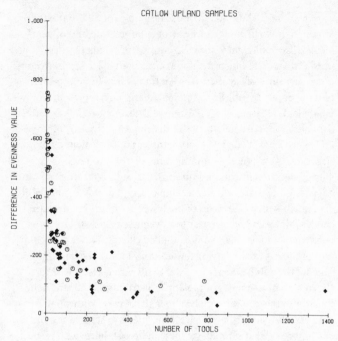

CATLOW UPLAND SAMPLES

Fig. 7.12. Absolute numerical difference between J₁ and J₂ evenness plotted against sample size for all Catlow Upland site assemblages (diamonds) and all Catlow Upland offsite assemblages (circles)

Table 7.1. *Diversity statistics for DC1-56 offsite and site assemblages*

Assemblage	N	N of classes	J_1	J_2
DC1-56	566	10	0.421	0.518
DC1-56/1A	227	12	0.509	0.580
DC1-56/1B	25	5	0.463	0.814
DC1-56/2	842	12	0.531	0.605
DC1-56/4	522	11	0.419	0.495
DC1-56/7A	323	6	0.365	0.577
DC1-56/7B	150	9	0.424	0.547

of class distributions in each of these locational settings. We have no models of subsistence or land use that parallel ecological models of competition or resource partitioning with distributional entailments. When we fall back on intuitive expectations for differences in class richness and evenness, we find, as this example illustrates, that our predictions as to the kind and degree of archaeological variability are not entirely satisfactory.

Why is this so? Why has this examination clearly failed to demonstrate functional differences between these distinct manifestations of artifact density? We have identified functional variability among these samples, but it has not taken fully expectable patterns. If these samples were drawn from sample spaces that exhibit a wide range of significant environmental variation, it might be argued that our analyses were conducted at inappropriate spatial scales. While we cannot pursue an exhaustive evaluation of this question, we will attempt a preliminary examination below, where we turn to an investigation of the difference between site and offsite samples within the context of a single sample unit in which some degree of control over environmental variation may be exerted.

Local functional variation

For our examination of functional differences between site and offsite phenomena at a finer spatial scale, we have chosen a single survey unit, DC1-56. In addition to possessing a sizable offsite artifact sample ($n = 584$), and a relatively large number of sites ($n = 6$), DC1-56 displays considerable environmental uniformity. The survey unit covers approximately 1.39 km². Over its 1.9 km length, there is an overall change in elevation of only 60 m. The unit has a constant northern aspect and today possesses a fairly uniform bunchgrass–small sagebrush vegetation association. In selecting this sample unit, we hope to reduce possible sources of context-specific functional variation, thus permitting us to focus on functional richness along gradients of artifact density.

Evenness estimates (J_1 and J_2) were calculated for the DC1-56 survey assemblage and each of the six DC1-56 site assemblages (Table 7.1). As the indices in this table indicate, the value for all offsite material falls relatively close to the values calculated for five of the six site assemblages. The sixth site, DC1-56/1B, has a J_2 diversity value of 0.814, far above that of the offsite assemblage; however, as noted earlier, evenness is very sensitive to small sample sizes and thus this value is attributable to the small size of the DC1-56/1B assemblage ($n = 25$). Thus, the diversity indices in Table 7.1 suggest that there is little functional difference between site and offsite assemblages on DC1-56.

In part, this failure to identify functional differences between site and offsite assemblages may be due to the masking effect of composing all offsite space as a single sample. As a consequence, the variation within the entire offsite sample might be as great as, if not greater than, the variation between that offsite sample and the site samples. Although site boundaries coincide with a sharp drop in artifact density, areas just beyond those boundaries do characteristically possess higher artifact densities than most offsite space. It is likely that not all centralized activities are equally constrained spatially and thus create diffuse boundary characteristics that were not recognized by site definition during survey. Thus, certain of the offsite areas (i.e., those adjacent to the sites) may be more similar in terms of functional diversity than other areas (i.e., those farthest from the sites). In an attempt to create more homogeneous offsite samples over gradients of artifact density (i.e., from highly clustered areas to nearly isolated occurrences of artifacts), concentric samples were created centered on each of the DC1-56 sites (Figure 7.13).

In subdividing the offsite area in this way, however, we created a technical problem. As noted earlier, the behavior of evenness is less stable at small sample size, and, in parceling the offsite area, we have greatly reduced the sizes of the samples being compared. Consequently, we must return to richness, which, though less informative, assumes a more predictable behavior as the sizes of samples change.

As shown in Figure 7.13, offsite samples were formed as

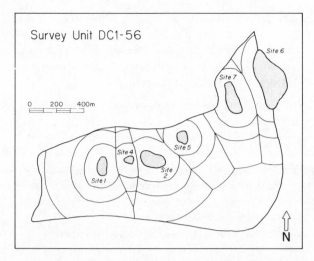

Fig. 7.13. Survey unit DC1-56 showing site locations and concentric offsite samples

Table 7.2. *Regression statistics for DC1-56 sample groups*

Sample group	N	r	r^2	Regression equation
Inner offsite	6	0.87	0.75	$Y = 0.062 + 0.357X$
Intermediate offsite	6	0.43	0.19	$Y = 0.289 + 0.194X$
Outer offsite	6	0.95	0.90	$Y = 0.035 + 0.503X$
Site	6	0.66	0.44	$Y = 0.528 + 0.177X$
All offsite	19	0.85	0.73	$Y = 0.060 + 0.392X$
All samples	25	0.89	0.79	$Y = 0.120 + 0.347X$

rings of 100-width encircling each cluster. A convenient figure, 100 m closely approximates the average radius of the DC1-56 sites. In addition to the six cluster samples, three offsite samples were created for each cluster (resulting in 18 offsite samples): (1) within 100 m of the site boundary (Inner), (2) 100–200 m (Intermediate), and (3) 200–400 m (Outer). A residual sample of artifacts lying beyond 400 m comprises a nineteenth offsite sample. Comparisons of sample richness employ these 25 samples.

Following the arguments raised earlier, we may ask if artifact-class richness drops with distance from artifact clusters. We might expect this to occur as extractive activities replaced domestic and maintenance activities, corresponding to a reduction in artifact density. If there are, in fact, differences in functional diversity between site and offsite areas, we might expect either that richness will gradually decline with distance from sites, or that it might drop abruptly at some point along the density gradient, coincident with an actual site boundary. Table 7.2 contains regression statis-

tics for each of the DC1-56 sample groups as well as combined sample groups. The sample size–richness relationship variously accounts for between 19% and 90% of the variance in class richness among the sample groups. While these generally follow our expectations, the more instructive information lies in the differences in the equations of the regression lines. As depicted in Figure 7.14, the slopes of the lines are visually different. A statistical test (Table 7.3), however, identifies only one pair of lines as differing significantly: the site-sample group and the outermost offsite sample. Although this particular outcome does follow expectations noted earlier, corresponding trends are not apparent in other cross-sample comparisons.

Importantly, although the slopes of these samples diverge, they do so in the reverse of our expectations if artifact clusters should represent a wider range of functions and offsite samples a smaller range. The regression slope, which relates to the underlying frequency structure of the samples comprising each group, indicates that new classes are added less frequently with increases in sample size among site samples than among offsite samples. This would occur if we were to sample from site assemblages that display low class proportionality (low evenness) and from offsite samples in which all classes occur in relatively more similar proportions. As suggested, this pattern runs counter to our expectations. However, because wider trends are not apparent among the other sample groups, and because there is little overlap in the distribution of sizes of the site and offsite samples, it is difficult to carry these points further without attention to the records of a wider number of individual survey units.

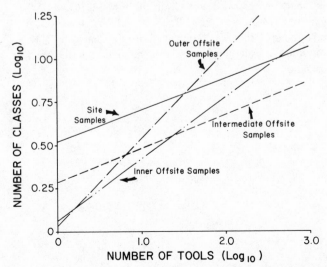

Fig. 7.14. Regression lines for three offsite sample groups and site sample group from DC1-56

Table 7.3. *Comparisons of slopes (b) for DC1-56 sample groups* ($H: b_1 - b_2 = 0$)

Samples compared	t^*	p
Inner–intermediate	0.76	< .50
Inner–outer	−1.06	< .40
Inner–sites	1.17	< .40
Intermediate–outer	−1.51	< .30
Intermediate–sites	0.08	< .90
Outer–sites	2.46	< .10

*t = 2.776, 95% two-tailed significance.

Table 7.4. *Differences in functional class composition between DC1-56 offsite assemblage and each of six DC1-56 site assemblages*

Assemblage	N	X^2	Significance
DC1-56/1A	227	28.78	0.005
DC1-56/1B	25	18.26	0.005
DC1-56/2	842	76.43	0.005
DC1-56/4	522	9.11	0.100
DC1-56/7A	323	5.14	0.500
DC1-56/7B	150	2.08	0.900

Summary and conclusions

Archaeological remains occur over the Catlow Upland, as we suspect they do over most landscapes, in distributions of varying density, which, we have argued, correspond to past spatial behavior of centralized and dispersed sorts. In this paper we have attempted to evaluate to what degree clustered (site) and unclustered (offsite) density configurations correspond to patterns of functional and technological artifact variation. Our results suggest that offsite areas were predominantly zones of tool use and discard, while sites appear to represent a more complex overlaying of events, combining both tool-using and manufacturing activities. Among the most interesting observations coming from these analyses, however, is that samples of both clustered and dispersed types are very similar with respect to their functional structure. Undoubtedly, the expedient nature of this technology, one reason why archaeological remains are so prevalent in this setting, is a primary contributor to similarity among samples. Almost certainly the generalized flake tools making up most of these assemblages served a wide variety of functions, yet without producing equally variable patterns of use-wear.

There is, however, a second factor that may be contributing to the lack of functional difference between clustered and dispersed phenomena. Many of these artifact clusters likely represent dense offsite accumulations, possibly the consequence of multiple episodes of resource procurement and artifact discard. As Ebert (1985:5) points out:

Analytically, it might be expected that if a density peak occurs at the overlap of two discarded assemblages resulting from similar functional activities, then the diversity of materials within the density peaks would be similar to that between the density peaks.

With respect to our examples, then, variations in functional diversity may well be masked by the inclusion of these clusters that actually represent dense accumulations from offsite activities rather than focal activities. Before any final statements concerning differences in functional diversity between clustered and dispersed phenomena can be made, those clusters that are similar to the dispersed phenomena in terms of functional class composition must be separated from those that are not.

Since our purpose in this exercise has been to assess the range of functional variability as it relates to artifact density, expressly in terms of the structural properties of samples, i.e., richness and evenness, we have not considered their compositional properties. Although a consideration of class composition is beyond the scope of this paper, a preliminary comparison of site and offsite assemblages from DC1-56 (Table 7.4) indicates differences among some, but not all, samples. These results are what might be expected, given the above discussion.

In sum, we have shown that differences between clustered and dispersed phenomena do exist along technological dimensions. Functional variations, on the other hand, do not approximate similarly robust patterns. This, we believe, is a complex issue that ultimately returns to the simple equation of dense artifact clusters with domestic and maintenance activities. Simple behavioral inferences such as this are often made concerning the record of simple, mobile human foragers, and it is fair to conclude, based on our studies here, that the broadened spatial perspectives brought to such analyses challenge such inferences.

Acknowledgments

We would like to thank Bob Leonard who read this paper in draft. The Steens Mountain Prehistory Project was funded by National Science Foundation Grants BNS-77-12556 and BNS-80-06277 to C. M. Aikens, D. K. Grayson, and P. J. Mehringer, Jr., and by a grant from Mr. Bingham's Trust for Charity to D. K. Grayson. We gratefully acknowledge the support of these organizations.

Chapter 8

Sample size and relative abundance in arch-aeological analysis: illustrations from spiral fractures and seriation

Donald K. Grayson

Some very basic archaeological problems require the analysis of the number of classes that comprise a series of assemblages (richness), and of the distribution of abundance across those classes (diversity). In a number of places, I have emphasized that both kinds of measures are prone to sample-size effects. For instance, I have pointed out that much of the variation in the numbers of taxa present in archaeological faunal assemblages can be accounted for by variation in the numbers of identified specimens across those assemblages (Grayson 1984), and, with my colleagues G. T. Jones and C. Beck, have applied the same observation to the numbers of lithic artifact classes in archaeological surface assemblages (Jones *et al.* 1983). I have also shown that the relative abundances of taxa in archaeological faunal assemblages are often correlated with the total number of identified specimens in those assemblages (Grayson 1981, 1984, 1985). In both settings, I have suggested ways in which the effects of sample size can be taken into account so that analysis can proceed without fear of confusing differences in true richness or diversity with what are merely differences in the size of the collected sample (see also Kintigh 1984a for an alternative to the approach suggested in Grayson 1984 and in Jones *et al.* 1983).

It is my perception that the scope of sample-size effects on the relative abundances of classes in archaeological assemblages has yet to be generally recognized. In this brief paper, I suggest that the possible presence of such effects should be sought whenever the relative abundances of classes are measured in an archae-ological setting. My goal is to emphasize the pervasive nature of correlations between sample size and the relative abundances of the classes that comprise archaeological assemblages. In the past, I have demonstrated such correlations only in the faunal setting, using biological taxa as my basic analytic unit. Here, I demonstrate the presence of such correlations in two very different contexts.

Spiral fractures at Old Crow

The broken bones provided by the Late Pleistocene localities in the Old Crow Basin, northern Yukon, provide one of the most intriguing, and one of the most widely discussed, cases for the human occupation of the New World prior to Clovis times. The first wide-ranging analysis of the Old Crow bones was conducted in the mid-1970s by Bonnichsen (1979), who was interested in assessing the evidence for a human role in the production of the fractured bones that characterize the Old Crow assemblages. Bonnichsen (1979) hypothesized that the distinctive breakage pattern known as spiral fracture is diagnostic of human activity, both 'indicative of man's presence' and reflecting 'patterned human behavior' (1979:69). Bonnichsen's use of spiral fractures as such a diagnostic was quickly shown to be incorrect, and his analysis as a whole replaced by Morlan's (1980) superb taphonomic study. Today, it is Morlan's work that is the prime focus of the Old Crow debate.

Because my focus here is on sample-size matters, and not on

the evidence Old Crow provides for the early peopling of the New World (but see Nelson *et al.* 1986), the fact that spiral fractures are no longer held to have the status attributed to them by Bonnichsen is not of concern. Of concern, however, are two subsidiary hypotheses specified by Bonnichsen (1979) in order to allow him to move from spirally fractured bones to other aspects of the record. Bonnichsen (1979 : 69) hypothesized that 'the geographic distribution of spirally fractured bones may indicate human activity localities' (hypothesis 1), and that 'spirally fractured mammal bones indicate the genera selectively exploited by man' (hypothesis 2) (original in italics).

Bonnichsen attempted to test the first of these statements by comparing the spatial distribution of spirally fractured bones to that of specimens that had not been altered in this fashion. If abundances of these two classes of specimens did not covary, he reasoned, support would be gained for the argument that spirally fractured specimens had been produced by some process that had not affected the remaining bones and, in particular, by people.

Bonnichsen gathered data from 116 Old Crow localities for his analysis (Table 8.1). Plotting the number of specimens in spirally fractured and non-spirally fractured classes by grouped collection localities, Bonnichsen (1979, Figure 10) found that 'the clusters of paleontological specimens and spirally fractured elements do not covary in an identical manner' (1979:76). The lack of such covariation, he concluded, lends support to the hypothesis that the frequency of spirally fractured bones could be used to indicate archaeological locations in the region.

Table 8.1 displays the rank order of localities in terms of both the total number of specimens they contain and in terms of the number of spirally fractured specimens contributed by those localities (Bonnichsen's analysis employed the percentage of the total number of specimens contributed by a given set of assemblages, as provided in columns 3 and 6 of Table 8.1; the ranks of these percentages are, of course, identical to the ranks of the number of specimens per assemblage). These two ranks are highly cor-

related (Spearman's *rho*, r_s = .900, p < .01), demonstrating that the larger the assemblage from a given set of localities, the greater the number of spirally fractured specimens found in that assemblage. No matter what caused the spiral fractures in these assemblages, their abundance is varying almost perfectly with sample size. Before it can be convincingly concluded that spiral fracture abundance in these assemblages is telling us anything secure about the phenomena that produced them, it would have to be shown that these abundances were, in fact, responding to something other than changes in the total number of specimens across the assemblages that contain them.

In treating the number of spirally fractured bones across taxa within the Old Crow assemblage, Bonnichsen (1979) found that, of the 525 identified spirally fractured specimens, 37% were on proboscidean bone, 20% on horse, 7% on bison, and 4% on caribou. He took this apparent differential distribution as confirming his hypothesis that spirally fractured bones indicate genera exploited by people, and then used that hypothesis to explore the selective use of mammals present in the large assemblage from locality 89. 'By comparing the distribution of spirally fractured specimens with specimens which have not been spirally fractured,' Bonnichsen (1979:87) argued, 'it is possible to discern those genera favored by man.' Table 8.2 provides the raw data employed by Bonnichsen in this assessment.

Using this information, Bonnichsen observed that a full 36.3% of the spiral fractures in the locality 89 collection were on proboscidean bone. He concluded that this pattern indicated 'a clear preference' (1979:87) for the exploitation of elephants. I observe, however, that the correlation between the total sample size for each taxon and the percentage of the total number of spirally fractured bones contributed by that taxon is quite high (r_s = .87, p < .01), showing again that, as sample size increases, the number of spirally fractured bones in that sample increases, regardless of the particular taxon involved. Because spiral fractures are relatively rare in the locality 89 collection, it might be thought that this

Table 8.1. *Total numbers of specimens and numbers of spirally fractured bones from 116 Old Crow localities (from Bonnichsen 1979)*

Locality	Number of specimens	% of total collection	Rank	Spiral fractures		
				Number	% of total	Rank
1–10	37	0.3	11	0	0.0	11.5
11–20	192	1.3	10	7	1.3	9
21–30	3181	22.0	1	42	8.0	3
31–40	1229	8.5	6	25	4.8	6
41–50	232	1.6	9	5	0.9	10
51–60	2113	14.6	4	18	3.4	7
61–70	923	6.4	7	12	2.3	8
71–80	2145	14.9	3	109	20.8	2
81–90	2388	16.5	2	243	46.3	1
91–100	602	4.1	8	28	5.3	5
101–110	1394	9.6	5	36	7.2	4
111–115, 999	12	0.1	12	0	0.0	11.5
Totals	14,448	99.9		525	100.3	

Table 8.2. *Numbers of identified specimens (NISP) and numbers of spirally fractured bones by taxon, Old Crow locality 89 (from Bonnichsen 1979)*

Taxon	NISP	Rank	Spiral fractures		
			Number	% of Total	Rank
Ursus	3	12.5	0	0.0	13
Symbos	1	16	0	0.0	13
Saiga	3	12.5	0	0.0	13
Rangifer	126	5	12	5.0	5
Ovibos	26	7	1	0.4	7
Proboscidea	440	2	86	36.3	1
Equus	776	1	76	32.0	2
Cervus	14	9	1	0.4	7
Camelops	4	11	0	0.0	13
Bison	183	3	15	6.3	4
Artiodactyla	48	6	0	0.0	13
Alces	20	8	1	0.4	7
Castor	1	16	0	0.0	13
Felis	2	14	0	0.0	13
Bovidae	9	10	0	0.0	13
Megalonyx	1	16	0	0.0	13
Unknown	137	4	45	19.0	3

relationship results from the incorporation of such extremely uncommon taxa as bovids (nine specimens), *Camelops* (four specimens), and *Megalonyx* (one specimen) in the analysis. However, removing all taxa that did not have spirally fractured specimens does not change the outcome ($r_s = .88, p < .01$), nor does removing all taxa that are represented by less than 20 specimens ($r_s = .93, p < .01$). The appropriate target of explanation in this situation may not be the distribution of spirally fractured specimens across taxa, but may instead be the distribution of sample sizes across those taxa. This is so because sample size itself may provide an adequate account of the variation in the number of spirally fractured bones across taxa at locality 89.

Seriation

There is nothing peculiar to bone assemblages that makes them especially prone to sample-size effects. Whenever the relative abundances of classes are examined, effects of this sort may be present. It is, for instance, distressingly easy to find seriations of archaeological ceramic assemblages that display these effects. Examples abound; I examine only one here.

Linares (1968) provided a detailed analysis of the prehistoric cultural sequence in the Gulf of Chiriquí, Panama, a sequence felt to have begun at about A.D. 300. Basing her work largely on four sites (IS-3, IS-7, IS-11, and SL-1) that she had excavated, Linares (1968) built the Gulf of Chiriquí chronology on the basis of frequency seriation (using changing relative abundances of ceramic classes through time), occurrence seriation (using the presence and absence of modes), and the appearance of trade wares. My emphasis here will be on the frequency seriation she

constructed. I emphasize that, while I will point out difficulties with that seriation, I do not mean to imply that Linares' resultant chronology was incorrect. Because her approach was eclectic, using multiple approaches to extracting relative chronological order (see Dunnell 1970), there is little reason to question the order she obtained. Instead, I use this example simply to point out that relative abundances of ceramic classes are often correlated with sample size, and that these correlations must be taken into account in building seriations. It so happens that Linares' approach was sufficiently broadly based that it survives the problems I will discuss.

The core of Linares' sequence was provided by Pit 3 at site IS-3; the frequencies of ceramic classes from the vertical excavation units provided by this pit were interleaved with those provided by other units at this and other sites to build the seriation. Table 8.3 presents the raw data for the two most common ceramic classes (Plain Wares D and I) in Pit 3, IS-3. Linares plotted the percentages of these two classes, as well as of six others, as bars to build the seriation by inspection. However, as Table 8.3 shows, the relative abundances of these two classes are significantly correlated with sample size (for Plain Ware D, $r_s = .65$, $p < .01$; for Plain Ware I, $r_s = .55, p < .05$). As sample size increases, so do the relative abundances of these two classes.

Table 8.4 presents comparable data for the two most common ceramic classes in Pit 1, IS-11. Again, sample size and the relative abundances of these classes are significantly correlated (for Plain Ware B, $r_s = - .72, p < .02$; for Tarragó Biscuit Ware, $r_s = .90, p < .001$). As sample size increases, the relative abundance of Tarragó Biscuit Ware increases, while that of Plain Ware B decreases.

Not all of Linares' units show such significant correlations. Table 8.5 displays total numbers of identified sherds and the relative abundances of the two most common ceramic classes in Pit 2, IS-7. Here, there is no significant correlation between sample size and relative frequency for either Plain Ware ($r_s = .02, p \gg .20$) or Villalba Streaked Red ($r_s = .45, p > .20$).

The meaning of the frequency data from Pit 3, IS-3 and from Pit 1, IS-11 is thus obscured. It may be that changing relative frequencies are reflecting time, but it may be that they are merely reflecting changing sample sizes across excavation units. Were it not for the fact that Linares' relative chronology is bolstered by a mode-based occurrence seriation and by evidence derived from trade wares, there would be good reason to question the adequacy of the seriation as a whole. Even though occurrence seriations are extremely prone to sample-size effects, the fact that all of Linares's approaches provide consistent results suggests that the general sequence she has derived is sound. Other seriations that lack such independent support but that are also characterized by correlations between sample size and relative frequencies of artifact classes are much less secure.

Fortunately, archaeologists have long been aware that both frequency and occurrence seriation are sensitive to sample size (e.g., Beals *et al.* 1945; Cowgill 1968; Drennan 1976; Dunnell 1970; Marquardt 1978). Cowgill (1968), for instance, has observed that occurrence seriation can be greatly affected by small sample sizes,

Table 8.3. *Total numbers of sherds and numbers of Plain Ware D (PWD) and Plain Ware I (PWI) sherds, Pit 3, Site IS-3 (from Linares 1968)*

Level	Total number of sherds	Rank	PWD	%	Rank	PWI	%	Rank
0–10	2085	1	1545	74.1	1	55	2.6	11
10–20	1279	2	921	72.0	2	71	5.6	9
20–30	501	11	324	64.7	6	52	10.4	7
30–40	921	9	563	61.1	8	122	13.3	5
40–50	1171	3	590	50.4	11	297	25.4	2
50–60	945	8	341	36.1	13	278	29.4	1
60–70	904	10	583	64.5	7	124	13.7	4
70–80	1041	5	705	67.7	4	99	9.5	8
80–90	997	6	664	66.6	5	124	12.4	6
90–100	1083	4	618	57.1	10	177	16.3	3
100–110	460	12	320	69.6	3	6	1.3	13
110–120	960	7	573	59.7	9	18	1.9	12
120–130	453	13	186	41.1	12	11	2.4	10
130–140	143	15	16	11.2	14	0	0.0	15
140–150	178	14	6	3.4	15	0	0.0	15
150–160	11	16	0	0.0	16	0	0.0	15
Totals	13132		7955			1434		

Table 8.4. *Total numbers of sherds and numbers of Plain Ware B (PWB) and Tarragó Biscuit Ware (TBW) sherds, Pit 1, Site IS-11 (from Linares 1968)*

Level	Total number of sherds	Rank	PWB	%	Rank	TBW	%	Rank
0–10	1019	1	268	26.3	5	492	48.3	1
10–20	358	6	84	23.5	6	158	44.1	3
20–30	370	5	80	21.6	7	111	30.0	6
30–40	566	2	76	13.4	10	271	47.9	2
40–50	493	3	82	16.6	8	197	40.0	5
50–60	478	4	79	16.5	9	196	41.0	4
60–70	306	7	105	34.3	3	71	23.2	7
70–80	122	8	48	39.3	1	15	12.3	9
80–90	97	9	35	36.1	2	21	21.7	8
90–100	44	10	15	34.1	4	4	9.1	10
Totals	3853		872			1536		

since the smaller the sample, the less the likelihood that a rare class will be represented. Along these lines, it is worth observing that many apparent violations of a key assumption required by frequency seriation, that historical classes are distributed unimodally through time (e.g., Dunnell 1970), may also be caused by fluctuating sample sizes.

Table 8.6 displays the total number of sherds, and the number of those sherds that are Linarte Zoned Red, in the uppermost six levels of Linares's Pit 1, site IS-7 (Linares 1968; Linares did not use the seventh, and lowest, level in her seriation). Also provided is the percentage of the ceramic assemblage for each level that is Linarte Zoned Red, and the percentage of the entire ceramic collection from these six levels that was contributed by each of those levels. These two sets of percentages are significantly correlated ($r_s = -.83, p = .05$). As sample size increases, the fraction of each level assemblage that is Linarte Zoned Red decreases. This is the case even though the most abundant type in Pit 1 – Plain Ware, which comprises from 50 to 79% of the assemblage of each level – is not significantly correlated with sample size ($r_s = .09$, $p \geqslant .20$). Figure 8.1 graphically displays the relationship between

Table 8.5. *Total numbers of sherds and numbers of Plain Ware (PW) and Villalba Streaked Red (VSR) sherds, Pit 2, Site IS-7 (from Linares 1968)*

Level	Total number of sherds	Rank	PW	%	Rank	VSR	%	Rank
0–10	925	2	518	56.0	3	212	22.9	8
10–20	534	5	251	47.0	8	154	28.8	3
20–30	719	4	357	49.7	6	182	25.3	6
30–40	1561	1	745	47.7	9	383	24.5	7
40–50	864	3	365	42.3	11	276	31.9	2
50–60	330	8	120	36.4	13	127	38.5	1
60–70	359	7	146	40.7	12	102	28.4	4
70–80	299	9	141	47.2	10	67	22.4	9
80–90	195	10	104	53.3	4.5	51	26.2	5
90–100	121	13	60	49.6	7	22	18.2	10
100–110	411	6	259	63.0	2	39	9.5	11
110–120	194	11	125	64.4	1	7	3.6	12
120–130	180	12	96	53.3	4.5	2	1.1	13
Totals	6692		3287			1624		

Table 8.6. *Total numbers of sherds and numbers of Linarte Zoned Red (LZR) sherds from Pit 1, Site IS-7 (from Linares 1968)*

Level	Total number of sherds	% of assemblage	Rank	LZR	%	Rank
0–10	362	13.98	4	1	0.28	3
10–20	416	16.07	3	1	0.24	5
20–30	272	10.51	5	4	1.47	2
30–40	789	30.48	1	2	0.25	4
40–50	688	26.57	2	1	0.15	6
60–70	62	2.39	6	3	4.84	1
Totals	2589	100.0		12		

sample size and the frequency of Linarte Zoned Red in this pit. Clearly, Linarte Zoned Red should not be used to seriate the levels of this unit: insofar as the resultant order depended on the relative abundances assumed by this class, that order would be based less on the critical assumptions of seriation than on the sizes of the

samples that happened to be recovered from the excavation unit. This is an extreme, and hence highly visible, case (there are only 12 sherds of Linarte Zoned Red from the six levels involved), but, as my discussion has hopefully shown, similar phenomena occur with much larger samples (see also Grayson 1985).

Conclusions

This paper presents nothing new: it simply extends to new ground observations I have made elsewhere on the relationship between sample size and relative abundance. The lessons should be fairly clear. Correlations between sample size and relative abundance must be sought before those abundances are used as the basis of more detailed analysis. If significant correlations are present, it is, of course, quite possible that no causal relationship exists between the two variables, but that some third factor is causing both to vary in concert. It is also possible that the two variables are related causally, but that sample size is the dependent variable. If, for instance, some technological innovation leads to an increase in the absolute abundance (through increased use, increased survivability, or even, in the case of such things as cer-

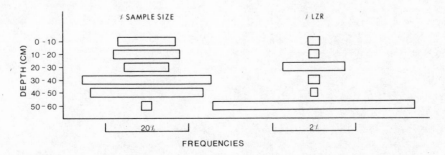

Fig. 8.1. Relationship between sample size (% sample size: the fraction of the total number of sherds in the collection contributed by each level) and relative abundance of Linarte Zoned Red (% LZR: the fraction of the assemblage from a given level that is Linarte Zoned Red)

amics, increased tendency to break) of a given class of material, the relationship between sample size and the frequency of that class will be correlated, yet sample size itself will not be driving the correlation (see also Grayson 1984:127–9). In none of the cases discussed above have I demonstrated that changes in sample size have caused changes in the relative abundances of the classes I have examined. All I have shown is that there is cause for concern.

Thus, after detecting significant correlations between sample size and relative abundance, the next analytic step must be a search for the cause or causes of the correlation. If sample size is causal, the problem can often be solved by step-wise removal of analytic units with small numbers of members (see, for instance, Grayson 1984, 1985). If the correlation cannot be removed and the cause cannot be shown to be something other than sample size itself, then independent corroboration should be brought into play. If neither approach can be taken, then at least the analyst will have avoided having mistaken what may be simply a sample-size phenomenon for an archaeologically meaningful pattern.

Acknowledgments

I thank R. C. Dunnell for telling me of Beals *et al.* (1945) and both R. C. Dunnell and R. D. Leonard for their insightful comments on a draft of this paper.

Assessments of archaeological diversity

Chapter 9

Diversity in hunter–gatherer cultural geography

David Hurst Thomas

Within the past decade, the systematic regional approach has become *de rigueur* in American archaeology.[1] An increasingly wide range of exacting field techniques has been proposed to extract relatively unbiased samples of archaeological items at a regional level. Probabilistic research designs are today commonly employed by both 'academic' and 'contract' archaeologists.

Despite these significant and far-reaching changes in field strategy, methods for analyzing such regional data have changed surprisingly little from the good old 'single site' days. The truth is that many regional studies continue to rely on simplistic, impressionistic, and often unrealistic analytical methods.

Bridging the gap between the archaeologically visible and the behaviorally viable remains a major headache. In the case of hunter–gatherer studies, many archaeologists, myself included, find it worthwhile to view regional patterning in terms of a *forager–collector continuum*, a spatially integrated strategic network consisting of discrete settlement components – base camps, field camps, procurement locations, hunting stations, and so forth (*sensu* Binford 1980).

But even granted this relatively workable framework, contemporary archaeology has enjoyed decidedly limited success in operationally defining these behavioral constructs in the archaeological record. How, for instance, does one empirically distinguish prehistoric base camps from task-specific field camps? Unless we can make such baseline distinctions with some certainty, the strategic decision-making behind the mosaic of prehistoric cultural geography will remain elusive.

We know that residential positioning among hunter–gatherers is generally conditioned by exigencies of adequate life-space, protection from the elements, and a location sufficiently central to key survival resources. Base camps inhabited for several months are closely bound by such factors. Short-term field camps are less heavily patterned by life-space considerations. Areas of strictly diurnal resource extraction ('locations') are selected without reference to life-space.

To date, the most reliable archaeological signatures for detecting residential areas derive from the following structural elements. Residential areas tend to have *service centers* (in the sense of Wagner 1960:170); many base camps tend to have patterned areas of sleeping, maintenance, and discard; some base camps (particularly those involved in logistic systems) tend to have visible storage facilities, etc. Analysis of faunal utility indices likewise provides clues as to relative settlement positioning (Binford 1978a; Speth 1983; Thomas and Mayer 1983).

But site-structural and ecofactual data are usually preserved in only a few sites within a region, and serious bias results when we define overall cultural geographic patterning from such a limited and obviously biased sample. The bulk of the regional archaeological record often consists of relatively sparse surface lithic assemblages. Assemblage-level signatures remain ill-defined, and the available base-camp diagnostics are notoriously difficult to apply to such surface remains (e.g., Binford 1978a, 1978b; Gould 1980:126; Thomas 1983a:78–9). It is critical that we integrate the diverse evidence from both surface survey and deep site excavation into a single, coherent, interpretive framework.

One is tempted to equate the degree of absolute diversity in such assemblages with the behavioral settlement components discussed above. Smaller, less diverse assemblages are commonly taken to be areas of diurnal extraction ('locations'). Larger, more diverse assemblages are often equated with residential utilization ('base camps'). Assemblages of intermediate size and absolute diversity are conventionally viewed as logistic settlements ('field camps'). The tacit equation of absolute assemblage diversity with discrete settlement types underlies many so-called behavioral interpretations in contemporary hunter–gatherer studies.

This line of reasoning is incorrect. In many (if not most) archaeological assemblages, the diversity of a sample is a direct, linear function of the size of that sample. Jones *et al.* (1983) have convincingly demonstrated the 'treacherous' relationship between class richness and sample size in archaeological assemblages (see also Beck 1984; Kintigh 1984a).

Assemblage diversity is not, of course, unrelated to site function, but the exact nature of that relationship can be appreciated only by focusing on the relative (rather than absolute) degree of diversity.

The overall relationship between number of tool classes and number of individual tools is influenced by ecological, technological, informational, and scheduling factors, and attempts at such hologeistic theory building are just beginning. Torrence (1983), for instance, has shown the intercorrelation of tool-kit diversity with latitude: high-latitude technologies are demonstrably more diverse than those employed in tropical areas.

But concern here is not with absolute degree of global assemblage diversity, but rather the relative degree of diversity within a given system. Long-term residential areas ('base camps') are where the greatest variety of artifact- and byproduct-producing activities occur; base camps comprise the 'hub' of hunter–gatherer cultural geography. Base camps should generally be characterized by technologically and typologically diverse assemblages – relative to the overall techno-economic systemic matrix.

Logistic encampments ('field camps') are typically task-specific, single-sex, short-term, and ephemeral. Field-camp activities are behavioral subsets of what occurs at the base camp, and tool inventories at logistic settlements are material cultural subsets of base-camp assemblages. But such patterning is not always directly translated into the archaeological record. Only rarely can logistic assemblages be defined in terms of specific artifact-level signatures; rather, the field camp can be expected to contain only a more homogeneous (i.e., relatively less diverse) assemblage than the mean base-camp inventory.

Daytime use areas ('locations') involve even more task-specific technology. Assemblages associated with locations should be the most homogeneous (i.e., least diverse relative to size) produced within a given system.

The general expectations can be arrayed in conventional size/diversity fashion (Figure 9.1); the X-axis represents absolute assemblage size, and the Y-axis scales absolute assemblage diversity. *Within a given system*, long-term residential base camps will generally be characterized by a steep profile: assemblage diversity increases rapidly relative to sample size. Assemblages generated from strictly diurnal activities will commonly define a flatter profile: assemblage diversity increases slowly relative to sample size. Logistic assemblages describe an intermediate profile:

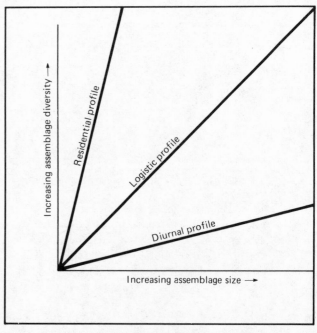

Fig. 9.1. Theoretical relationship between assemblage size and diversity in hunter–gatherer assemblages

assemblage diversity is expected to increase moderately with increasing sample size.

Figure 9.1 is a general model; exceptions will occur, even within a single techno-economic system. The base camp occupied for ten months per year will be expected to contain a relatively more diverse assemblage than the residence lived in for only two months a year. Some procurement locations are known to involve more heterogeneous assemblages than others, depending on the resources exploited, the size of the foraging radius, and the specific tool kits, byproducts, and use-lives of artifacts involved. Certain procurement loci will generate more diverse assemblages than some short-term, task-specific field camps. The degree of intra-assemblage level variability merits detailed study *per se* (Thomas 1983a:12–17).

The degree of observable assemblage diversity is also significantly blurred in the translation from behavioral to archaeological contexts. Hunter–gatherer cultural geography tends to be redundant: abandoned base camps are reoccupied as temporary field camps; functionally diverse field camps are reestablished at the same camp site; diurnal exploitative areas overlap spatially as seasonal resources ripen. Given sufficient time, residential assemblages commonly become physically commingled with various logistic assemblages. Discrete logistic assemblages accumulate in certain favorable loci, one behavioral accumulation inextricably mixing with another. Rarely is a given location utilized in only one way, and the palimpsest accumulation is an archaeological fact of life.

But as a coarse-grained empirical generalization, Figure 9.1 satisfactorily anticipates the relative variability in assemblage size and assemblage diversity across an idealized archaeological landscape. In effect, Figure 9.1 defines a continuum, grading from the highly diverse assemblages produced in areas of predominantly residential utilization to assemblages of low relative diversity generated from mostly diurnal activities. Logistic zones fall toward the middle.

We explore the implications of this approach to diversity by turning briefly to the archaeological record of Monitor Valley, Nevada.

The Monitor Valley Project

Interdisciplinary archaeological fieldwork was conducted in Monitor Valley, Nevada between June 1970 and August 1981. The general and mid-range theoretical orientations of this inquiry are addressed in the first of five volumes dealing with the archaeology of this area (Thomas 1983a).

Fieldwork commenced with stratigraphic and living-floor excavations at the 10 m-deep Gatecliff Shelter. The archaeology, geomorphology, paleontology, and paleobotany of Gatecliff Shelter are reported in the second volume of the Monitor Valley series (Thomas 1983b).

Field inquiry also included excavations at Alta Toquima Village, a multi-component site located at an elevation of 11,000 ft. Preliminary results of the 1981 field season are available (Thomas 1982); the 1983 field results are currently being analyzed and will be presented in the Monitor Valley series (Thomas, in press b).

The Monitor Valley fieldwork employed a sampling strategy designed to generate data from a large range of archaeological observations. Ten additional rock-shelters and caves were excavated. These excavations were supported by a variety of probabilistic and opportunistic site surveys, resulting in the recording and collection of hundreds of additional prehistoric sites and non-sites. A dozen rock-art localities were recorded. Numerous satellite sites – drift fences, hunting blinds, rock ambushes, and soldier cairns – were also mapped, collected, and, in some cases, excavated.

The overall sampling strategy and empirical results of the Monitor Valley fieldwork are described in detail elsewhere (Thomas 1983a, 1983b, in press a, b). For present purposes, we group the hundreds of site and non-site assemblages into a series of topographic catchment categories.

How pervasive is sample-size bias in Monitor Valley?

This paper explores how much of observed assemblage diversity must be attributed to sample-size effects. Only after the relationship between sample size and absolute diversity is understood, can one hope to explain the behavioral nature of that variability.

We previously examined the sample-size effect operating among the various horizon assemblages at Gatecliff Shelter (Thomas 1983b;428–30). This exploration began by defining 'sample size' as raw artifact count per horizon; the sample sizes varied from $n = 2$ (for Horizons 11 and 16), to $n = 399$ for Horizon 5. Our first measure of 'sample diversity' was simply the summation of the typological categories used as primary artifact description. This approach magnified the absolute degree of assemblage diversity to encompass 88 different categories: Desert Side-notched points were tallied separately from Elko Eared points; splinter bone awls were distinguished from scapula bone awls; block metates were differentiated from slab metates.

The log–log relationship on Figure 9.2 has a correlation coefficient of $r = 0.96$ (df $= 13$, $p < 0.000$). In statistical terms, this means that more than 95% of the variability in density and diversity across the Gatecliff horizons can be accounted for strictly in terms of sample size. As expected, the artifact-rich horizons at Gatecliff Shelter manifest the greatest absolute diversity. It likewise comes as small surprise that artifact-poor living surfaces contain a very narrow range of artifact categories. Given only sample size, one can almost precisely predict the degree of assemblage diversity.

One might observe that 'number of artifacts' and 'number of artifact types' are subjective measures. This is true because, in practice, no two archaeologists classify their artifacts in the same way. Does the assemblage size/diversity problem plague only Thomas' categories?

To explore the definitional issue, we modified our definitions of both 'sample size' and 'sample diversity' for the Gatecliff Shelter data: the size of the sample was increased to include unmodified debitage counts, and sample diversity was remeasured in a typological scheme employing only 30 categories. Instead of using 88 artifact categories, we grouped the artifacts into fewer,

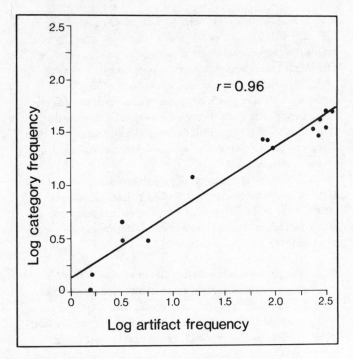

Fig. 9.2. Scattergram relating assemblage size and assemblage diversity across the horizons of Gatecliff Shelter. 'Sample diversity' is plotted for 88 descriptive artifact categories; 'sample size' is defined as the total artifact count per horizon (after Thomas 1983b, Figure 218).

more generalized types. Rather than distinguishing, say, between Desert Side-notched and Elko Eared types, we simply call all of them 'projectile points.' Similarly, block and slab metates are merely called 'metates.' Splinter and scapula bone awls are tallied simply as 'awls,' and so forth.

Despite these major definitional modifications, the overall degree of autocorrelation was not significantly lowered (Thomas 1983b:428–31). Demonstrably different definitions of basic variables produced remarkably similar profiles: regardless of how size and diversity were measured at Gatecliff Shelter, size effects never accounted for less than 70% of the observed variability in absolute diversity.

Considerably more such experimentation is required before one can confidently conclude that sample-size effects transcend all typological considerations; but our initial experiments certainly suggest this to be the case.

With these cautions in mind, we can expand the scope of diversity analysis by adding the ten additional excavated Monitor Valley sites to the Gatecliff Shelter data: Triple T Shelter, Toquima Cave, Grenouille Verte Cave, Butler Ranch Cave, Little Empire Shelter, Boring-as-Hell Shelter, Jeans Spring Shelter, Ny1059, Hunts Canyon Shelter, and Bradshaw Shelter.[2]

We begin in Figure 9.3 by considering the total artifact assemblages (including ceramic totals), so 'sample size' is defined as raw artifact count per site. Sample diversity ranges from $n = 1$ for Grenouille Verte Cave to $n = 88$ at Gatecliff Shelter. The log–log plot of this relationship has a correlation coefficient of

$r = 0.98$ (df $= 9, p < 0.001$). Over 96% of the variability in these archaeological assemblages from 11 sites can be accounted for by sample size alone.

It is desirable to replicate the definitional experiment on the sample of 11 excavated sites from Monitor Valley, lumping the 88 initial categories into the 30, more general artifact groupings. Although the operational definition of one variable was changed markedly, the relationship remains virtually unchanged. The correlation coefficient remains high, $r = 0.97$ (df $= 8, p < 0.001$): sample size still accounts for 94% of the observed diversity.

The data in Figure 9.3 can be combined in somewhat different fashion, but again with similar results. When sherd counts are removed and sample size computed only for the aceramic artifact assemblage, the correlation coefficient remains high, at $r = 0.98$; the same correlation coefficient results when sherd frequencies are dampened by division by ten.

In these calculations, sample size varies between $n = 1$ at Grenouille Verte Cave to $n = 2046$ for Gatecliff Shelter. These disparate values can be partially equalized by splitting the overall Gatecliff Shelter assemblage into its component 15 horizons, thereby increasing the data set from 11 to 25 points. The value of r decreases slightly to 0.97 (df $= 22; p < 0.001$).

Regardless of how we compute size/diversity relationships among the 11 excavated sites in Monitor Valley, the sample size effect never accounts for less than 94% of the observed variability.

Exploration of the sample/size diversity relationship can be expanded by supplementing the 11 excavated sites with the rest of the archaeological assemblages recovered from throughout Monitor Valley, inventories associated with spring catchments, low-

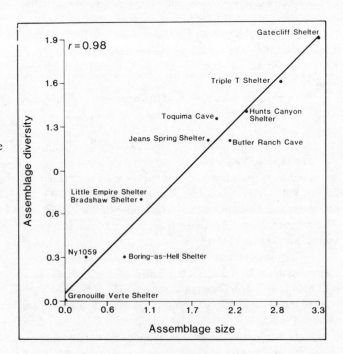

Fig. 9.3. Size/diversity regression for 11 caves and rock-shelters excavated in Monitor Valley. Horizontal and vertical axes are plotted on a log scale. 'Sample diversity' is plotted for 88 descriptive categories; 'sample size' is defined as the total artifact count per site.

land lacustrine zones, rock-art localities, drift-fences, hunting blinds, rock ambushes, and soldier cairns (Figure 9.4). This scattergram plots the pooled assemblages with both variables defined as before and Gatecliff tallied as independent horizons. The correlation coefficient remains quite high ($r = 0.88$, df $= 80$, $p < 0.001$).

La627 is a significant outlier in this relationship. The Upper Ackerman Spring Site (La627) is a concentration of 385 Shoshone ware sherds in the Hickison Summit catchment. These heavily crushed and indurated sherds are almost certainly from a single vessel. Here is a prime example of the differential fragmentation effect; the extreme position of this outlier is determined strictly by the spurious comparison of lithic and ceramic frequencies. When outlier La627 is dropped, the correlation increases to $r = 0.94$ (df $= 79$, $p < 0.001$) for the remaining 81 data points.

Regardless of which specific algorithm is imposed on the data, there can be no question that the correlation between sample size and diversity is very high for the aggregate Monitor Valley assemblage. Despite the differential sampling strategies and the variety of post-depositional factors, sample size accounts for much, if not most, of the overall variability in the Monitor Valley database.

Therefore, extreme caution is in order when the behavioral meaning of absolute diversity in archaeological assemblages is interpreted. Large accumulations will almost always be diverse; small assemblages will almost invariably contain very few artifact types – regardless of which types are present and irrespective of what behavior actually produced the assemblages (see also Jones *et al.* 1983; Beck 1984).

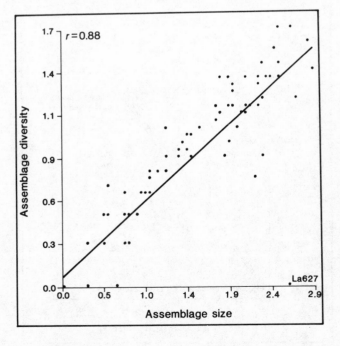

Fig. 9.4. Pooled size/diversity regression for the overall Monitor Valley database (including individual horizons at Gatecliff Shelter)

A regression approach to sample-size effects

The assemblage size/diversity relationship is commonly described by the log–linear regression function involving two variables and two constants:

$$\log Y' = \log a + b \log X$$

where X is the independent variable and Y' is an estimate of the dependent variable. Sample size is usually taken to be the independent variable in order to explore the effects of variable assemblage size on apparent diversity. The constant a is the Y-intercept and b is the coefficient of regression, commonly called *slope*.

The regression format allows one to examine size/diversity interactions on a site-by-site basis, and the analysis of slope permits one to scale these data points along a more behaviorally relevant settlement continuum.

To illustrate, the highly correlated linear relationship on Figure 9.3 is described by the simple equation:

$$\log Y' = 0.08 + 0.57 (\log X)$$

where X = assemblage size (the raw number of artifacts recovered) and Y' = estimated assemblage diversity (the number of artifact types present).

Regression equations permit projection, within a definable degree of error, of the expected values of Y. At least in Monitor Valley, sample size and assemblage diversity are known to be heavily dependent on one another: given the raw number of artifacts present, one can predict – with a high degree of accuracy – the number of types at an archaeological site.

Consider the case of Toquima Cave, where we recovered a total of 92 artifacts, classified into 22 artifact classes. This is an 'observed,' 'known,' 'empirical' relationship. But to what extent can this relationship be attributed to sample-size effects?

Since assemblage size is $X = 92$, we project the following:

$$\log Y' = 0.08 + 0.57 (\log X)$$
$$\log Y' = 0.08 + 0.57 (\log 92)$$
$$Y' = 15.8$$

Rounding the results, the regression relation predicts that – all else being equal – Toquima Cave should contain about 16 artifact types. As it turns out, the observed value ($Y = 22$ types) is within the 95% confidence interval surrounding each Y'. In other words, the observed value cannot be distinguished statistically from that predicted strictly from the sample size.

Similar relationships hold for the other sites on Figure 9.3: the closer the observed point to the line, the better the prediction. Ten artifacts were found, for instance, at Little Empire Shelter. Linear regression predicts that $Y' = 4.47$ artifact types should be recovered. Six types occurred at Little Empire, well within the 95% confidence intervals surrounding Y'.

At Jeans Spring Shelter, $X = 78$, and the predicted number of artifact classes is $Y' = 14.4$. This result easily falls with the 95% confidence intervals around the observed value of $Y = 16$ typological categories. These results underscore the dangers of interpreting results expressed in terms of absolute assemblage diversity.

This is not a remote concern; sample-size bias influences the everyday business of archaeological interpretation. It is convenient and comfortable to assume that the kinds of artifacts found at any given site should directly reflect the activities that went on there.

We now know that this assumption is usually incorrect: the absolute degree of assemblage diversity at, say, Toquima Cave is almost totally conditioned by the number of artifacts recovered in the excavations.

We also know that very small sites will almost invariably display limited absolute diversity. The same is true of very small samples from large sites: When the assemblages are set out on a lab. table, one cannot distinguish between the completely recovered small site and the incompletely tested large site. Absolute diversity depends on the sample size recovered, not the potential samples remaining in the ground.

So long as site function is assessed on the residential–logistic–diurnal continuum, the basis of absolute diversity, our conception of prehistoric cultural geography will depend heavily on our field strategy. Dig all of a large site, and you might get a base camp; dig half of the same site, and you've got a field camp; take a surface collection, and it will look like a location.

The more intensively we investigate, the more the apparent diversity that we discover. There must be a better way.

Slope reconsidered

The regression constant, b, offers a way of assessing relative assemblage diversity independently of absolute sample size – *so long as assemblage size and diversity are found to be highly correlated.*

Slope measures the rate of change in Y per unit change in X. In the case of perfect correlation ($r = 1.00$), a slope of 1.0 shows that one unit of change in the dependent variable, Y, is expected to correspond to one unit of change in the independent variable, X. A slope of -1.0 shows that Y decreases one unit for each unit increase in X. The predictive value of b decreases as r decreases.

This elementary statistical relationship provides an operational measure of relative assemblage diversity. As the regression lines become steeper (i.e., as diversity increases), the regression constant (b) becomes greater (Figure 9.1). As assemblage diversity decreases, the slope approaches the horizontal (i.e., b approaches zero). This is so, regardless of what the sample sizes may be.

Given sufficient experimentation, we may some day find that the magnitude of b is directly correlated with specific components within a settlement system. But we presently lack adequate mid-range theory, and this analysis is restricted to posited scaling along a residential–logistic–diurnal axis.

Residential activities produce, in the long run, the greatest relative diversity within a given behavioral system. This diversity will be apparent in those assemblage groupings characterized by a relatively steep slope (as measured by increasing values of b). By contrast, relatively low diversity assemblage groupings commonly result from diurnal procurement activities. Such homogeneous

assemblages are characterized by a nearly horizontal slope (a value of b approaching zero). Intermediate values of b occur for assemblages in the middle range of the residential–logistic–diurnal continuum.

There will be exceptions. Whenever a series of unrelated, homogeneous, non-residential assemblages co-occur at a single locus, one complex and diverse palimpsest accumulation will result. The non-residential character of such assemblages will be apparent only from supra-assemblage data such as positioning relative to resources, presence of on-site facilities and structures, or ecofactual evidence. Similarly, among low-latitude groups with relatively little overall technological diversity, base-camp accumulations will sometimes be relatively homogeneous, even when compared with strictly diurnal assemblages. Relative assemblage diversity is doubtless conditioned by multiple behavioral and post-depositional factors; the proportional contribution of each factor must be considered in each case (see also Beck 1984:187–9).

But for most mid-latitude assemblages, relative assemblage diversity is demonstrably graded along a residential–logistic–diurnal continuum. The operational challenge is to perceive such diversity independently from biasing effects of differential sample size, and the regression coefficient, b, is one way to do this.

Consider Figure 9.5, a size/density plot showing the variability among the various pooled assemblages from Monitor Valley (listed on Table 9.1). Although the curves are superficially rather similar, the differential slopes provide a means of monitoring relative assemblage variability.

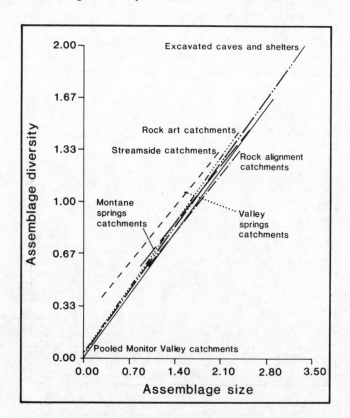

Fig. 9.5. Size/diversity regression profiles for major site and non-site assemblages in Monitor Valley (see also Table 9.1)

Table 9.1. *Regression coefficients (b values) for the major pooled assemblages in Monitor Valley[a]*

Assemblage	Slope b	Correlation r
Pooled Monitor Valley total ($n = 81$)	0.56	0.94[b]
Streamside catchments ($n = 7$)	0.49	0.98
Montane spring catchments ($n = 12$)	0.48	0.95
Valley-floor spring catchments ($n = 3$)	−0.22	−0.95[c]
Rock alignment catchments ($n = 4$)	0.55	0.97
Excavated caves and shelters ($n = 11$)	0.57	0.98
Rock art catchments[b] ($n = 13$)	0.64	0.98
Pictograph catchments ($n = 11$)	0.59	0.98
Petroglyph catchments[b] ($n = 4$)	0.57	0.92[d]

[a] n denotes the number of discrete assemblages within each site or catchment type.

[b] Outlier La627 removed.

[c] Approximate value for comparison only

[d] Correlation coefficient not significantly different from zero

First of all, Figure 9.5 demonstrates that the valley-floor catchment assemblages are markedly different from the other assemblages, and from each other. Whereas the Dianas Punch Bowl sample is rather small ($X = 36$), it is also relatively diverse, with $Y = 11$ types present. Conversely, the White Sage Spring assemblage contains $X = 188$ items (when ceramic frequencies are included), but only $Y = 7$ types are present. In this rather distorted case, assemblages become less diverse as sample size increases; as discussed above, the differential fragmentation between lithics and ceramics makes the heterogeneous assemblages difficult to compare.

The remaining slopes are all positive; the slope of the pooled Monitor Valley assemblages is $b = 0.56$, and individual assemblage values vary between $b = 0.48$ to $b = 0.64$. The overall impression conveyed by Figure 9.5 is one of invariant, size-dependent relationships, a characteristic of Monitor Valley assemblages in general.

Diversity scaling is but a first step in understanding the overall variability in the prehistoric cultural geography of Monitor Valley. These inferences are, incidentally, supported by additional, independent lines of evidence from the regional database (as elaborated in Thomas in press a).

Summary and implications

This paper began on a decidedly pessimistic note. Archaeologists have been sorely tempted to view larger sites as representing 'base camps,' and to interpret thin lithic scatters as 'chipping stations': or as 'task-specific field camps.' Graphic analysis forcefully demonstrates why that temptation must be resisted. We now know that sample size heavily biases our perception of the artifact-level diversity evident in the Monitor Valley assemblage.

Yet once the sample-size effect is recognized, it is possible to control the bias to some degree. Analysis of regression constants effectively holds sample size constant and allows one to examine the relative degree of assemblage diversity (assuming that the correlation coefficients remains high).

Relative measures of diversity cannot be used to classify specific assemblages as base camps, field camps, and so forth. But it is quite reasonable to rank these assemblages along a sliding scale of relative residential intensity. Diversity analysis can thus become an initial step toward defining the settlement structure inherent in diverse archaeological data sets.

Notes

1. This paper is an abbreviated version of Chapter 8 in *The Archaeology of Monitor Valley: 3. Survey and Additional Excavations* (Thomas, in press a).
2. Bradshaw Shelter, located 80 km. south of Monitor Valley proper, has been included here only for comparison.
3. The major funding for the Monitor Valley fieldwork and analysis was provided by the following sources: the Frederick G. Voss Fund for Anthropology, the James Ruel Smith Fund, Earthwatch, the University of California (Davis), the National Geographic Society, and the National Science Foundation (grant BNS77-24179). A generous grant from the Richard Lounsbery Foundation significantly aided in the preparation and publication of this manuscript. We also thank the Taylor Foundation for their assistance in the latest stages of the Monitor Valley project.

Dennis O'Brien is responsible for the artwork. I also thank Margot Dembo, Lorann S. A. Pendleton, and the editors of this volume for helpful comments on an earlier draft of this manuscript.

Chapter 10

The effect of urbanization on faunal diversity: a comparison between New York City and St Augustine, Florida, in the sixteenth to eighteenth centuries

Nan A. Rothschild

The existence of diversity in human behavior is clearly an important fact which has the potential for conveying information on many aspects of culture. Many of us believe that this behavioral diversity is reflected in material culture, in artifact types, or foods, or other such objects made or made use of by people. While behavioral diversity and diversity in 'things' are real and observable, the measurement of diversity is in many ways difficult (Hill 1973; Hurlbert 1971; Kintigh 1984a).

Formulas which measure diversity have been adopted in a number of disciplines, to examine, for example, taxa in a natural system or collections of artifacts, designs, and faunal specimens. It has been suggested that they have the ability to quantify organization and patterning in ecosystems, and identify complexity in social and cognitive structure (Conkey 1981b; Hill 1973; Peebles 1972; Pielou 1969; Rothschild n.d.b.; Tainter 1977a, b; Wing and Brown 1979). Many of the applications of these measures carry implications as to the significance of differences among them. In ecology, for example, discussion has focused on whether a more diverse ecosystem (having more species, and organisms distributed more evenly among these species) is, either in theory or in fact, a more stable one than a less diverse system (Margalef 1968; May 1973; Pielou 1975). In this paper, two measures of diversity are evaluated with data from two sets of faunal material from historic sites. The goal is to consider the utility of diversity measures, and their appropriate use, and also to observe the effect of changes such as urbanization on diet.

Most indices of diversity include in one measure the number of different groups of something (artifacts, taxa, etc.), which is also called 'richness' and the proportional representation of each of these groups, or 'evenness.' Thus a higher diversity index can be the result of either more groups or of a more even distribution of individuals among these groups. Further, most indices are based on the probability of achieving certain results from successive trials; these results derive from the composition of the population being sampled. A commonly used diversity measure originates in information theory; while it is phrased in terms of the structure of a given language and the chances of 'surprise' in the next sample or element selected, it is similar in function to other measures of diversity; 'information' in this sense is the opposite of redundancy. Such measures are related in concept to variance, although the variance being observed is multidimensional as it is sensitive to both the number of groups in a population and the number of members of each group.

The application of diversity measures to historic-period fauna
Recently it has been suggested that diversity measures have the ability to delineate socioeconomic differences in faunal material from historic-period sites. Reitz and Cumbaa (1983), for example, suggested that in eighteenth-century St Augustine, Florida, families at the lower and upper ends of the socioeconomic scale ate a wider variety of animals than those in the middle. Individuals of greater wealth had either the leisure to hunt for culturally desirable exotic foods or the ability to hire surrogate hunters. Those at the lower end of the scale would be more likely to eat hunted meat (including some species which may not have been so culturally desirable) than to have access to domestic animals. These latter individuals were also more likely to be from ethnic backgrounds where domestic animals did not make up any significant portion of the diet. Those in the middle, Reitz and Cumbaa felt, were probably eating primarily meat from domestic animals (pork and

beef), yielding faunal assemblages lower in diversity than those of family units lower or higher on the socioeconomic scale.

Another research area in which diversity changes may well be relevant relates to urbanization during the historic period. It is suggested that increasing urbanization would correspond to decreasing diversity in food species, for a number of reasons. For one, building a city implies environmental change, particularly the loss of certain econiches due to filling, other land alterations, and pollution. It should be noted that, while some fauna lose their homes, cities provide hospitable environments for certain new animals, usually not part of the diet, such as pets and pests.

A second influence on decreased diversity is the increasing participation of an urban community in a market economy, and an increasing reliance on specialist provisioners (butchers and commercial fishermen) which will lead to greater standardization in foods consumed and consequent lower diversity. This should be true in the community as a whole in spite of ethnic and socio-economic differences because of the logistics of provisioning a city. As it grows larger and any self-sufficiency for its inhabitants (kitchen gardens and the keeping of domestic animals) becomes impossible, a city requires increasingly efficient foods: large, cheap, and easy to raise or procure. The major constraints involve transport costs and efficiency. Thus we would expect that domestic animals and fowl, and large deepwater fish, will become par-ticularly significant food sources over time.

St Augustine and New York

In this paper, the impact of urbanization on the diversity of faunal assemblages will be examined by comparing material from New York City, in the seventeenth through the late eighteenth centuries, to material from St Augustine, Florida in the sixteenth and eighteenth centuries (Deagan 1983). During this time, St Augustine was becoming a town whose population went from 625 at the end of the sixteenth century (Reitz and Scarry n.d.:50) to 3104 by 1763, at the end of the First Spanish period (Deagan 1983:30). New York during the period in question was becoming a city; in 1675 the population was 2000 and in 1800 it was 60 489 (Rosenwaike 1972). While population size alone is not enough to establish urbanism, the differences in size and growth-rate bet-ween these two communities clearly signal different scales of development. It is expected, therefore, that there should be less change in faunal diversity through time seen in St Augustine than in New York.

The St Augustine material includes three sites, excavated under the direction of Kathleen Deagan. One dates from the six-teenth century (SA 26-1) and is described in a manuscript by Reitz and Scarry (n.d.), while two (SA 34-6, SA 34-2) are eighteenth-century sites with fauna analyzed by Reitz and Cumbaa (Deagan 1983). The New York material comes from one site in Manhattan (7 Hanover Square) excavated by Arnold Pickman, Diana Wall (Rockman) and me. Faunal analysis of the Hanover Square material has been funded by NSF and is being done by Cumbaa and Balkwill of the Zooarchaeological Identification Centre in Ottawa, and Greenfield, Janowitz, and Morgan of the City University of New York.

The St Augustine sites may represent households from upper socioeconomic strata (Deagan 1983:162; Reitz and Scarry n.d.:96). The New York material is a bit more difficult to interpret. The block that was excavated as 7 Hanover Square was created between 1687 and 1697 by landfilling; it consists of a number of building lots, each of which is, in some sense, a site, since each has its own history of use. It is difficult to assign specific archaeologi-cal deposits to particular individuals because of the relatively broad date ranges for most diagnostic artifact types (e.g. glass, ceramics, and pipes) and the frequent turnover of building owners or occupants. However, while we may not be able to say which family is responsible for the creation of a specific archaeological deposit, we can often establish the socioeconomic position of a group of occupants by means of information on profession and tax records.

It is clear that this section of New York City was a relatively affluent one during the period in question. Its early inhabitants in-cluded Dutch and English families whose homes and workplaces were there. Captain Kidd owned land on the block as did Robert Livingston, a wealthy Scottish merchant. It can also be assumed that waterfront land, in a community whose economy was based on water-borne trade, would be valuable and would be the locus of upper level home–workplaces. The two early faunal assemb-lages come from landfill, dating to before 1700 (Pickman and Rothschild 1981), and a midden located inside a basement, with a mean ceramic date of 1708. By the end of the eighteenth century the area had changed slightly; the 7 Hanover Square block was no longer on the waterfront, but the occupants of the lot on which the third deposit, a cistern, was located, were all merchants, and therefore members of an upper socioeconomic stratum.

The measurement of diversity

For each of the three components from two communities, diversity was measured in two ways, and these measures were then

Table 10.1. *Two measures of diversity*

	N	Simpson's[a]	Shannon–Weaver[b]
New York City			
7 Hanover Square			
Landfill	48	0.943	0.771
Midden	32	0.911	0.691
Cistern	59	0.936	0.740
St Augustine			
26-1	400	0.801	0.597
34-2	128	0.867	0.622
36-4	173	0.872	0.676

[a] Simpson $\quad D = 1 - \dfrac{1}{N(N-1)} \Sigma N_j (N_j - 1)$

[b] Shannon–Weaver $\quad J = H/H_{max}$

$$H = -C \sum_{j=1}^{n} p_j \log p_j \qquad H_{max} = \log s$$

Table 10.2. *Minimum numbers of individuals in New York City and St Augustine data*

New York City data (MNI)

Species (common name)	Fill	Midden	Cistern
Chicken	9	9	11
Domestic turkey	1	1	1
Wild turkey	1	1	2
Canada goose	2	1	0
Snow goose	1	1	1
Mallard	1	1	1
Puddle duck	1	2	1
Robin	1	1	0
Snipe	2	0	0
Passenger pigeon	1	1	1
Bob white	0	0	2
Shad	2	0	1
Striped bass	4	2	7
Cod	1	1	3
Black sea bass	0	1	8
Sheepshead	6	3	3
Tautog	4	2	5
Flatfish	1	0	1
Eel	0	0	2
Total	38	27	50

In addition to the above, there are ten species unique to the fill, five unique to the midden and eight unique to the cistern, each representing one individual only. These are not listed.

St Augustine data (MNI)

Species (common name)	26-1	36-4	34-2
Raccoon	5	3	1
Rabbit	7	4	2
Deer	10	11	6
Chicken	17	10	10
Domestic turkey	2	4	2
Domestic goose	2	0	1
Green-winged teal	2	0	0
Blue-winged teal	3	0	0
Mallard	3	1	0
Bob white	2	0	0
Spot	2	0	0
Sheepshead	22	1	2
Hard headed catfish	39	19	13
Gaff topsail catfish	5	5	1
Sea trout	12	4	2
Kingfish	6	3	1
Croaker	8	4	1
Black drum	16	5	4
Red drum	23	12	10
Southern flounder	9	5	2
Mullet	168	53	42
Bluefish	2	0	0

Requiem shark	4	0	0
Tiger shark	0	1	1
Hammerhead shark	3	6	1
Bonnet head shark	2	0	1
Bull shark	2	0	0
Box turtle	1	0	1
Diamondback turtle	6	2	2
Gopher tortoise	12	5	14
Sea turtle	0	1	2
Total	395	159	122

In addition there are seven species from 26-1, 14 from 36-4 and six from 34-2 which are unique to the site and which are represented by one individual apiece. These are not listed.

evaluated in terms of sample-size problems (Grayson 1984) and the relative contribution of 'richness' and 'evenness' to diversity. Simpson's Diversity Index (Pielou 1969:223) and the Shannon–Weaver Diversity Index (Pielou 1969:229) were both calculated. The former is less sensitive to the presence of rare elements (e.g., a single bone from a species) than the latter; it is thus a measure of 'dominance concentration' (Whittaker 1972, cited in Hill 1973). Urban excavations in particular are subject to varied disturbances and the ability to exclude single representatives of a species seems useful. Simpson's measure of diversity for a sample (see Bobrowsky and Ball: equation 24, this volume) was calculated. The values for the six components are shown in Table 10.1.

The Shannon–Weaver Diversity Index (see Bobrowsky and Ball, equation 25, this volume), standardized by maximum diversity (see Bobrowsky and Ball, equation 19, this volume), was used. This statistic is widely used by faunal analysts (Wing and Brown 1979), and this measure also allowed the use of Kintigh's technique (1984b, this volume) to evaluate the effect of sample size and distinguish between richness and evenness within diversity. The Shannon–Weaver figures are also seen in Table 10.1.

Diversity measures in both cases were calculated on MNI (minimum number of individuals), but excluded large domestic mammals (cows, pigs, and sheep or goats) because one cannot make the assumption that a bone from a cow, representing meat which may have been bought from a butcher, implies the presence of the whole animal, whereas fish, birds and small mammals were probably whole, with the exception of a very few large fish found during the period of occupation resulting in the later New York deposit. Only those species thought to have been used for food were included (Table 10.2 presents these data).

An examination of the diversity measures shows several interesting comparisons. For one thing, each set of three components from a community maintains the same internal relationship with both measures, in terms of rank order and relative

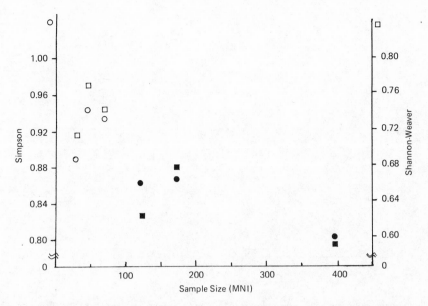

Fig. 10.1. Relationship between sample size (MNI) and Simpson's index (circles) and Shannon–Weaver index (squares) for New York City (open symbols) and St Augustine (closed symbols)

differences between components. Further, the New York City components are more diverse by both measures than the St Augustine sites. This is particularly interesting, given the location of the two sets of components. One might expect a more diverse fauna in St Augustine simply because of its semi-tropical environment. However, it is clear that assemblage diversity cannot be assumed to be a simple mirror of environmental diversity. Cultural factors have a very strong influence on food choice, especially perhaps in the case of recent migrants (here, colonial settlers) to a new environment.

The New York components do not demonstrate the expected decline in diversity; the landfill component appears to be the most diverse, followed by the late eighteenth-century cistern (landfill fauna could, of course, be affected by taphonomic factors to produce different results from those of other deposits), but in fact all three values are fairly similar. The St Augustine sites show an increase in diversity between the one sixteenth-century site and the two eighteenth-century ones.

Figure 10.1 shows the relationship between diversity value and sample size to be an unclear one, mostly because of the limited number of data points for each set, although there is a slight suggestion of an inverse effect for the St Augustine material. In order to examine sample-size effects further, Kintigh's (1984a) technique for evaluating a given set of data in terms of a set of randomly derived values for the same sample size was applied. An alternative method of assessing the effect of sample size using regression (Grayson 1984; Jones *et al.* 1983) is not possible with so few data points. Kintigh's technique has the important additional quality of being able to separate the contribution of richness from that of evenness in the diversity measure. The method, which Kintigh graciously ran for me, simulates a series of assemblages (in this case 200 or 300) for a given sample size (number of MNI). In the case of the assessment of evenness, the method also assumes a certain

number of sub-units, in this case species. The method has been described elsewhere (Kintigh 1984a, 1984b; this volume). The final step in both cases is to compare the specific value for richness or evenness computed for a particular assemblage with the range of expected values in terms of confidence intervals.

Evaluation of results

The figures for sample size, richness, evenness and the percentile value of the latter two numbers compared with the simulated results can be seen in Table 10.3 and Figures 10.2–10.5. Several interesting points emerge from the examination of these data. The first is that, for the New York City material, the earliest component was both the richest and the most even, while the late eighteenth-century cistern deposit is the lowest in richness and as

Table 10.3. *Sample size, richness, and evenness*

	Sample size	Evenness (H/H_{max})		Richness	
	(MNI)	No.	%	No.	%
New York					
Landfill	48	0.771	94	26	99
Midden	32	0.691	63	19	88
Cistern	59	0.740	64	25	78
St Augustine					
26-1	400	0.597	7	35	6
34-2	128	0.622	79	29	89
36-4	173	0.676	100	35	99

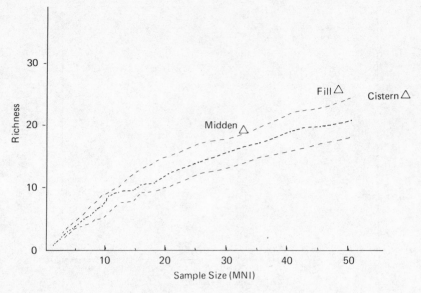

Fig. 10.2. Simulated relationship between sample size (MNI) and taxonomic richness based on New York City data

uneven as the early eighteenth-century midden deposit. This change in richness supports the original hypothesis, although it is clear that much more extensive testing of this idea will be necessary before it can be supported with any confidence. Taphonomic differences between landfill and features will also need to be considered carefully.

In St Augustine, on the other hand, the sixteenth-century site had very low values for both richness and evenness, while the eighteenth-century sites were both quite rich and even, especially SA36-4, the Ponce de Leon site, occupied by 'an old and prominent criollo family' whose head 'probably occupied the most prestigious position' (of the sites examined in St Augustine) (Deagan 1983:162). It is interesting to note that, for all components examined, richness and evenness values were relatively similar to each other in terms of confidence-interval position.

The interpretation of richness in terms of actual subsistence practices has very different implications from that of evenness, however, which is why it is important to consider them separately. Richness alone simply refers to the number of species which make their way into the household diet. It is often tempting to use richness alone as a measure of diversity, but it is strongly influenced by sample size. If it could be freed from this effect, it might well reflect the kind of socioeconomic factors Reitz and Cumbaa (1983) discuss, and it could also reflect the loss of econiches suggested here as a by-product of urbanization.

A re-examination of the New York material from this point

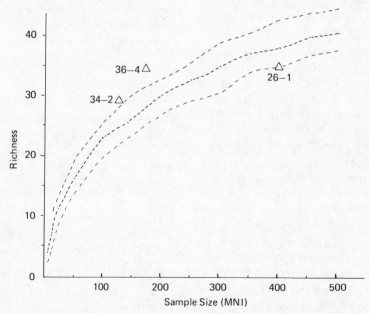

Fig. 10.3. Simulated relationship between sample size (MNI) and taxonomic richness based on St Augustine data

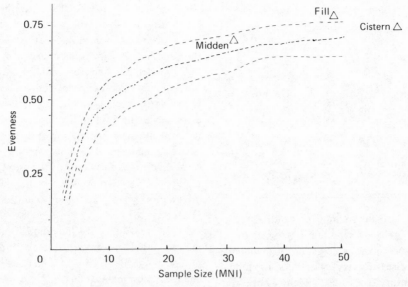

Fig. 10.4. Simulated relationship between sample size (MNI) and taxonomic evenness based on New York City data

of view shows that there is a gradual decrease over time in richness, with sample size taken into account, so that the position of richness values in terms of confidence intervals declines from 0.99 to 0.78. Thus, even if landfill represents a deposit that has bones in it which do not represent the remains of meals consumed, there is still a considerable decline in richness between the midden deposit and the late eighteenth-century cistern. The fact that there is no such decline in St Augustine suggests that the effect of urbanization in a relatively small town was not as environmentally destructive as it was in a city. Certainly the pollution of environments would not have been as great with a population of 3,000 as with one of 60,000. The explanation as to why richness increases from the sixteenth to the eighteenth century is beyond the scope of this

paper; there are a number of possibilities, but they require more information on St Augustine than is available to the author.

The interpretation of evenness, however, is very suggestive of the degree of specialization in a food system, indicating whether most of the meat and fish eaten came from only a few species or from many, evenly apportioned taxa. From this perspective, the most interesting result is the earliest St Augustine site, with very low evenness. Most faunal remains representing food were fish bones, with mullet and catfish making up half of the number of MNI analyzed (Reitz and Scarry n.d.:230).

The degree of specialization of fauna representing food cannot really be discussed without considering the contribution of large domestic mammals which have been excluded from diversity

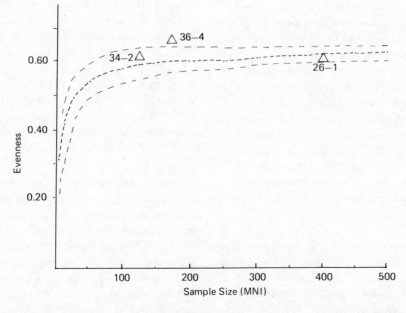

Fig. 10.5. Simulated relationship between sample size (MNI) and taxonomic evenness based on St Augustine data

Table 10.4. *Ratio of domestic mammal to total food bone (NISP)*

New York City	
7 Hanover Square	
Landfill (before 1700)	275/565 = 0.48
Midden (early eighteenth century)	147/239 = 0.62
Cistern (end of eighteenth century)	71/436 = 0.16
St Augustine	
SA 26-1 (sixteenth century)	161/4026 = 0.04
SA 34-2 (eighteenth century)	481/1831 = 0.26
SA 36-4 (eighteenth century)	414/2158 = 0.19

calculations based on MNI. Using the number of identified specimens (NISP) as the base, Table 10.4 shows the proportion of bones at each site or component representing domestic mammals. St Augustine shows an increase from very little domestic mammal to 26% in the eighteenth century. The addition of these bones would do little to change the richness index for these sites. Further, if we are interested in evenness as an indicator of specialization, it does not appear that there was a major change in the type of food system between the earlier and later time periods in terms of an economy heavily weighted towards these large, efficient food sources.

The New York components present a very different picture. Domestic mammals are an important part of the early food assemblage, making up 48% of the seventeenth-century deposit and 62% of the early eighteenth-century deposit. While richness measures would not change significantly, evenness would, if there were a meaningful way of including these bones in diversity measures. What is most interesting about these figures, however, is the decline in importance of these animals in the turn-of-the-century cistern deposit. This is matched by an increase in the consumption of a variety of birds, some of them domestic (duck, goose, pigeon), and an increase in the quantity and frequency of fish eaten, some of them for the first time, including such large deep-sea fish as Atlantic salmon, tomcod, and haddock. This suggests that there would be a smaller difference in evenness between the early fill and the late cistern than there is presently, the former deposit being more even and the latter being more uneven than at present. Apart from these numerical changes, however, the food remains in the cistern deposit seem to represent a more specialized and rather more exotic diet than those from the earlier deposit. While this may only represent sampling error, it may also be a valid reflection of the food habits of at least some portion of the upper socio-economic strata of society, during a period when these strata were becoming more differentiated.

Conclusions

The purpose of this paper has been the preliminary analysis of a series of historic-period faunal assemblages from two different parts of North America, in terms of the effect of increasing urbanization on that part of the diet seen in faunal material. A comparison between two measures of diversity, the Simpson and the Shannon–Weaver measures, shows them to be, for the most part, consistent in their results. While this conclusion needs further testing, it suggests that a researcher is free to choose whichever measure seems more appropriate, with particular regard to the question of the inclusion or exclusion of classes represented by only one element. The use of Kintigh's technique made possible the evaluation of the effect of sample size and the separation of richness from evenness in the Shannon–Weaver measure. This is extremely useful, even though in this case they were mostly similar, because the interpretation of richness and evenness is intuitively quite different. The choice of a technique of measurement is a complex one; in other contexts the use of other measures such as regression analysis (Grayson 1984), rarefaction (Styles 1981), or k-dominance curves (Lambshead *et al.* 1983) may be more appropriate.

In New York City, the process of becoming urban, reflected in rapid population growth, does seem to be accompanied by a decline in faunal diversity, in both richness and evenness. This change is presumably influenced by environmental change, specifically the loss of econiches and by the increasing use of specialist food providers and purveyors. A very different picture is presented by the St Augustine material where the sixteenth-century site is less diverse and even (i.e., more specialized) than the later sites. Further evidence of the nature of this difference, and particularly of the impact of marketing and the use of specialists, is seen in the importance of large domestic mammals. These make up a large part of early New York components, and are less important in the later deposit, signalling perhaps that, as industrial capitalism became prevalent, class differences were manifest in such things as more exotic foods. The use of large domestic mammals increases gradually in St Augustine, where, during the eighteenth century, class may be reflected by faunal remains (Reitz and Cumbaa 1983).

The impact of class, urbanization, and the system of production on faunal diversity is a very complex issue. Before the influence of these factors can be evaluated with any confidence, a number of things needs to be done. The possible influence of other factors, as yet unidentified, and including taphonomic ones, on the variety of fish, fowl, and animals consumed in a household, needs to be addressed. Many more deposits and larger samples need to be analyzed, using similar methods and techniques. The present paper can only be taken as a suggestion that the use of diversity measures, adjusted for sample size, may provide answers to some important questions about the nature of life in early cities and towns in the United States.

Acknowledgements
I am grateful to a number of people who have helped me in a number of very significant ways. Meta Janowitz, Kate Morgan, and Haskel Greenfield did the analysis of domestic fauna in New York, while Darlene Balkwill and Steve Cumbaa analyzed the birds and fish in Ottawa. Steve and Betsy Reitz have been very generous with their time and data, answering innumerable questions with great patience. Don Grayson got me interested in faunal analysis in the first place, mostly because of the way he taught it. Keith Kintigh has run my data on his computer several

times, and I am very thankful for his tremendous help. George Cowgill, Bob Leonard, Tom Jones, Keith Kintigh, Bill MacDonald, and Betsy Reitz made very useful comments on an earlier version of this paper, presented at the Society for American Archaeology meetings in Portland in 1984. Finally, I thank the New York City Landmarks Preservation Commission for initiating the projects from which the data come, and Diana Wall (Rockman) and Arnold Pickman, without whom I would not have had such a good time.

Chapter 11

Changing strategies of Anasazi lithic procurement on Black Mesa, Arizona

Robert D. Leonard, F. E. Smiley, and Catherine M. Cameron

The relationship between the kinds of stone tools recovered from archaeological sites and the kinds of raw materials from which they are manufactured is not always easily understood. Interpretation of the information content of such assemblages is also a vigorously debated issue. In any case, it is clear that technological and functional considerations are an important component of raw-material selection and use. Oftentimes particular material types are utilized preferentially over other available materials because they possess certain useful characteristics evident in either manufacture or end-product. While these considerations may be overriding, it also appears that the use of one material over another may have little to do with technology, and that its utilization may be a product of certain aspects of social organization, structure, or even stochastic events.

In this paper, we explore the connection between prehistoric chipped-stone technology and raw-material procurement on Black Mesa, northeastern Arizona. Diversity measures will be used to monitor changes in lithic raw-material procurement strategies, and it will be suggested that documented strategic shifts through time are, for the most part, either directly related to changing technological concerns, or a product of considerations involving the tactics of procurement. It will also be suggested that, while technological needs may in part determine which materials are procured, aspects of social organization and structure may well influence not only *which* materials are obtained, but also *how* they are obtained.

The discussion will begin with a description of lithic raw-material procurement strategies and tactics. The following sections present information concerning the environmental and cultural settings of Black Mesa as well as a description of lithic raw-material characteristics. A final section details the application of the model to the Black Mesa data.

The procurement of lithic raw materials

The variability in the types and frequencies of lithic material represented on archaeological sites can be viewed as the product of a set of decisions involving procurement strategies and tactics. Strategic decisions determine which materials, out of the total available population (or known population) of materials, are to be procured. Strategic decisions are made in the context of knowledge of source locations, the value (for whatever purposes) of these materials, and the costs or energy expenditures needed to procure them. If the value of a particular material exceeds, by some margin, the costs incurred in obtaining it, it is likely that the representation of this material will be at least in proportion to need. Where costs exceed value, materials are unlikely to be procured. In an archaeological context, we observe a sample of the cumulative set of strategic procurement decisions made by site inhabitants over the period of site occupation.

Tactical decisions are those which determine how materials are going to be obtained, or, in an archaeological context, how they were obtained. Binford (1979) discusses two possible tactics of procurement of raw materials, direct procurement and embedded procurement. In the case of direct procurement, the scheduling of procurement of raw materials is independent of other activities, and all costs can be assigned to the specific resource being procured. In an embedded mode, lithic raw materials are obtained in the context of another continually functioning system. Costs of the different kinds of resources obtained can be diffused among all benefits accrued, e.g., items obtained or transferred. The procurement of lithic raw materials can often be efficiently embedded in subsistence scheduling, trade networks, or in exchange in the context of social interaction . Elsewhere (Leonard *et al.* 1983), we have concluded that direct procurement is most cost effective when distances from sites to sources are small. As distances increase, embedded tactics become less costly than direct procurement. Embedded tactics may also differ in cost from one another, and vary in effectiveness in regard to distance and direction of procurement.

A human population in any given area may employ a variety of strategies and tactics. In the Black Mesa instance, it is highly unlikely that all materials were obtained in identical frequencies in either an absolute or relative sense, when more than 38 different material types were available for procurement. Likewise, these materials may not all have been procured in the same manner. Problems with what appears to be equifinality, i.e., the use of different tactics leaving similar or identical patterns, make the identification of procurement *tactics* in the archaeological record extremely difficult, and perhaps in most cases, forthcoming only with further resolution of exactly what the end products of alternative tactics are. The definition of procurement strategies, however, is somewhat easier.

Possible procurement strategies range from exploiting one resource exclusively to exploiting *all* available materials in equal numbers. The first can be termed a specializing strategy, the second a generalizing strategy. A number of situations can be adduced for which generalizing and specializing strategies might be employed. The examples proffered here are by no means exhaustive of the possibilities and merely provide a starting point for further analyses. Specializing strategies might be expected when (1) the number of available material types is restricted either in quantity or as a result of cost and value considerations and/or (2) only a few materials exhibit all characteristics necessary and sufficient for the manufacture of all needed tools. If only a few kinds of tools are needed, *and* a specializing procurement strategy is employed, the small number of materials used might also be of limited utility, needing only to display those characteristics required of the few tools. If the variety of tools employed were larger and a small number of materials were used, the few materials must exhibit characteristics required for the manufacture of more kinds of tools.

In contrast, more generalizing strategies might be expected when (1) the number of available material types is restricted by neither quantity nor cost and value considerations, and/or (2) many kinds of available materials exhibit characteristics necessary and sufficient for the manufacture of all needed tools. If only a few types of tools are needed and a generalizing strategy is employed,

then a wide range of materials possesses the characteristics required of these few tools. If a large number of tool-types is needed, more material types might be employed because of the varying needs for material characteristics in the manufacture of different tools.

Generalizing and specializing strategies represent the extremes of a continuum, and strategies may be compared in ordinal terms along this dimension. As a first step in comparing procurement strategies, two categories of information are required: (1) the number of material types represented (richness) in each assemblage and (2) the proportional representation of those types (evenness). Assemblages with high richness *and* evenness values are more diverse than assemblages with low richness and evenness values. Thus, indices of both richness and evenness are useful in assessing the degree to which generalizing or specializing strategies were employed. A generalizing strategy would be indicated by high richness and evenness values, whereas a specializing strategy would yield low values of richness and evenness. Prior to the application of this model to the Black Mesa material, background information regarding the environmental and cultural settings is provided in the following sections.

Environmental setting

Black Mesa, one of the major land forms of northeastern Arizona, rises on the north in a precipitous escarpment from the Klethla Valley and Laguna Creek drainages (Figure 11.1). Some 120 km in diameter, the Black Mesa land surface dips gently to the southwest, terminating in the high mesa-extensions upon which the modern-day Hopi villages lie. The study area consists of lands leased to the Peabody Coal Company by the Navajo and Hopi tribes and is situated in the northeastern portion of the mesa. Elevations in the study area average 2,000 m ASL, and the terrain varies from deeply incised canyons on the north and east to rolling hill country toward the southern end. The area is drained by Moenkopi Wash and its tributaries and by Dinnebito Wash, both tending southwest and eventually debouching into the Little Colorado River. Pinyon pine and juniper are the overwhelmingly preponderant woody species in the area, and sage communities dominate at lower elevations and on deeper soils. Precipitation is highly variable within the limits of the semi-arid climatic regime, falling primarily in late summer.

The prehistoric cultural setting of Black Mesa

Black Mesa has never supported large human populations. Both short- and long-term climatic variability make subsistence by hunting, gathering, and farming a chancy enterprise. However, the sporadic prehistoric occupation of the study area spans almost 8,000 years. Small Archaic groups are known to have made only temporary use of northern Black Mesa at approximately 6,000 B.C. and again at about 1,200–900 B.C. (Smiley and Andrews 1983).

More than 16 years of intensive survey and excavations provide only sketchy evidence for use of the area between the early and late Archaic manifestations. The same is true of the period between 900 B.C. and A.D. 100–200. However, with the arrival of

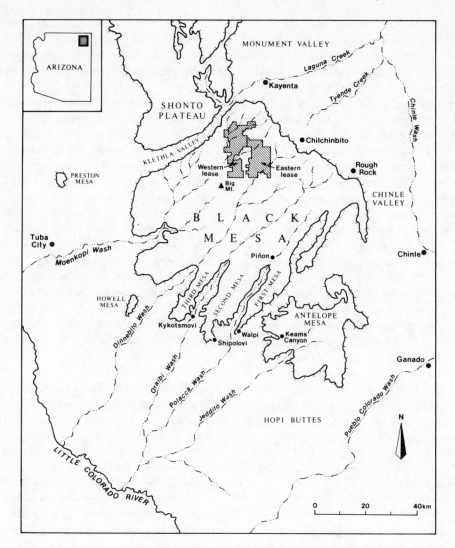

Fig. 11.1. Map of Black Mesa, Arizona

maize and squash, two elements of the upper Sonoran agricultural complex (Ford 1981), probably from west-central New Mexico, a more intensive exploitive period began.

The Lolomai (Basketmaker II) phase had its beginnings at about A.D. 100–200 (Smiley 1985) when small, semi-mobile groups of hunter–gatherer/farmers moved onto the mesa top as part of the expansion of small-scale agriculture over much of the Colorado Plateau. This occupation, like the previous ones, proved to be temporary and is not likely to have lasted more than approximately 150 years, possibly much less. The comparatively substantial record left by the Basketmaker II peoples attests to multiseasonal use of the area, although probably not year-round occupation of particular sites. The variation among sites ranges from small clusters of hearths and lithic debris, to pithouse settlements with as many as 12 structures and dozens of storage and heating and cooking features.

Another hiatus followed the Lolomai occupation and, although large, nucleated settlements were occupied during Basketmaker III times to the north near Skeleton Mesa and to the south in the Hopi Buttes vicinity, there is no evidence that Black Mesa was inhabited between A.D. 300 and A.D. 800. By about A.D. 800–850, the mesa was reoccupied by transitional Basketmaker III/early Puebloan groups living in small, but relatively formalized sites consisting of storage facilities, deep earthen pithouses, and accumulating midden deposits. Population grew until about the tenth century A.D., when a cessation in building activity, evidenced by the almost complete lack of tree-ring cutting dates, indicates either population decline or another, though relatively short, cultural hiatus (Nichols and Smiley 1985).

By the middle or late eleventh century, small settlements were once again being constructed in the study area and prehistoric population levels reached their highest level (Layhe 1981). About 150 years prior to the general abandonment of the Kayenta region of A.D. 1300, the last Anasazi groups had left the northern Black Mesa study area. The study area remained essentially unoccupied until the arrival of the Navajo in the late eighteenth and early nineteenth centuries.

Thus, Black Mesa has continually proved to be a great challenge to prehistoric human exploitive skills, apparently winning every contest. Groups using the area were unlikely ever to have enjoyed any period of stasis and, as the previous comments should indicate, even times of 'colonization' and growth were comparatively brief. It is likely that a complex interaction of environmental, technological, social-organizational, and demographic factors enabled or compelled the periodic occupation and abandonment of Black Mesa by the Anasazi.

The assemblages considered in this discussion consist of materials recovered from 35 prehistoric sites excavated by the Black Mesa Archaeological Project between 1979 and 1982. The sites range in age from ca. A.D. 100 to A.D. 1150. The cultural sequence includes the preceramic Lolomai phase (Basketmaker II) and all of the ceramic period Puebloan phases extant on the mesa (Pueblo I–III).

Lithic procurement on Black Mesa

Lithic materials suitable for the manufacture of chipped-stone tools may be classified in many ways. Examples include grain size, source location, trace-element composition, and the kinds of natural formation processes which produced them, i.e., volcanism, sedimentation, metamorphic forces, and so on. The materials available in the greater Black Mesa region and those recovered in archaeological contexts from Black Mesa prehistoric sites lend themselves, rather fortuitously, to simultaneous classification according to grain size and source location. Fortunately, an extensive survey early in the history of Black Mesa lithic research has provided a great deal of specificity as to the kinds of materials available and the locations of potential sources (Green 1982).

At least 38 different material types from a minimum of 29 different sources were used to varying degrees within and across time periods. Following Green (1982:140), we have placed these material types into three categories based on distance from the sources to the prehistoric habitation sites. Local materials are those coming from sources on Black Mesa. Non-local materials come from sources off the mesa but within 50 km of the study area. Distant materials are those obtained from sources over 50 km away.

The number of locally available lithic raw materials is limited to three or four types. These tend to be relatively large-grained products of sedimentary and metamorphic processes which are not ideal for flaking in most respects. A variety of grades of metamorphosed siltstones comprise the bulk of prehistorically utilized materials. The better grades of Black Mesa siltstones range from bone-white to gray-brown and are fairly fine-grained material. Other varieties grading to pink and yellow are coarser-grained and very brittle. Finally, a number of outcrops of a massive, coarse-grained gray material with a high percentage of inclusions are known and many site assemblages include this material. The higher-quality white material tends to be badly fractured and often occurs naturally as small tabular pieces less than two cm thick. While suitable for biface manufacture, the tabular materials lack the blocky, more massive structure necessary for the manufacture of even relatively small flake tools. The remaining varie-

ties are either too brittle, too chalky, or too coarse-grained to be suitable for anything but core or large, imprecise flake tools.

A second locally available material, a coarse-grained, intractable, petrified wood, is generally useful only for very crude flake or core tools, or for percussion implements. A third type is a variable, fine-grained sandstone, which, by lithic-technological standards, is actually quite coarse. Finally, there are several materials including small coarse-grained, quartzitic lag gravels, siderites, and limestones, which were used in varying frequencies.

All materials in the first category were available to inhabitants of study-area sites within a few hours' walk. However, the source locations of the materials in the next category probably required trips of 15–30 km as well as descent of the north rim of the mesa. Alternatively, they might have been procured by 20–30 km treks to the west. These *intermediate*-distance materials are better suited to flake-tool manufacture since they generally occur in non-tabular pieces and in more massive outcrops. In addition, the wide variety of medium-quality cherts and quartzitic cobbles in the intermediate-distance class are finer-grained and thus produce much better cutting edges than the locally available materials. Particular source locations for these and other materials are shown in Figure 11.2

It should be noted that the intermediate-distance material sources cannot be defined strictly on straight-line distance criteria. We have attempted to take topographic obstacles, such as the north escarpment, into consideration. Thus, while some intermediate source locations lie less than ten km by air from the center of the study area, a straight-line route would be very difficult, particularly on the return trip, due to the rough terrain.

The third category contains raw materials from distant sources which are exclusively high-quality cherts, chalcedonies, jaspers, and obsidians. These materials come from locations at greater than a 100-km radius, including the Little Colorado drainage and the Flagstaff area to the southwest, and the Four-Corners and the Washington Pass areas to the northeast and east respectively. Such high-quality materials are never present in abundance on Black Mesa in archaeological contexts, but most sites typically yield at least a few specimens.

An interesting aspect of the Black Mesa location is, thus, the very different technological properties of lithic raw materials available within fairly clear-cut distance-to-source categories. In the following sections, the technological attributes of various general material classes will be evaluated in terms of their relationships to procurement strategies, tactics, and mobility patterns.

Analysis

In order to determine the particular strategies employed by the Black Mesa Anasazi, two measures of assemblage diversity will be applied. The first measure of assemblage diversity to be examined is richness, the number of material types represented. In terms of richness of material-type representation, Basketmaker II and Puebloan sites are remarkably similar. Basketmaker sites have a mean of 18.8 material types represented, Puebloan sites a mean of 19.1. This difference in mean number of material types represented is not statistically significant at the 0.05 level ($p = 0.634$).

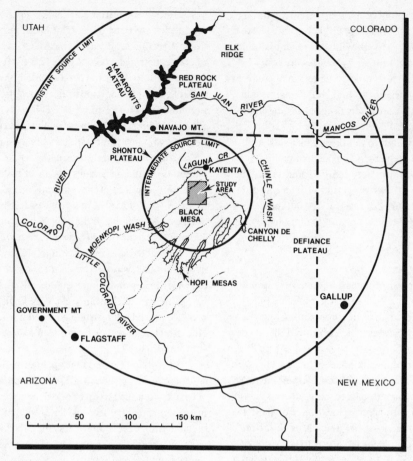

Fig. 11.2. Source distance limits defined for raw materials found in prehistoric contexts on Black Mesa. Local area sources are situated on northern Black Mesa within easy travelling distance of the study area sites. Virtually all intermediate-distance sources lie to the northwest, north, and northeast of the northern scarp (ticked line) of Black Mesa. Note the Government Mountain source at the southwestern limit of the distant source area.

Simple richness, however, cannot be our sole measure of diversity, nor consequently of the relative preference for particular strategies. As argued by Jones *et al.* (1983) and Kintigh (1984a), respective sample sizes should be taken into account, given these authors' conclusion that class richness values are often demonstrably a function of sample sizes. Following procedures outlined by Jones *et al.* (1983), it becomes apparent that, when sample sizes are considered, significant differences in richness exist across Basketmaker and Puebloan assemblages. Figure 11.3 depicts the number of material types represented on Basketmaker and Puebloan sites plotted against the total number of artifacts recovered from each site. From Figure 11.3, it can be seen that a slight correlation does exist between site sample sizes and material class richness ($r = 0.46$), when both Basketmaker and Puebloan sites are considered in the same equation. One Basketmaker site, D:11:3172, is a 2 standard-deviation outlier from the regression line. D:11:3172 has significantly fewer material types represented than would be expected given the total number of artifacts recovered. No attempts will be made here to account for this anomalous value. With the removal of this site from the regression equation, the correlation value increases considerably ($r = 0.58$), and a change in slope is evidenced (see Figure 11.4). When Basket-

maker and Puebloan sites are considered separately it becomes apparent that this relationship differs for each period (Figure 11.5). Correlations increase in significance (Basketmaker II, $r = 0.68$ when D:11:3172 is considered in the equation, $r = 0.81$ when it is omitted; Puebloan, $r = 0.80$), and the steeper slope generated by Puebloan sites indicates that additional material types are added to Puebloan assemblages at comparatively lower sample sizes. When D:11:3172 is omitted from the equation, slope differences become more pronounced (Figure 11.6). This difference in slopes indicates that Puebloan samples are comparatively richer in terms of material types than Basketmaker sites. From this perspective, greater richness at comparable sample sizes for Puebloan sites would suggest that a more specializing strategy was favored in Basketmaker times, and a more generalizing strategy in Puebloan times.

Calculations of diversity measures which consider evenness, the proportional representation of each type, as well as richness, support this conclusion. Figure 11.7 displays diversity values for Basketmaker and Puebloan assemblages calculated using the Shannon–Weaver information statistic (Pielou 1975). A calculation of this index provides two values: (H') a diversity measure which considers both richness and evenness in obtaining a value

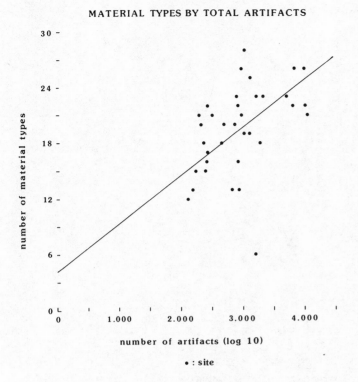

Fig. 11.3. Relationship between number of material types and number of artifacts in Basketmaker and Puebloan assemblages

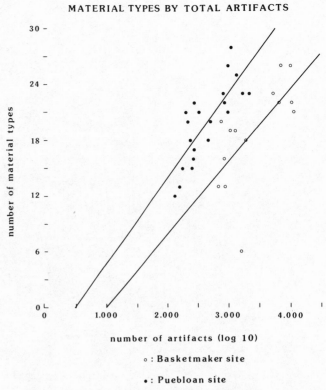

Fig. 11.5. Relationship between number of material types and number of artifacts. Regression lines are plotted separately for Basketmaker (open circles) and Puebloan (closed circles) assemblages.

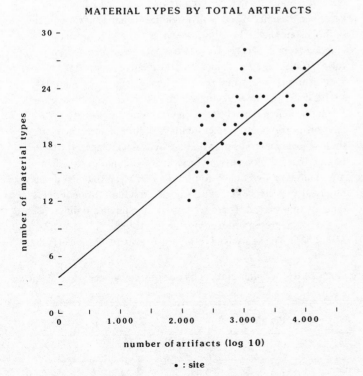

Fig. 11.4. Relationship between number of material types and number of artifacts in Basketmaker and Puebloan assemblages with Basketmaker site D:11:3172 omitted

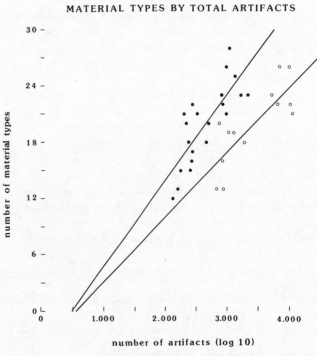

Fig. 11.6. Relationship between number of material types and number of artifacts with Basketmaker site D:11:3172 omitted. Regression lines are plotted separately for Basketmaker (open circles) and Puebloan (closed circles) assemblages.

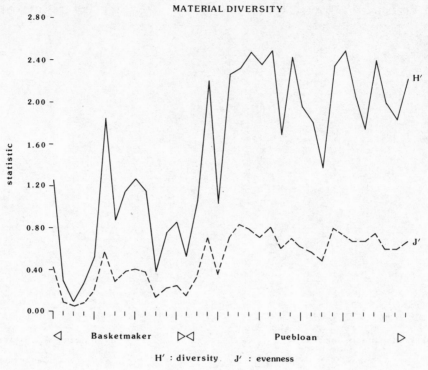

Fig. 11.7. Evenness values (H′ and J′) for Basketmaker and Puebloan assemblages

and (J′) a measure of evenness. From this figure, it can be seen that, when evenness is considered, significant differences between Basketmaker and Puebloan assemblages exist. Materials on Puebloan sites are for the most part much more evenly represented, indicating that, following the reoccupation of Black Mesa c. A.D. 850, there had been a shift to a more generalizing strategy during Puebloan times.

Puebloan peoples were not only utilizing a relatively greater number of material types in more even frequencies than the earlier Basketmaker inhabitants, but they were also obtaining the bulk of materials from more distant sources. Basketmaker sites contain between 74.0% and 100.0% local materials with a mean percentage falling at 94.0%. Puebloan sites range from 20.0% to 87.1% with a mean value of 48.0%. Basketmaker assemblages were primarily composed of locally available materials, and Puebloan assemblages of non-local materials.

The change in strategies from the use of a few local mat-

erials in Basketmaker times to that of using a greater number of non-local materials in more even frequencies during Puebloan times occurred in concert with a significant change in the content of tool assemblages. For this discussion we have grouped all chipped-stone tool classes into two categories, expedient and formal tools. Figure 11.8 indicates the relative proportions of tools grouped into formal and expedient categories by material source distances for Basketmaker and Puebloan assemblages. From this figure, it can be seen that Basketmaker assemblages have proportionately greater numbers of formal and expedient tools of local materials than do Puebloan assemblages. It can also be seen that Puebloan assemblages are dominated by expedient tools manufactured out of non-local materials. Table 11.1 displays observed, expected values, and adjusted residuals for material types by time period. There are statistically significant differences in material representation across these categories ($\chi^2 = 600.37$; $p \ll 0.001$). The analysis of residuals (Everitt 1977) indicates that

Table 11.1. Observed values (O), expected values (E) and adjusted residuals (AR) for material types by distance categories ($\chi^2 = 600.37$; $p < 0.001$)

Source distance	Basketmaker II				Puebloan			
	O	E	AR	p	O	E	AR	p
Local	769	526.92	24.09	< 0.001	141	383.07	− 24.09	< 0.001
Non-local	160	396.06	− 23.79	< 0.001	524	287.93	23.79	< 0.001
Distant	38	44.01	− 1.43	> 0.05	38	31.99	1.43	> 0.05

ASSEMBLAGE COMPOSITION

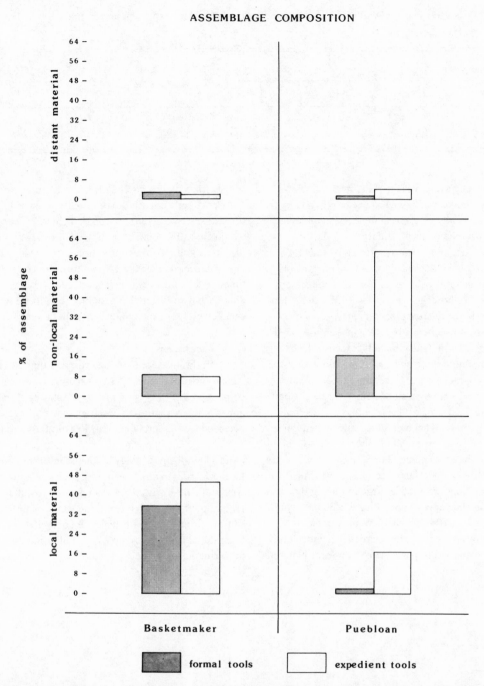

Fig. 11.8. Relative abundances of formal and expedient tools made from local, non-local, and distant lithic source materials

Basketmaker assemblages have a significantly greater number of tools from local sources than would be expected and that Puebloan assemblages have a significantly greater number of tools from non-local sources than expected. In addition, Table 11.2 indicates that expedient tools are significantly under-represented in Basketmaker assemblages and over-represented in Puebloan ones ($\chi^2 = 115.40$; $p \ll 0.001$). A change in technological concerns is apparent.

The previously noted shift in strategic decisions regarding lithic raw-material procurement in Puebloan times may be related to these changing technological concerns. An examination of the flaking characteristics of the materials involved suggests that locally available siltstones are often of uneven quality and extremely brittle. As a result, they are less suitable for flake-tool production than are higher-grade non-local materials, and consequently of less value. Yet, these siltstones were obviously quite suitable for both the formal and expedient tool technology required in Basketmaker times, given their considerable representation in site assemblages, and may well have been adequate for Puebloan needs. It is also possible that finer-edged high-grade materials were required by the Puebloan expedient tool technology, and that materials from non-local and distant sources became relatively

Table 11.2. Observed values (O), expected values (E) and adjusted residuals (AR) for expedient and formal tools by Basketmaker and Puebloan periods ($\chi^2 = 115.86; p < 0.001$)

Time period	Expedient				Formal			
	O	E	AR	p	O	E	AR	p
BM II	529	632.30	− 10.76	< 0.001	438	334.69	10.76	< 0.001
Puebloan	563	459.68	10.76	< 0.001	140	243.30	10.76	< 0.001

more valuable than locally available materials. Regardless, it is clear that, while Basketmaker technological needs were met by the almost exclusive use of locally available materials, Puebloan technology utilized non-local materials preferentially.

This preferential use of non-local materials by Puebloan peoples may also have been independent of any significant considerations regarding technological value. Instead, changes in the tactics of procurement, or how the materials were procured, may have affected changes in the relative procurement costs of these more distant materials, subsequently resulting in their increased utilization and representation. Unfortunately, exactly which tactics were employed to obtain these raw materials is not easily outlined. Based on site characteristics, preceramic Basketmaker peoples appear to have been more mobile than later Puebloan groups (Powell 1983). Basketmaker peoples may have simply utilized sources on the mesa whenever subsistence scheduling placed them near these sources. Small numbers of non-local and distant materials may have been curated specifically for tasks for which locally available materials were unsuitable. Puebloan groups were comparatively less mobile, though during the early periods of occupation they appear not to have been year-round residents in the study area (Powell 1983). While Puebloan groups were not entirely sedentary, the increased reliance on agriculture, and the increased importance of non-local materials

suggest that the procurement of lithic materials was for the most part embedded in a continually functioning system other than subsistence. If lithic procurement was operating embedded within the subsistence system it would suggest that these peoples were going further for subsistence needs, contrary to existing evidence for increased agricultural reliance during these times. The tactical shift evidenced may have been from embedding within subsistence scheduling to embedding within an exchange system in the context of social interactions.

Conclusions

In this discussion we have argued that the study of prehistoric lithic procurement systems requires the delineation of two components of those systems: (1) the strategies of procurement, and (2) tactics relating to procurement. We have stated that a shift occurred from a specializing strategy in Basketmaker times where a few locally available materials were utilized preferentially, to a more generalizing strategy in Puebloan times incorporating non-local materials in more even frequencies. We suggest that this strategic shift was likely either as a response to different technological requirements, or to changes in the tactics of procurement. While shifts in procurement strategies can be well documented, the identification of the tactics employed to obtain these materials remains problematical.

Chapter 12

Ceramic diversity, production, and use

Prudence M. Rice

The organization and aims of this paper are threefold. First, I summarize some of the problems and limitations of the archaeological database relating to the investigation of ceramic production. Secondly, I outline the assumptions of diversity measures as they can be used to organize the dimensions of variability in ceramics in order to infer production strategies. Thirdly, I examine the congruence between diversity measures and their interpretation within the realm of ceramic production and use. My focus is more on the nature of variability within ceramic materials, and less on the mathematics of the diversity indices themselves.

Ceramic production

The large quantities of pottery fragments at archaeological sites sooner or later prompt questions concerning where they came from and how they were made, i.e., questions of commodity production. An understanding of ancient productive arrangements is important because the relations of production are among the most fundamental points of integration between members of a society, between societies, and between societies and the environment. Many kinds of variables can be specified in these relationships, but, with respect to pottery specifically, the following are among those most frequently addressed: the socioeconomic status of producers, the local and regional interdependencies of commodity production and exchange, the degree of administrative control of production, and the role of specialist producers. (The last two are particularly associated with complex societies or their evolution.)

Craft specialization is one of the major issues to which archaeological analyses of ceramic diversity have been directed (Hagstrum 1985; Rice 1979, 1981; Stark and Hepworth 1982; Toll 1981; Wright 1983). The problem is that there is little correspondence between prehistoric and ethnographic criteria, either definitional or operational, for identifying specialization; hence, it is difficult to develop strategies for its archaeological study. Evolutionary schemes postulate a series of arrangements, varying from intermittent household production through large-scale industrial manufacture (van der Leeuw 1977; Peacock 1981, 1982), on the basis of ethnographic or historical data, but the ability to discriminate these developmental stages by means of archaeological data alone is questionable.

In addition, other factors may further confound the archaeological visibility of specific productive arrangements. Earle (1981) has called attention to the importance of 'attached' specialists producing specifically for an elite, as distinct from 'general' specialists. Stark (n.d.) points to 'ratio' or scale effects, i.e., the need to consider the relationship between numbers of producers and numbers of consumers. Feinman *et al.* (1984) illustrates the role of fluctuations in administrative control of commodity production as a function of broader overall concerns of agricultural productivity and defense. A related matter concerns part- versus full-time specialization. This is a particularly elusive distinction to which archaeologists are wont to attach great significance. The ethnographic and ethnoarchaeological literature, however, suggests that much production – even involving workshop organization – is seasonally adjusted to the agricultural cycle, and thus is really only part-time (e.g., Peacock 1982:9, 31, 39; Voyatzoglou 1974). Full-time year-round pottery making is associated primarily with an 'urban nucleated workshop' mode of production.

More important, perhaps, is the fact that the concept of 'specialization' is itself vague and unwieldy. Muller (1984:490–2) has clarified the concept by drawing attention to the distinction between 'site' and 'producer' specialization. Site or locus specialization denotes areas of limited or intensive activity, such as production of certain goods. Producer specialization, on the other hand, refers to the allocation of labor, i.e., the time, skill, and/or training invested in producing goods for one's primary livelihood (apart from specialization by gender or age). This is a useful distinction with respect to pottery specialization studies, because in some cases it is possible to identify *areas* of production (site specialization) but little information may be available as to the amount of time spent in the activity (producer specialization).

For pottery studies, a third kind of specialization might also be hypothesized, and that is 'resource specialization.' This could prove to be a useful heuristic where particular clays and tempers are selected for special functions. The concept is also applicable to the growing body of archaeometric studies which focus on pottery paste and glaze compositions, and define 'reference groups' whose members have similar mineralogical and chemical properties indicating common raw materials. For example, in the case of wares such as Fine Orange pottery (Bishop and Rands 1982), neither locus nor personnel specialization can be specified. A restricted geochemical range of resources, however, is a crucial variable, not only in hypothesizing the origins of the ware, but as an underlying rationale of provenience studies in general.

Pottery production is ideally studied through all these lines of information, combining locus and personnel specialization, scale and mode of production, and analysis of the kinds of resources used. Unfortunately, however, in many archaeological situations it is impossible to retrieve all these kinds of data giving direct evidence of production (see Stark 1985). In these instances, alternative lines of reasoning and inferential data must be pursued in order to understand the nature of productive arrangements. What has emerged as the focus of attention in studies of specialization is the ceramic objects themselves, as an indirect pathway toward determining production locations and strategies.

This focus exists for several reasons. First, lacking abundant comparable ethnographic data on definitions and characterization of specialist production, and without direct indicators of workshop locations, archaeologists have had to concentrate on information they *do* have available: the pottery itself. Thus the study of production has sometimes been initiated by identifying the manufacturing technique of individual vessels (molds, or coiling, for example), or identifying individual producers by their skill or errors (Hardin 1977; Hill 1977).

In most cases, however, production is more broadly conceived as a socioeconomic process, rather than as a set of manufacturing techniques, and the basis of study is the ceramic assemblage. Thus, a second reason for the focus on ceramic objects in production studies is to investigate the variability or lack of variability in the products. Different degrees of variability in ceramics are associated with differential skills of the producers, reduction in the number of producers, or mass production and quality control of the products, which leads to standardized products (see Balfet 1965; Rathje *et al* 1978:171–3; Rice 1981; Rottlander 1966, 1967; Stark n.d.; van der Leeuw 1977; Wright 1983). On an assemblage basis, then, the study of production may proceed by means of attention to internal variability of the products, or by studying the standardization or lack of variability evident in the collection.

Ceramic variability and diversity

The increasing attention to variability in ceramic collections is an outgrowth of archaeologists' responses to repeated calls for the study of patterns of artifact variability (Binford 1962; Clarke 1968) as a source of information on cultural behavior. As a result, there has been a proliferation of developments with respect to how variability in pottery is conceptualized, measured, and interpreted. Variability may be studied on an artifact or an assemblage level, and it may involve changes in the numbers of artifacts or attributes, the number of functions the pottery vessels serve, the skill with which they are produced, the kinds of contexts in which they are used, and the resources from which they are manufactured. New behavioral contexts for interpreting variability have also been explored. Among the most significant of these have been the relationship of pottery decorative style to social interaction (e.g., Deetz 1965; cf. Friedrich 1970; Longacre 1964; S. Plog 1980), use-functional variability (Braun 1980; Ericson *et al.* 1972; Hally 1983), 'ethnicity' (Hodder 1979), and status, in addition to continuing attention to spatiotemporal variability (Adams 1979).

These interpretations have increasingly availed themselves of a number of graphical, metric, and multivariate models of variability. Aside from the long-popular frequency seriations, more recent innovations include the use of: cumulative percentage graphs (Mortenson 1973), histograms (Johnson 1975; Rice 1980), an ordinal 'production step index' (Feinman *et al.* 1981), comparisons with known ancient units of measurement (Rottlander 1966, 1967), various formal coefficients or informal proportional measures of homogeneity (Braun 1980; Bronitsky 1978; Dickens 1980; Leone 1968; Whallon 1968; Whittlesey 1974), and multivariate cluster, factor, and scaling analyses (Fry 1980; Fry and Cox 1974; Rice and Saffer 1982; also a vast literature on physicochemical provenience studies too voluminous to cite here: see, for example, Bishop *et al.* 1982). Finally and most explicitly, the concept of diversity, a measure borrowed from population ecology, has been employed in analyzing assemblage variability as a function of ceramic production strategies (Rice 1979, 1981; Rice and Saffer 1981; Stark and Hepworth 1982; Toll 1981).

The idea of diversity has long been used in a non-quantitative or intuitive sense to describe the variability of ceramic collections, and to draw inferences about production, trade, and use (e.g., Otto 1975:161, 219; Rothschild and Rockman 1982:13; Shepard 1958; Whittlesey 1974; Wright 1983). More recently, however, the quantitative concept of diversity has been borrowed from ecology to treat these same problems. Diversity is a descriptive measure used in mathematical ecology to represent the structure and complexity of living communities. Calculation of a diversity measure (of which there are many) permits evaluation of the heterogeneity of a system in terms of its constituent units. This allows analysis of a property that is in some ways analogous to the statistical quantity of 'variance,' but which uses frequencies or counts within nominal categories, such as species. Diversity is commonly expressed as the numbers of categories present in a population (its 'richness'), as well as the relative proportion of the units within the whole (its 'evenness'). Richness is a rather straightforward concept, but evenness (also expressed as heterogeneity, dominance, or equitability) is more controversial and tenuously defined.

Despite the prominence of the idea of diversity in population ecology studies (see Pielou 1975, 1977:291–311), it has no clear definition and there is no real consensus on its interpretation. Diversity is 'in essence . . . defined by the indices used to measure it' (Peet 1974:285), and different indices emphasize different facets of the compositional variability of a community.

Three levels of diversity have been identified (Whittaker 1972, cited in Peet 1974:286), which are important in terms of parallels to archaeological objectives in the study of pottery variability. These levels are:

(1) intra-community diversity, within a habitat (in archaeology this corresponds to the diversity within a site)
(2) between-habitat diversity, e.g., along a gradient (in archaeology, the gradient might be time or distance)
(3) landscape diversity, which is a combination of (1) and (2) (in archaeology, this would probably be equivalent to regional studies).

Arguing from diversity to production

The diversity approach to the study of pottery production is appropriate because pottery has a large number of production-related attributes that can be described at all levels of measurement, nominal, ordinal, and interval. These attributes can be grouped into four broad systems: attributes relating to ceramic resources (kind, particle size, and amounts of various raw materials), manufacturing technology (techniques of forming and the variables of firing), vessel form (primary and secondary shape characteristics, and dimensions), and decoration or 'style,' broadly conceived. (Additional important properties relate to use and depositional context, but only indirectly inform on the production process via the other traits mentioned above.)

Regardless of whether a collection of pottery is divided into type classes or categories of shape or size, variability in any of these primary attribute systems may occur from one example to another for any of a number of reasons. These include: (1) generally imperfect processes of replication; (2) random events in the production activity (a bad day, shortage of time, interruptions); (3) lack of skill; (4) conscious decision to vary; (5) infrequency of the activity; (6) number of producers involved; and (7) lack of strong controls (over access to resources, shapes, sizes, decorative patterns).

Excessive variability in production is generally limited by a combination of forces, including intended use, consumer preferences, and traditional ideas ('costumbre;' see Reina and Hill 1978) about the proper way to do something.

For an understanding of pottery production, especially specialized organization and diversity/standardization of the products, the role of these sources of variability in the major attribute systems must be investigated and explained. This is true both in terms of their reliability as indicators of specialized production, but also as regards their appropriateness for diversity measurements. It is entirely expectable that different attribute systems will behave differently with respect to registering in standardization or diversity, because each system is responsive to different constraints within the overall social and economic system of relations of production, distribution, and 'consumption' (Rice 1984). In addition, there are different kinds of variability or diversity, to which different attributes may respond differently.

Stated very simply, the arguments from diversity measures to ceramic production are based on broad analogies between the population sizes, complexity (numbers and proportions of species), and occupied habitats of biotic communities, and the socioeconomic relationships of production and consumption in human societies of varying degrees of complexity. Social systems exercise different kinds and degrees of demand for a variety of commodities, including ceramics, and produce and use them in different ways. In terms of inferring production, a ceramic assemblage with high diversity would suggest the presence in the society of many kinds of products serving many needs, the presence of many producers, a lack of controls or regulation of the production process, or some combination of these factors. A ceramic assemblage with low diversity, on the other hand, would be characteristic of a society with fewer kinds of products (or more products with less variability in each), fewer producers, the presence of controls or regulation of the production process, or pots that could be put to multiple uses. This latter situation of low diversity is believed to obtain in very large complex societies with craft specialists producing pottery, which in its most developed form is characterized by mass production, quality control, and/or standardization of the products.

Depending upon the cultural contexts of the samples for which diversity is computed, differences in the index values may be informative as to a variety of behavior patterns interpretable in terms of ceramic production, but they also relate to use. These patterns include: access to resources for manufacture; status variables that relate to distribution and access to finished goods; differing functions or activities involving pottery at different sites or parts of sites; and changes through time.

From the viewpoint of pottery studies, then, these measures are useful because, rightly or wrongly, the emphasis in the study of production is most frequently and directly placed upon the products of ceramic production and only indirectly on the processes or actual organization of production relations. Because much of the data on the pottery products is at the nominal level (type classes, form classes, colors, temper categories, etc.), the focus of diversity indices on similar nominal categorizations is especially welcome as a way of extracting maximum information from the sherds or vessels.

On the other hand, there is good cause for reflection on the relationship between diversity indices and ceramic production. Many different kinds of diversity exist, and there is no real agreement among ecologists as to what diversity, despite its precise quantification, actually means (Peet 1974). Its use in archaeology is one example of many difficulties with adopting ecological concepts into this discipline (see, for example, Hardesty 1980; Rhoades 1978), and may be viewed as somewhat premature or incautious in this light, because our understanding of the nature of ancient production and its visibility in the archaeological record is not well developed. Diversity measures become another instance of 'clear answers to vague questions' (Rice 1978), or 'solutions in search of problems.' It should be argued, however, that diversity is a measurement of a characteristic of a statistical distribution of any collection of items, rather than a property possessed only by plant and animal communities. The application of diversity indices to archaeological data then corresponds to that of any other statistical measure: meeting the criteria or assumptions necessary for its use, and interpreting the results in a proper manner (without regard, for our purposes, to ecological processes such as dominance, predation, etc.).

Criteria for using and evaluating diversity indices

An important criterion in the application of diversity indices to ceramic data is sample size. Questions about diversity are questions about the structure and relations between classes within large, complex assemblages; a diversity index is not a parameter of a population, nor is it an inferential statistic. Although no specific size limits are given in ecological studies, which often illustrate indices with samples that are 'indefinitely large' or with small 'fully censused' communities, samples are usually on the order of several hundred individuals in size. Comparisons of artifact-class richness (numbers of classes) are particularly susceptible to sample-size effects (see Jones *et al.* 1983): small samples will tend to leave rarer categories unrepresented, and thereby distort the diversity measure downward. This is of some importance in archaeological studies in which access to rare resources is often assumed to be a prime correlate of socioeconomic status. Certain of the diversity measures, for example H', are more sensitive than others to rare categories (Peet 1974:296).

Apart from absolute size of the sample, relative sizes are also important if two assemblages are being compared, because no diversity indices are completely independent of sample size. Comparison of diversities between different assemblages should be made only if they are of equal (or approximately equal) size. Comparability of proveniences, or contexts of use and recovery, is another important variable in determining the significance of differences in ceramic assemblages (see Boone 1982 for calculations of heterogeneity of dump contents), and this too relates to sample size. This is particularly a problem in view of the relationship between sample size, number of classificatory units (richness) identified, and the length of occupation represented by a particular

assemblage (Jones *et al.* 1983:71–2). In addition, different breakage and replacement rates of different kinds of pottery (which are a function of several technical and use-related factors; see David 1972; DeBoer 1974; DeBoer and Lathrap 1979; Foster 1960) will affect class richness. Thus, the period of occupation of a site may be a factor in determining the apparent diversity of an assemblage, apart from absolute quantities of pottery. The presence of rare categories at a site may be partly a function of length of occupation (a briefly occupied site is analogous to a small sample).

Properly comparing and interpreting diversity indices is more easily recommended than achieved, and much depends on the kinds of questions which diversity measures are expected to answer. In studies of pottery production and specialization, the research framework is usually comparative: comparing certain kinds of pottery from different sites, areas, or time periods to determine whether or not the assumptions of increasing standardization with respect to specialized pottery production hold true.

Problems arise with respect to the reliability of inferring differences in production or use behavior for comparisons of diversity indices calculated for pottery assemblages. One problem is that, because diversity is not a 'real' or intrinsic property with an absolute standard of measurement, there is no easy way to determine whether or not the observed differences between sampled sites or populations represent bona fide differences between them. That is, some independent test of the significance of the differences in diversity between two pottery samples must be made. Tests of significance, such as the chi square (Toll 1981) and *t*-test (Stark and Hepworth 1982), have been used to determine whether the samples represent the same population (statistically speaking) of variability, or represent distinct populations.

In archaeological applications, a further consideration involves the selection of samples for diversity or standardization comparisons. The samples or populations being compared should ideally have some real links, either through temporal continuity or geographical contiguity, as a control of extraneous variables. This is because no absolute criterion exists for evaluation of diversity figures; consequently their interpretation is very much context-based. The need for comparable contexts does not mean that geography or time alone can bring about a difference in the variability of pottery; rather, the links between samples establish a 'background' or baseline range of variability (perhaps related to differences in available clays, for example) against which differences in diversity can be meaningfully interpreted in terms of production.

In the present state of imperfect understanding of pottery production arrangements, it is inappropriate to select the ceramic products of widely separate societies in order to compare their diversity and infer different degrees of productive specialization. Without the presence of some known relationship between the units being compared, the differences in diversity of their ceramic products may not be a real reflection of differences in production strategies but rather a function of any of a number of other historical, ecological, or demographic phenomena. It should be added that, once the relationship between product diversity and production strategy is better understood, this stricture will very likely prove less significant, and can be relaxed.

Diversity in individual ceramic attribute systems

It is important to consider in more detail the relationship between pottery attributes and the validity of inferences of production. Just as the size and constitution of the samples have a considerable impact on the interpretation of diversity measures in terms of production, so too do the attributes selected for investigation. At least four attribute systems of pottery can be identified that relate to production, as described above: resources, manufacturing technology, form, and decoration/style. (These and other attributes can be interpreted in other terms as well, of course.)

The point is that not all ceramic attributes can be expected to register diversity in a manner that is directly responsive to issues of production organization or specialization. Emphasis on attributes representing a combination of these systems (as opposed to simply typological categories) allows investigation of the *structure* of variability in pottery. This then provides a basis for further interpretations concerning productive arrangements and patterns of 'consumption' within or between societies. For example, it can be asked whether there is more variability or less in the attributes of resources, of form, or of decoration within or between the pottery categories of interest.

Are attributes of the resource and technological systems highly variable? Variability in resources, on the one hand, has to be interpreted in the context of knowledge of the 'ceramic environment': background information on the geological variability of the local environment and the availability of a variety of clay and temper sources. At the same time, there is a cultural element operative in terms of the *effective* 'ceramic environment': the potters' recognition and selection of few or many of the sources potentially available. Very limited diversity in the resource attribute system of a pottery collection may be interpretable in terms of restricted access to resources, and/or standardization of production activities, for example in clay or glaze preparation (see Peacock 1982:120–1 for discussion of Arretine manufacture; Rye and Evans [1976] and Wright [1983] discuss ethnographic Pakistani glaze preparation). With respect to technological attribute systems, which primarily involve forming and firing, the diversity of specific traits within this system relates to the general level of technological development (e.g., use of wheels versus hand-building), and the degree of standardization and/or mass production in the manufacturing process. A similar point of view was expressed by Shepard (1958:452):

> standardized wares and types may be considered products of pottery-making communities having well established techniques; classes that are variable in composition suggest that style was more widely established than technique; uniformity within a site may reflect self-sufficiency in pottery production; diversity may indicate a community depending in large measure on trade for its pottery. These explanations are without doubt glaring oversimplifications. There are other factors that must be weighed, especially exchange of

raw materials, potters of a community practicing a number of different techniques or passing through a period of experimentation, and different degrees of standardization in different centers.

Attributes of form may or may not be highly variable. If they are, variability in primary forms (shapes, usually in gross functional terms such as jar, bowl, etc.) is significant in terms of interpreting the variety of functions and activities among the archaeological contexts being compared (see Kohler 1978:29). Variability in secondary-form characteristics (lip or base variations, vessel dimensions, appendages), while usually partially functional, is perhaps more likely than primary variables to inform on production; extremely low diversity, for example, may be indicative of standardization and specialization. On the other hand, differences in rim form and size (of almost 2 cm) were noted within a single size-class of vessels produced by specialist potters in Rajasthan, India (C. Kramer, personal communication, 1984; see Solheim 1984 for a similar example from Thailand).

The decorative or stylistic attribute system is more removed from direct inferences of production and more complex in terms of its interpretation. Stylistic and decorative data are extremely sensitive to a broad range of social-interactional phenomena (e.g., Friedrich 1970; S. Plog 1980; see also the papers in Washburn 1983a) as well as to overall cultural changes, although perhaps less directly to the latter (see Adams 1979; Rice 1984). It is that very sensitivity which confounds their utility in interpretations restricted solely to productive arrangements. Thus, a clear one-to-one relationship between the degree of standardization, diversity, or elaboration in the decorative attribute system and the actual productive arrangements, especially intensiveness, is unlikely. This circumstance is hinted by Earle's comments on attached versus general specialists (1981) and Feinman *et al.*'s (1981) production step index.

In part, the anticipated greater variability in decorative attributes can be ascribed to the fact that styles carry information that is intended to be sent and received (Wobst 1977). This information (its content and diversity) may be more closely related to the context of use of the vessels (DeBoer and Moore 1982) or to the outside contacts of the makers (Dickens 1980), than to the actual production process *per se*. The point here is not that diversity measures are inappropriate for stylistic analysis; on the contrary, the complexity of styles and their components makes them attractive for diversity analyses. Rather, unless the stylistic information can be related directly to the production process, as through the actual gestures of painting, for example (Hagstrum 1985), style as measured by diversity (unlike the earlier correlation interaction analyses) does little to inform on productive location or organization.

Diversity, production, and use: some examples

Barton Ramie: temporal change and diversity

Diversity indices were used to investigate the structure of ceramic variability and production at Barton Ramie, a small lowland Maya site in Belize, Central America. The sherds from five ceramic complexes, spanning a time range from *c*. 900 B.C. to

Table 12.1. Diversity of slipped vs unslipped ceramic groups at Barton Ramie, Belize (by time phase)[a]

	Jenny Creek	Barton Creek	Hermitage	Tiger Run	Spanish Lookout
Slipped groups					
N groups	4	4	8	8	10
N sherds	2,351	5,562	8,927	16,604	41,532
H (richness)	0.87	0.94	1.58	1.23	1.60
e (evenness)	0.62	0.68	0.76	0.59	0.69
Unslipped groups					
N groups	2	2	4	3	3
N sherds	5,105	2,503	20,312	21,014	16,171
H (richness)	0.52	0.69	0.98	0.74	0.51
e (evenness)	0.75	1.00	0.71	0.67	0.46

[a] Phasing and classification from Gifford 1976; calculations of diversity from Rice 1981.

A.D. 900, had been classified into wares, groups, types, and varieties (Gifford 1976), the standard units in the type-variety system employed by Maya archaeologists. Variability between slipped (red, black, and polychrome) and unslipped utilitarian ceramics within each complex was compared by calculating richness and evenness values using H (Table 12.1; see also Rice 1981:224–5). Slipped groups showed a sine-wave or S-curve pattern of increasing richness and evenness from the Preclassic through the Early Classic, then a drop in the early part of the Late Classic, followed by a sharp rise. Unslipped pottery showed a different pattern, however. The richness of unslipped pottery was far lower than that of slipped (i.e., there were fewer classificatory units) in all periods; richness peaked in the Early Classic, then declined sharply. Evenness, in contrast, was generally higher than that of slipped groups (suggesting little selectivity or preference in use),

peaking in the Late Preclassic, after which it declined markedly through the Late Classic.

Because the individual typological units within slipped and unslipped categories are relatively heterogeneous units, subsuming a great deal of variation within them, the variability in form, decoration, and technological attributes within each group was investigated separately, complex by complex. Variability (or standardization) in these attribute systems was measured not by diversity indices, but rather by counting the number of identified modes and calculating the variants per 1,000 sherds of each type (Table 12.2). The sine-wave pattern of alternating increases and decreases from period to period continued to be evident, with generally much higher variability in the Preclassic than in the Late Classic.

These data were interpreted to mean that specialized manufacture (as evidenced by standardization) appeared earliest in paste technological variables and in elite wares; significant fluctuations occurred after utilitarian wares became standardized and mass-produced, when elite wares experienced increased elaboration and variability (Rice 1981:226–7).

Further consideration of these data called attention to the fact that, throughout the entire Barton Ramie sequence, form is less variable than technology, and decoration is far more variable than either form or technology. Unslipped vessels used in the generally conservative, non-display activities of food preparation were far less variable than any of the slipped categories (Rice 1984). These observations point to the need for investigation of each of the attribute subsystems of ceramics, because each behaves differently with respect to changing circumstances of production organization, and any one does not predict the patterning in any other.

Coastal Georgia: technological and resource diversity
The 'use-functional' roles of pottery are likely to be detectable through measurement of diversity. Braun's (1980) work with Navajo pottery suggests this to be the case, on the basis of variability in vessel (rim) form categories. Similar interpretations may

Table 12.2. Variability in attributes of technology, decoration, and form by time phase in ceramic groups at Barton Ramie, Belize (calculated as n types/1,000 sherds)[a]

	Technological variables				Decorative variables				Form variables			
	Unslip.	Red	Black	Poly.	Unslip.	Red	Black	Poly.	Unslip.	Red	Black	Poly.
Phase												
Jenny Creek	11.5	41	87	–	6.6	37.5	63.7	–	10	28	32.5	–
Barton Creek	27.5	11	50	–	7.3	100.4	148.5	–	8	6	20	–
Hermitage	8	15.5	22	33	0.4	110.1	35.3	126.4	5	8	5	7
Tiger Run	7.4	14	9.7	30	0.7	138.4	26.9	92	1	5	9	11
Spanish Lookout	13.9	5.5	14.5	4	0.5	10.0	91.9	324.4	2	2	6.5	4

[a] Phasing and classification from Gifford 1976; calculations from Rice 1981.

Table 12.3. *Diversity values for selected technological variables of pottery from Sapelo and St. Simons Islands, Georgia*[a]

	Total sample	Cord-marked	Check-stamped
Variables			
Degree of coring	0.66	0.34	0.49
Hardness (Mohs')	0.68	0.27	0.51
No. of classes of sand-sized particles	0.50	0.38	0.48
Fired color	0.90	0.62	0.87
N sherds	100	50	50

[a] Data taken from Saffer 1979, and Rice and Saffer 1981

be derived from technological characteristics as well. Samples of aboriginal pottery from the Georgia coast, consisting of 50 check-stamped sherds and 50 cord-marked sherds, were analyzed for a number of technological properties, including color, coring, hardness, porosity, thickness, size of aplastics, and proportion of aplastics (Saffer 1979). Differences between the two surface treatment categories of pottery were revealed by the H' diversity index (Rice and Saffer 1981). If the total sample of 100 sherds is considered, the total diversity is very high, but when the sample is separated by surface treatments the diversity values decrease; in the case of the cord-marked pottery the decreases are dramatic (Table 12.3).

The check-stamped pottery has lower porosity, thinner and harder walls, and less dark coring than does the cord-marked pottery. In addition, the two categories occur in different relative proportions in two contemporary structures at the site at which they were recovered, and were produced from different clays; check-stamped pottery was produced from coarse mainland clays, while cord-marked pottery was from finer marsh clays (Saffer 1979). Although the general level of cultural complexity of the late prehistoric inhabitants of the Georgia coast is not such that locus or producer specialization is any real possibility for production of these vessels, the possibility of resource specialization – selection of resources for functional properties – is likely, with check-stamped pottery used for (dry) storage and cord-marked for cooking or water storage.

Shipibo–Conibo: stylistic diversity

Examinations of stylistic behavior in a variety of media are calling attention to the ways styles 'function' in information transmission. Thus diversity analyses of ceramic stylistic variables call attention to questions of the relationship between diversity measurements and pottery use. Stylistic diversity in Shipibo–Conibo rim designs (measured by the frequency distribution procedure suggested by Kintigh [1984a]), revealed that vessels with greater public exposure have greater diversity (DeBoer and Moore 1982). Although the authors call this a 'significant correlation

which lacks a theoretical context' (DeBoer and Moore 1982:152), the homogeneity of decoration *within* compounds at least suggests a lack of messaging behavior that conforms to the predictions of Wobst (1977:323–5): stylistic behavior decreases between closely related individuals and is redundant. The diverse messages of the rim designs that operate at compound boundaries, however, are difficult to interpret and apparently do not signal compound affiliation.

As the authors note (DeBoer and Moore 1982:153), 'artifacts do not soak up style uniformly; rather they participate differentially in style and they do so on the basis of the social context in which they are used.' In terms of interpreting diversity measures of style in particular, as well as other attributes, it is clearly necessary to have some grasp of the context of recovery and use. It is also important to know the precise location of production because the portability of pottery both increases its geographical distribution and expands the contexts in which its messaging functions can operate.

Metepec: taxonomic and functional diversity

Another example, related to both use and production, comes from modern pottery in Metepec, a pottery-producing village in highland Mexico (Kirkpatrick 1977). Pottery vessels from six households were classified into six ceramic groups, of which three are locally produced and three are non-local products from other locations (i.e., 'tradewares' in archaeological parlance). The variable frequencies of the types are important in the context of family size and number of children (Table 12.4).

Comparisons between the richest and poorest of the households suggest significant differences that serve as cautions to archaeological interpretations (Rice and Saffer 1981). The wealthiest household, household L, has neither the largest number of vessels nor the largest number of 'tradewares.' This may be a telling point, given archaeologists' predilections for assuming that tradewares are signs of status. What the wealthiest household does exhibit is the highest diversity (richness) statistic (H') and the highest evenness statistic. Household L thus has both more different kinds of vessels and more equitable access to or acquisition of each of those kinds, than do any of the other households (see Kohler 1978:28–9 for a similar example at a plantation site in the Southeastern U.S.).

The non-locally manufactured Saraguato ceramic group is fairly abundant in virtually all Metepec households. This group is a functional complement to the locally made Teporingo group: Teporingo vessels are *ollas* and *cazuelas* used in cooking, while Saraguato vessels, made of clay with poor thermal stress resistance, are principally small drinking mugs. They tend to be common in households with children, and are broken and replaced frequently. Again, there is a caution to traditional archaeological interpretations: high frequency of at least one kind of non-local good in the Metepec households correlates not with status but with composition of the family and with formal functional specialization in village-level manufacture. This latter, at least in Metepec, reflects regional-level production adjustments to resources and recognition of their special properties.

Table 12.4. Diversity of ceramic inventories of six Metepec households[a]

| | Households | | | | | | | | | | |
| | Wealthy | | | | | | | | Poor | | |
	L		M		N		O		P		Q
Family size	10		9		3		6		9		8
Number of children	6		4		1		3		7		6
Ceramic group											
Local	No.	%	No.	%	No.	%	No.	%	No.	%	No.	%
Teporingo	19	30	68	71	31	84	6	19	20	48	11	31
Zacatuche	–	–	–	–	1	3	–	–	2	5	–	–
Marsopa	4	6	1	1	–	–	–	–	–	–	–	–
Non-local											
Coyotl	10	16	–	–	1	3	3	9	5	12	3	8
Saraguato	11	17	19	20	–	–	20	63	12	28	21	58
Cacomixtle	3	5	–	–	–	–	–	–	–	–	–	–
Other	17	26	8	8	4	10	3	9	3	7	1	3
Total	64		96		37		32		42		36
Diversity											
Richness	0.71		0.35		0.23		0.41		0.50		0.37
Evenness	0.92		0.51		0.32		0.67		0.80		0.69

[a] Data from Kirkpatrick 1977: Tables 10 and 14

Discussion and summary

The study of pottery production, especially specialization, is frequently pursued by describing the nature of variability in the pottery products and trying to interpret the structure of that variability in terms of the behavior that was responsible for it. The concept of diversity, a descriptive measure borrowed from population ecology, has increasingly been employed in these endeavors because it is oriented toward understanding the structure of large, complex data sets.

In the application of any mathematical construct, such as a diversity index, it is important to be aware of the underlying assumptions and the general requirements of the data sets to which the measure is directed. For purposes of studying diversity of pottery, the following criteria can be identified, and are summarized here in terms of their archaeological application.

(1) Diversity measures are based on assemblages (of vessels or sherds), and the objectives are usually comparative: comparing certain kinds of pottery from different sites, areas, or time periods to determine whether or not the assumptions of increasing standardization with respect to production hold true. The assemblage is divided on the basis of taxa (nominal levels of measurement) which must be: (a) mutually exclusive, (b) common to all assemblages that will be compared, and (c) equivalent and equally different. As an example, the pottery should be all type classes or form classes, not a mixture of both; similarly, hand-built and wheel-made pottery should not be combined into single classes.

(2) The sample size must be 'adequate,' and, although absolute sample-size requirements in archaeological applications of diversity measures cannot be specified, they are probably in the same range as in ecological studies. The best rule of thumb to use is that the sample size is adequate when the log-based distribution curve of frequencies of individuals in the observed classes, arranged from most to least frequent, would not be changed if additional classes were included through continued sampling (cf. Jones *et al.* 1983; Kintigh 1984a). Although the size will vary from situation to situation, I would hazard a guess that most archaeological pottery samples should consist of at least 30 individuals at a minimum, and 100 is probably a preferable number, depending on the number of significant classes of interest. Because diversity is a characteristic of large, complex assemblages, if the data sets consist of fewer than 30 sherds or whole pots, it is difficult to imagine that mathematical diversity measures are really of any utility in understanding the variability of the collection. In such small samples, other characteristics are likely to be more important and 'diversity' in an intuitive sense can be assessed by inspection and/or non-parametric statistics.

(3) There should be some real link between the samples or populations being compared, either temporal or geographical. It is inappropriate to select the ceramic products of widely disparate (temporally, geographically, or sociopolitically) societies in order to infer different degrees of productive specialization (see, for example, the 'levels' of diversity noted above: intra-community, between-habitat, and landscape). In addition, arguments can be made for the need to select archaeological samples representing approximately equal time spans

of occupation (Stark 1981:235; cf. Rice 1981:238).

(4) Ceramics may be characterized by a number of attribute systems, and diversity in any of these may or may not be a response to differences in production organization. Technological variables of composition and firing may be more sensitive registers of producer and resource specialization than are variables of form and decorative style. In all cases, breakage rates and contexts of use and recovery will be significant in confounding direct relationships between diversity and production.

Problems are inherent in both components of the production–diversity relationship. On the one hand, diversity indices are susceptible to sample-size effects and there is no agreement on precisely how to interpret them in ecology. On the other, the concept of specialization and how to treat it archaeologically has not been addressed satisfactorily. Models relating product standardization to the organization of production have not been widely or adequately tested, either with ethnographic or archaeological data, or with or without diversity indices. Different attribute systems of pottery will vary in their sensitivity to production organization, as opposed to use (including status, public visibility, function) or historical factors.

The study of pottery production is very much in a nascent stage, and diversity measures show considerable promise for illuminating the structure of variability in complex data sets. Until a larger corpus of relational propositions concerning variability and production organization can be verified, however, studies aimed at understanding production through diversity indices need to be very carefully designed in terms of choice and size of sample, and attributes analyzed.

Chapter 13

The use of diversity in stylistic analysis

Margaret W. Conkey

This chapter is concerned with the use of the concept of diversity and of diversity measures in the archaeological study of style. Two broad questions will be addressed: (1) How has the aspect of homogeneity and heterogeneity in style been treated, and how can we work towards a better theoretical framework for understanding why there is diversity in style? (2) How have different approaches in the archaeological study of style used diversity measures, and what kinds of problems have been encountered when we try to measure heterogeneity and homogeneity?

Given the number of us who have tried to use diversity both as a concept and as a measure in our archaeological inquiry into style, there are now enough examples to assess the state of the field. Although there have been abundant 'theories' of style in the archaeological literature of the past two decades (e.g., Binford 1962, 1965; Conkey 1978; Dunnell 1978; Friedrich 1970; Lechtman 1977; Sackett 1977, 1982; Wiessner 1983, 1984; Wobst 1977), an appraisal of how archaeologists have *used* style may be helpful, particularly if we are interested in understanding why diversity might occur in style. To a great extent, the uses of diversity in stylistic analysis exemplify problems and issues in the broader archaeological concept of diversity and its measurement. Thus, this review will hopefully contribute both to a rethinking of how archaeologists have used style and to the general topic of diversity in archaeological analysis.

Some historical background

The past two decades have been a time of heightened and explicit inquiry into theories of style and how to carry out stylistic analysis. Although the question of relative similarity and dissimilarity among archaeological assemblages has long been of concern to archaeologists, particularly as a way of inferring cultural units, it seems as if diversity has come to play an increasingly prominent role in stylistic analysis and interpretation (e.g., Braun 1977, 1985a; Conkey 1980; DeBoer and Moore 1982; Dickens and Chapman 1978; Kintigh 1984a; Rice 1981; Tainter 1977b, 1983). Following the Binfordian programmatics (e.g., 1962, 1965), stylistic analysis came to be considered a likely access route to understanding social variation; similarities and dissimilarities in stylistic attributes were thought to inform on social variation. Coupled with increasing experimentation with computer analysis of attribute data (e.g., Hill 1965; Longacre 1963), the 1960s approaches to style set the stage for what is a continuing debate and discussion over the use of measures of diversity in the archaeological study of style.

This section of the chapter will consider some general trends over the past two decades of archaeology that may have promoted the interest in diversity and how to measure it. The following is one possible historical pathway to a period in archaeology that has been marked by intellectual discussion and debate over stylistic analysis. One way to characterize this pathway is that the analysis of *pattern* came to be of central concern to contemporary archaeologists. With an emphasis on patterns as central to stylistic analysis, ways to characterize or describe patterns, such as with diversity indices, became increasingly of interest.

Because American archaeology has its roots in anthropology, we might be able to make a case for the archaeology of the 1960s having inherited and perpetuated a certain view of human material culture. That is, among the more general theoretical perspectives in anthropology, the archaeology of the 1960s drew more on the views of White than of Kroeber or of Boas. Kroeber, for example, considered material culture to be part of the on-going workings of human culture. Although Kroeber considered artifacts to be participants in cultural life, he did not believe that material traits were active in the sense held by some current theorists (e.g., Bourdieu 1977; Hebdige 1979; Hodder 1982, 1985): artifacts as agents with the potential to inform or constitute the cultural creation of social context.

It was not this Kroeberian view of artifacts as participants, but a view more akin to that of Leslie White that seems to have influenced archaeological concepts of artifacts in human life. It is well known and well cited (e.g., Binford 1965; Leone 1972; Martin 1971) that Binford and other new archaeologists of the 1960s were explicitly influenced by White's ideas on culture as an adaptive system, and on the concept of cultural evolution and its energetics (White 1949). The adaptive systems approach to culture became a core guiding concept of American archaeology. The concomitant perspective on material culture and artifacts, however, was that they were seen more as products than as participants; they were outputs of the human cultural system.

Coupled with this perspective on artifacts as coded products of cultural subsystems, there may have been an increasing emphasis on the study of artifacts as objects for scientific analysis, increasingly studied for themselves rather than as features or participants of wider cultural contexts. This shift to a 'more autonomous role for artifacts' involves what Miller has called (1983) a 'symbolic inversion.' That is, although objects began by standing for the prehistoric peoples we want to study, the people or 'cultures' (such as the Magdalenians, the Hopewell, the Hohokam) became *labels* for artifacts. It was the artifacts that became the immediate subjects of analysis.

Therefore, it is not surprising that many archaeologists became interested in how to measure homogeneity and heterogeneity as a way to characterize artifact assemblages, as a way to specify the nature of variation and patterns in archaeological data. These observations on archaeological analysis in general also apply to the archaeological studies of style.

Stylistic patternings in artifacts, usually measured by attribute patternings, were also conceived of as cultural products and as the output of cultural behaviors, comprising codes for us to read. Emphasis has thus been placed on strategies for recognizing patterns, in contrast to understanding in more detail why or how such patterns might have been generated. This emphasis comes from the assumption that patterns inform *us* about style, about its social contexts, and about its spatio-temporal distributions.

Sackett (1977, 1982) has been explicit about this concept of style: style is a passive aspect of material culture that speaks to us about such things as social groupings or ethnic geography. He advocates viewing style from the 'outside,' as an analyst; he wants to identify style, not explain it (1977:372).

This kind of concept of stylistic patterning is often confounded with the inquiry into style as a social or cultural process, into how style or stylistic behaviors or products worked, were recognized, generated, given meaning in, or indeed gave meaning to prehistoric social situations. Analysts of style (e.g., Wiessner 1984) often move back and forth in the same discussion between style as 'speaking' to us and 'having spoken to' past peoples.

The logic that allowed us to accept the idea that stylistic (or other) patterns are readable and can inform us about the past involves not only the implicit notion of material traits as cultural products, more than as participants, but also that these traits therefore reflect sociocultural phenomena, as material correlates. Once artifacts have been characterized in terms of their stylistic patternings, which may include observations on diversity of decoration or form, the observation is then said to *reflect* certain features of prehistoric life, such as the development of craft specialization or forms of social organization. For example, as is well known from the pioneering studies in the 1960s of stylistic patterning (e.g., Hill 1970, originally 1965), a particular pattern of variation in ceramic decorations was taken to reflect the prehistoric practice of matrilocality.

Of course it was Binford who had the greatest influence on the actual analysis of style in archaeological materials (e.g., 1962, 1965). The Binfordian directive emphasized the search for what he called formal variability (more properly stated, it would be formal variation). His concept of style stressed the formal variability that relates to the social context of manufacture or use, other than that related to function (Binford 1965:208). Since 1965, style has primarily been defined in terms of formal variability in material culture.

A succeeding concept of style that challenged some of the Binfordian premises still retained a definition that focused on formal variability: 'formal variability in material culture that can be related to the participation of artifacts in processes of information exchange' (Wobst 1977:321). Unfortunately, the notion that style is neither equivalent nor reducible to formal variation has often been overlooked; much stylistic analysis has been carried out as if style and formal variation were equivalent.

Given persistent views that attributes of formal variability were the archaeological correlates of past human behavior, and the directive that we search for and demonstrate the nature of variability, the stage was set for the continued archaeological interest in how to measure homogeneity and heterogeneity. It follows that archaeologists would be attracted to the use of diversity measures that characterize or describe formal variability as well as make a relative or comparative statement about that variability.

In general then, the emphasis has primarily been on how to recognize and describe patterns (pattern-recognition) and how these patterns reflect social variation. In retrospect, we see that this emphasis has been at the expense of inquiry into how or why patterns came into existence in the first place (pattern-generation). It is therefore not surprising that we are still working on a substantive theory of material culture, of style in human life, and on why diversity might occur in style.

Before turning to a discussion of differing approaches to style and to the use of diversity measures, this next brief section will add one more aspect of the intellectual context from which these differing approaches sprang. Here we should consider the general context of anthropological archaeology.

The general archaeological context of stylistic analysis

As was suggested above in the discussion on the influence of Leslie White in American archaeology of the 1960s, it was a systemic concept of culture that most obviously linked White to Binford. Ultimately, many stylistic analyses and their approaches to diversity can be shown to be rooted in the concept of culture as a system. At the core of this concept was the assumption that 'differences and similarities between different classes of archaeological remains reflect different subsystems [of culture]' (Binford 1965:203). These different subsystems (e.g., subsistence, social) were expected to have differing archaeological correlates, which could be isolated by the archaeological analyst primarily by a heightened sensitivity to recognizing the nature and the sources of variation in archaeological remains.

Thus, there were at least two arguments that directed archaeological attention to the search for variability: (1) that culture should be considered as a multivariate phenomenon, so that the nature of its operation and changes could not be reduced to changes in or persistence of a single variable, such as ideas (about how to make or do things) (Binford 1965): and (2) that 'classes or items are articulated differently within an integrated system, hence the pertinent variables with which an item is articulated, and exhibit concomitant variation are different' (Binford 1962:220). These systemic assumptions reinforced the notion that patterns in archaeological data are coded information about variability in past cultural systems (Clarke 1968). They resulted in a methodological dissection of culture into subsystems, with their archaeological correlates: function and style were separated, as were the technical, the social, the ideological. The methodological guidelines were to isolate relevant variables and to partition one's observational fields (Binford 1962, 1965).

In general this concept of culture promoted the view that stylistic patterns in archaeological data reflected social phenomena. The analysis of style, or at least of formal variability, was highly valued and given research priority because social groupings, such as post-marital residence units, must have been reflected by certain kinds of patternings in material culture. Thus, we could 'know' prehistoric social life. This is archaeology-as-anthropology, or 'ceramic sociology' (Sackett 1977), and it was a hallmark of a particularly exciting and optimistic period in archaeology. Given that stylistic expression carries information about social relations and social affiliations, then ways to recognize and characterize stylistic expression were the necessary pathway to identifying these past social relations.

The 1970s saw the rise of what was called processual analy-

sis, and archaeology was promoted (and given relevance) as 'diachronic anthropology' (e.g., F. Plog 1973). However, in retrospect it appears that a synchronic framework prevailed, even in studies that hoped to be processual. Rather than seeking *how* the observed patterns in archaeological data were generated in a particular context, patterns were taken as givens at particular points in time. They were seen as patterns to be recognized and characterized.

When diversity measures were used to characterize patterns of this sort, such measures were primarily typological in application. Diversity in ceramic production, for example, would be used to characterize a certain type of society in contrast to another type; how or why diversity came into existence or why it was minimal were infrequently addressed processual questions. Although the systems perspective gave us the concept of 'trajectory,' this concept was more often used to give readings of serial events or decontextualized patterns than to provide processual histories (Lathrap 1983:37). Particularly in studies attempting stylistic analysis with diachronic intentions (e.g., Braun 1977; Rice 1981), it has more often been the case that patterns have been characterized for different periods or synchronic slices, and these characterizations have then been compared.

Ultimately, much of the archaeological use of diversity measures, as one attractive way to characterize sets of archaeological data, derives from the strong *comparative* approach of an archaeology that has been explicitly evolutionary, or at least *transformational* in its underpinnings. Diversity measures depend upon viable typologies (e.g., Braun 1985a; Conkey 1980), and they provide comparable units. Diversity is, by definition, a *relative* measure: certain assemblages can be characterized as more (or less) heterogeneous. Furthermore, the use of comparable units promotes empirical generalizations. Although empirical generalizations are now most strongly criticized by anti-positivists, they are not necessarily a 'problem to be avoided' (Wuthnow *et al.* 1984:257) or an interpretive mode to be rejected (as Binford has often claimed, e.g., 1972). Empirical generalizations are probably impossible to avoid in archaeology, but what needs more attention, perhaps, is that such generalizations 'are not objective but mediated by culture; empirical facts are "known" only through the filtering lens of available language' (Wuthnow *et al.* 1984:257; see also Hodder 1985:22 for some good examples of changes in available language in archaeology). The 'available language' and the models of culture change that have primarily been served by the use of diversity measures in archaeology and in stylistic analysis are what Dunnell (1980) has referred to as *transformational*. That is, the question of homogeneity and heterogeneity in style have primarily been addressed through the lens of transformational models of culture change. Following a discussion of different approaches to style and how diversity has been used by them, this underlying transformational preference will be addressed further.

Differing approaches to the study of style and uses of diversity

The archaeological study of style is of continuing prominent interest although a single concept of style itself is not agreed upon: 'the very definition of style remains elusive and continues to exasperate many archaeologists; style is a perfect black box: its works are omnipresent; its internal workings remain problematic' (DeBoer and Moore 1982:147; see also Wobst 1977).

The past two decades of stylistic studies have been a time of examination, re-examination, evaluation, reconsideration, challenge, and refinement (e.g., Sackett 1982). I have no pretensions to clarify the concept of style here, if there even exists *a* concept of style for archaeological research. In discussing how diversity measures have been used in some stylistic analyses, I have to take into consideration that there have been varying concepts of style and underlying associated assumptions. Our notions of why stylistic diversity occurs and why it is interesting have depended upon our definition(s) of style and on our models of how social and other contextual factors may have been at work. However, given the continuation of a historical trajectory of controversy and debate over concepts of style, it is not surprising that we have not yet agreed upon or come to understand *why* heterogeneity or homogeneity might occur in style.

The following discussion finally gets to the substance of this chapter; I hope to illuminate some particular ways in which stylistic studies have used diversity measures. I hope this will lead to some insights into the basic assumptions about style and about the meaning of diversity. Although I would like to avoid the explicit grouping of stylistic studies in terms of types or 'schools' of stylistic analysis as is often done (e.g., the normative, the iconological), the discussion will tend to group stylistic studies of diversity that proceed from similar assumptions and analytical emphases. Such a review should highlight both the theoretical and methodological challenges of understanding diversity in style and its cultural significance.

Normative assumptions in stylistic analysis

In the early 1960s, Lewis Binford brought an explicit rejection of the normative view of culture into the archaeological literature (e.g., 1965). In his opinion, this view reduced the operation of culture to the single variable of shared norms or ideas about how to do things. However, despite Binford's proclamations against normativism in archaeological inquiry, no archaeological concept or analysis of style is without some normative underpinnings. Rather than making explicit and direct reference to the very general source of 'shared ideas about how to do things,' we have shifted our terms for the source(s) of style to somewhat more particular social, systemic, or processual phenomena, such as social interaction (e.g., S. Plog 1978) or social comparison (e.g., Wiessner 1984).

Two basic normative assumptions have not gone away, particularly if we agree that style is, at its base, how things are done. These two assumptions stress that learning is how things are passed on between generations (enculturation), and diffusion is how things are transmitted between individuals and social units (acculturation). Neither assumption says anything about the hows or whys of such phenomena, and we have certainly attempted more precise and detailed explanations for such phenomena as people coming to decorate ceramic rim sherds in an increasingly similar way (e.g., Braun 1985a, 1985b; Braun and Plog 1982); that is, why diffusion and of what sort?

Given the powerful influence of the rejection of normativism, it is rare to find explicitly normative studies in archaeology, in the sense that the source for observed or hypothesized changes is thought to reside in changes in *ideas* about how to do or make things. One such rare example, which also happens to employ diversity anlaysis, is that by Dickens (1980; Dickens and Chapman 1978; Dickens and Fraser 1984). This is a study of diversity in the surface finish on some assemblages of ceramics from archaeological sites of the Woodland 'South Appalachian ceramic province.' Dickens uses a gene-flow analogy to set up his asumptions and analysis. That is, he assumes that at times of increased contact and exchange among groups, new ideas are expected and expressed, including ideas about how to make pots.

However, in evaluating Dickens' use of diversity in style to make inferences about culture change, the weaknesses of the study cannot be attributed so much to the underlying basic normative assumption that changing ideas about surface finish are due to increased contact and could lead to diversity in manufacturing. Rather, it is the methods used and the way in which inferences are drawn, particularly with regard to what diversity might mean, that illustrate some current problems.

First, the assessment of whether the expected increase (and then decrease) in diversity took place considers only one attribute (surface finish). Secondly, as the author is well aware, the sample size is a problem, in that ceramics from only 17 sites over a 2000-year time period are considered. As with some of the 1960s' studies of ceramic-design variation that did not yet control for sampling at several sites and for the sample formation processes, Dickens is faced with the persistence of these constraints. Given such limits on what the analytical methods allow, the resulting sociocultural implications must be questioned. These are not only sweeping, but apparently assumed before the analysis was undertaken.

That is, it was assumed that there *was* an apogee of (and then a decrease in) Hopewellian contact and interaction. The changing diversities noted in surface finish were then used to support the interpretation of an increase (and then a decrease) in interaction. As is often the case with stylistic studies, there was not much attention to alternative hypotheses, either of the cultural trajectory or concerning the sources of the observed change in surface finish. Diversity measures on ceramic-surface finish were said to support the very general notion that this was a dynamic cultural context; accompanying the changing ideas about surface finish were unspecified changing ideas about social relations and ideological concepts.

This study is an example of how easily a speculative leap can be made, a leap from the very specific level for which diversity is shown to the very general level of sociocultural processes that are inferred to be 'causing' such diversity. And, as is the case with many stylistic studies that depend upon differences in diversity, there is no real consideration as to why the particular attribute (surface finish) would so easily be varied in a contact situation, either in its manufacture or in its use. That is, the author does not make any compelling linkages between the particular attribute and the historical context of contact and 'idea pools.' The study is thus *de*contextualized; there are no clues as to why or how diversity in the surface finish of ceramics was meaningful in this given prehistoric context.

Style from the perspective of social interaction

As archaeologists have tried to specify the sources for stylistic variation, some have turned to social interaction (e.g., S. Plog 1978, 1983). Social interaction still rests upon an implicit recognition of the normative component of style, but this component is conceived of in more active or processual terms: as enculturation and/or acculturation. Furthermore, because there is explicit concern for the contexts in which learning or being exposed to 'other ways of doing things' takes place, there is recognition that these contexts can be varied – ranging from the household to the so-called regional interaction sphere. Thus, there can be different levels of stylistic patterning.

In investigating the social-interaction dimension of style, the variation in material culture or the increase/decrease in diversity is not easily reduced to a single broad inclusive variable such as changing ideas. For example, in Braun's earliest work on diversity in style (1977), using Illinois Woodland ceramics, he assumed that, if ceramic design attributes become less diverse through time, it could be a supralocal interaction process that was responsible for the diversity. More specifically, he hypothesized this process to be one of more contact and integration among previously localized units, which might be called 'tribalization' (see also Braun and Plog 1982).

If one takes the view that stylistic variability is 'symptomatic' (as does Sackett 1977:370), another way of phrasing the relation between diversity and tribalization would be that the decrease in diversity reflects tribalization. Although the kinds of contexts within which diversity might change are somewhat better specified, there remains a failure to make linkages between contexts and stylistic changes. With the advantage of hindsight, we can now point out that diversity could easily be used as a way of avoiding specifying the exact sorts of stylistic changes we might expect under the particular local and historical conditions we were investigating (see Braun 1985b for an attempt at revising his study along these latter lines).

The now classic study of style in terms of social interaction is Margaret Hardin Friedrich's ethnoarchaeological analysis (Friedrich 1970; see also Hardin 1983). Although she did not employ diversity concepts or measures, she was concerned with decorative variability and the contexts within which stylistic similarities and differences occur. Furthermore, her study strongly influenced later studies that do use diversity both as a general concept (e.g., Washburn 1977; 1983a) and as a statistical measure (e.g., Conkey 1980).

Consistent with, and going beyond, the emphasis on the vague notion of formal variability as the essence of style, Hardin argued for analysis of decorated artifacts in terms of design structure, which she employed to replace style as the analytical framework. She argued for a more structural and hierarchical approach than that used by early 'ceramic sociologists' (e.g., see Longacre,

Hill, Deetz and others in Binford and Binford 1968), which focused on the correlation of patterns in design-element distributions and social networks.

Her major finding does not, however, contradict the underlying assumptions of the social-interaction approach. What she found is that design *structure*, more than design elements, reflects potters' interaction patterns and their intensity. The structural approach, which involves the identification of coding and decoding strategies of those making the artifacts, does promote analytical consideration of at least the technological and operational processes that brought the artifacts into existence. For example, with Hardin's ceramic analysis, there is concern for the spatial divisions of the vessel in the decorative process, and with the rules for the selection and placement of design elements. The basic assumption of stylistic analysis as symptomatic of social interaction is, however, retained, in that Hardin sought design correlates for socially interacting units, and she attempted to 'read' design structure to measure social patternings.

The continued emphasis on formal variability and the extension of this into an emphasis on design structure has the potential to remove the study of patterns even further from the particular contexts within which patterns were generated and used. Many design-structure studies suffer from the same concern expressed above in regard to Dickens' study. That is, there is rarely attention to why diversity might be expected not just in the particular context, but also in the particular class of material culture (such as ceramics or engraved bones) and in those attributes (e.g., rim designs or surface finish) selected for measurement.

This decontextualization, which inhibits access to the meaning of diversity, is perhaps due to the way that cross-cultural and general principles about the sources and meanings of diversity are invoked. Is it really and often the case that we can expect the degree of contact to covary directly with stylistic patterning in such objects as engraved bones or decorated cooking pots, objects that happen to be archaeologically abundant? Is it so highly probable that, with more individuals, with longer site occupation, or with more visitors to a site, diversity in the formal variability of almost anything will increase?

Because style has been assumed to be passive and reflective of social demography and social interaction, diversity measures tend to be used as symptomatic indicators. One criticism worth thinking about is that, in using diversity measures or notions of stylistic similarity in these ways, we have only generated what appears to be a more sophisticated version of the fossil-director approach. This approach employs typical objects or groups of artifacts as indicators for past cultures or culture groups. Instead of using diagnostic artifact types (e.g., Clovis points) to reflect or define a pasture culture for us, the relative amount of diversity in certain sets of archaeological data reflects or defines certain broad sociocultural phenomena of the past, such as tribalization or social aggregation.

Just as we have not made it particularly clear why one form of pot should be an index of a particular culture, it is not often made clear why diversity in certain artifacts or attributes should have been meaningful in a social context of tribalization, aggregation, or the like. That is, even given a passive notion of style, we need to argue much more clearly for the processes that produce a specific kind of diversity.

Style as active

Although they are very much rooted in the idea that style has something to do with social interaction and contexts of social proximity and distance, there are other approaches to style that are predicated on a more active concept. Here, for example, style is more than just the way certain things are done and more than enculturation or acculturation; style has a function in human cultural life. The first explicit developments of this concept of style specify the function of style to be in the domain of cultural communication and information systems (e.g., Conkey 1978; Wiessner 1983; Wobst 1977); these systems are, of course, the essence of situations of inter- and intracultural social contact and interaction.

Certain classes of material culture are thought to be invested with iconic style as a means of transmitting symbolically encoded information about ethnic affiliation and identity to various target populations (after Sackett's summary 1982). To a certain extent, there is an expanded approach to style here, which conceives of style as more than formal variability or design structure; art and decorative behavior are viewed as functioning in communication (e.g., Lathrap 1983) or social marking (e.g., Braun 1985a).

The analytical appeal of the more active concept of style has been that there have been direct and explicit expectations put forth on how the analyst can identify style in archaeological materials. At least three of the core expectations can be easily related to the use of diversity measures. Given these expectations, the use of diversity measures and concepts seems particularly appropriate. There is the expectation that (1) stylistic messages or elements will be consistent or standardized; (2) styles should be *unevenly* distributed over material culture, and those classes (or attributes) of material culture considered to be active or signalling are of a certain sort, which is related to (3) the role that these artifacts play in processes of information exchange. Thus, for example, this kind of active, signalling, or 'iconic' style is expected to be manifest in those artifacts with a high visibility, in order to maximize their being seen by the intended target population (after Wobst 1977).

With such expectations, it is easy to see why a measure of diversity is appealing: diversity is a comparative characteristic, and style can be comparatively scaled with the concept of diversity (DeBoer and Moore 1982:151). However, there are certain problems with the ways in which diversity measures and statistics have been brought into stylistic analysis. The next section will address some of these problems.

Some problems in the use of diversity measures

Some archaeologists have come to recognize the possibility that style is not simply a passive outcome of social processes but is often an active part of social process. Many have specified that the kind of social processes most likely to involve stylistic phenomena

are those relating to communication and information exchange. Coincidentally, one statistic for measuring diversity in archaeological assemblages that has been widespread in ecology and popular in archaeology is characterized as an 'information' statistic. Although the 1960s work on homogeneity (e.g., Deetz 1965) did try out quite a few ways to measure diversity, none of the measures were borrowed from ecology. Instead of elaborating on the general problems of applying statistics developed in other fields, such as plant ecology, to archaeological collections (see Keene 1983), this consideration of diversity measures will address some of the specific problems of the 'information statistic' and why complementary or alternative measures have recently been introduced into archaeology.

The 'information statistic' is also known as the Shannon–Weaver information index, which was originally proposed as a measure of the information content of a code; or, 'of the information content per symbol of a code composed of s kinds of discrete symbols whose probabilities of occurrence are $p_1, p_2, \ldots p_s$' (Pielou 1977:298). The Shannon index measures the diversity per individual in a population which includes many species, but it is based on the assumption that the population being sampled is infinitely large. That is, the communities are 'infinite in the sense that removing samples from them causes no perceptible change in them' (Pielou 1975:10).

Although widely used in all sorts of archaeological analysis (e.g., Freeman 1981; Peebles 1972; Tainter 1977b; Yellen 1977), the fact that the Shannon index is 'valid only for an infinite population' (Peet 1974:293) is almost never addressed (but see Rothschild n.d.a., who feels uncomfortable with the assumption). Whether or not archaeological collections meet this assumption, or even whether this matters, needs to be addressed if the statistic is to be used in archaeology. In fact, one of the general problems of borrowing, adopting, or developing new statistics is that different methods have different properties, different assumptions, and different effects on data. An example of this will be given below, where results from the Shannon statistic are compared to results from another diversity statistic (Simpson's), when both are applied to the same data. Too infrequently, the different underlying assumptions and expected effects on data are not made explicit in the archaeological use of statistics and measures.

Given the intellectual affinities of anthropological archaeology with the systems approach of the 1960s and 1970s, it is easy to see why a measure of 'information' or 'entropy' has been attractive. Some applications of the measure, however, have been as a 'direct, not even as an analogical, indicator of entropy and information, such as in Tainter's use (1977b) of the Shannon index. In his study of Woodland mortuary practices in prehistoric Illinois, Tainter uses the statistic as a way to measure directly not only the amount of organization or entropy of past sociocultural systems, but also the comparative degree of organization among them, which can then be used to imply certain evolutionary or developmental stages in the course of cultural transformations.

More recently, Tainter (1983) has criticized and reinterpreted Braun's early study (1977) of Woodland ceramic stylistic diversity. Again, Tainter takes the position that we must take seriously – and not just analogically or heuristically – the information–theoretic implications of the Shannon information function. Given that the concept of information in information theory is 'closely related to the concepts of entropy and organization,' Braun's analysis, Tainter argues, '*directly* measures changes in the organization of Woodland ceramic design distributions' (1983:153, emphasis added).

That is, Braun's diversity indices for the Middle–Late Woodland transition indicate increasingly organized ceramic design systems. Thus, *if* one accepts the assumption that ceramic designs function to convey social information (Braun 1977:117–22; 1985a), 'then the patterns he [Braun] observed would seem to signal some fundamental change in inter-community relations' or 'increasing organizational stringency in local-level symbolic systems' (Tainter 1983:153). This kind of interpretation elevates the inference of ceramic-design diversity to the level of a description of the amount or organization and information not just in the ceramic design systems but in the 'local-level symbol systems.' In ecology, where the Shannon index has been widely used and discussed, there is great debate as to whether this diversity index (H) is a suitable measure of ecological diversity (e.g., Hill 1973; Pielou 1977:293–9, especially 298). To the ecologist who has worked extensively with measures of diversity (Pielou 1966, 1969, 1975, 1977), the fact that this index is said to measure information or entropy is beside the point.

Although it is 'mathematically interesting' that Shannon's (and Simpson's) index measures entropies (of different orders), resemblances between codes or messages and communities or ecological collections 'are only superficial' (Pielou 1975:10). Put more strongly, both information and entropy are fashionable words that have been 'bandied about out of their proper context (the mathematical theory of information) and have led to false analogies' (Pielou 1977:298).

In actually carrying out a stylistic analysis that produces some understanding of the homogeneity and heterogeneity of archaeological materials, we find at least two recurring problems which must be considered before we approach any literature for statistical formulae to apply to archaeological data. Although archaeologists have tried to measure diversity in a number of ways, the simplest measure has been to assess the number of different classes of items represented in a collection, especially when compared with another collection. And although this is a pretty reasonable way to start out, Kintigh (1984a) reminds us there are immediate archaeological problems which may not be soluble with statistics developed in other fields or that have underlying assumptions about infinite populations.

These are the issues of significance: (1) whether one distribution is significantly more diverse than another and (2) the relative sizes of the samples, since we usually try to compare archaeological units with collections of different size. In addition, we have only recently become more aware of the effect that a variety of formational and sampling processes can have on apparent diversity (e.g., Graves 1981). It may be a mark of the development or maturation of diversity studies in archaeology that we are now turning to these more fundamental issues and seeking archaeological solutions, rather than continuing to rely on only the equivocal ecological literature and derived sociocultural implications.

Kintigh's recent work (1984a, this volume) has addressed the first two of these issues (significance and sample size), using, in part, engraved bone and antler assemblages that I had analyzed using diversity measures (Conkey 1980). This study constituted an attempt to support the hypothesis that a particular Upper Paleolithic site in Spain had been an aggregation site for otherwise-dispersed hunter–gatherers. In other studies addressing these issues, Braun (1985a, b) is explicitly reconsidering his own original (Braun 1977) and subsequent (Braun and Plog 1982) analyses. Here he is giving more attention to the inferences derived from the diversity measures than, as Kintigh has done, to the measures or statistical attributes of the assemblages. Although Braun admittedly finds that his original analysis gave us only a 'low resolution picture of regional social dynamics,' it was there (and in other studies) that some persistent features of the use of diversity measures in stylistic analysis were apparent.

First, although specific sets of expectations are usually laid out as to the relative diversity expected (in a class or attribute of material items), these are often stated in terms of quite broad sociocultural circumstances. For example, Braun predicts that if localization (i.e., social isolation) was occurring, then the diversity values (for certain ceramic rim-sherd decorative attributes) for each locality should decrease, although such values should *not* decrease (and should maybe even increase) at the regional level, as a whole (Braun 1985a:27).

In my analysis of diversity among engraved bone and antler assemblages from Magdalenian sites of north-coastal Spain, certain expectations were also generated regarding the relative diversity of assemblages *if* one site (Altamira) had been used as a regional aggregation site (Conkey 1980:616). Similarly, Rice (1981) spells out specific expectations regarding diversity if a certain model had obtained for the evolution of craft specialization in Maya ceramic production. Despite our own disclaimers and cautionary points about the fact that our 'present bridging concepts lack sufficient precision to deal with such issues' (Braun 1985a:32) as the details of local and supralocal networks, aggregation and dispersion settlement patterns or the evolution of craft specialization, we inevitably appeal to such issues for our starting assumptions and our closing inferences.

It is not often enough that alternative generative sources for any observed increase or decreases in diversity are explored. To draw again from the Braun example (1985a), the noted diversity decrease is accounted for in terms of some kind of cultural convergence among rim-decorators, but Braun does not make a convincing argument as to why only convergence is at work here. What other, and perhaps more specific, processes might also account for what specific changes in rim decoration? What other contextual features of the site, of the location of which sherds within the site, might be observed and related to decreases in diversity? Here is where more refined understanding of sample formation processes might also affect diversity results.

Finally, as with the less theoretically developed analyses

(e.g., Dickens 1980), there is still relatively little concern with why things like ceramic rim-sherd designs on cooking pots, or surface finish, should reflect or constitute social proximities and relative social 'connectedness.' Although we make assumptions that the decoration of so-called domestic vessels or individually transported bone and antler artifacts *should* be affected by factors that are social and that structure the 'contexts of visibility' (Braun 1985a:33), we have not yet developed the social and material culture theory to justify these notions further. We have also *not* worked enough on the particular historical record or wider contextual features of the very archaeological situation we are concerned with for 'clues' or substantiation of these assumptions (see Lathrap 1983 for some ethnoarchaeological perspectives).

These problems suggest that, in addition to recognizing that style is often more than a passive outcome of social processes and that it is an active part of social process, we must also address our case studies in more detail. That is, we must determine the specific context in which diversity is studied, and we need to develop models of social and stylistic processes appropriate to that context. It may be that the root of at least some of the persistent problems in diversity studies and stylistic analysis that have inhibited the development of such models has been the current underlying models about cultural change. The next section will return to the idea that the transformational models of culture change have been a particular problem in our diversity studies.

Transformational approaches

At the same time that social-interactional approaches to style have spawned the more active, iconic, and information-theory framework for stylistic analysis, many social-interactional studies have retained the view that style is reflective of past sociocultural phenomena, such as of social demography or social relations. Many social-interactional studies are also transformational studies. That is, those sociocultural phenomena that are reflected, such as tribalization or craft specialization, are part of underlying schemes about cultural evolution, which take the form of progressive transformations (see Dunnell 1980 for elaboration). Concepts and measures of diversity, variability, elaboration, or standardization are primarily used as part of a methodological repertoire to identify features or events of 'system-evolution,' or of a sequential model of cultural transformation from simple to complex. Our own inherent high cultural value on diversity, as well as its long-standing association with the progressive evolution of 'simple to complex' have certainly provided the transformational roots of most studies.

The most explicit and critical treatment of the persistence of the transformational approach in archaeology is that by Dunnell (1980). He argues that archaeology has retained the social–philosophical and transformational, rather than the scientific, selectionist, evolutionary paradigm. Given that cultural evolution sees evolution as a particular history, and evolutionary theory as a set of abstractions about that history, stages or other similar typological concepts are a 'natural outcome' (Dunnell 1980:45–6). In stylistic studies, as in archaeology as a whole, we have produced and contributed to extrapolations from the course of history that

point to a general progression, and, more seriously, without clear causative mechanisms for such an evolution (Dunnell 1980:45).

It was the programmatics of the new archaeology that advocated strongly a change in the kinds of explanations sought – from empirical generalizations about particular histories and events to the *processes* that account for the occurrences of these histories and the generalizations we make about them. However, Dunnell argues (1980:76) that theoretical developments in archaeology have not (yet) gone in this direction. Furthermore, because the definition of culture and the approach to cultural analysis were both considered within the systemic framework, a certain other kind of explanation was produced. That is, what prevails has been the more functional explanation of the sort associated *not* with the selective evolutionary models of biology, but with the transformational, evolutionary models of social philosophers. Thus, Dunnell characterizes archaeological inquiry as directed by the combination of a functional framework with assumptions that emphasize progress and a focus on a particular history, stages, and a transformational view of change (Dunnell 1980).

Some examples of studies that use diversity concepts and that depend upon some sort of underlying transformational assumptions include Braun (1977), Dickens (1980), Rice (1981), Rothschild (n.d.a), and Tainter (1977b). Most of these date to early stages of experimentation with large data sets, formal statistical diversity measures, and processual questions. Examples of underlying transformational assumptions or empirical generalizations include the notions that relative richness of burials should be defining criteria of social complexity (e.g., Rothschild n.d.b; Tainter 1977a, b); that variety and elaboration in ceramics ought to be correlates of social status and also correlates of the evolution, by stages, of craft specialization (e.g., Rice 1981); or that system evolution, as a whole, is characterized by a changing trajectory in the diversity of material culture, from general variability, to standardization, to local instances of elaboration and diversity (Rathje 1975). As guiding and/or as resulting assumptions, these do not get us very far toward explaining, in causative terms, the general processes or conditions that underlie diversity in style and material culture; nor do they contribute much to explaining the particular instance or situation being investigated.

For example, in Rice's (1981) trial model for the evolution of specialization of pottery production, in which she uses diversity measures to assess relative standardization and variability, we can see two of the problems of inherently transformational models and of the use of diversity measures in such models. At the more theoretical level, there is the implication that the empirical generalizations drawn from the particular case study constitute a set of abstractions that, in turn, support a general progressive model of evolutionary history.

Both Adams (1981:227–8) and Davis (1981:228–30) appropriately question this aspect of her study, suggesting that she tries to promote a general model that is of wider applicability than to the particular historical context from which it was derived. 'Social stratification sometimes involves craft specialization..., but this is hardly a necessary or universal relationship' (Davis 1981:230). Davis has also identified the methodological weakness of serving a transformational paradigm: 'reasoning from preconceived theory to archaeological fact, paradoxically, the theory seems to be in turn founded upon a narrow reading of a particular set of archaeological facts' (Davis 1981:230). Because the concepts underlying Rice's trial model are 'not generalizable,' it is difficult to assess its 'test.'

With regard to the concepts and measures of diversity, there are some of the same persistent concerns. Expectations are set out, in terms of degree of standardization and diversity, for the different steps along the progressive continuum of development towards craft specialization. Although the statistics, such as the *H* diversity measure, can describe a state of relative diversity or standardization, the ultimate causes of theses particular states cannot be specified without some specific theoretical roots as to *why* diversity or standardization might occur. Nor can the particular states of diversity or standardization be necessarily linked to the presence or absence of specialization without the underlying transformational assumptions that somehow link diversity, standardization, and specialization in some predictable relationship. The question of the study cannot really be answered: that is, how do we actually identify specialization? One response to the Rice article suggests that, in the study of specialization, 'only the historical investigation of the *meaning* of what is made [ceramics or otherwise] will be revealing' (Davis 1981:230).

As with most other analyses in the service of transformational models, the Rice study also exhibits the commonly large gap between the observed diversity and the level of sociocultural phenomena invoked to account for such a pattern. For example, the author describes a phase in which ceramic forms were becoming 'slightly standardized,' although a wide range of technological characteristics and decorative styles still obtain, suggesting a 'lack of pressure toward conformity, a variety of acceptable styles or personal tastes, and probably a large number of producers' (Rice 1981:226). To account for this phase, she appeals to extremely broad sociocultural phenomena of the Late PreClassic Period. This is characterized as a period of 'population growth,' 'land shortage,' and 'general social stress.' One response to this kind of stress may have been for a greater number of people to enter the pottery business, especially producing low-value/high-consumption goods (Rice 1981:225).

The linkages among social stress, more producers, and the nature of variation in what they produced are not made. Why would it be the case that more people began producing pots, and how would one support this? And why would the particular patterns of diversity have been meaningful in these given social contexts?

Because diversity measures are relative and comparative, because they are used to describe or characterize not just patterns in archaeological data but also the sociocultural phenomena assumed to have caused them, despite the lack of bridging arguments, they are particularly amenable to being used in the service of the comparative, typological, transformational models of cultural evolution that have prevailed in archaeological research. But how might we restructure our inquiry, particularly in the archaeological study of style? The next section tries to address this question.

Expanding the conceptual framework

As a prelude to some comments on where we might most productively direct our attention, I will summarize two case studies. First, there is DeBoer and Moore's interesting attempt (1982) to measure and interpret stylistic diversity, using an explicitly active or iconic approach to style. They study an ethnoarchaeological situation and use the simulation measure developed by Kintigh (1984a, this volume) that is designed to deal with some of the statistical issues that characterize archaeological collections. Secondly, I will review some recent developments in my own attempt to use diversity measures and concepts in stylistic analysis (Conkey 1980, 1981b, 1982; see also Kintigh 1984a, this volume).

In their ethnoarchaeological study of some Shipibo–Conibo ceramics, DeBoer and Moore (1982) suggest that the social contexts of ceramic use can be related, on an ordinal scale, to the degree of public exposure, that is, to visibility. They ask: how does the style of rim designs relate to the social context of vessel use? As a measure of diversity they use Kintigh's simulation approach (1984a), and conclude that the greater the public exposure of a vessel category, the greater the diversity of its rim designs.

However, they are adamant that this correlation is neither universal nor necessarily applicable to other 'style-bearing media' in this particular society. They call for comparative studies within Shipibo–Conibo society as 'rim designs, after all, are a rather small and inconspicuous part of the Shipibo–Conibo decorative style' (DeBoer and Moore 1982:153). Whereas most stylistic studies have used diversity measures to 'address the variability rather than the modal characteristics expressed in style' (p. 151) or to characterize patterns or variation in assemblages in order to identify the implied sociocultural correlates of relative diversity, the decision to use a diversity measure in this Shipibo–Conibo study came from *more than* these usual motivations.

DeBoer and Moore present an explicitly active approach to style, which directs their research; style is an active aspect of social communication and negotiation. Given the observation on their data that vessel categories can be distinguished by differing ranges of rim designs (e.g., one vessel type had 17 different designs, while another had only five), DeBoer and Moore suggest that it is not the rim designs themselves that carry social information, but the *diversity* of such designs. Thus, there are compelling contextual reasons why it might be relevant to understand diversity itself in the study of style and its functioning – in this particular medium, in this particular society, given the particular features of ceramic decoration and of their social contexts.

The same kind of compelling contextual reasons for the relevance of diversity in a stylistic analysis have yet to be spelled out for the prehistoric and archaeological case study of engraved bones and antler from Magdalenian sites that first got me involved in the use of diversity concepts and measures. However, there have been some developments in this study beyond my early published paper (Conkey 1980) that might help in restructuring our inquiry.

Originally, I used the Shannon–Weaver diversity indices (*H'*) to characterize engraved bone and antler assemblages from five Lower Magdalenian levels in Cantabrian Spain (Conkey 1980; see Table 13.1). This study was directed at answering questions about hunter–gatherer site use – was Altamira an aggrega-

Table 13.1. *Diversity'scores' for engraved design elements on Lower Magdalenian bones/antlers from Cantabrian Spain*

Lower Magdalenian units	Number of decorated objects	Total N design elements	Different design elements (n)	H'	H_{max}	H'/H_{max}	Simpson's
Altamira (AL)	58	152	(38)	1.51	1.64	0.92	0.957
El Juyo (J)	25	53	(19)	1.05	1.64	0.64	0.923
El Cierro (CI)	11	35	(15)	1.11	1.64	0.68	0.925
Cueto de la Mina (CM)	36	69	(27)	1.22	1.64	0.74	0.942
La Paloma (PL)	22	23	(12)	0.91	1.64	0.55	0.929

tion site? – and to lend support to a model that involved social and symbolic factors as well as the more usual ecological and economic models for hunter–gatherer site use. This was not as explicitly a transformational study as some other stylistic studies cited, although there are transformational implications. For example, there is the notion that the kind of aggregation/dispersion pattern hypothesized was an Upper, not a Middle or earlier, Paleolithic phenomenon, coming at a more recent point in the cultural evolution of hunter–gatherers (Conkey 1980:610–11). One might also argue that the study employed a somewhat passive view of style and design variation, in that variation was being used, in part, as a reflection of a settlement pattern. More emphasis could have been placed on the inquiry into how and/or why certain design variation in engraved bones would have been meaningful in an aggregation site context.

The results of the original study raised many problems and questions concerning the relation of sample size to diversity. It was clear that the number of different design elements engraved on the objects was directly related to the number of engraved bones and antlers recovered from the sites and to the total number of design elements engraved on these objects. I could show (Conkey 1981b, 1982) that there was a significant linear regression ($r = 0.9$, $p < 0.005$) between the diversity indices and the number of incised design elements per site.

Still constraining myself by the statistical bonds of the diversity statistics that were prevalent in the ecological literature, I tried to work at the sample-size problem. In addition to the H' indices of the 1980 study, I used both another index (Simpson's; see Simpson 1949) and a comparison of the Simpson's results with those based on the H' calculations (Conkey 1982; see Table 13.1). Neither of these two approaches was as successful as what Kintigh has subsequently done (1984a). However, I did conclude from this case that those diversity statistics developed in plant ecology and information theory are not best employed in archaeology as answers; they certainly cannot be direct statements on entropy, organization, or complexity.

Some exploratory use of diversity statistics might help direct analysis that must be anthropological and archaeological: Why, for example, would we expect diversity in engraved bones/antlers at a Cantabrian Magdalenian aggregation site? How can we, furthermore, control for sample-formational processes so that any

assessment of relative diversity – once shown to be a relevant variable in the cultural question – can be pursued with some confidence?

There were some interesting results (Conkey 1981b, 1982) from comparing two of the common statistics applied to the same data set. This was particularly suggestive when used in combination with the basic archaeological data, the design-element counts for each archaeological level. This combination and comparison approach aided in characterizing the use of particular design elements in more detail, and in suggesting how this use might account for the relative diversity of the assemblages. This exercise was also a good example of how different measures have differing assumptions and properties, and differing effects on the same data.

The Shannon and Simpson indices gave very different results (Table 13.1); the latter was chosen as a more conservative approach to diversity. In all the Magdalenian assemblages studied (Lower through Upper), there are many single occurrences of different design elements; this alone makes this a relatively poor case study for statistics such as diversity indices. However, this is one attribute of certain populations for which the Simpson measure is said to control (Hill 1973:427; Peet 1974:295). It is often referred to as a measure of dominance or concentration (Pielou 1975:9). Note that all five Lower Magdalenian collections scored extremely high and very close to each other; all within the 0.900 range (Table 13.1).

With two very different rankings of the five assemblages in terms of diversity indices, I returned to the original counts of design elements at each site. I found that in all five Lower Magdalenian sites just a few design elements could account for up to 40% of all the engraved design elements; in most assemblages just two or three different elements accounted for 30% of the elements incised. Most of these elements were those I had called 'core' or dominant elements of the engraving repertoire; these tended to be found throughout the Magdalenian in the region (Conkey 1978). At only two Lower Magdalenian sites are there concentrated occurrences of elements that are *not* core elements: at Altamira and Cueto de la Mina. Thus, the two assemblages with the highest H' were represented by elements not found at all or in low frequency at other less diverse (as measured by H') sites.

Although it was instructive to pursue the comparative approach of the H' and Simpson's indices as a way to characterize in more detail the use of different design elements, and how this might account for the relative diversity of an assemblage, the comparative parameters set by the *H'* on one hand and the Simpson's index on the other are *only suggestive* of – if not a time-consuming means to get to – the relative design composition of engraved-bone assemblages. This comparison of techniques indicated that it was necessary to rephrase the inquiry into diversity, particularly if one views style or even simply the engraving of bone as an active process. One question then becomes how we might approximate the selection process whereby certain design elements were 'chosen' and incised. Can we characterize Magdalenian engraving activities (or even Magdalenian style) as a set of probabilities that certain elements would be selected and that, for example, at Altamira, we are far less certain as to which elements would be used/found?

It seems that the Altamira assemblage is characterized by a high diversity/uncertainty index because, in part, elements there have been used, and used in greater numbers, than the probability of their use in the region would predict. Thus, by rephrasing the question about diversity in style at Altamira, we need at least two further avenues of inquiry. First, we need a method that is sensitive to the archaeological issues of significance and sample size; the development of the simulation method by Kintigh has been in direct response to these issues. Using this method, he has shown that there is additional support for the hypothesis that the diversity of design elements at Altamira is more than we would expect even given its larger sample size (Kintigh 1984a).

Secondly, behind all this we need better development of the cultural and contextual questions. The relevance and the validity of a diversity study depends upon our theories as to why homogeneity or heterogeneity might occur in style. The methods and measures used in the actual analysis of diversity depend upon what aspect of style we are trying to investigate. Thus, we need an explicit approach to stylistic analysis that must be linked to the methods. One approach that might help focus on the particular reasons why diversity might occur is based on the idea that, in a given prehistoric context, there are ways of doing things that are taught, reinforced, and modified (i.e., an active or dynamic 'isochrestism,' to use Sackett's [1982] term). Certain choices are made in the production and use of material culture, and the selection process and its context are of archaeological concern. That is, we can characterize painting pots, engraving bones, or making bronze earspools as a set of probabilities that certain raw materials, elements, techniques, and so forth, would be selected, and would occur on artifacts in certain contexts. The probability that certain attributes were selected and used is not universal but relative to the specific contexts and past histories of manufacture and use. Furthermore, in a given prehistoric cultural situation we might expect different probabilities of designs to vary for very different reasons.

If we find variations or departures from the expected probabilities, this is our key to look more closely at the particular situation, not to appeal to some tranformational assumptions, such as the evolution of craft specialization or social stress that leads to increased ceramic manufacturing. For example, DeBoer and Moore (1982) expected diversity in rim designs based on their preliminary analysis of the Shipibo–Conibo decorative structure. But when they looked at this diversity in terms of specific social context, they found departures from the way they expected the diversity to be distributed. These departures were then correlated with specific Shipibo–Conibo contexts of use.

Furthermore, their findings actually call into question some of the usual, more universal assumptions on stylistic signalling: that stylistic indicators should be standardized and unambiguous at the level of the social group, that is, between residential compounds. Instead they found the greatest diversity of rim designs at this social level. This suggested to them that it is diversity itself, not the content of the rim designs, that may be meaningful at the Shipibo–Conibo between-compound level. This makes diversity all the more interesting, *not* as a way for us to characterize our data, but as an aspect of material culture that was significant to the users in specific social contexts.

Although there has been relatively little discussion in this chapter of the use of specific diversity measures, it should be apparent that congruent with this 'probability' approach to stylistic variation would be simulation methods such as that proposed by Kintigh (1984a). In addition to confronting the issues of significance and sample size, this method has a certain contextual baseline that is rooted in the particular archaeological data set.

To the extent that the underlying frequency distribution in the Kintigh method (i.e., the expected) is not a universal or high-level cross-cultural generalization, and is more often derived from relevant data of the particular case study, the method is closely tied to the specific context of inquiry and the specific contexts of use of the stylistic objects and attributes in question. This was the case in Kintigh's analysis of the Magdalenian engraved bone and antler data, the rock art data, and the surface collection data used to illustrate the method (Kintigh 1984a, this volume), and in the application of the method to the Shipibo–Conibo data on ceramic rim designs (other applications include Benco 1985; Larick 1983; Steponaitis 1985).

Some concluding remarks

The chapter began with some historical background as to why diversity measures have become attractive in stylistic studies. I noted how the archaeological preference for the study of objects and patterns contributed to the use of diversity measures as a popular method. More specifically, I suggested that the recent historical development of archaeology as based on a systemic concept of culture and its functioning has promoted the application of statistical methods developed in ecology to describe and characterize archaeological data, particularly in comparative approaches.

Primarily, I discussed some varying approaches to stylistic analysis. I tried to stress how the aspect of homogeneity and heterogeneity has been treated and how different approaches have used diversity measures in the archaeological study of style. Above all, I wanted to stress the interpretive and theoretical problems.

These problems seem to converge on two related issues. First, I have tried to point out the prevalence of decontextualized analogues in stylistic interpretation that derive from several sources. On the one hand, there has been the continued search for general laws or principles of style and how our analysis of style might 'capture' past sociocultural phenomena for *us*. On the other hand, there is the more inclusive theoretical source, which is the persistence of the transformational paradigm of cultural evolution.

The second of these related issues is that we have not yet made many inroads into the *meaning* of diversity in stylistic forms: why is there diversity in style? In the discussion of expanding our conceptual frameworks, I used two case studies to illustrate how we might rephrase questions of method, theory, and interpretation when we use diversity in stylistic studies. Beyond these particular illustrations, we might ask if there are, more generally, any revised frameworks that can address these concerns of stylistic analysis.

To a great extent, we may first have to enrich our social theory, and there is considerable activity along these lines (see references in Hodder 1985 or Miller 1983). Archaeologists realize how we have tried to use the concept and analysis of style as a way to reveal 'the social group,' as if it were a continuous, integrated entity, and an entity that changes transformationally and gradually. From this view of 'group' has come the concern for interaction of groups and the use of stylistic analysis to reveal this as well.

There are, in general, some alternative concepts of culture to the systemic one, and alternative concepts of the relation between style and the social group. For example, there is the view of culture as a constitutive process, as a 'series of productive and individual acts aimed towards the construction of meaning' (Dougherty and Fernandez 1981:415). Social action is constitutive (e.g., Giddens 1979), just as culture is always 'in production.' 'Stated radically, cultures do not exist but are always in the process of formation' (Drummond 1981:638). From this, it follows that material culture itself is an active, productive, social force (Csikszentmihalyi and Rochberg-Halton 1981; Williams 1985; Wolff 1981).

Given these assumptions, style is more about context than about group or status positions. What we can learn about from the study of style are the contexts in which groups, or other sociocultural phenomena, are mobilized or brought into existence; what style can or does 'reveal' with regard to social groups may be the mobilization of group as process. Furthermore, we are not limited to 'group' in the study of style.

If style is mostly about process and context, and if we recognize that we have not yet made many inroads into the meaning of diversity in stylistic forms, then one way to approach diversity in stylistic analysis is to ask the kinds of questions posed frequently in the chapter: Why do we expect diversity in style? Why or how is an observed diversity meaningful in the given prehistoric situation? What is it about the particular attribute(s) that they should vary in the particular context? What are the particular and compelling linkages between the stylistic forms and the contexts within which stylistic diversity, or its lack, was generated?

Thus, we should not excuse the weaknesses of our diversity studies in stylistic analysis because the concept of style is too elusive, multifaceted, or arbitrary. Nor can we turn only to the inappropriateness or problems of the statistical measures for archaeological and stylistic questions. Rather, our weaknesses can be linked more to our asking questions that seek to characterize and manipulate patterns in the data, usually in the hope of confirming some underlying assumptions about the progressive nature of cultural evolution.

The implications, of course, are that we not only need to reconsider how we conceptualize and use style, but also need to work more with the very materials that archaeologists have at hand – the archaeological record. Given that the sociocultural contexts of the past were, at least in part, activated or constituted by material culture, we are the most appropriate students of those contexts and constitutive processes.

Acknowledgements

Particular thanks must go to the editors of this volume for their patience and encouragement. I especially want to thank them for scheduling me as the last paper in the day-long SAA session, for I then had to hear everyone else's contribution. Several people made extremely helpful and important suggestions: David Braun, Keith Kintigh, Roy Larick, and Jim Moore waded through a very dense version and I have tried to clarify this to meet their standards. I am particularly grateful to David Braun for a most frank critique. Thanks go to Jan Simek for several hours of collaboration on calculating the diversity statistics for the 1981 SAA paper summarized here, and to Vin Steponaitis for a lot of bibliographic assistance.

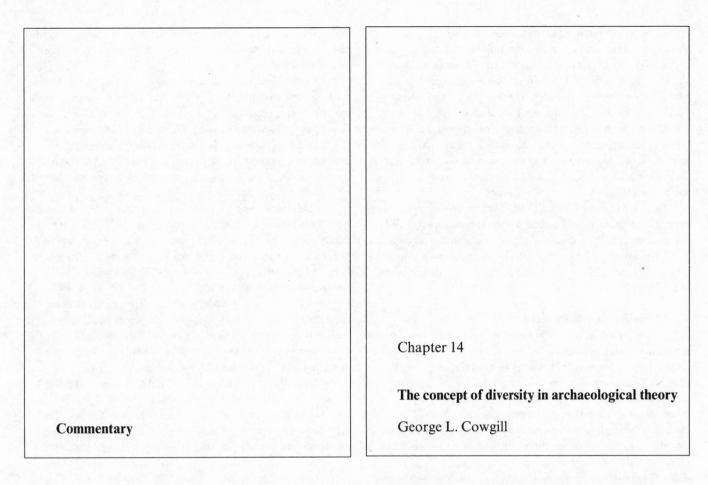

Commentary

Chapter 14

The concept of diversity in archaeological theory

George L. Cowgill

I want to begin by raising some general questions about the roles of the concept of 'diversity' in archaeological method and theory. The concept has been current for some time in biology, especially in ecology, where there has been time to use it, refine it, and criticize it. Unquestionably it is also useful for archaeologists, but we must not simply import it from the ecologists. We must think rather carefully about just how and why it will be useful for us. Most of the papers in this volume give evidence of such thought, but there are a few that seem unduly bent on applying diversity statistics simply because it is something other archaeologists are doing. There are several cases in which the measures of 'richness' and 'evenness' add little, if anything, to what can be learned from more straightforward approaches to the data presented.

Above all, we must pay more attention to differences in the sorts of entities to which measures of diversity may apply. For the ecologists, it appears that the entities have mainly been the populations of individual organisms existing within some specified tract at a certain time. Basic data are the species (or other taxonomic units) represented, and counts or estimates of the numbers of individuals in each species. In this volume, Rindos often seems to have some such set of entities in mind, but few other chapters are about such entities. Instead, most are about archaeological data sets, and the basic data are the archaeological categories represented and the numbers of examples of each category in various deposits. This difference from ecological studies probably has little importance for the specific mathematical techniques that might be applied, but it makes a tremendous difference in the *meaning* of the numbers. The essential point is that diversity in an archaeological data set is an aspect of what Binford (1983a and elsewhere) calls 'statics.' Diversity in the archaeological record often bears a complex relationship to diversity (or any other aspect) of ancient behavior (Binford's 'dynamics'). I do not know how much agreement about the meaning of species diversity there is among ecologists. In any case, that is their concern. We, as archaeologists, do not need simply to develop techniques to measure diversity in archaeological data sets. We must also think much more about the meanings of such diversity.

In the following section, I will leave the problem of meanings aside temporarily and discuss some technical aspects of measuring diversity in the archaeological record. With this preparation, I will then elaborate on some aspects of giving meaning to archaeological diversity. Finally I will take up problems raised by some of the chapters.

Diversity in archaeological data sets

One obvious difference between our data and those of biologists is that our categories are far more problematic. Taxonomic difficulties may seem large to biologists, but I think ours are far greater. If inappropriately defined categories are used, no amount of mathematical finesse can remedy the trouble. There is, of course, no single 'right' set of categories for all purposes. The essential thing is that, for a given purpose, we must not lump in ways that obscure important differences and we must not split on the basis of differences that are irrelevant for that purpose. In practice, there are strong pressures to accept categories that have been used previously, often either for obscure reasons or because they work well for time–space systematics, and to use these categories for other purposes, such as inferring ancient activities. There are some examples of this kind of use of inappropriate categories in this volume. It is hard to avoid doing this because, at best, to use more relevant categories requires restudy of collections. Often the collections are no longer available, so that one has no choice but to try to make some sense of categories designed for other purposes, or else reject the data as useless for studies of diversity.

The matter of techniques and concepts for arriving at good categories for specific purposes is a large topic (Whallon and Brown 1982), and of great importance, although it receives little analysis in this volume. For that reason, and to keep my own chapter shorter, I too will only underscore its importance and move on to other things.

A central theme that is emphasized in many chapters is that small samples misrepresent assemblage diversity. Richness of categories will be underrepresented, and evenness in the numbers of individuals in the categories is also likely to be lower in the sample than in the parent population. Thus, comparisons between data sets are deeply flawed and likely to be highly misleading if the sizes of the data sets are ignored. However, all is not lost. Although corrections for sample size must remain probabilistic, there are ways of making such corrections, and they often permit one to make comparisons that can be accepted, if not with perfect certainty, then at least with a satisfactorily high level of confidence. Grayson

and Kintigh have alternative approaches to this problem, and they and other contributors give a number of examples of the application of these techniques.

Kintigh's method is an appealing application of the 'Monte Carlo' approach, wherein a problem that it does not seem feasible to solve by exact methods is solved, to a satisfactory approximation, by probabilistic simulation. I have only a few suggestions. One is that I am teased by the suspicion that there may be an easier approximation, not requiring simulation, that is just as accurate, and that would require substantially less computer power or time. The exact solution can be found, in principle, by expanding the expression $(p_1 + p_2 + p_3 + \ldots + p_m)^n$, where m is the number of categories and n is the sample size, and finding the cumulative probability of all the terms for which any given number of the p_i's have a zero exponent. If m and n are even moderately large, however, the full expansion will involve an enormous number of terms. For example, for $n = 30$ and $m = 10$, there will be about 20 trillion terms. Many of these terms need not be calculated, however, and I wonder if there is some good approximation that can be computed more easily than running Kintigh's simulation program. However, I offer this only as a suggestion and a challenge to the statistically inclined.

A second point is that I do not think the jagged 'stairstep' shapes of Kintigh's graphs are useful or necessary. They are due only in part to the probabilistic aspects of his simulations. The main reason is that, with a small number of types, only a limited number of discrete sample outcomes are possible. For example, if there are 20 types, then in any real data set, the number of types present can only be 20, 19, 18, and so on. Suppose that, in a given case and for a given sample size, Kintigh's technique finds all 20 types present in about 0.4% of the simulation runs, exactly 19 types present in about 4.0%, 18 types present in about 14.0%, and so on. Suppose we would like to show a symmetrical 80% confidence interval; that is, an interval such that 10% of the simulation outcomes are at or higher than its upper limit, and another 10% are at or below its lower limit. When we try to obtain such an upper limit in the hypothetical case I have described, however, we find that about 4.4% of the outcomes have 19 or more types present, while about 18.4% of all outcomes have 18 or more types present.

We are, thus, faced with a dilemma. Either we adopt an upper limit for the confidence interval that cannot correspond to any possible real outcome (such as 18.6 types present) or we adopt an upper limit that excludes more or less than the uppermost 10% of outcomes (such as 19 types present or 18 types present). Kintigh makes the latter choice. But this means that the lines representing confidence limits in his displays do not actually correspond to the stated confidence interval. Generally, they show intervals that are narrower by amounts that vary considerably and unpredictably as one moves across the graph.

Kintigh's graphs would be easier to interpret and more useful if he made the first choice, even though that requires some interpolation between whole numbers, and will lead to values that no real sample can possibly show, such as 18.6 types present. Such graphs should not be hard to interpret or misleading. A real data set with 18 of 20 types present is just within the 80% confidence interval, while a data set with 19 types present is somewhat above it.

The same argument applies to estimates of the most likely number of types expected in samples of a given size from a specific postulated population. A further advantage of plotting non-integer values is that the curves should move smoothly from one sample size to another. Kinks in the curves will flag points where the simulation runs accidentally led to a poor result.

Instead of Kintigh's simulation, Grayson, Thomas, and others use a much simpler technique for relating richness to sample size. They merely use linear regression to estimate the logarithm of the richness as a function of the logarithm of sample size. The results are often quite good, at least in the sense that the correlations are quite high. It is reasonable to ask, then, whether anything is to be gained by using Kintigh's technique. I suggest there are three possible advantages. First, the log–log method does not work well when there are very few data sets, as Simek and Rothschild point out. Secondly, the log–log regression cannot continue to be linear when the expected richness closely approaches the total number of defined categories. Thirdly, Kintigh's method seems to offer a more sensitive way to identify outliers. Extreme outliers can be spotted by eye on the log–log graphs, but no way is provided to identify cases that are not so extreme, yet significantly more or less rich than expected. One might, of course, derive probability ellipses, but unless the data points are from nearly bivariate–normal populations the meaning of these ellipses will be doubtful. Kintigh's method, however, provides direct estimates of confidence intervals.

A further point on which I suspect that there is conceptual difficulty concerns the nature and size of the population that is being sampled. The situation is clear if we think of the problem as that of estimating the richness and diversity that would be found in an entire archaeological deposit, if only a part of the deposit has been excavated, or if we only have information obtained by surface collecting. To be sure, even in this situation there may be very serious questions about the representativeness of the sample. But, if these can be satisfactorily settled, then I see no conceptual problems in using the Kintigh or Grayson techniques to estimate the richness and/or evenness that *would have been found* if the rest of the deposit had been excavated by similar techniques.

But suppose that one has *all there is* from a number of deposits, and these total collections differ considerably in size. Does that mean that we should directly compare their richness and evenness, without making any allowances for differences in size? If we only want to compare one piece of the archaeological record with another piece of that record, then there is a sense in which we are comparing populations, and perhaps we need not control for size. If, however, we hope to give cultural meaning to our data, it is *essential* to control for size. Most contributors to this volume understand this, but the reasons are not discussed very fully.

A nearly universal view is that there is a significant degree of structure, of orderliness, in human behavior. Archaeologists (and others) differ sharply about whether this structure is almost wholly given by the historically contingent manners and customs of specific societies in specific times and places, or whether much of it can be formulated as the consequences of more general laws or principles. I will avoid that interesting debate here because, for present purposes, I emphasize that *it doesn't matter* where the structure comes from or what explains it; it is the fact of its existence that is important. A consequence is that anything that a finite number of people actually do, in a finite amount of time, can be seen as a *sample* of what more bearers of the same culture, or the same people, given more time, would be likely to do. If a site was occupied only briefly or by a few people, and then forever abandoned (for reasons that might well have been external to their own society and culture), we have *only a sample* of what these same people, or others bearing essentially the same culture, would have added to the local archaeological record, if they had continued longer doing the same kinds of things in the same place. For this reason, our attempts to give meaning to the archaeological record will always go astray if we do not control for size effects in comparing data sets. It makes no difference if we have obtained everything that was ever there. The relevant population is not any finite set of actual objects. The relevant population is the infinite set of objects that would be generated by some set of behavioral propensities.

One point that should be abundantly clear from the discussions of richness in this volume is that it is altogether mistaken to suppose that retreating to presence/absence scoring is generally a good way of coping with poor data. Actually, two situations should be sharply distinguished. One is the case in which counts of materials have not been reported or have been arrived at in ways that make the interpretation of the counts highly problematic, but the total mass of material is large enough to warrant the belief that any category not reported is very probably absent in the sampled population, or at any rate extremely uncommon. In this case, presence/absence tabulations are often reasonable. But if the sample size is so small that many categories that are only moderately uncommon in the population may easily be absent in the sample, then reliance on presence/absence tabulations is no help. If anything, it magnifies the distortions caused by smallish sample sizes and by differences in the sizes of different samples.

The papers in this volume concentrate on the biases small samples cause for estimates of diversity measures such as richness and evenness. Small samples cause other systematic distortions as well. For example, even if all other sources of error are eliminated, counts of numbers of objects in each category in small samples are subject to random sampling errors that are large relative to the counts themselves. This means that correlations will have low reliability, whether the correlations are based directly on counts or on percentages (which are ratios between counts). It might be thought that the effect of a reduction in the reliability of correlations due to small sample size is simply to increase the variance of sample correlations, with values higher than the true population value being just as likely as lower values. In fact, Spearman (1904) showed long ago that unreliability of correlation coefficients systematically biases them toward zero. That is, positive population correlations are usually represented by lower positive values in samples, while negative population correlations are usually represented by more weakly negative values in samples. Spearman labelled this effect 'attenuation' and gave a formula for estimating its effect, if one also has estimates of the reliability of each variable. If r is the correlation between variables x and y computed from the sample data, rx is the reliability of x, and ry is the reliability of y, then $\hat{p} = r/\sqrt{rx*ry}$ where $\hat{p}$ is the estimated correlation between x and y in the population. Cowgill (1970:165, 1986) and Nance (1987) discuss this further.

For correlations based on counts or on percentages derived from counts, an upper limit to the reliability can be computed from the numbers of objects in the relevant categories. The implications of the attenuation effect are far more serious than has been recognized for either bivariate or multivariate statistics based on small samples. In this connection, it is unfortunate that one contributor to this volume (Rice) suggests that 'adequate' sample sizes may be somewhere in the range of 30 to 100. I recently (Cowgill 1986) suggested that we are often in trouble with samples less than about 300. This vague suggestion deserves elaboration.

What really matters is not the total sizes of the samples, but the numbers of objects in the least abundant categories about which one would like to be able to make good inferences. To take an extreme example, suppose two samples consist of 1000 sherds each. One sample has 996 sherds of plainware, three sherds of decorated type A, and one sherd of decorated type B. The second sample also has 996 plainware sherds, one of type A, and three of type B. The samples suggest, of course, that the first comes from a population with three times as much type A as type B, while the second comes from a population with the reverse proportions. However, in assessing the confidence we should place in these suggestions, the 1992 plainware sherds don't count; they simply provide extremely strong evidence that both decorated types are quite uncommon in both populations. With respect to inferences about type A relative to type B, for practical purposes we have two samples of size four each, and these eight sherds warrant only very tentative suggestions about the true ratios of type A to type B in the two populations. A 2×2 contingency table and a Fisher's exact test of the hypothesis that both samples are from populations with identical proportions of types A and B yields a two-tailed significance level of 0.49. Thus, the observed differences could very easily be accidental differences in samples from populations with identical proportions of types A and B.

I have presented an extreme example to illustrate the point. I fear that with less extreme data sets, the problem is very often not recognized. One approach to the question 'how much is enough?', from the viewpoint of correlation studies, is to get some estimate of the average proportion of a category in the entire set of populations being sampled (where each collection represents a different population). One might reasonably do this, as Kintigh does, by pooling data from all the samples in one's study. A criterion for a minimal sample size, then, could be that it is large enough so that it offers the possibility of reliably detecting evidence that the sample is from a population with a substantially below-average proportion of the given category.

To illustrate, suppose that pooling the data from all collections yields a grand total of 10,000 specimens, of which 100 belong to category x. A reasonable null hypothesis is that category x constitutes 1% of each of the different populations represented by each sample. Notice that this does not lead us into circular reasoning. We expect that, in fact, category x may constitute considerably more than 1% of some populations, and less than 1% of other populations. However, it is by comparing the number of specimens actually found in a particular sample with the number expected if the sample were from a population with 1% of category x that we can identify the samples that really give evidence that the actual population proportion is *not* close to 1%.

Suppose, then, we have a sample with a total of 1,000 objects. If it is from a population with 1% of category x, the sample should include about ten examples of category x. Assuming that the sampling procedure reasonably approximates simple random sampling, we can compute (using the normal approximation to the binomial expansion) that the probability that the sample will have four or fewer examples of category x is 0.04. If, for example, the sample actually has only three examples of category x, then it provides strong evidence that the population proportion of category x is not 1%, but is instead considerably less.

Now suppose that another sample has a total size of 100. We expect that it will include one item of category x. But, using the binomial expansion, we can compute that 36.6% of such samples from populations with 1% of category x will have no examples at all of category x. Hence, it is not possible, with only 100 objects, to obtain strong evidence that the true proportion of category x is less than 1%. Samples no larger than 100 are *necessarily* ambiguous with respect to this question. A further calculation shows that if we want to reduce to 5% the risk of incorrectly concluding that a category is absent from a population when in fact the category constitutes 1% of the population, we will need an approximately simple random sample of 298 or more objects. To reduce the risk to 1%, we will need at least 458 objects.

In some situations, it would be quite possible to get larger archaeological collections, once the need for larger numbers is understood. In many other cases, of course, this is just not possible. In these cases, one must apply corrections, such as those discussed in this volume for richness and evenness and the attenuation correction discussed above for correlations.

It seems worth calling attention to a relationship between the Shannon H statistic and the 'likelihood ratio' version of chi-square. This version, often called G^2, is defined as $2\Sigma f_o \ln (f_o/f_e)$, where the f_o are observed frequencies, the f_e are expected frequencies, and 'ln' stands for natural logarithms (to base e) (Blalock 1979:281). After some algebraic struggle, I have established that, if we have two samples, where n_1 is the size of one sample, n_2 is the size of the other sample, N is the combined size of the two samples, H_1 pertains to sample 1 and H_2 to sample 2, and H is computed from the pooled samples, then, if the Hs are computed using natural logarithms, $G^2 = 2(NH - n_1 H_1 - n_2 H_2)$. Since G^2/N is very close to chi-square/N, which equals the strength of association measure phi-square, phi-square is about $H - n_1 H_1/N -$

$n_2 H_2/N$. One consequence of this is that if $H_1 = H_2$, they must both equal H, and G^2 must be zero. If phi-square is nearly zero, then H_1 must be close to H_2. In addition, I conjecture that if n_1 is not very different from n_2, but H_1 is quite different from H_2, phi-square is also necessarily large. This is another challenge that I set before the mathematically inclined. Further development of these relations may add useful insight into the H measure of diversity. Among other things, since the approximate sampling distribution of G^2 is known, it may be possible to get a good approximation to the sampling distribution of H/H_{max}, which could be used in place of Kintigh's simulation technique. Also, when there are three or more collections, some useful generalization of my analysis may be possible. At least, one can compare any one collection with the pooled numbers for all the other collections.

Finally, I offer some suggestions about further concepts related to diversity. I think these will be especially useful for discussions of ceramic production and style, but they will probably also be useful for considering diversity in other phenomena. Figure 14.1 sketches these ideas.[1] First, of course, is *richness*, the number of categories present. Second is *evenness*, which expresses the extent to which the categories are represented by similar quantities of objects. A third concept is *range*, by which I mean the amount of difference between the most different categories. Range can easily be measured separately for each interval variable used to describe a data set. For nominal variables, an indicator of range is the number of distinct categories represented for each variable. There is an obvious and quite simple sense in which an assemblage that exhibits wider ranges in descriptive variables is more diverse than an assemblage that exhibits narrower ranges. For example, are all pots in a collection more or less the same size, or do they range from tiny to huge? Preoccupation with richness and evenness can blunt one's sensitivity to such a simple question. A fourth concept is *standardization*. This has been used too loosely, to mean several different things, including relatively low richness. I suggest we distinguish between richness and standardization, and use the latter term to refer to low variation within categories. Fifthly, since some categories in a data set may show high standardization while other categories show low standardization, it seems worth defining *uniformity of standardization* as the extent to which some categories are more standardized than others. At Teotihuacan, for example, Paula Krotser points out (personal communication) that some wares appear to be far more standardized than others. This adds to other evidence that suggests there were several different ceramic production subsystems simultaneously in operation.

Equipped with these terms, one can suggest several possible reasons for relatively low richness in the ceramics produced by a workshop. Among these are that the consumers of the pots used pots for a limited number of activities; that the workshop did not produce all the kinds of pottery locally used; and that some kinds of pots served multiple purposes, so that a few kinds of pots were used for a large number of different activities. In all these cases, the common theme is that the producers had a limited number of distinct kinds of pot in mind. I will not rehearse lengthy arguments on this matter, but will simply point out that one can regard an-

cient ideas as a subject for research without falling into a 'normative' model of prehistory. Also, although we cannot be sure that we have correctly captured essential aspects of ancient ideas (namely, how many different kinds of things people thought there were), we cannot be scientifically sure of anything else either, and there are scientifically valid procedures for making and improving inferences about anciently recognized categories.

Low standardization, in contrast, as I urge we define it, means that there is considerable variation between different examples of a given category. There are at least three plausible reasons for low standardization. One is that there is simply little value placed on standardization by the culture. A second is relatively low skill, and/or conditions not conducive to uniformity of products or raw materials. A third is relatively high skill and control over techniques, which can be taken advantage of to vary monotony. Greater skill and greater control over materials and techniques doubtless appear when producers spend a higher proportion of their time in making ceramics (or lithics, or whatever), but low standardization, *per se*, may reflect low skill, high skill, or have little to do with skill. Even distinguishing richness and range from standardization is not enough. Studies of artifact production must take explicit account of more than this, such as sensitive indicators of skill. Unfortunately, many attempts to deal with craft production and specialization, such as those of Rice (1981, this volume) have been seriously flawed by vagueness about some of the distinctions I have discussed.[2]

Diversity in ancient phenomena

The papers in this volume bear on diversity in at least four aspects of ancient life: diet, raw materials, style, and activities. These are such different phenomena that, when we turn from simply measuring diversity in the archaeological record to giving meaning to that diversity, quite different concepts seem to be needed. My discussion here will focus on diversity in activities, and I will make only a few observations about diversity in diet or style. Concerning diet, I wonder about the relevance of biological taxa. It seems to me that more relevant categories would be those reflecting differences in microenvironments exploited, in techniques used, and in nutrition. Among other things, does low diversity in food remains reflect low diversity in what was available, or concentration on a limited part of what was available? As to style, I suggest that attention to range, standardization, and uniformity of standardization may usefully supplement measures of richness and evenness. But I am especially struck by the absence, in this volume, of any reference to the concepts current in art history and related fields. Surely they have at least as much to offer as ecology or information theory.

Concerning ancient activities,[3] it is natural to assume that there is a reasonably simple relationship between diversity in the archaeological record and diversity in the activities that generated that record. This would probably be so, if for each activity that we wished to distinguish, we could identify at least one 'diagnostic' category that (a) was practically never used for any other activity, and (b) as a consequence of this activity, entered the archaeological record in such numbers that absence of the category in a de-

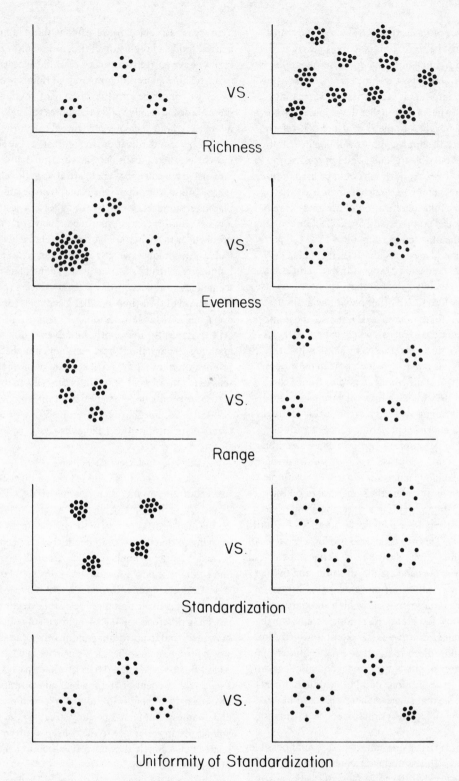

VS.

Richness

VS.

Evenness

VS.

Range

VS.

Standardization

VS.

Uniformity of Standardization

Fig. 14.1. Five concepts related to diversity

posit would assure us that the activity in question had contributed practically nothing to the deposit in question.

Often, we do not seem to have any categories of objects that meet these criteria. However, to judge from everything in the literature and my own struggles to derive formal techniques for

dealing with less than ideal situations, I conclude that we should do our utmost to identify good 'diagnostics.' Note that by a diagnostic category I do not mean simply a formal or stylistic category; I mean any possible combination of form, style, material, use-wear, and spatial pattern of discard that can be shown to be strongly associated with a specific activity. Studies in ethnoarchaeology, experimental archaeology, and taphonomy must be pursued to the fullest in order to expand the number and quality of recognized 'diagnostics.'

Consider the situation when no single category is diagnostic of any single activity. That is, given some set of ancient activities that we would like to be able to identify in the archaeological record, and given some set of recognized categories of objects, there is no one category whose presence or absence in a deposit provides strong evidence that a specific activity did or did not contribute to that deposit. In general, two or more categories may have been used for each activity, and each category may have been used to some extent in two or more activities. Note, incidentally, that low richness in the archaeological record can be due to low richness of ancient activities, or it can reflect multiple uses for many categories, together with a possibly high richness of ancient activities.

If there is not a one-to-one relationship between activities and categories, it is easy to show that evenness of activities need not be the same as evenness of categories in deposits generated by these activities. Suppose that activity A uses categories X and Y and, on the average, generates twice as many fragments of X as of Y. Suppose activity B uses the same two categories but on the average generates four times as many fragments of Y as of X. Thus, the contribution of activity A to a deposit will, on average, consist of 2/3 X and 1/3 Y, while the contribution of activity B to a deposit will consist of 1/5 X and 4/5 Y. If half the material in a given deposit was generated by activity X and half by activity Y, the expected assemblage proportions will be (1/2)(2/3)X + (1/2)(1/5)X, or (13/30)X, and (1/2)(1/3)Y + (1/2)(4/5)Y, or (17/30)Y. The assemblage proportions are not equal, and hence do not show the highest possible evenness. On the other hand, if 9/14 of the material in the deposit was generated by activity A and only 5/14 by activity B, then the expected assemblage proportions are (9/14)(2/3)X + (5/14)(1/5)X, or (1/2)X, and (9/14)(1/3)Y + (5/14)(4/5)Y, or (1/2)Y. Thus, assuming that both activities add absolute amounts of material to the archaeological record at about the same rate, a less even mix of the two activities can generate more even proportions in the archaeological record.

The above numerical example is, of course, merely illustrative, and I am not suggesting that any ancient people made such calculations, or were necessarily aware of the point I have made.

To deal more fully with the connections between ancient activities and the archaeological record let us begin with a model of activities and deduce consequences for the archaeological record, rather than beginning with archaeological data and trying to imagine what might have caused them. Consider the following general model. Suppose that there were L different activities, A_1, $A_2, \ldots, A_k, \ldots, A_L$. Suppose we have defined M types, and j is the index over types. Suppose also we have N archaeological deposits, and i is the index over deposits. From a formal viewpoint, it does not matter whether the deposits are whole sites, whole layers, or spatial loci within layers. Assume that each activity has a set of propensities to contribute different proportions of each category to the archaeological record. Let the average proportion of activity k's total contribution to the archaeological record that consists

of category j be symbolized by p_{jk}. The value of p_{jk} will be the resultant of several factors, including the extent to which category j was used in performing activity k, the wear and tear on this category typically produced by this activity, people's preferences for discarding or continuing to use damaged examples of this category, different ways of dealing with discarded or lost examples of this category, and so on. All these factors will vary from situation to situation. Moreover, at best, the p_{jk}s represent statistical tendencies; expected proportions rather than actual proportions, so actual proportions in actual cases will show variance about the average p_{jk}s.

In order to take this model seriously, we have to assume that, for each pair of activities, A_k, and A_r, there is at least one category, j, for which the difference between p_{jk} and p_{jr} is large relative to the variances of p_{jk} and p_{jr}. In view of what is now known of the many factors that can affect the quantities and proportions of things that enter the archaeological record, this may seem like a large assumption. However, it seems to me that to deny the reasonableness of this assumption is tantamount to rejecting the possibility of ever identifying ancient activities by any possible archaeological technique.

Incidentally, notice that if, in this model, we split what is, for practical purposes, one category into two categories, j and r, we will find that p_{jk} is practically the same as p_{rk} for all k. Of course, it would still be a good idea to avoid excessive splitting, if for no other reason than that splitting will reduce category counts and thus increase effects of sampling errors.

Also notice that, if some category j is 'diagnostic' of activity k, we can express this formally by saying that p_{jr} equals zero, with negligible variance, for all p_{jr} for which r is not equal to k.

Since the p_{jk} are proportions, they add to unity for any activity. That is, $\Sigma_{j=1}^{M} p_{jk} = 1$, for each value of k. Consider, now, that each deposit may be the sum of contributions from each activity, where A_{ik} is the proportion of the material in deposit i contributed by activity k. Note that $\Sigma_{k=1}^{L} A_{ik} = 1$. Now, the expected proportion of category j in deposit i is $e_{ij} = \Sigma_{k=1}^{L} A_{ik} p_{jk}$; that is, the sum of the products of the proportion of each activity times the average proportion of that activity's contribution to the archaeological record that consists of category j. In fact, because of variance, the observed proportion of category j in deposit i, o_{ij}, will not generally equal e_{ij}.

In a real situation, we observe the o_{ij}, and our problem is to infer the A_{ik} and the p_{jk}. There are NL activities, ML categories, and NM observed proportions of categories in deposits. However, since the proportions of activities, categories, and observed proportions each must add to unity, the actual number of unknowns will be $N(L - 1) + L(M - 1)$, and the number of independent known quantities will be $N(M - 1)$. If $N(M - 1)$ is greater than $N(L - 1) + L(M - 1)$; that is, if N is greater than $L(M - 1)/(M - L)$, there will be more knowns than unknowns, and at first it seems that a unique solution is possible. For example, we could, by analogy with multiple regression models, solve for the values that minimize the mean squared deviations between observed and expected frequencies. That is, we could minimize $\Sigma_{i=1}^{N} (o_{ij} - e_{ij})^2$ for each j, which is the same as $\Sigma_{i=1}^{N} (o_{ij} - \Sigma_{k=1}^{L} A_{ik} p_{jk})^2$. Note, however, that we have to estimate the p_{jk} as well as the A_{ik}. An appealing approach would be to assume that only one activity accounted for all the observed deposits, find the best solution, then repeat the process for two postulated activities, three activities, and so on, until the postulation of a further activity failed to yield any statistically significant further reduction in mean squared error.

If unique solutions could be found for the above set of equations, the method would constitute a truly enormous breakthrough in the linked problems of inferring ancient activities, ancient activity sets (or 'tool kits'), and, to a certain extent, the spatial organization of ancient activities. The principal difficulty about spatial organization, as I see it, is that we cannot assume that all the debris generated by the activity was simply dropped in place. We must at least assume that often some fraction was tossed out of the way (Binford 1983a:153) or collected and dumped elsewhere. In many cases, it may be adequate to distinguish between the average composition of 'dropped' fractions left in place and the different average composition of 'dumped' fractions accumulated elsewhere. If the compositions of these fractions themselves remain reasonably stable, we can perfectly well think of the dropped fraction of the materials generated by a given activity as one activity set, while the dumped fraction of the materials generated by the same activity can be regarded, formally, as a second activity set. As long as our archaeological techniques permit us to judge whether the contents of a given deposit (or excavation unit within a deposit) were generated by dropping or dumping, the fact that a fraction of the material resulting from an activity is dropped and the remainder is dumped should cause no insurmountable problems. The greatest worry is that, it seems, the fractions dumped or dropped may be highly dependent on factors such as whether the activity was carried out indoors or outdoors, plans to conduct other activities in the vicinity, and the intended duration of occupation of a site. If this is the case, the formal implication is that the variances about average values may be excessively large, thus frustrating the attempted analysis.

Assuming the variances are not too large, however, notice that there is no need to begin by identifying deposits or segments of deposits whose contents were generated by a single activity. We could simply bypass the vexing problems discussed by Whallon (1984), by Carr and others (1985), and in this volume by Simek. We could take provenience units and their contents as given, solve the above equations for the A_{ik}s and the p_{jk}s, and, for each activity, plot spatially the proportion it contributed to the contents of each provenience unit. To be sure, the smaller the provenience units are, the more detailed and meaningful will be the pictures given by such spatial plots. But problems of overlapping activity drop areas, and problems of dumps that pool a fraction of the materials from different activities, would no longer be nearly so difficult.

Unfortunately, after this tantalizing glimpse of what the approach seems almost to offer, I have to report that investigation of imaginary 'perfect' data in which observed proportions of categories in deposits are identical to expected proportions

shows that, if two or more activities are postulated, there is usually no unique solution for the A_{ik}s and the p_{jk}s. It does seem that one can often show that the A_{ik}s and p_{jk}s have to lie within certain limits. Table 14.1 shows the expected proportions of four artifact categories for eight deposits generated by two activities. It is assumed that the fraction of a deposit generated by activity 1 consists of 20% of category 1, 30% of category 2, 40% of category 3, and 10% of category 4, while the fraction of a deposit generated by activity 2 consists of 5% of category 1, 20% of category 2, 30% of category 3, and 45% of category 4. It is further assumed that the fraction contributed by activity 1 is none of deposit 1, 10% of deposit 2, 20% of deposit 3, 30% of deposit 4, 40% of deposit 4, 50% of deposit 6, 60% of deposit 7, and 100% of deposit 8. The remainder of each deposit is contributed by activity 2. Finally, it is assumed that the observed values are identical to the computed expected values.

The problem, then, is to take the observed values and see if the values of the A_{ik} and p_{jk} actually used can be recovered. In fact, one can show that there are some proportional relationships that necessarily hold among the various p_{jk}, but these are not strong enough uniquely to determine their values. For example a set of 'wrong' values of p_{jk} and the A_{ik} is shown in parentheses in Table 14.1. These wrong values generate the observed values perfectly. They are among the most extreme wrong values that will do this. They include the largest workable values for p_{11} and p_{42} and the smallest workable values for p_{41} and p_{12}. One could find the range of all workable values by finding the largest values of p_{41} and p_{12} that will generate the correct observed values.

My feeling about these results is disappointment that unique solutions are not generally possible, tempered with gratification that the method seems to do well enough to be of some use. The range of possible values of p_{jk} and the A_{ik} is, after all, fairly narrow. Notice that the assumed true values imply that, except for category 4, the two activities generate rather similar proportions of the various categories. An example in which the two activities contrasted more sharply in their contributions to deposits would probably yield better results.

Consideration of Table 14.1 suggests two important further points. First, whenever the proportion of any one of the four categories in a deposit is specified, the proportions of the other three categories can be predicted. This would not be the case if three or more activities were contributing to the contents of the deposits. Thus, the structure of the 'observed' data tells us that two, and only two, activities contributed to these deposits. Secondly, the 'wrong' values allow for the possibility of a deposit in which category 1 is wholly absent (if the deposit represents only activity 2) and for the possibility of a deposit in which category 1 constitutes 24% of the contents (if the deposit represents only activity 1). The true values, however, imply that the observed proportion of category 1 will not be less than 5% in any deposit nor more than 20%. Similarly for the other categories, the true values predict limits on observable proportions that are different from the limits predicted by various wrong guesses. If one has data on a large number of deposits, it can be assumed that it is unlikely that the possible ranges

Table 14.1. *Eight hypothetical deposits, derived from different proportional contributions of four artifact categories by two activity sets. Numbers in parentheses are one set of incorrect values that are consistent with the observed data values.*

Activity set 1:

$p_{11} = 0.20\,(0.24)$	$p_{21} = 0.30\,(0.33)$	$p_{31} = 0.40\,(0.43)$	$p_{41} = 0.10\,(0.00)$

Activity set 2:

$p_{12} = 0.05\,(0.00)$	$p_{22} = 0.20\,(0.17)$	$p_{32} = 0.30\,(0.27)$	$p_{42} = 0.45\,(0.57)$

Proportions of each activity in each deposit:

$A_{11} = 0.00\,(0.21)$	$A_{12} = 1.00\,(0.79)$
$A_{21} = 0.10\,(0.27)$	$A_{22} = 0.90\,(0.73)$
$A_{31} = 0.20\,(0.33)$	$A_{32} = 0.80\,(0.67)$
$A_{41} = 0.30\,(0.39)$	$A_{42} = 0.70\,(0.61)$
$A_{51} = 0.40\,(0.45)$	$A_{52} = 0.60\,(0.55)$
$A_{61} = 0.50\,(0.52)$	$A_{62} = 0.50\,(0.48)$
$A_{71} = 0.60\,(0.58)$	$A_{72} = 0.40\,(0.42)$
$A_{81} = 1.00\,(0.82)$	$A_{82} = 0.00\,(0.18)$

Observed data (identical to expected values in this example):

$o_{11} = 0.050$	$o_{12} = 0.200$	$o_{13} = 0.300$	$o_{14} = 0.450$
$o_{21} = 0.065$	$o_{22} = 0.210$	$o_{23} = 0.310$	$o_{24} = 0.415$
$o_{31} = 0.080$	$o_{32} = 0.220$	$o_{33} = 0.320$	$o_{34} = 0.380$
$o_{41} = 0.095$	$o_{42} = 0.230$	$o_{43} = 0.330$	$o_{44} = 0.345$
$o_{51} = 0.110$	$o_{52} = 0.240$	$o_{53} = 0.340$	$o_{54} = 0.310$
$o_{61} = 0.125$	$o_{62} = 0.250$	$o_{63} = 0.350$	$o_{64} = 0.275$
$o_{71} = 0.140$	$o_{72} = 0.260$	$o_{73} = 0.360$	$o_{74} = 0.240$
$o_{81} = 0.200$	$o_{82} = 0.300$	$o_{83} = 0.400$	$o_{84} = 0.100$

in observed proportions are much greater than the observed ranges. This can be used to narrow further the range of *probably correct* guesses about the true values of the p_{jk}s and A_{ik}s.

It remains to be seen how this approach will fare when it is applied to real data, where (a) there will be more or less large differences between observed and expected proportions, and (b) there may well be three or more activities contributing to the contents of deposits. At any rate, I think it is finally possible to say that we have a model that is concordant (in the sense of Carr 1985) with the situation. I believe it offers a valid and appropriate way for thinking of the connections between the archaeological record and ancient human activities. I am, however, far from satisfied with my current mathematical analysis of the model. I hope very much that others will be challenged to carry this work further.[4]

In this connection, it is useful to look at the results of applying some alternative approaches to the data in Table 14.1. For example, R-mode correlations between proportions of the four categories in the eight deposits show (Table 14.2) that all pairs of the first three categories have correlations of plus 1 with one another, while category 4 has correlations of minus 1 with all the other categories. All correlations are plus or minus 1, of course, because in this example all observed values are identical to expected values. A straightforward principal components analysis would yield one component, which would account for 100% of the variance. The variables representing proportions of categories 1, 2, and 3 would have loadings of plus 1 on the one component, while the variable for

Table 14.2. *Product-moment correlations between the proportions of the four categories in the deposits of Table 14.1*

Variables	1	2	3	4
1				
2	$+1.00$			
3	$+1.00$	$+1.00$		
4	-1.00	-1.00	-1.00	

category 4 would have a loading of minus 1. Up to a point, such an analysis seems appropriate and useful. The data in Table 14.1 have been constructed in such a way that all the variation in observed category frequencies can be attributed to just one thing: the proportion of the contents of each deposit that was generated by activity 1. Since there are only two activities in this example, the remainder of the contents of each deposit is, necessarily, due to activity 2. The fact that all the observed variation can be attributed to just one factor is just what a principal components analysis would tell us. Indeed, it seems highly likely that principal components analysis would be an appropriate and effective way to determine how many distinct activity sets are implied by other data sets. I hope to test this soon with invented examples based on three or more distinct activities.

In other respects, however, customary interpretations of a principal components analysis of the data in Table 14.1 are more problematic. Characterizing the deposits by their scores on component 1 may or may not prove to be appropriate. I am especially concerned, however, that one might conclude that categories 1, 2, and 3 constituted one activity set (or 'tool kit'), while category 4 constituted a second activity set. In fact, of course, this is very different from the activity sets used to generate the data of Table 14.1. The principal components analysis is quite correct in the implications of loadings; the more activity 1 contributes to a deposit, the higher the proportions of categories 1, 2, and 3 there will be in the deposit, and the lower the proportion of category 4. The difficulty is not that the principal components analysis will give a wrong answer, but that we may be mistaken about what the question was. My earlier analysis showed one way to get an approximation to the actual constitution of the activity sets responsible for the data. It is not clear at present whether principal components analysis could also aid in this task. It is certain, however, that it is wrong simply to interpret a set of categories whose proportions share high loadings on a single component as an activity set.

Table 14.3 gives the Brainerd–Robinson similarity coefficients between the eight deposits of Table 14.1. An attempt to cluster the deposits would yield one large cluster consisting of deposits 1 through 7 that could not be decomposed into sub-clusters, and a second cluster consisting of the somewhat distinctive deposit 8. These results are valid, but they reflect no more than that deposits 1 through 7 represent evenly varying proportional contributions from activity 1, while deposit 8 stands somewhat apart because it represents a much higher contribution from activity 1 than does any other deposit. This is correct, but it does not seem to offer a very effective lead for further analysis of the observed data.

Comments on some papers

All of the chapters in this volume are interesting and useful. I will not attempt to summarize them individually, or to adjudicate between all the differences that crop up. There are, however, a few problems that call for discussion.

As will be apparent from the preceding section, I cannot agree with Simek's insistence that the attempt to infer activity sets from archaeological data is not warranted unless it can be shown that there is considerably less diversity within deposits (or segments of deposits) than between them. I am also baffled by his discussion of global versus local patterning and his distinction between 'homogeneous' patterns and 'heterogeneous' structures. I agree with Whallon (1984) and Carr (1985) that archaeological records are built up by local, rather than global (i.e., site-wide) processes. But what I understand by this is that different activities will be concentrated in different places and that the dropped and dumped materials resulting from these activities will be concentrated in different places, and that the concentrations themselves will be quite variable in size and shape and density and will often overlap. All this is consistent with the model I discussed in the preceding section of this chapter. Simek, however, seems to argue that localized processes are inconsistent with high site-wide correlations, and that it is *good* news when correlations between

Table 14.3. Brainerd–Robinson similarity coefficients between the eight deposits of Table 14.1

Deposits	1	2	3	4	5	6	7
1							
2	193						
3	186	193					
4	179	186	193				
5	172	179	186	193			
6	165	172	179	186	193		
7	158	165	172	179	186	193	
8	130	137	144	151	158	165	172

categories, across all the deposits (or segments of deposits) of a site are low. This is simply not so.

At the same time, Simek has a good point in arguing that it is useful to identify segments of a site that are distinctive or anomalous in their contents. However, before employing measures of richness and evenness to identify anomalies, it would be better to begin with simpler techniques such as contingency table analysis. Such an investigation of Simek's nine spatial clusters for Couche V of Le Flageolet I leads to an overall chi-square of 72.3, which, for 40 degrees of freedom, is significant at better than the 1% level. Thus, we are justified in thinking that not all the differences in composition among the nine clusters are accidental. However, the most striking difference is that cluster 5 has 12 bladelets, rather than the 3.5 that would be expected if the distribution of bladelets across clusters were random. It is also notable that cluster 3 has no bladelets at all, while 5.1 would be expected. Cluster 7 has 9 end-scrapers, whereas only 3.7 would be expected. Cluster 8 has 9 retouched pieces, but only 4.4 would be expected. There are a few other cases where there are somewhat more or fewer examples of a category in a cluster than would be expected, but the ones I have just listed are all the striking anomalies. It seems to me that efforts to give meaning to Simek's data would do better to focus on these observations rather than to concentrate on richness and evenness indices. Of course, the approach I sketched earlier might be tried, but the low counts for many categories in many clusters suggest that large sampling errors will cause difficulties.

I wonder, indeed, how much meaning one can hope to extract from the six categories used by Simek. Since his chapter is intended merely to illustrate an approach, this is not a major criticism. Nevertheless, I wonder if it would not be highly useful to distinguish different kinds of burins, perhaps to use finer subdivisions of some of the other categories, and to use evidence of use-wear, if it is available.

Some of the other chapters also call for comments. I am puzzled by the passage in which Rice says that diversities should be compared only between assemblages of approximately equal sizes. A central theme of this book is the possibility of controlling for wide ranges of sample size in making diversity comparisons.

I am also puzzled by Rothschild's figures for her New York City samples. Like children in Lake Wobegon, all three seem to be above average in both richness and diversity.

Thomas, like Jones, Beck, and Grayson, shows different regression slopes for different data subsets. Unlike them, he does not provide information about the significance of these slope differences. The method is excellent in principle, but I seriously doubt whether these particular differences are significant at, say, the 5% level.

I wonder if the lower richness of Basketmaker raw materials found by Leonard, Smiley, and Cameron may be simply because most of the Basketmaker materials came from a relatively short distance, within which one would expect less diversity of sources.

Some of Kintigh's examples seem to use collections known to combine material from several periods. This is unobjectionable as long as the examples merely illustrate the technique, but when one is more interested in the meaning of the analyses it is important to use collections believed to pertain to single periods.

Jones, Beck, and Grayson ask whether evenness should be computed on the basis of all categories used in an analysis, or only those actually present in a given collection. It seems to me that the former choice is preferable. This will, of course, make the maximum possible evenness depend on the sample size whenever the size of the sample is smaller than the number of categories used. However, there is no escaping the fact that such very tiny samples must be problematic. The techniques discussed in this volume for controlling for variable sample sizes cannot work miracles.

To sum up, I think the greatest contributions of the studies in this book are, first, that they show that comparisons between samples of small and large size will be very misleading if corrections for sample size are not made, and, secondly, they show us some good ways to make those corrections. Proper allowance for different sample sizes is a necessary condition for giving meaning to diversity in the archaeological record, but it is not a sufficient condition. The most interesting chapters in this volume deal with various possible meanings of various kinds of diversity. It is along these lines that future work should proceed.

Notes

1. The horizontal and vertical axes in Figure 14.1 are intended to suggest a multivariate descriptive space. Each dot stands for an object and each cluster of dots stands for a category of objects.
2. My ideas on ceramic production have benefitted from discussions of this topic with Mary R. Hopkins.
3. In the terms used by Binford (1983a:147), what I refer to in this chapter as 'activities' should probably be called 'tasks.'
4. There is, in fact, a substantial literature on this topic under the name of 'linear unmixing.'

Chapter 15

Diversity in archaeology: a group of measures in search of application?

Robert C. Dunnell

The chapters that constitute this volume represent contemporary thinking about and attempts to employ an increasingly rigorous notion of diversity in archaeological contexts. Some common concerns, or better, attitudes are expressed. Diversity is properly addressed in quantitative terms rather than by intuitive assessment. The attempt to quantify diversity has led directly to attempts to refine the notion itself and to assay the relation between measures of diversity and both the data employed (e.g., the effects of sampling) and the questions being addressed.

As in the larger arena, much of the difficulty presented in synthesizing this collection of essays stems from ambiguous terminology. Most authors have been explicit and precise about diversity and associated concepts; the bulk of the ambiguities obtain in the archaeological concepts that are employed in conceiving diversity as a useful archaeological tool. That this tangential ambiguity adversely affects the integration of each chapter's contribution into a larger understanding of diversity is striking evidence that the value of diversity, both as a concept and as a set of measures, is wholly dependent upon its own integration with equally robust archaeological concepts. Several of the chapters in this volume (e.g., Conkey, Rice, Rothschild)[1] make this point, often quite strongly. Diversity displays all of the classic symptoms of concept borrowing, symptoms largelys initiated by the efforts to treat it quantitatively. Obviously, neither the previous chapters in this volume nor these comments are appropriate contexts in which to construct a theoretically and conceptually robust archaeology.

There are, however, other problems, methodological problems *sensu stricto* (cf. Osbourn 1968) that must be solved before a rigorous application of diversity measures to archaeological problems can be effected. Some are specific to diversity and some are not, but all are associated with the archaeological context and it is this to which I direct my attention here. Inevitably, this focus constrains me to look more closely at some of the contributions than others because of the varied foci of the chapters themselves. The other major class of concerns, the technical issues in formulating and employing measures of diversity, have been critically assessed by Professor Cowgill in Chapter 14.

The terminology of diversity

Most of the chapters recognize that early efforts to make use of diversity as a quantitative characterization of phenomena suffered because of imprecision associated with the term 'diversity.' It is imperative to separate the concept from the various measures that attempt to give it an empirical interpretation. Taking an operationalist stance (diversity is whatever a diversity index measures) simplifies discussion, but it does not clarify it or forward the integration of diversity as a useful archaeological concept. Hereafter, I will use 'diversity' to denote the concept, the thing about which information is being sought when measures are proposed. By extensional analysis of the chapters in this volume, I take diversity to mean the *structure of the distribution of cases among categories*. Diversity is thus a statement about an empirical property; it involves both distributions (counts of one kind or another which must be obtained from observation) and association (cases with categories, which must also originate in empirical observations). Less obviously, there is a further association, cases with cases, to create the thing about which diversity is a characterization. In those chapters which involve applications, the things are usually assemblages (most chapters) or subassemblages (e.g., Schiffer and Simek). Rindos treats this matter extensively, and I return to it later in another context. *Contra* Rice's contention (cf. Rindos), a diversity measure is a statistic much like mean or variance; the difference lies in the scale. Diversity is a property of all aggregated sets of things.

Following the terminology advanced and justified by Bobrowsky and Ball and seconded by Jones and Leonard, there are three major groups of indices[2] that are currently used to interpret the concept (Figure 15.1), each of which supplies different information about the structure of the distribution of cases over categories. Richness is a group of indices denoting the number of categories over which cases are distributed; evenness is a group of indices denoting the proportional assignment of cases to categories. Both are first-order indices in that they are calculated directly from measurements. Heterogeneity is a group of indices denoting structure arising jointly from the number of categories and the proportional assignment of cases to them. Heterogeneity is a second-order index because it is derived from richness and evenness; it is calculated from them and not vice versa. Whereas one layer of potential differences is introduced in calculating richness or evenness, an additional layer is interposed for heterogeneity – there are different ways to calculate both richness and evenness and different ways to calculate heterogeneity from them. Consequently, for simple structural reasons, heterogeneity is always more problematic than either richness or evenness. Even though heterogeneity may seem intuitively more nearly coterminous with the concept of diversity, as it is currently employed, heterogeneity is a less, not more, fundamental interpretation of diversity.

One might argue, as is occasionally but not consistently implied by some of the contributions, that evenness is derived from richness because the number of categories (richness) is requisite for a calculation of the proportional distribution of cases. Inconsistency arises because everyone who explicitly recognizes the differences between richness and evenness and who comments on the relation asserts that they are *independent* indices of diversity. My rendition of the relation between richness and evenness as equivalent in Figure 15.1 does not rest upon a denial of the obvious calculation requirements for evenness but rather on a distinction touched on by only a few of the papers, that between populations and samples (Chapters 1 and 3).

Conceptually, richness and evenness are regarded as independent because analysts imagine that the processes responsible for their manifestation in phenomena may be different. Evenness and richness are imagined, at least potentially, to have different causes. In application, this conceptual distinction is carried over to populations; it is not, however, maintained in samples. In samples, a knowledge of the proportional assignment of cases to classes is just as necessary to an assessment of richness as an assessment of

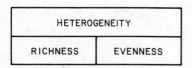

Fig. 15.1. Relation among indices of diversity

richness is to the estimation of evenness. In this situation, they are *equally dependent.* Presumably, were diversity thoroughly integrated into archaeological concerns, there would be concepts analogous to the indices of richness and evenness and the relations between the concepts would be different from those between the indices currently in use. One virtue of distinguishing concepts and indices is that it allows us to frame the general methodological problems. The indices have been borrowed from ecology; the concept, as many of the papers show, has a long archaeological history but one that has not been distinguished by careful dissection. The result is that the indices in use are not empirical interpretations of comparable archaeological concepts. It is this uncrossed synapse that makes the meaning of diversity indices so problematic in archaeological contexts.

Before addressing the methodological issues suggested by this analysis (the phenomena characterized by diversity indices, the relation and impact of sampling to such indices, and the source[s] of meaning for indices), one ancillary terminological ambiguity should be noted, the term 'relative.' Several authors assert (e.g., Conkey, Rice, Thomas) that diversity indices are 'relative.' For some, relative appears to mean 'in relation to sample size.' For others it appears to mean only that the typical current usage of such indices lies in comparing assemblages and thus relative means 'comparative.' Related to this is the usage that implies a contrast between relative and absolute, not in the sense these terms are applied in dating to designate age assignments to ordinal/interval and ratio time scales respectively, but in the sense that, lacking any theoretical expectations for any of the indices, their use is constrained to a comparative mode. Further, the meaning of relative does not always appear to be constant within a given contribution. These characterizations of diversity indices, and perhaps the concept, are not conclusions based on arguments, but simple assertions about the nature of diversity. Fortunately, the impact of this ambiguity is limited to semantic confusion; in no case does the characterization of diversity as relative actually enter into substantive conclusions.

The components of diversity indices
The making of any observation, the creation of a value for a variable, can always be shown to involve the use of at least two categories or sets of categories – a category that identifies the thing about which the observation pertains and the category or categories in which the observation is rendered. Thus when we say a book weighs 545 grams or is blue, we have had to identify objects with a classification that includes a class 'book,' and we have had to employ some classification with a root called weight or color. If we want to say something about book*s*, a third category enters, that which determines the search space within which the books were aggregated. The total weight, the range of weights, the mean

weight, the variance, are all a function of which particular books were considered.

Statistics, including the diversity indices treated in this volume, are generalizations about such observations, developed by employing one or another algorithm for their construction. As generalizations they contain much less information than do the measurements on which they are based. A histogram of class frequencies, for example, contains more information than does any single numerical summation of those frequencies, be it a mean or an evenness value, a point explicitly appreciated in some of the chapters. That two or more sets of different numbers can yield identical means or evenness values while employing identical algorithms is a clear demonstration of this information loss. Whether the loss is advantageous (i.e., suppresses extraneous variability) or disadvantageous (i.e., entails equifinality) is a function of the nature of the categories that generated the measurements.

In all of the contributions in this volume, with the notable exception of Chapter 9, there is an appreciation of the general role of categories in making diversity indices meaningful. For the most part, however, this appreciation is limited to those categories which provide the terms of measurement (e.g., types of artifacts or species of organisms). The categories analogous to 'book' in the previous discussion (e.g., artifacts and organisms) are universally taken for granted. The search space (e.g., communities and assemblages), the thing to which a diversity value is assigned, is largely adopted uncritically from the traditional and highly variable archaeological usage. Lack of attention to this last kind of category appears to be largely responsible for the confusion between samples and populations inasmuch as the expression of this distinction correlates strongly with a recognition of the role of the search space. For instance, Rindos (Chapter 3) carefully outlines the kinds of categories involved and sporadically recognizes the population/sample distinction, whereas the other chapters that ignore the origin of the 'things,' which can be diverse, fail to operationalize, and usually even to note, the population/sample distinction.

Rindos treats these measurement parameters in far greater detail than any of the other contributions. He terms the thing to be characterized by an index U. Measurements are made on what he calls the 'working data set,' d. If $U = d$, then a censused population is characterized; if $U > d$, then a sample is being used to characterize a population. The first operation is descriptive, the latter inferential. The individuals, n, correspond to the book, artifacts, or organisms of earlier examples. Finally, Rindos uses c to denote the categories that provide the terms for the measurements. Rindos provides more than a handy set of terms with which to discuss the creation of measurements; he also illustrates some of the ways in which each component influences the meaning of an index. For example, he points out that some indices are designed for use under the condition $U = d$ (Brillouin's function) while others assume that $U > d$. While lumping different sources of variation, he argues that differences in level (e.g., species vs genera) in c, or differences in scale (e.g., pots vs sherds) that inhere in n all influence the meaning of the indices. But his discussion embodies an important confusion.

In setting forth the requirements for each set of categories, Rindos skirts the character of U in favor of noting the large literature that exists on the character of d when $U > d$. He goes on to assert that both n and c must be 'real,' a notoriously snaky term. This entails a confusion between class *significata* and *denotata* (Dunnell 1971), for, to make sense of his discussion, 'real' must be interpreted variously as 'empirical' (in the context of n) and 'not capricious' (in the context of c). It is clear that n categories *must* be units about which an empirical claim of setness can be sustained. Without this empirical connection, no measurement or observation can be made. Artifacts have to be empirical for counts of them to be derived. U might be distinguished as a set empirically, i.e., the set boundaries may be observational. Alternatively U, while constituted by 'real' ns, might be an association identified only by an algorithm (as, for example, assemblages and communities are treated and as Simek's clusters and Schiffer's subassemblages are). It is certainly conceivable, however, that one might want to calculate diversity values for arbitrary units of space such as areas or volumes, much in the way in which archaeologists use artifact density. Rindos' reluctance to analyze the requirement of U categories may only reflect the rather shaky notion of 'community' in ecology, from which the indices are borrowed.

That the indices have been borrowed from ecology may be the cause of the confusion over the characterization of c categories. Species, the common c units in ecology, have both the properties of classes (taxa) and groups of things about which existential claims are made (and can be sustained in the synchronous settings presented by ecological time [Pianka 1974]). Since taxonomic classes entail such a large assumptive input (Dunnell 1971), species are almost always operationalized as empirical entities, 'real' things in Rindos' terms. The c units clearly can be groups, but this cannot be generalized to a requirement of c units. Most measurements are made with classes for which no empirical reality is claimed, or even desired. Distance is not rendered meaningless because it is measured in terms of wholly arbitrary and conventional units such as meters, wavelengths of light, or feet. Distance is meaningless only if the units in which it is rendered are *undefined*. Thus, to understand Rindos' discussion of c categories, 'real' has to be interpreted as 'not whimsical, capricious, or *ad hoc*,' even though elsewhere he apparently means 'empirical.' If the definitions of c units are not to be capricious, they must be justified theoretically, a point made quite strongly in other terms by Conkey and Rice in this volume. The same requirement holds for the identification of empirical groups, be they U, n, or c categories. Variations in the algorithms for constructing communities or assemblages and variations in the identification of organism or artifact, as well as in the algorithms for recognizing species, affect the meaning of indices calculated from them.

In the rest of the chapters, little attention is paid to U type units *per se*, although a major focus of many of them is on the U/d relation when $U > d$. Only in the contribution from Jones *et al.* (Chapter 7) is this parameter actively manipulated when they consider site/non-site comparisons, and various partitions of the latter. No doubt the lack of interest in this component of diversity lies in the unquestioned status of the notion of site and its empirical derivative, the assemblage. Similarly, the *n* categories receive no attention at all, even though Rindos warns that this may be quite problematic in archaeology. Again, the uncritical use of a traditional archaeological concept, here usually artifact, seems to occasion the lack of interest.

The *c* categories, on the other hand, are prominent, probably because archaeological classifications generate the *c* type units. True, adoption of preexisting classification is common enough (e.g, Thomas, Schiffer) and *de rigueur* when archaeofaunas are involved (Rothschild). But even in these cases there is concern about the meaning of the classes. Most dramatically, Thomas 'tests' the influence of classification on the behavior of his richness index by comparing the performance of what are apparently two levels (Dunnell 1971) of classes drawn from the same classification. The classification involved is apparently either a taxonomy or simply an *ad hoc* set of artifact type definitions, because there are no empty classes that would characterize a dimensional classification such as a hybrid or a paradigm. Parenthetically, it should be noted that Jones *et al.* point out the potential of 'absolute' assessments of richness when dimensional classifications, specifically paradigms, are used. That Thomas finds no difference in the behavior of the richness index, when this is calculated using one or the other level of classes, tells us only that his lower-level classes (analogous to Rindos' species) are more or less randomly distributed among his higher-level classes (analogous to Rindos' genera).

The most sophisticated manipulation of the *c* categories is apparent in the use by Jones *et al.* of two different classifications, one 'functional' and one 'technological,' to derive two different estimates of diversity on the same set of materials. This allows them to show that technological diversity behaves differently in space than does functional diversity, clearly demonstrating that the meaning of a diversity index is a function of the *c* categories. Their demonstration does not, however, bear upon the superficially contradictory results obtained by Thomas because Thomas compares levels of the same classification whereas Jones *et al.* compare the results of two different classifications. Jones *et al.* do not, however, develop the justifications for the classifications they use in detail. We must simply assume that the functional classification actually measures function in some archaeological sense and that their technological classification does measure technology. No doubt some of the ambiguity they report in the behavior of functional diversity derives from this lack of theoretical sophistication. Their models for the behavior of functional diversity are couched in terms of 'activities' (cf. Simek), yet there is no activity classification involved. Artifact function is not generally equivalent to activity since a given function (e.g., cutting) can be expected to participate in a variable number of different activities (cf. Simek) which themselves can be expected to have variable representation in the archaeological record. In many different kinds of activities, for example, the cutting function may be the only function that finds its way into the preserved archaeological record.

Chapter 11 by Leonard *et al.* is more sophisticated in this regard. The *c* categories are stone types defined by attributes that identify spatially segregated sources, a parameter that is of direct relevance to the problem they address. But, unlike Jones *et al.*, this chapter employs only one classification; other potentially valuable parameters such as 'workability' are treated intuitively. If these parameters can be addressed with robust classifications so that measurements rather than impressions are generated, they may well be able to identify the causal mechanisms controlling diversity of stone type with more certainty.

The efforts of Jones *et al.* and Leonard *et al.* to give their *c* units a foundation in archaeological theory are congruent with the programmatic statements pertaining to this relation (e.g., Conkey, Rice), but they are not typical of practice. Bobrowsky and Ball describe the typical practice when they note that 'a conceptual substitution of artifact types for species allows researchers to formally apply the concept of diversity to archaeology' (p. 8). It is true that species and artifact types, like *c* units, play identical roles in calculating diversity indices. It is this functional identity, in spite of the gross differences between species and artifact types and the necessity for different theoretical justification, that allows the technique to be transferred from one field to another in advance of the appropriate theoretical development.

That most archaeological uses of diversity represent the application of a technique without a theoretical warrant receives high-level expression throughout the volume. In spite of the programmatic appreciation that the meaning of any diversity index is a function of the *a priori* meanings of the three sets of categories required for their calculation (e.g., Conkey, Rindos, and Rice) and the practical demonstration of this relation (e.g., Jones *et al.*), the *interpretation* of diversity assessments occurs as a minor element in all but a few chapters and is the main focus of both Conkey and Rice. That archaeologists pursue this curious course is, of course, only a manifestation of the poverty of archaeological theory and the inability to create meaningful *U*, *n*, and *c* units. All good intentions aside, the meaning of diversity indices is mechanically *determined* by the definitions of the categorical inputs; if the *measurements* on which diversity indices are based do not unambiguously measure the parameter of interest, then no interpretations are warranted. Of course, a certain amount of movement back and forth between inductive and deductive strategies is to be expected, and in fact is necessary, in the development of theory, but one senses a larger commitment to the inductive interpretive mode than simply as a phase in theory construction. One can only hope that this impression is illusory, because, if it persists, theory development will be thwarted and the value of rigorous efforts to assess diversity negated. Archaeological data will continue to speak for themselves from their black box, only through a different hole.

Samples, sampling, and populations

As noted earlier, *U* categories bear one of two relations to the set of things measured, *d*: $U = d$, in which *d* is a population; and $U > d$, in which case *d* is a sample. In the first instance, $U = d$, measurements and indices based on them *describe* a population; in the second case, $U > d$, measurements and indices based on them describe a sample which is used to infer a description of a population. Although there is programmatic recognition of this distinction in several of the papers, almost everyone proceeds on the assumption that $U > d$. The substantial interest in the sample situation is undoubtedly due to the work of Grayson who demonstrated that diversity correlates strongly with sample size in faunal assemblages (Grayson 1981, 1984) and more generally (Jones *et al.* 1983 and Grayson Chapter 8). The pragmatic confusion between population and sample is, however, due in part to terminology, and in part to conceptual, properly metaphysical, differences. As Bobrowsky and Ball and Rindos indicate, this distinction is important in the selection of the appropriate index of diversity, but the implications are far more extensive and fundamental than choice of technique. Failure to distinguish rigorously between the two relations of d to U accentuates what Gould (1985:22) has identified as the most serious and persistent error in all scientific reasoning, the conflation of cause and correlation. More pragmatically, it can lead to nonsense conclusions and negate the efforts to quantify diversity in a meaningful manner.

The key to these problems lies in the multiple meanings attached to 'sample.' Sample is sometimes used in the sense of $U > d$, i.e., sample in a statistical sense. As is generally appreciated in archaeology, but not infrequently ignored, to infer a description of U from d, where $U > d$, the relation between U and d must be known *a priori*. A large body of sampling theory, and algorithms to effect it, has grown up around this point. One of the salient requirements, noted by Rindos and pertinent to later discussion, is that U must be known if one is to sample it in a statistically valid way. Some d categories are thus samples, $U > d$; others are not, $U = d$. Of course, some ds bear an unknown relation to U and strictly speaking are not appropriate subjects of quantification when the intent is to draw conclusions about U rather than d. This knowledge does not always prevent the use of such 'samples.'

Sample is also frequently used to mean simply 'case,' i.e., it is used as a synonym for d regardless of whether $U > d$ or $U = d$. Because of the overlap between the two meanings, it is easy to slip unremarked from one usage to the other. This is the principal source of confusion between d as a sample in the statistical sense and d as a population.

Sample is also used metaphorically, approximating the meaning of 'example.' In these usages, U is an hypothesized whole, unrealized and unrealizable empirically. This meaning of sample is apparent when individual ds and ds collectively are said to be samples of 'culture,' 'human behavior,' or 'cultural systems' (e.g., Jones and Leonard). This is simply the fallacy of misplaced concreteness. A conceptual quality is substituted unremarked for an empirical one, precluding any possibility of empirical evaluation of the conclusions drawn. Although a sampling terminology is often employed in this context when it is said that human behavior or culture is 'inferred' from ds, the inference is not statistical inference but rather interpretation. Such interpretation is typically a substitution for explicit theory as noted earlier. Since the thrust of contemporary interest in diversity lies in rigorous measurement and quantification, exploration of this use of sample is beyond the scope of this chapter except to the degree that it conflates other issues.

That sample size ($U > d$) affects diversity statistics is uncontestable (Figure 15.2). The number of individuals comprising d, Σ_n, places absolute limits on the total number of c categories (i.e., richness) that may be present in a given d, as noted by several authors in this volume. Even when Σ_c is significantly exceeded by Σ_n, whenever the distribution of c categories in U is not perfectly even (i.e., when the proportion of ns assignable to the various c categories is not identical from one c to the next and therefore not equal to 1 divided by Σ_c categories), sampling interacts with the distribution of ns over cs partly to determine richness. Further, as the number of classes present, richness, partly determines evenness, the apparent evenness of sample is influenced, albeit in a more complex way, by the interaction of c distributions in U with sample size.

The relation between sample size and indices of diversity was not, however, first identified by deductive argument; sensitivity to the issue arose directly from the empirical observation that a strong correlation obtains between Σ_n and Σ_c (e.g., Grayson 1984 and references therein). Because of the strength of this correlation and its appearance in studies unrelated by subject or location, all chapters in this volume and recent studies elsewhere appreciate the significance of sample size on diversity indices, at least in a general way. Research is usually founded on the assumption that such correlations obtain generally. For many workers, the general strategy pursued is to ascertain how much of the variability in diversity indices may be accountable as a consequence of sampling. It is at this point that the conflation between cause and correlation can occur, for many investigators conclude, when a high correlation between Σ_n and Σ_c occurs, that diversity values obtained are 'explained by' sample size. Only Jones *et al.* are circumspect enough on this issue to modify the account to read 'may be explained by.' The stronger 'explained by' conclusion is not warranted for the very reasons that archaeologists are interested in measuring diversity; there are an indefinite number of empirical correlations of the same direction, if not magnitude, that may obtain in the phenomenological world. For example, assemblages that represent diverse activities may also typically be larger; assemblages that represent longer spans of time may also typically be larger. These correlations may be causally linked by cultural and natural processes.

Ironically, Thomas, who is the worst offender in terms of the 'explained by' terminology, is also the author most cognizant of the potential for equifinality with empirical correlations. Perhaps it was the conflict between the two positions that led Thomas (cf. Jones *et al.* 1983) to suggest that since correlation *per se* (i.e., r, r^2) cannot be accorded unambiguous cultural meaning, the differing *slopes* exhibited by regressions of different cases (and presumably different c categories) offer the greatest potential for cultural interpretation. Differences in slope record differing rates at which an increase in the size of the sample is accompanied by an increase in richness. Other contributors (Jones *et al.*; Leonard *et al.*) also see a potential for this approach. Thomas goes even further to sketch the outline of an archaeological framework for the interpretation

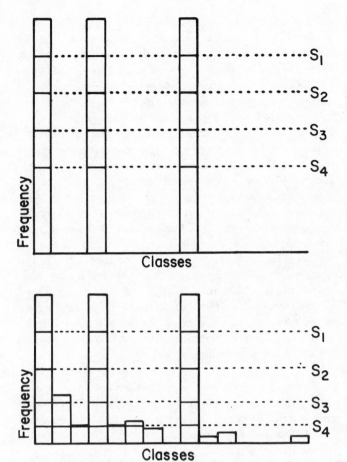

Fig. 15.2. Richness, evenness, and samples. S_1–S_4 represent successively larger, equivalent samples of two different populations. Note that larger samples are required in populations that are uneven: once Σ_n exceeds Σ_c increases in population richness exert no influence on sample-size requirements. Note also that regression slopes, the rate at which increases in sample size are accompanied by increases in richness, are a function of evenness.

of regression slopes. As Figure 15.2 suggests, however, slope in regressions of Σ_n and Σ_c is a function of evenness, again demonstrating the interdependence of richness and evenness.

Differentiating empirical and artificial sources of correlations between Σ_n and Σ_c is not, however, hopeless. Indices of diversity, as noted earlier, suppress most of the information contained in the measurements on which they are based. Which classes are present in what specific abundances should differentiate sampling error from other nonrandom sources of correlations, much as the class frequencies can be used to evaluate similar coefficients of similarity in seriation applications (Dunnell 1970).

This discussion presumes that the cases, ds, are actually samples in the statistical sense, $U > d$. While many archaeological ds are samples in this sense, at least in the loosest interpretation, where representativeness cannot be asserted, many are not. Populations, $U = d$, are also employed frequently. Further, sampling error is confined to an increasingly minor role in samples that comprise very large segments of the parent populations, especially in terms of evennes (cf. Lipe 1964). Be-

cause this distinction is not clearly drawn in those papers that supply substantive applications, it is difficult to know which kind of d is involved in any given study or whether they may have been mixed. Because of the ds in Chapter 7 (Jones *et al.*) were obtained from stable or deflating surfaces, those which were collected in their entirety are probably populations rather than samples. Similarly, Simek's Couche V at Le Flagolet 1 is probably a population rather than a sample. The same is probably true of Schiffer's d units.

This is a crucial point. *There can be no effects of sample size when there is no sample!* When the correlation between Σ_n and Σ_c is said to be explained by sample size under the conditions that d is identical to U or approaches identity with U, the conflation of cause and correlation yields nonsense conclusions. That such correlations do obtain in some analyses that operate on populations is clear and substantial proof that other, empirical, correlations do exist between Σ_n and Σ_c. When populations are the ds on which a diversity index is based, the diversity index is a *description* of a population parameter, not an estimation of it. Presumably, no one would regard the meaning of identical diversity indices derived from two cases, in both of which $n = 15$ and $c = 2$ with identical numbers of members in the corresponding categories, as identical if one case were a population (i.e., all the artifacts deposited = 15) and the other a small sample of a larger population. To use some of the terminologies of this volume, our population case would never be regarded as a base camp, whereas the possibility that our sample case is a base camp cannot be ruled out *a priori*.

What the growing literature on the effects of sampling on diversity indices should tell us is simple, but not diminished in importance by its simplicity. If $U > d$, then artificial correlations between Σ_n and Σ_c may be present and if present may mimic some empirical correlations of interest. The meaning of diversity indices cannot be assumed *a priori* to be cultural when samples are involved. The charge to the researcher is to differentiate the causes of correlations (cf. Grayson). Here, as elsewhere in science, conflation of cause and correlation may truncate the search for causal mechanisms and the techniques to detect them. The ultimate utility of indices of diversity in archaeology is very much tied to research on these questions.

Before leaving sampling questions, note should be taken of the two strategies for modeling the diversity/sample size relationship, Kintigh's simulation approach (Kintigh 1984a, Chapter 4 above) and the regression approach discussed earlier. Leaving aside the confusion about the nature of d units and the conflation of cause and correlation, both efforts share a common feature that serves to illustrate a further sampling issue, the relation *between* ds. As Conkey notes explicitly (and others imply by example), the principal archaeological interest in using diversity indices lies in comparing samples of different assemblages rather than different samples of the same assemblages.[3] In these instances, ds are treated as samples of some larger entities because the assemblages from which the ds are derived are conceived as samples of a larger entity (e.g., the 'culture type' of Conkey or the 'culturally determined underlying frequency distribution' of Kintigh). Indeed, to make inferences about the diversity of such larger entities, the d units would have to be strict samples of them. Both approaches assume that such is the case.

Kintigh's model makes this easiest to appreciate when, to generate his expectations, he simply sums the five data sets and uses those totals to compute the parameters for simulation. But the five data sets cannot be shown to be a statistically representative sample of anything, either by derivation or other characteristics. There is no list of all Lower Magdalenian deposits and, without such a list, there is no way to show that the five assemblages from which samples have been drawn are themselves representative samples of Lower Magdalenian assemblages. Indeed, as most archaeologists would readily admit, the known record, unless generated by a probabilistic-based modern survey, never even approaches this condition.

While less evident, the regression approach employs the same assumptions; all characteristics of the regression are functions of the assemblages included. Even if the archaeological record were known in its totality or close to it,[4] any variation in the algorithms for selecting what cases (i.e., what constitutes being Lower Magdalenian and what space is to be searched for things that are Lower Magdalenian) are to be included will influence the results. The lack of appreciation of this problem may arise in the regression approach simply because the issue is structurally more obscure than in simulation. But it may also simply be a matter of convenience (as seems to be the case in Chapter 4 above) or an appeal to a metaphorical universe. Whatever the reasons, the lack of a defined *U* and consequently the problematic nature of the *d*s employed would seem to deprive both the regression and simulation models of any warrant in this comparative context. Deviations and outliers may be deviations and outliers only because of the particular suite of *d*s used and bear no relation to the distribution of diversity in the archaeological record.

In these larger comparative contexts, we would be far better off if we were to ask straightforward sampling questions. In Kintigh's example, for instance, the substantive questions really appear to be 'Is Cueto de la Mina more or less rich than Altamira? Is El Juyo more or less rich? . . . etc.' Given a sampling interpretation, these questions amount to asking 'What is the probability that a sample the size of Cueto de la Mina would have the same richness value, within a given confidence interval, as Altamira if the distribution of cases over classes were the same?' Or, more generally, 'What is the probability that a class which has a frequency *X* in a parent population will be represented in a sample of *Y* size?' These do not exhaust the range of straightforward sampling hypotheses that would appear to address the concerns of researchers without committing them to unwarranted models. Solutions of this sort are foreshadowed in the work of Beals *et al.* (1945) to evaluate frequencies. Efforts specific to diversity indices are also being made (Rhode 1985).

These comments should not be taken to mean that simulation models and regression approaches are without value. On the contrary, whenever there is known or knowable *U* from which the *d*s have been drawn or whenever the models are used to describe, rather than infer, relationships, both approaches seem on firm ground. Simek's paper provides an excellent positive case in point

when he uses Kintigh's approach to describe the activity structure of Couche V, Le Flageolet I. His clusters, which serve as the *d* units, are subassemblages of the Couche V assemblage, itself probably a population. He asks only whether it is reasonable to interpret the diversity indices of his subassemblages as a consequence of their size or whether these indices represent significant departures from the Couche V assemblage characteristics as a whole. Here, the diversity of the total assemblage is clearly the relevant parameter to generate a simulation. The assemblage is an empirically bounded entity and the relation between it and the subassemblages is known, in fact, spelled out in detail by Simek. Schiffer's paper in which unrecognized 'whole pots' (sherd count interdependences) are suggested as responsible for erroneous interpretations of the Broken K Pueblo sherds distributions is a different but nonetheless legitimate usage. Kintigh's model is employed, but again there is a relevant empirical population (actually a sample, but functioning as a population in Schiffer's application) from which to generate the simulation, and the *d* units are samples of that population. Further, no inferences are drawn about the larger unit. Similarly, many of the applications of the regression approach are probably descriptive rather than inferential, although this is difficult to determine in many cases.

Significance, explanation, and metaphysics

While the exploration of the conception and use of diversity indices is still too primitive to be integrated with the general research strategies of the discipline as a whole, the use of metaphorical populations and the occasional use of 'significance' (e.g., Kintigh; Leonard *et al.*) in a comparative context foreshadow an issue which may become of paramount importance once the technical problems have been resolved.

As Rindos argues from ecological contexts, the *U*s are typically categories about which empirical claims can be made. For an index of diversity of a community to be meaningful, the community itself must be an empirical entity – internally coherent, externally contrastive with other such units. It has to be a thing to which it is reasonable to ascribe a property. Such entities, loosely things, exist only in a space-like conception of reality (Dunnell 1982). Such a framework is the context of *difference*. This essentialist metaphysic is empirically operable *at any given point in time*. Consequently, disciplines which conceive of their phenomena as timeless (e.g., physics and chemistry) and those which operate in the here and now take decidedly essentialist views of reality and their analytic tools are designed to isolate difference. Ecology, the source of contemporary indices of diversity, is just such a discipline. Inferential statistics have a similar metaphysical basis. Significance testing, for example, presumes the existence of discreteness or difference.

Archaeologists, and scientists in other historical disciplines, face a much more complicated situation. The archaeological record is a phenomenon of the here and now. Artifacts are discrete entities and various higher-level orders of artifacts may also be potentially discrete. Methodologically, though not of course theoretically, methods and techniques developed in ahistorical disciplines are quite compatible with analyses of the record *per se*.

But archaeologists are also, and many would claim primarily, interested in change, a concept rooted in a time-like conception of reality linked to a materialist metaphysic (Dunnell 1982). In this framework, things do not exist; rather they are always in a state of becoming (cf. Prigogine 1980 for a similar view in physics). This condition deprives archaeologists of the use of methods and techniques borrowed from space-like disciplines because the 'things' they require do not exist. This has had two common results. As Conkey notes, one avenue of response has been the increasing restriction of archaeology to synchronic applications. The traditional interest of the discipline in change has been subtly replaced by the study of difference for which methods and techniques already exist. The other avenue of response, the creation of fictive or metaphorical things to take the place of the absent empirical entities is widely evident in these essays. This approach in the role of an heuristic device is reasonable enough. For example, Leonard *et al.* note 'significant differences' in the richness of lithic raw materials between Basketmaker and Pueblo. That significant differences exist between two arbitrarily defined segments of a continuous development is valuable insofar as it demonstrates that lithic source richness of assemblages is worth exploration; it is variable and very likely that variation is patterned over time. But when it comes to explaining that variation, they encounter difficulties, not only for the theoretical inadequacies that they note, but also because they have converted change into difference.

The point is simple. The measurement of diversity, at least as presently conceived, is a business properly confined to the empirical record. The explanation of diversity thus measured, however, is going to take us into largely unexplored methodological ground if archaeology is to be more than a dog wagged by a borrowed technical tail or an exercise in the writing of uncontestable fiction. While I would not go so far as Rindos to claim that evolutionary theory provides the only context in which diversity will prove explicable in a scientific sense, Rindos does show that it can be explained by that kind of theoretical construct.

Summary

Diversity in archaeology has moved quite rapidly from a wholly intuitive notion about complexity to serious efforts at quantification. The papers in this volume illustrate the difficulties entailed in taking an intuitive notion and attempting to apply it in a rigorous fashion. They also serve to illustrate the liabilities of uncritical technique borrowing. At the same time, they also illustrate the very substantial gains in clarity of thought that occur as a result of these efforts. There already have been spinoffs of general value to archaeology in the discussions of sampling. The ultimate value of the notion of diversity to archaeology will be determined by the larger strategy pursued by the discipline as a whole and its realization will hinge on solving some long-standing and knotty methodological problems. Yet it is clear from these essays that it can be feasible to measure diversity in archaeological contexts and that such measurements can open major new avenues of understanding of the archaeological record and its makers.

Notes

1. All undated references cited pertain to the contributions contained in this volume.
2. None of the various diversity 'figures' are properly termed measurements, i.e., they are not derived from the direct application of measurement scale to phenomena. All must be calculated from measurements, *sensu stricto*, a point well made by Rindos. This feature interposes an additional source of variation, not entailed in the phenomena themselves, and affects both the meaning and the use of diversity indices.
3. The strategy of comparing different samples (ds) of the same assemblage (U) is, of course, the ideal way in which to explore the relation between sampling and samples, *sensu stricto*, and indices of diversity. Not distinguishing among ds, when $U = d$ and when $U > d$ is probably partly responsible for the absence of this approach in the literature. Further, to the extent that many 'samples' are actually populations, or closely approach being populations, this strategy is physically impossible.
4. Because the archaeological record is empirical, it is at least theoretically possible to treat it as a population and to draw inferences about it from the examination of assemblages which can be acquired in such a manner as to constitute samples of that population. This possibility does not mean, of course, that assemblages always or even usually are samples of the archaeological record in a statistical sense. Assemblages, on the other hand, can never be presumed to be samples, *sensu stricto*, of cultures or cultural systems, or even of all of the remains that were deposited. The first two are metaphorical entities which, despite their frequency of use and their value in interpretations, cannot be sampled. The last, the remains originally deposited, while at one point empirical, is no longer, and the contemporary record cannot be presumed to be a representative sample of it because the processes by which elements of it have been removed are demonstrably not random.
5. This paper was read in draft by D. K. Grayson, G. T. Jones, and R. D. Leonard and has benefited from their comments. M. D. Dunnell provided helpful editorial assistance. R. Rodriguez typed the manuscript. To all these individuals, and any inadvertently omitted, I am most grateful.

REFERENCES

Adams, W.Y. 1979. On the argument from ceramics to history: a challenge based on evidence from medieval Nubia. *Current Anthropology* 20(4): 727–44.

    1981. Reply to P. Rice, Evolution of specialized pottery production: trial model. *Current Anthropology* 22 (3): 227–8.

Aikens, C. Melvin, Donald K. Grayson, and Peter J. Mehringer, Jr 1982. *Final Project Report to the National Science Foundation on the Steens Mountain Prehistory Project*. Department of Anthropology, University of Oregon.

Ammerman, Albert and Marcus Feldman 1974. On the making of an assemblage of stone tools. *American Antiquity* 39 (4): 610–16.

Ammerman, Albert, Keigh Kintigh, and Jan Simek 1983. Recent developments in the application of the *k*-means approach to spatial analysis. Paper presented at the Fourth International Flint Symposium, Brighton, England.

Antia, D.D.J. 1977. A comparison of diversity and trophic nuclei of live and dead molluscan faunas from the Essex Chenier Plain, England. *Paleobiology* 3: 404–14.

Arnold, D.E. 1971. Ethnomineralogy of Tical, Yucatan potters: etics and emics. *American Antiquity* 36: 20–40.

Ayala, F.J. and J.W. Valentine 1979. *Evolving: The Theory and Process of Organic Evolution*. Menlo Park, CA: Benjamin Cummings.

Balfet, H. 1965. Ethnographical observations in North Africa and archaeological interpretation: the pottery of the Mahgreb. In *Ceramics and Man*, edited by F.R. Matson, pp. 161–77. Chicago: Aldin.

Basharin, G.P. 1959. On a statistical estimate for the entropy of a sequence of independent random variables. *Theory of Probability and its Applications* 4: 333–6.

Beals, Ralph L., George W. Brainerd, and Watson Smith 1945. *Archaeological Studies in Northeast Arizona*. University of California Publications in American Archaeology and Ethnology 44 (1).

Beck, Charlotte 1984. *Steens Mountain Surface Archaeology: The Sites*. Ph.D. Dissertation, University of Washington. Ann Arbor: University Microfilms.

Benco, Nancy L. 1985. Ceramic diversity and political centralization: a case study from medieval North Africa. Paper presented at the 50th annual meeting of the Society for American Archaeology, Denver, CO.

Berlinski, D. 1976. *On Systems Analysis: an Essay concerning the Limitations of some Mathematical Methods in the Social, Political and Biological Sciences*. Cambridge, MA: MIT Press.

Binford, Lewis R. 1962. Archaeology as anthropology. *American Antiquity* 28 (2): 217–25.

    1965. Archeological systematics and the study of culture process. *American Antiquity* 31 (2): 203–10.

    1972. *An Archaeological Perspective*. New York: Seminar Press.

    1977. Forty-seven trips: a case study in the character of some formation processes of the archeological record. In *Contributions to Anthropology: The Interior Peoples of Northern Alaska*, edited by E.S. Hall Jr., pp. 299–351. Archaeological Survey of Canada Paper 49.

    1978a. *Nunamiut Ethnoarchaeology*. New York: Academic Press.

    1978b. Dimensional analysis of behavior and site structure: learning from an Eskimo hunting stand. *American Antiquity* 43 (3): 330–61.

    1979. Organization and formation processes: looking at curated technologies. *Journal of Anthropological Research* 35 (3): 255–73.

    1980. Willow smoke and dogs' tails: hunter–gatherer settlement systems and archaeological site formation. *American Antiquity* 45 (1): 4–20.

    1981. Behavioral archaeology and the "Pompeii premise." *Journal of Anthropological Research* 37 (3): 195–208.

    1982. The archaeology of place. *Journal of Anthropological Archaeology* (1) 1: 5–31.

    1983a. *In Pursuit of the Past: Decoding the Archaeological Record*. New

York: Thames and Hudson.

1983b. Long term land use patterns: some implications for archaeology. In *Lulu Linear Punctated: Essays in Honor of George Irving Quimby*, edited by Robert C. Dunnell and Donald K. Grayson, pp. 27–53. Anthropological Papers No. 72, Museum of Anthropology, University of Michigan, Ann Arbor.

Binford, Lewis R., and Sally R. Binford 1966. A preliminary analysis of functional variability in the Mousterian of Levallois facies. In *Recent Studies in Paleoanthropology*, edited by J.D. Clarke and F. Clark Howell, pp. 238–95. *American Anthropologist* 68 (part 2).

Binford, S.R. and L.R. Binford, eds. 1968. *New Perspectives in Archaeology*. Chicago: Aldine.

Bishop, R.L. and R.L. Rands 1982. Maya fine paste ceramics: a compositional perspective. In *Analyses of Fine Paste Ceramics*, no. 2 of *Excavations at Seibel, Department of Peten, Guatemala*, edited by J.A. Sabloff. Memoirs of the Peabody Museum of Archaeology and Ethnology, vol. 15, no. 1–2, pp. 283–314.

Bishop, R.L., R.L. Rands, and G. Holley 1982. Ceramic compositional analysis in archeological perspective. In *Advances in Archaeological Method and Theory*, vol. 5, edited by M.B. Schiffer, pp. 275–330. New York: Academic Press.

Blalock, Hubert 1972. *Social Statistics*. New York: McGraw-Hill.

1979. *Social Statistics* (2nd edition, revised). New York: McGraw-Hill.

Bobrowsky, Peter T. 1983. Estimation of adequate sample size for biological remains. Paper presented at the 16th Annual Meeting of the Canadian Archaeological Association, Halifax.

Bølviken, Erik, Ericka Helskog, Knut Helskog, Inger Marie Holm-Olsen, Leiv Solheim, and Reidar Bertelsen 1982. Correspondence analysis: an alternative to principal components. *World Archaeology* 14 (1): 41–60.

Bonnichsen, R. 1979. Pleistocene bone technology in the Beringian refugium. *Archaeological Survey of Canada Paper* 89.

Boone, J.L., III 1982. Defining and measuring refuse catchment. Paper presented at 47th Annual Meeting of the Society for American Archaeology, Minneapolis.

Bourdieu, F. 1977. *An Outline of a Theory of Practice*. Cambridge: Cambridge University Press.

Braun, David P. 1977. Middle Woodland–(Early) Late Woodland Social Change in the Prehistoric Central Midwestern U.S. Ph.D. Dissertation, Department of Anthropology, University of Michigan. Ann Arbor: University Microfilms.

1980. Experimental interpretation of ceramic vessel use on the basis of rim and neck formal attributes. In *The Navajo Project, Archaeological Investigations*, edited by D. Fiero, R. Munson, *et al.* Museum of Northern Arizona Research Paper 11.

1985a. Ceramic decorative diversity and Illinois Woodland regional integration. In *Decoding Prehistoric Ceramics*, edited by Ben A. Nelson, pp. 128–53. Carbondale, IL.: Southern Illinois University Press.

1985b. Making an impression: Illinois Woodland pottery design and social interactions. Paper presented at 50th Annual Meeting of the Society for American Archaeology, Denver, Co.

Braun, D.P. and S. Plog, 1982. Evolution of "tribal" social networks: theory and prehistoric North American evidence. *American Antiquity* 47 (3): 504–25.

Brillouin, Leon, 1962. *Science and Information Theory*, 2nd edition. New York: Academic Press.

Bronitsky, G. 1978. Postclassic Maya plainware ceramics: measures of cultural homogeneity. In *Papers on the Economy and Architecture of the Ancient Maya*, edited by R. Sidrys, UCLA Institute of Archaeology Monograph B. pp. 142–54.

Burgh, Robert R. 1959. Ceramic profiles in the Western Mound at Awatovi, northeastern Arizona. *American Antiquity* 25 (2): 184–202.

Buzas, M.A. 1979. The measurement of species diversity. In *Foraminiferal Ecology and Paleoecology*, Short Course 6: 3–10. Society of Economic Paleontologists and Mineralogists.

Cahen, Daniel and Lawrence H. Keeley. 1980. Not less than two, not more than three. *World Archaeology* 12 (2): 166–80.

Cannon, Aubrey 1983. The quantification of artifactural assemblages: some implications for behavioral inferences. *American Antiquity* 48 (4): 785–92.

Caplan, A.L. 1979. Darwinism and deductivist models of theory structure. *Studies in History and Philosophy of Science* 10: 341–53.

Carniero, R.L. 1973. Classical evolution. In *Main Currents in Cultural Anthropology*, edited by R. Naroll and F. Naroll, pp. 57–121. New York: Appleton-Century Crofts.

Carr, Christopher, 1981. The polythetic organization of archaeological tool kits and an algorithm for defining them. Paper presented at 46th Annual Meeting of the Society for American Archaeology, San Diego.

1984. The nature of organization of intrasite archaeological records and spatial analytic approaches to their investigation. In *Advances in Archaeological Method and Theory*, vol. 7, edited by M.B. Schiffer, pp. 103–222. New York: Academic Press.

Carr, Christopher, ed. 1985. *For Concordance in Archaeological Analysis: Bridging Data Structure, Quantitative Technique and Theory*. Kansas City, Missouri: Westport Publishers, Inc.

Cavalli-Sforza, L.L., and M.W. Feldman 1981. *Cultural Transmission and Evolution: A Quantitative Approach*. Princeton, NJ: Princeton University Press.

Clarke, D.L. 1968. *Analytical Archaeology*. London: Methuen.

Conkey, Margaret W. 1978. An analysis of design structure: variability among Magdalenian engraved bones for north coastal Spain. Unpublished Ph.D. dissertation. University of Chicago, Chicago.

1980. The identification of prehistoric hunter–gatherer aggregation sites: the case of Altamira. *Current Anthropology*, 21 (5): 609–30.

1981a. The measurement and meaning of diversity in archaeological assemblages. Paper presented at 46th Annual Meeting of the Society for American Archaeology, San Diego, CA.

1981b. What can we do with broken bones? Paleolithic design structure, archaeological research and the potential of museum collections. In *The Research Potential of Anthropological Museum Collections*, edited by A.M. Cantwell, J.B. Griffin and N.A. Rothschild. *Annals of the New York Academy of Sciences* 376: 35–53. New York.

1982. The measurement of stylistic diversity: a reassessment. Paper presented to New York University Anthropology Colloquium.

Connell, Joseph H. 1978. Diversity in tropical rain forests and coral reefs. *Science* 199: 1302–10.

Cook, Thomas Genn 1980. Tools, debris and tasks at the excavated sites. In *Archaeological Salvage Excavations at Patoka Lake, Indiana: Prehistoric Occupations of the Upper Patoka River Valley*, edited by Cheryl Ann Munson, pp. 504–33. Glen A. Black Laboratory of Archaeology, Indiana University, Bloomington.

Cowgill, George L. 1968. Review of *Computer Analysis of Chronological Seriation*, by Frank Hole and Mary Shaw. *American Antiquity* 33 (4): 517–19.

1970. Some sampling and reliability problems in archaeology. In *Archeologie et Calculateurs*, edited by J.C. Gardin, pp. 161–75. Paris: Centre National de la Recherche Scientifique.

1986. Archaeological applications of mathematical and formal methods. In *American Archaeology Past and Future*, edited by D.J. Meltzer, D.D. Fowler, and J.A. Sabloff, pp. 369–93. Washington, D.C.: Smithsonian Institution Press.

Csikszenthmihalyi, M. and E. Rochberg-Halton 1981. *The Meaning of Things: Domestic Symbols and the Self*. Cambridge: Cambridge University Press.

Dacey, Michael 1973. Statistical tests of spatial association in the locations of tool types. *American Antiquity* 38 (3): 320–8.

David, N. 1972. On the lifespan of pottery, type frequencies, and archaeological inference. *American Antiquity* 37 (1): 141–2.

Davis, W.M. 1981. Reply to P. Rice, Evolution of specialized pottery production: a trial model. *Current Anthropology* 22 (3): 228–30.

Deagan, Kathleen 1983. *Spanish St. Augustine: the Archaeology of a Colonial Creole Community*. New York: Academic Press.

DeBoer, W.R. 1974. Ceramic longevity and archaeological interpretation: an example from the Upper Ucayali, Peru. *American Antiquity* 39 (2): 335–43.

DeBoer, W.R. and D. Lathrap 1979. The making and breaking of Shipibo–Conibo ceramics. In *Ethnoarchaeology: Implications of Ethnography for Archaeology*, edited by C. Kramer. pp. 102–38. New York: Columbia University Press.

DeBoer, Warren R. and James A. Moore 1982. The measurement and meaning of stylistic diversity. *Nawpa Pacha* 20: 147–62.

de Caprariis, Pascal, and Richard A. Lindemann 1978. Species richness in patchy environments. *Journal of the International Association for Mathematical Geology* 10: 73–90.

1981. Maximum diversities from cumulative species curves. *Lethaia* 14: 134.

de Caprariis, Pascal, Richard H. Lindemann, and Catharine M. Collins 1976. A method for determining optimal sample size in species diversity studies. *Journal of the International Association for Mathematical Geology* 8 (5): 575–81.

de Caprariis, Pascal, Richard Lindemann, and Robert Haimes 1981. A relationship between sample size and accuracy of species richness predictions. *Journal of the International Association for Mathematical Geology* 13 (4): 351–5.

Deetz, J. 1965. *The Dynamics of Stylistic Change in Arikara Ceramics*. Urbana: University of Illinois Series in Anthropology, No. 4.

Diaconis, Persi, and Bradley Efron 1983. Computer intensive methods in statistics. *Scientific American* 248 (5): 116–30.

Dickens, R.S. 1980. Ceramic diversity as an indicator of cultural dynamics in the Woodland period. *Tennessee Anthropologist* 5: 34–46.

Dickens, R.S. and J.H. Chapman 1978. Ceramic patterning and social structure at two late historic Upper Creek sites in Alabama. *American Antiquity* 43 (3): 390–8.

Dickens, R.S. and M.D. Fraser 1984. An information-theoretic approach to the analysis of cultural interaction in the Middle Woodland period. *Southeastern Archaeology* 3 (2): 144–52.

Dougherty, J. and J. Fernandez 1981. Introduction: In *Symbolism and Cognition*, I. *American Ethnologist* 8 (3): 413–21.

Drennan, R.D. 1976. A refinement of chronological seriation using nonmetric multidimensional scaling. *American Antiquity* 41 (3): 290–302.

Drummond, L. 1981. The serpent's children: semiotics of cultural genesis in Arawak and Trobriand myth. *American Ethnologist* 8 (3): 633–60.

Duffield, Rose, and James E. King 1979. Sample size and palynology: a Midwestern test. *Illinois State Academy of Science Transactions* 72 (2): 1–7.

Dumond, Don E. 1977. Science in archaeology: the saints go marching in. *American Antiquity* 42 (3): 330–49.

Dunnell, Robert C. 1970. Seriation method and its evaluation. *American Antiquity* 35 (3): 305–19.

1971. *Systematics in Prehistory*. New York: Free Press.

1978. Style and function: a fundamental dichotomy. *American Antiquity* 43 (2): 192–202.

1980. Evolutionary theory and archaeology. In *Advances in Archaeological Method and Theory*, vol., 3, edited by M.B. Schiffer pp. 35–99. New York: Academic Press.

1982. Science, social science, and common sense: the agonizing dilemma of modern archaeology. *Journal of Anthropological Research* 38 (1): 1–25.

Dunnell, Robert C., and Sarah K. Campbell 1977. *History of Aboriginal Occupation of Hamilton Island, Washington*. Reports in Archaeology No. 4, Department of Anthropology, University of Washington, Seattle.

Earle, T.K. 1981. Comment on Rice. *Current Anthropology* 22 (3): 230–1.

Ebert, James I. 1985. Modeling human systems and "predicting" the archaeological record: the unavoidable relationship of theory and method. Paper presented at 50th Annual Meeting of the Society for American Archaeology, Denver, CO.

Eldredge, N. and S.J. Gould 1972. Punctuated equilibria: an alternative to phyletic gradualism. In *Models in Paleobiology*, edited by T.J.M. Schopf, pp. 82–115. San Francisco: Freeman, Cooper.

Elton, C.S. 1942. *Voles, Mice and Lemmings: Problems in Population Dynamics*. Oxford: Oxford University Press.

1958. *The Ecology of Invasion by Animals and Plants*. London: Methuen.

Ericson, J.E., D. Read, and S.P. DeAtley 1972. Research design: the relationship between the primary functions and the physical properties of ceramic vessels and their implication for ceramic distributions on an archaeological site. *Anthropology UCLA* 3: 85–95.

Everitt, B.S. 1977. *The Analysis of Contingency Tables*. New York: Halsted Press.

Fager, E.W. 1972. Diversity: a sampling study. *American Naturalist* 106: 293–310.

Feinman, G., S.A. Kowalewski, and R.E. Blanton 1984. Modelling Ceramic production and organizational change in the pre-Hispanic Valley of Oaxaca, Mexico. In *The Many Dimensions of Pottery: Ceramics in Archaeology and Anthropology*, edited by S.E. van der Leeuw and A.C. Pritchard, pp. 295–337. Amsterdam: University of Amsterdam.

Feinman, G.M., S. Upham, and K.G. Lightfood 1981. The production step measure: an ordinal index of labor input in ceramic manufacture. *American Antiquity* 46 (4): 871–84.

Fisher, R.A., A. Steven Corbet, and C.B. Williams 1943. The relation between the number of species and the number of individuals in a random sample of an animal population. *Journal of Animal Ecology* 12 (1): 42–58.

Foley, Robert 1981a. Offsite archaeology: An alternative approach for the short-sited. In *Patterns of the Past, Studies in Honour of David Clarke*, edited by I. Hodder, G. Isaac, and N. Hammond, pp. 157–83. London: Cambridge University Press.

1981b. A model of regional archaeology structure. *Proceedings of the Prehistoric Society* 47: 1–17.

Ford, J.A. 1954. On the concept of types. *American Anthropologist* 56 (1): 42–54.

Ford, Richard I. 1981. Gardening and farming before A.D. 1000: patterns of prehistoric cultivation north of Mexico. *Journal of Ethnobiology* 1 (1): 6–27.

Foster, G.M. 1960. Life expectancy of utilitarian pottery in Tzintzuntzan Michoacan, Mexico. *American Antiquity* 25 (8): 606–9.

Freeman, Leslie G. 1978. The analysis of some occupation floor distributions from Earlier and Middle Pleistocene sites in Spain. In *Views of the Past*, edited by L. Freeman, pp. 57–116. The Hague: Mouton.

1981. The fat of the land: notes on paleolithic diet in Iberia. In *Omnivorous Primates: Gathering and Hunting in Human Evolution*, edited by R. Harding and G. Teleki, pp. 104–65. New York: Columbia University Press.

Friedrich, M.H. 1970. Design structure and social interaction. Archaeological implications of an ethnographic analysis. *American Antiquity* 35 (3): 332–43.

Fry, R.E. 1980. Models of exchange for major shape classes of Lowland Maya pottery. In *Models and Methods in Regional Exchange*, edited by R.E. Fry, pp. 3–18. Society for American Archaeology Papers 1.

Fry, R.E. and S. Cox 1974. The structure of ceramic exchange at Tikal, Guatemala. *World Archaeology* 6 (2): 209–25.

Giddens, A. 1979. *Central Problems in Social Theory: Actions, Structure, and Contradiction in Social Analysis*. Berkeley: University of California Press.

Gifford, Diane P. 1978. Ethnoarchaeological observations of natural processes affecting cultural materials. In *Explorations in Ethnoarch-*

aeology, edited by R.A. Gould, pp. 77–101. Albuquerque: University of New Mexico Press.

Gifford, J.C. 1976. *Prehistoric Pottery Analysis and the Ceramics of Barton Ramie in the Belize Valley*. Cambridge, MA: Memoirs of the Peabody Museum, vol. 18.

Gleason, H.A. 1922. On the relation between species and area. *Ecology* 3 (2): 158–62.

1925. Species and area. *Ecology* 6 (1): 66–74.

Goldman, S. 1953. Some fundamentals of information theory. In *Information Theory in Biology*, edited by H. Quastler, pp. 7–11. Urbana, IL.: University of Illinois Press.

Good, I.J. 1953. The population frequencies of species and the estimation of population parameters. *Biometrika* 40: 237–64.

Gould, R.A. 1980. *Living Archaeology*. Cambridge: Cambridge University Press.

Gould, Steven J. 1980. Is a new and general theory of evolution emerging? *Paleobiology* 6 (1): 119–30.

1985. A short way to big ends. *Natural History* 95 (1): 18–28.

Gould, S.J. and N. Eldredge 1977. Punctuated equilibria: the tempo and mode of evolution reconsidered. *Paleobiology* 3 (2): 115–51.

Gould, S.J., D.M. Raup, J. Sepkoski, Jr., T.J.M. Schopf, and D. Simberloff 1977. The shape of evolution: a comparison of real and random claces. *Paleobiology* 3 (1): 23–40.

Graham, Ian 1980. Spectral analysis and distance methods in the study of archaeological distributions. *Journal of Archaeological Science* 7 (2): 105–29.

Grassle, J.F., G.P. Patil, W. Smith, and C. Taillie, eds., 1979. *Ecological Diversity in Theory and Practice*. Statistical Ecology Series, vol. 6. Fairland, MD: International Cooperative Publishing House.

Graves, Michael 1981. Ethnoarchaeology of Kalinga ceramic design. Ph.D. dissertation, University of Arizona, Tucson. Ann Arbor: University Microfilms.

Grayson, D.K. 1978. Reconstructing mammalian communities: a discussion of Shotwell's method of paleoecological analysis. *Paleobiology* 4 (1): 77–81.

1981. The effects of sample size on some derived measures in vertebrate faunal analysis. *Journal of Archaeological Science* 8 (1): 77–88.

1983. The paleontology of Gatecliff Shelter: small mammals. In *The Archaeology of Monitor Valley: 2. Gatecliff Shelter*, by D.H. Thomas. *American Museum of Natural History Anthropological Papers* 59: 99–126.

1984. *Quantitative Zooarchaeology. Topics in the Analysis of Archaeological Faunas*. Orlando: Academic Press.

1985. The paleontology of Hidden Cave: birds and mammals. In *The Archaeology of Hidden Cave, Nevada*, edited by D.H. Thomas. *American Museum of Natural History Anthropological Papers*, 61 (1): 126–61.

Green, Margerie 1982. Chipped stone raw materials and the study of interaction. Unpublished Ph.D. Dissertation, Department of Anthropology, Arizona State University, Tempe.

Greenberg, J.H. 1956. The measurement of linguistic diversity. *Language* 32 (1): 107–15.

Hagstrum, M.B. 1985. Measuring prehistoric ceramic craft specialization: a test case in the American Southwest. *Journal of Field Archaeology* 12: 65–75.

Hally, D.J. 1983. Use alteration of pottery vessel surfaces: an important source of evidence for the identification of vessel function. *North American Archaeologist* 4 (1): 3–26.

Hardesty, D.L. 1980. The use of general ecological principles in archaeology. In *Advances in Archaeological Method and Theory*, vol. 3, edited by M.B. Schiffer, pp. 157–87. New York: Academic Press.

Hardin, M.A. 1977. Individual style in San Jose pottery painting: the role of deliberate choice. In *The Individual in Prehistory*, edited by J.N. Hill and J. Gunn, pp. 109–36. New York: Academic Press.

1983. The structure of Tarascan pottery painting. In *Structure and Cognition in Art*, edited by D.K. Washburn, pp. 8–24. Cambridge: Cambridge University Press.

Harris, M. 1968. *The Rise of Anthropological Theory*. New York: Harper and Row.

Hayden, B. 1981. Research and development in the Stone Age: technological transitions among hunter–gatherers. *Current Anthropology* 22 (5): 519–48.

Hayden, Brian, and Aubrey Cannon 1983. Where the garbage goes: refuse disposal in the Maya Highlands. *Journal of Anthropological Archaeology* 2 (2): 117–63.

Hebdige, D. 1979. *Subculture, the Meaning of Style*. London: Methuen.

Heck, K.L., Jr., G. Van Belle, and D. Simberloff 1975. Explicit calculation of the rarefaction diversity measurement and the determination of sufficient sample size. *Ecology* 56 (6): 1459–61.

Heltsche, J.F., and D.W. Bitz 1979. Comparing diversity measures in sampled communities. In *Ecological Diversity in Theory and Practice*, edited by J.F. Grassie, G.P. Patil, W. Smith and C. Taillie. Statistical Ecology Series, vol. 6. Fairland MD: International Co-operative Publishing House.

Hill, James N. 1965. *Broken K: a prehistoric society in eastern Arizona*. Ph.D. dissertation in Anthropology, University of Chicago.

1970. *Broken K. Pueblo: Prehistoric Social Organization in the American Southwest*. University of Arizona, Anthropological Papers, vol. 18.

1977. Individual variability in ceramics and prehistoric social organization. In *The Individual in Prehistory*, edited by J.N. Hill and J. Gunn, pp. 55–108. New York: Academic Press.

Hill, M.O. 1973. Diversity and evenness: a unifying notation and its consequences. *Ecology* 54 (2): 427–32.

Hodder, Ian 1979. Economic and social stress and material culture patterning. *American Antiquity* 44 (3): 446–54.

1982. *Symbols in Action. Ethnoarcheological Studies of Material Culture*. Cambridge: Cambridge University Press.

1985. Postprocessual archaeology. In *Advances in Archaeological Method and Theory*, vol. 8, edited by M.B. Schiffer, pp. 1–26. Orlando: Academic Press.

Hodder, Ian and Eric Okell 1978. An index for assessing the association between distributions of points in archaeology. In *Simulation Studies in Archaeology*, edited by Ian Hodder, pp. 97–108. New York: Cambridge University Press.

Hodder, Ian and Clive Orton 1976. *Spatial Analysis in Archaeology*. New York: Cambridge University Press.

Holmes, William H. 1919. *Handbook of Aboriginal American Antiquities. Part I: Introductory: The Lithic Industries*. Bureau of American Ethnology Bulletin 60.

Hull, D.L. 1976. Are species really individuals? *Systematic Zoology* 25 (2): 174–91.

Hurlbert, S.H. 1971. The nonconcept of species diversity: a critique and alternative parameters *Ecology* 52 (4): 577–86.

Isaac, Glynn 1981. Stone Age visiting cards: approaches to the study of early land use patterns. In *Patterns of the Past: Studies in Honour of David Clarke*, edited by I. Hodder, G. Isaac, and N. Hammond, pp. 131–55. Cambridge: Cambridge University Press.

Ives, J.W. 1981. Small site assemblages and prehistoric economic patterns in the Birch Mountains, northeastern Alberta. Paper presented at 14th Annual Meeting of the Canadian Archaeological Association, Edmonton.

Jefferies, Richard W. 1982. Debitage as an indicator of intraregional activity diversity in northwest Georgia. *Midcontinental Journal of Archaeology* 7 (1): 99–132.

Johnson, G.A. 1975. Locational analysis and the investigation of Uruk local exchange systems. In *Ancient Civilization and Trade*, edited by J.A. Sabloff and C.C. Lamberg-Karlovsky. Albuquerque: University of New Mexico Press.

Jones, George T. 1984. *Prehistoric land use in the Steens Mountain area, southeastern Oregon*. Ph.D. Dissertation, University of Washington. Ann Arbor: University Microfilms.

Jones, George T., Donald K. Grayson, and Charlotte Beck 1983. Artifact class richness and sample size in archaeological surface assemblages. In *Lulu Linear Punctated: Essays in Honor of George Irving Quimby*, edited by R.C. Dunnell and D.K. Grayson, pp. 55–73. Museum of Anthropology, University of Michigan Anthropological Papers 72.

Keene, A. 1983. Biology, behavior and borrowing: a critical examination of optimal foraging theory in archaeology. In *Archaeological Hammers and Theories*, edited by J.A. Moore and A.S. Keene, pp. 137–55. New York: Academic Press.

Keesing, R.M. 1974. Theories of culture. *Annual Review of Anthropology* 3: 73–97.

Khinchin, A.I. 1968. *Mathematical Foundations of Information Theory*. New York: Dover.

Kilburn, P.D. 1966. Analysis of the species–area relation. *Ecology* 47 (5): 831–43.

Kimura, M. and T. Ohta 1971. *Theoretical Aspects of Population Genetics*. Princeton: Princeton University Press.

King, J.L., and T.H. Jukes 1969. Non-Darwinian evolution. *Science* 164: 788–98.

Kintigh, Keith W. 1984a. Measuring archaeological diversity by comparison with simulated assemblages. *American Antiquity* 49 (1): 44–54.

1984b. Sample size, significance, and measures of diversity. Paper presented at 49th Annual Meeting of the Society for American Archaeology, Portland.

Kintigh, Keith, and Albert Ammerman 1982. Heuristic approaches to spatial analysis in archaeology. *American Antiquity* 47 (1): 31–63.

Kirkpatrick, M. 1977. The application of the type-variety method of ceramic analysis to a collection of contemporary pottery from Metepec, Mexico. M.A. thesis, Department of Anthropology, Temple University, Philadelphia.

Kohler, T.A. 1978. The social and chronological dimensions of village occupation at a North Florida Weeden Island period site. Ph.D. dissertation, Department of Anthropology, University of Florida, Gainesville.

Lambshead, P.J.D., H.M. Platt, and K.M. Shaw 1983. The detection of differences among assemblages of marine benthic species based on an assessment of dominance and diversity. *Journal of Natural History* 17 (6): 859–74.

Lamont, B.B., S. Downes, and J.E.D. Fox 1977. Importance-value curves and diversity indices applied to a species-rich healthland in Western Australia. *Nature* 265: 438–41.

Larick R. 1983. The circulation of Solutrean foliate point cherts: residential mobility in the Perigord. Ph.D. dissertation, Department of Anthropology, State University of New York, Binghamton. Ann Arbor: University Microfilms.

Lathrap, D. 1983. Recent Shipibo–Conibo ceramics and their implications for archaeological interpretation. In *Structure and Cognition in Art*, edited by D.K. Washburn, pp. 25–40. Cambridge: Cambridge University Press.

Laville, Henry, Jean-Philippe Rigaud, and James Sackett 1980. *Rockshelters of the Periogord: Geological Stratigraphy and Archaeological Succession*. New York: Academic Press.

Layhe, Robert 1981. A locational model for demographic and settlement system change: an example from the American Southwest. Unpublished Ph.D. dissertation, Southern Illinois University at Carbondale.

Lechtman, Heather 1977. Style in technology–some early thoughts. In *Material Culture: Styles, Organization, and Dynamics of Technology*, edited by H. Lechtman and R.S. Merrill, pp. 3–20. Proceedings of the American Ethnological Society. West Publishing.

Leonard, Robert D., Catherine M. Cameron, and F.E. Smiley 1983. Diversification in Anasazi lithic assemblages: implications for the study of social and technological change on Black Mesa. Paper presented at 48th Annual Meeting of the Society for American Archaeology, Pittsburgh.

Leone, Mark P. 1968. Neolithic economic autonomy and social distance. *Science* 162: 1150–1.

1972. Issues in contemporary archeology. Introduction to *Contemporary Archeology*, edited by M. Leone, pp. 14–27. Carbondale: Southern Illinois University Press.

Leroi-Gourhan, Andrea, and Michel Brezillon 1972. *Fouilles de Pincevent: Essai d'Analyse Ethnographique d'un Habitat magdalenien*. 7eme Supplement a *Gallia Prehistoire*. Paris: C.N.R.S.

Levi-Strauss, Calude 1963. *Structural Anthropology* (Trans. by C. Jacobson and B. Schoeof). New York: Basic Books.

Lewontin, Richard C. 1969. The meaning of stability. In *Diversity and Stability in Ecological Systems*. Brookhaven Symposia in Biology No. 22. Springfield, VA: National Bureau of Standards, U.S. Department of Commerce.

1974. *The Genetic Basis of Evolutionary Change*. New York: Columbia University Press.

1977. Sociobiology–a caricature of Darwinism. *Proceedings of the 1975 Biennial Meeting of the Philosophy of Science Association*, vol. 2, edited by F. Suppe and P. Asquitn. pp. 22–31.

Lieberson, S. 1969. Measuring population diversity. *American Sociological Review* 34 (6): 850–62.

Linares, O. 1968. Cultural chronology of the Gulf of Chiriqui, Panama. *Smithsonian Contributions to Anthropology* 8.

Lipe, William D. 1964. Comments on Dempsey and Baumhoff "The statistical use of artifact distributions to establish chronological sequence." *American Antiquity* 30 (1): 103–4.

Lischka, Joseph J. 1975. Broken K revisited: a short discussion of factor analysis. *American Antiquity* 40 (2): 220–7.

Lloyd, Monte, and R.J. Ghelardi 1964. A table for calculating the "equitability" component of species diversity. *Journal of Animal Ecology* 33 (2): 217–25.

Longacre, W.A. 1963. Archeology as anthropology: a case study. Ph.D. dissertation, Department of Anthropology, University of Chicago.

1964. Sociological implications of the ceramic analysis. In *Chapters in the Prehistory of East Arizona* II, edited by P. Martin *et al. Fieldiana Anthropology* 55: 155–70.

MacArthur, Robert H. 1965. Patterns of species diversity. *Biological Review* 40: 510–33.

Margalef, Ramon 1958. Information theory in ecology. *General Systems* 3: 36–71.

1968. *Perspectives in Ecological Theory*. Chicago: University of Chicago Press.

Marquart, W.H. 1978. Advances in archaeological seriation. In *Advances in Archaeological Method and Theory*, vol. 1, edited by M.B. Schiffer, pp. 257–314. New York: Academic Press.

Martin, Paul S. 1971. The revolution in archaeology. *American Antiquity* 36 (1): 1–8.

Martin, Paul S., James N. Hill, and William A. Longacre 1966. Documentation for chapters in the prehistory of Eastern Arizona, III. *Society for American Archaeology, Archives of Archaeology* 27.

Martin, Paul S., William A. Longacre, and James H. Hill 1967. Chapters in the prehistory of Eastern Arizona, III. *Fieldiana: Anthropology* 57.

May, Robert M. 1973. *Stability and Complexity in Model Ecosystems*. Princeton, NJ: Princeton University Press.

1974. *Stability and Complexity in Model Ecosystems*, 2nd edition. Princeton: Princeton University Press.

1975. Patterns of species abundance and diversity. In *Ecology and Evolution of Communities*, edited by M.L. Cody and J.M. Diamond, pp. 81–120. Cambridge, MA: Belknap Press.

1981. Patterns in multi-species communities. In *Theoretical Ecology: Principles and Applications*, edited by Robert M. May, pp. 197–227. Sunderland, MA: Sinaver Associates.

Maynard Smith, J. 1974. *Models in Ecology*. Cambridge: Cambridge University Press.

Mayr, Ernst 1942. *Systematics and the Origin of Species from the Point of View of a Zoologist*. New York: Columbia University Press.

1982. *The Growth of Biological Thought*. Cambridge, MA: Harvard University Press.

Menhininck, E.F. 1964. A comparison of some species–individuals diversity indices applied to samples of field insects. *Ecology* 45 (4): 859–61.

Miller, D. 1983. *Things* ain't what they used to be. *Rain*, Royal Anthropological Institute News. 59.

Montagu, M.F.A., editor, 1968. *Culture: Man's Adaptive Dimension.* London: Oxford University Press.

Morlan, R.E. 1980. Taphonomy and archaeology in the Upper Pleistocene of the Northern Yukon territory: a glimpse at the peopling of the New World. *Archaeological Survey of Canada Paper* 94.

Mortenson, P. 1973. On the reflection of cultural changes in artifact materials, with special regard to the study of innovation contrasted with type stability. In *The Explanation of Culture Change*, edited by C. Renfrew, pp. 155–9. Pittsburgh: University of Pittsburgh Press.

Muller, J. 1984. Mississippian specialization and salt. *American Antiquity* 49 (3): 489–507.

Nance, Jack 1981. Statistical fact and archaeological faith: two models in small-sites sampling. *Journal of Field Archaeology* 8: 151–65.

1983. Regional sampling in archaeological survey: the statistical perspective. In *Advances in Archaeological Method and Theory*, vol. 6, edited by M.B. Schiffer, pp. 289–356. New York: Academic Press.

1987. Reliability, validity and quantitative methods in archaeology. In *Quantitative Research in Archaeology: Progress and Prospects*, edited by Mark S. Aldenderfer, pp. 244–93. Newbury Park: Sage Publications, Inc.

Nelson, D.E., R.E. Morlan, J.S. Vogel, J.R. Southern, and C.R. Harrington 1986. New dates on Northern Yukon artifacts: Holocene not upper Pleistocene. *Science* 232: 749–51.

Nichols, Debra L., and F.E. Smiley 1985. An overview of Northern Black Mesa archaeology. In *Excavations on Black Mesa, 1983: A Descriptive Report*, edited by A.C. Christenson and W.J. Tarry, pp. 47–82. Southern Illinois University at Carbondale, Center for Archaeological Investigations, Research Paper No. 46.

Odum, E.P. 1959. *Fundamentals of Ecology.* Philadelphia: W.B. Saunders.

Odum, H.T., J.E. Cantlon, and L.S. Kornicker 1960. An organizational hierarchy postulate for the interpretation of species–individual distributions, species entropy, ecosystem evolution, and the meaning of a species-variety index. *Ecology* 41 (2): 395–9.

Otto, J.S. 1975. Status differences and the archaeological record: a comparison of planter, overseer, and slave sites from Cannon's Point Plantation (1794–1861), St. Simon's Island, Georgia. Ph.D. Dissertation, Department of Anthropology, University of Florida.

Osbourn, D. 1968. Jargon, jabber, and long words. *American Antiquity* 33 (3): 382–3.

Patil, G. P., and C. Taillie 1982. Diversity as a concept and its measurement. *Journal of the American Statistical Association* 77: 548–67.

Peacock, D.P.S. 1981. Archaeology, ethnology and ceramic production. In *Production and Distribution: A Ceramic Viewpoint*, edited by H. Howard and E.L. Morris, pp. 187–94. Oxford: BAR International Series 120.

1982. *Pottery in the Roman World: an Ethnoarchaeological Approach.* London: Longman.

Peebles, C.S. 1972. Monothetic divisive analysis of the Moundville burials: an initial report. *Newsletter of Computer Archaeology* 8: 1–12.

Peet, R.K. 1974. The measurement of species diversity. *Annual Review of Ecology and Systematics* 5: 285–307.

1975. Relative diversity indices. *Ecology* 56 (2): 496–8.

Phillips, David A., Jr. 1972. The use of non-artifactual materials in hypothesis-testing, Broken K Pueblo: a case study. MS, Department of Anthropology, Field Museum of Natural History, Chicago.

Pianka, E.R. 1974. *Evolutionary Ecology.* New York: Harper.

1978. *Evolutionary Ecology.* 2nd edition. New York: Harper.

Pickman, Arnold, and Nan A. Rothschild 1981. 64 Pearl St.: a limited excavation in 17th century landfill. Ms. on file, New York Landmarks Conservancy.

Pielou, E.C. 1966. The measurement of diversity in different types of biological collections. *Journal of Theoretical Biology* 13: 131–44.

1969. *An Introduction to Mathematical Ecology.* New York: Wiley-Interscience.

1975. *Ecological Diversity.* New York: Wiley-Interscience.

1977. *Mathematical Ecology.* New York: John Wiley and Sons.

Plog, Fred T. 1973. Diachronic anthropology. In *Research and Theory in Contemporary Archaeology*, edited by C.L. Redman, pp. 181–98. New York: John Wiley and Sons.

1974. *The Study of Prehistoric Change.* New York: Academic Press.

Plog, Stephen 1978. Social interaction and stylistic similarity: a reanalysis. In *Advances in Archaeological Method and Theory*, vol. 1, edited by M.B. Schiffer, pp. 143–82. New York: Academic Press.

1980. *Stylistic Variation in Prehistoric Ceramics: A Design Analysis in the American Southwest.* New York: Cambridge University Press.

1983. Analysis of style in artifacts. *Annual Review of Anthropology* 12: 125–42.

Popper, K. 1963. *The Poverty of Historicism*, revised edition. London: Routledge and Kegan Paul.

1974. Darwinism as a metaphysical research programme. In *The Philosophy of Karl Popper*, edited by P.A. Schilpp. LaSalle, IL: Open Court.

Powell, Shirley 1983. *Mobility and Adaptation: the Anasazi of Black Mesa, Arizona.* Carbondale: Southern Illinois University Press.

Preston, F.W. 1948. The commonness, and rarity, of species. *Ecology* 29 (3): 254–83.

1962. The canonical distribution of commonness and rarity. *Ecology* 43 (2, 3): 185–215, 410–32.

Prigogine, I. 1980. *From Being to Becoming: Time and Complexity in the Physical Sciences.* New York: W.H. Freeman.

Raab, L.M., and A.C. Goodyear 1984. Middle-range theory in archaeology: a critical review of origins and applications. *American Antiquity* 49 (2): 255–68.

Rathje, W. 1975. The last tango in Mayapan: a tentative trajectory of production–distribution systems. In *Ancient Civilization and Trade*, edited by J. Sabloff and C.C. Lamberg-Karlovsky, pp. 409–48. Albuquerque: University of New Mexico Press.

Rathje, William L., David A. Gregory, and Frederick M. Wiseman 1978. Trade models and archaeological problems: Classic Maya examples. In *Mesoamerican Communication Routes and Cultural Contacts*, edited by T.A. Lee, Jr. and C. Navarrete. Papers of the New World Archaeological Foundation, No. 40.

Raup, D.M. 1975. Taxonomic diversity estimation using rarefaction. *Paleobiology* 1 (4): 333–42.

Raup, D.M., S.J. Gould, T.J.M. Schopf, and D. Simberloff 1973. Stochastic models of phylogeny and the evolution of diversity. *Journal of Geology* 81 (5): 525–42.

Reher, C.A. ed., 1977. *Settlement and Subsistence Along the Lower Chaco River: The CGP Survey.* Albuquerque: University of New Mexico Press.

Reid, J. Jefferson 1973. Growth and response to stress at Grasshopper Pueblo, Arizona. Ph.D. dissertation, Department of Anthropology, University of Arizona. Ann Arbor: University Microfilms.

1978. Response to stress at Grasshopper Pueblo, Arizona. In *Discovering Past Behavior: Experiments in the Archaeology of the American Southwest*, edited by P.F. Grebinger, pp. 195–213. New York: Gordon and Breach.

Reid, J. Jefferson, ed., 1982. Cholla Project archaeology (5 volumes). *Arizona State Museum Archaeological Series* 161.

Reid, J. Jefferson and Izumi Shimada 1982. Pueblo growth at Grasshopper: methods and models. In *Multidisciplinary Research at Grasshopper Pueblo, Arizona*, edited by W.A. Longacre, S.J. Holbrook, and M.W. Graves, pp. 12–18. University of Arizona, Anthropological Papers 40.

Reina, R.E., and R.M. Hill 1978. *The Traditional Pottery of Guatemala.* Austin: University of Texas Press.

Reitz, E.J., and S.L. Cumbaa 1983. Diet and foodways in 18th century Spanish St. Augustine. In *Spanish St. Augustine*, edited by K. Deagan, pp. 151–85. New York: Academic Press.

Reitz, E.J., and M. Scarry n.d. Herbs, fish and other scum and vermin: subsistence in 16th century St. Augustine.

Rhoades, R.E. 1978. Archaeological use and abuse of ecological concepts and studies: the Ecotone Example. *American Antiquity* 43 (4): 608–14.

Rhode, D. 1985. Note on the use of the binomial formula in archaeology. Unpublished manuscript in author's possession.

Rice, P.M. 1978. Clear answers to vague questions: some assumptions of provenience studies of pottery. In *The Ceramics of Kaminaljuyu*, edited by R.K. Wetherington, pp. 511–42. University Park: Pennsylvania State University Press.

1979. Some considerations for the study of specialized pottery production. Paper presented at the annual meeting of the Society for American Archaeology, Vancouver.

1980. Peten Postclassic pottery production and exchange: a view from Macanche. In *Models and Methods in Regional Exchange*, edited by R.E. Fry. SAA Paper 1: 67–82.

1981. Evolution of specialized pottery production: a trial model. *Current Anthropology* 22 (3): 219–40.

1984. Change and Conservation in pottery-producing systems. In *The Many Dimensions of Pottery: Ceramics in Archaeology and Anthropology*, edited by S.E. van der Leeuw and A.C., Pritchard, pp. 231–93. Amsterdam: University of Amsterdam.

Rice, P.M., and M.E. Saffer 1981. Pottery production: a look at a model. Paper presented at 46th annual meeting of the Society for American Archaeology, San Diego.

1982. Cluster analysis of mixed-level data: pottery provenience as an example. *Journal of Archaeological Science* 9 (4): 395–409.

Rigaud, Jean-Philippe 1969. Note preliminaire de la stratigraphie du gisement du "Flageolet I" (Commune de Bezenac, Dordogne). *Bulletin de la Société Préhistorique Française* 66 (3): 73–5.

1978. The significance of variability among lithic artifacts: a specific case from southwestern France. *Journal of Anthropological Research* 34 (3): 299–310.

1982. Le Paleolithique en Periogord: les donnees du sud-ouest Sarladais et leurs implications. These de Doctorat d'Etat et Sciences. Universite de Bordeaux, No. 737.

Rindos, D. 1984. *The Origins of Agriculture: An Evolutionary Perspective*. New York: Academic Press.

1985. Darwinian selection, symbolic variation and the evolution of culture. *Current Anthropology* 26 (1): 65–88.

1986. The genetics of cultural anthropology: toward a genetic model for the origin of the capacity for culture. *Journal of Anthropological Archaeology* 5 (1): 1–38.

Rosenwaike, Ira 1972. *The Population History of New York City*. Syracuse, NY: Syracuse University Press.

Rothschild, N.A. n.d.a Sex, status and social complexity: an analysis of six Midwestern sites. *Occasional Papers in Anthropology*, Northwestern University, Department of Anthropology.

n.d.b. Are burials mirrors of cultural complexity? An analysis of six midwestern sites. Manuscript in possession of the author.

Rothschild, N.A., and D. Rockman 1982. Method in urban archaeology: the Stadt Huys block. In *Archaeology of Urban America: the Search for Pattern and Process*, edited by R.S. Dickins, Jr., pp. 3–18. New York: Academic Press.

Rottlander, R.C.A. 1966. Is provincial Roman pottery standardized? *Archaeometry* 9: 76–91.

1967. Standardization of Roman Provincial pottery II: function of the decorative collar on Form Drag. 38. *Archaeometry* 10: 35–45.

Rouse, I. 1960. The classification of artifacts in archaeology. *American Antiquity* 25 (3): 313–23.

1970. Classification for what? *Norwegian Archaeological Review* 3; 4–12.

Ruse, M. 1973. *The Philosophy of Biology*. London: Hutchinson.

1982. *Darwinism Defended: a Guide to the Evolution Controversies*. London: Addison–Wesley.

Rye, O.S., and C. Evans 1976. *Traditional Pottery Techniques of Pakistan, Field and Laboratory Studies*. Smithsonian Contributions to Anthropology no. 21. Washington, D.C.

Sackett, J.R. 1977. The meaning of style in archaeology: a general model. *American Antiquity* 42 (3): 369–80.

1982. Approaches to style in lithic archeology. *Journal of Anthropological Archaeology* 1 (1): 59–112.

Saffer, M.E. 1979. Aboriginal clay resource utilization on the Georgia coast. M.A. thesis, Department of Anthropology, University of Florida, Gainesville.

Sahlins, M.D. 1976. *Culture and Practical Reason*. Chicago: University of Chicago Press.

Sahlins, Marshall, and Elman R. Service, eds., 1960. *Evolution and Culture*. Ann Arbor, MI: University of Michigan Press.

Sanders, H.L. 1968. Marine benthic diversity: a comparative study. *American Naturalist* 102 (925): 243–82.

Schiffer, Michael B. 1972. Archaeological context and systemic context. *American Antiquity* 37 (2): 156–65.

1973. The relationship between access volume and content diversity of storage facilities. *American Antiquity* 38 (1): 114–16.

1975. Behavioral chain analysis: activities, organization, and the use of space. In *Chapters in the Prehistory of eastern Arizona*, IV. *Fieldiana: Anthropology* 65: 103–19.

1976. *Behavioral Archeology*. New York: Academic Press.

1983. Toward the identification of formation processes. *American Antiquity* 48 (4): 675–706.

1985. Is there a "Pompeii premise" in archaeology? *Journal of Anthropological Research* 41 (1): 18–41.

Seagraves, B.A. 1982. Central elements in the construction of a general theory of the evolution of societal complexity. In *Theory and Explanation in Archaeology*, edited by C. Renfrew, M.J. Rowlands, and B.A. Seagraves, pp. 287–300. New York: Academic Press.

Shannon, C.E. 1948. A mathematical theory of communication. *Bell System Technology Journal* 27: 374–423.

Shannon, C.E. and W. Weaver 1949. *The Mathematical Theory of Communication*. Urbana, IL: University of Illinois Press.

Sheldon, A.L. 1969. Equitability indices: dependence on the species count. *Ecology* 50 (3): 466–7.

Shepard, A.O. 1958. Ceramic technology. *Carnegie Institution of Washington, Year Book* No. 57.

Simberloff, D. 1972. Properties of the rarefaction diversity measurement. *American Naturalist* 106 (949): 414–18.

Simek, Jan 1984. *A K-means Approach to the Analysis of Spatial Structure in Upper Paleolithic Habitation Sites: Pincevent Section Le Flageolet I*. Oxford: B.A.R. International Series No. 205.

Simek, Jan, and Roy Larick, 1983. The recognition of multiple spatial patterns: a case study from the French Upper Paleolithic. *Journal of Archaeological Science* 10: 165–80.

Simek, Jan, and Paul Leslie 1983. Partitioning chi-square for the analysis of frequency table data: an archaeological application. *Journal of Archaeological Science* 10 (1): 79–85.

Simpson, E.H. 1949. Measurement of diversity. *Nature* 163: 688.

Simpson, G.G. 1953. *The Major Features of Evolution*. New York: Columbia University Press.

Smiley, Francis E. IV 1985. The chronometrics of early agricultural sites in northeast Arizona: approaches to the interpretation of radiocarbon dates. Unpublished Ph.D dissertation, University of Michigan.

Smiley, F.E. and Peter T. Andrews 1983. An overview of Black Mesa Archaeological research. In *Excavations on Black Mesa, 1981: A Descriptive Report*, edited by F.E. Smiley, D.L. Nichols, and P.T. Andrews, pp. 43–60. Southern Illinois University of Carbondale Center for Archaeological Investigations, Research Paper No. 36.

Smith, Wollcott, and J. Frederick Grassle 1977. Sampling properties of a family of diversity measures. *Biometrics* 33 (2): 283–92.

Smith, Wollcott, J. Frederick Grassle, and David Kravitz 1979. Measures of diversity with unbiased estimates. In *Ecological Diversity in Theory and practice*, edited by J.F. Grassle, G.P. Patil, W. Smith, and C. Taille, pp. 177–91. Statistical Ecology Series, vol. 6. Fairland, Maryland: International Cooperative Publishing House.

Solheim, W.G., II. 1984. Pottery and the prehistory of Northeast Thailand. In *Pots and Potters: Current Approaches in Ceramic Archaeology*, edited by P.M. Rice, pp. 95–105. UCLA Institute of Archaeology, Los Angeles. Monograph 24.

Spaulding, A.C. 1953. Statistical techniques for the discovery of artifact types. *American Antiquity* 18 (4): 305–13.

   1960. Statistical description and comparison of artifact assemblages. In *The Application of Quantitative Methods in Archaeology*, edited by R.F. Heizer and S.F. Cook, pp. 60–83. Viking Fund Publications in Anthropology No. 28. New York: Wenner Gren.

   1974. Review of Robert Dunnell's *Systematics in Prehistory*. *American Antiquity* 39 (3): 513–16.

Spearman, Charles 1904. The proof and measurement of association between two things. *American Journal of Psychology* 15: 72–101.

Speth, John D. 1983. *Bison Kills and Bone Counts: Decision Making by Ancient Hunters*. Chicago: University of Chicago Press.

Speth, John D., and Gregory A. Johnson 1976. Problems in the use of correlation for the investigation of tool kits and activity areas. In *Culture Change and Continuity: Essays in Honor of James Bennett Griffith*, edited by Charles E. Cleland, pp. 35–57. New York: Academic Press.

Stanislawski, Michael B. 1969. What good is a broken pot? *Southwestern Lore* 35: 11–18.

   1973. Review of *Archaeology as Anthropology: a Case Study*, by William A. Longacre. *American Antiquity* 38 (1): 117–22.

Stanley, S.M. 1979. *Macroevolution: Pattern and Process*. San Francisco: W.H. Freeman.

Stark, B.L. 1981. Comment on Rice. *Current Anthropology* 22 (3): 234–5.

   1985 Archaeological identification of pottery-production locations: ethnoarchaeological and archaeological data in Mesoamerica. In *Decoding Prehistoric Ceramics*, edited by B.A. Nelson, pp. 158–94. Carbondale: Southern Illinois University Press.

   n.d. Standardization and specialization in pottery: an ethnographic view. Ms.

Stark, B.L., and J.T. Hepworth 1982. A diversity index approach to analysis of standardization in prehistoric pottery. *Computer Applications in Archaeology: 1982 Conference Proceedings*, pp. 87–104. University of Birmingham.

Steponaitis, L.C. 1985. Assemblage diversity and prehistoric settlement patterns in the lower Patuxent drainage, Maryland. Paper presented at the Middle Atlantic Archaeological Conference, Rehobeth Beach, Delaware.

Steward, Julian H. 1955. *Theory of Cultural Change: the Methodology of Multilinear Evolution*. Urbana, IL: University of Illinois Press.

Stevenson, Marc G. 1982. Toward an understanding of site abandonment behavior: evidence from historic mining camps in the southwest Yukon. *Journal of Anthropological Archaeology* 1 (2): 237–65.

Styles, B.W. 1981. *Faunal Exploitation and Resource Selection: Early Late Woodland Subsistence in the Lower Illinois Valley*. Evanston, IL: Northwestern University Archaeological Program.

Sullivan, Alan P. 1978. Inference and evidence in archaeology: a discussion of the conceptual problems. In *Advances in Archaeological Method and Theory*, vol. 1, edited by M.B. Schiffer, pp. 183–222. New York: Academic Press.

Tainter, Joseph A. 1977a. Modeling change in prehistoric social systems. In *For Theory Building in Archaeology*, edited by Lewis R. Binford, pp. 327–51. New York: Academic Press.

   1977b. Woodland social change in west-central Illinois. *Mid-Continental Journal of Archaeology*, 2 (1): 67–98.

   1978. Mortuary practices and the study of prehistoric social systems. In *Advances in Archaeological Method and Theory*, vol. 1, edited by M.B. Schiffer, pp. 106–41. New York: Academic Press.

   1983. Woodland social change in the central Midwest: A review and evaluation of interpretive trends. *North American Archaeologist* 4 (2): 141–61.

Tainter, J.A., and R.H. Cordy 1977. An archaeological analysis of social ranking and residence groups in prehistoric Hawaii. *World Archaeology* 9 (1): 95–112.

Thomas, David H. 1971. Prehistoric subsistence–settlement patterns of the Reese River Valley, Central Nevada. Ph.D. Dissertation, University of California, Davis. Ann Arbor: University Microfilms.

   1975. Nonsite sampling in archaeology: up the creek without a site? In *Sampling in Archaeology*, edited by J.W. Mueller, pp. 61–81. Tucson: The University of Arizona Press.

   1976. *Figuring Anthropology: First Principles of Probability and Statistics*. New York: Holt, Rinehart and Winston.

   1982. The 1981 Alta Toquima Village Project: a preliminary report. Desert Research Institute, Social Sciences Center Technological Report Series No. 27.

   1983a. The archaeology of Monitor Valley: 1. Epistemology. American Museum of Natural History, Anthropological Papers 58 (1). New York.

   1983b. The archaeology of Monitor Valley: 2. Gatecliff Shelter. American Museum of Natural History, Anthropological Papers 59 (1). New York.

   In press a. The archaeology of Monitor Valley: 3. Survey and additional excavations. American Museum of Natural History, Anthropological Papers.

   In press b. The archaeology of Monitor Valley: 4. The Alta Toquima Complex. American Museum of Natural History, Anthropological Papers.

Thomas, David Hurst, and Deborah Mayer 1983. Behavioral faunal analysis of selected horizons. In *The Archaeology of Monitor Valley*: 2. *Gatecliff Shelter*, by David Hurst Thomas. American Museum of Natural History, Anthropological Papers 59 (1): 353–91.

Tipper, John C. 1979. Rarefaction and rarefiction–The use and abuse of a method in paleoecology. *Paleobiology* 5 (4): 423–34.

Toll, H.W. 1981. Ceramic comparisons concerning redistribution in Chaco Canyon, New Mexico. In *Production and Distribution: A Ceramic Viewpoint*, edited by H. Howard and E.L. Morris, pp. 83–121. Oxford: BAR International Series 120.

Torrence, Robin 1983. Time budgeting and hunter–gatherer technology. In *Hunter–Gatherer Economy in Prehistory: A European Perspective*, edited by Geoff Bailey, pp. 11–22. Cambridge: Cambridge University Press.

van der Leeuw, S.E. 1977. Towards a study of the economics of pottery making. In *Ex Horreo*, edited by B.L. van Beek *et al.*, pp. 68–76. Amsterdam: I.P.P.

Voyatzoglou, M. 1974. The jar makers of Thrapsano in Crete. *Expedition* 16: 18–24.

Wagner, P.L. 1960. *The Human Use of the Earth*. Glencoe, IL: Free Press.

Wallace, Henry 1983. The mortars, petroglyphs, and trincheras on Rillito Peak. *The Kiva* 48 (3): 137–246.

Washburn, D.K. 1977. *A Symmetry Analysis of Upper Gila Area Ceramic Design*. Papers of the Peabody Museum of Archaeology and Ethnology, vol. 68.

   1983a. Symmetry analysis of ceramic design: two tests of the method of Neolithic material from Greece and the Aegean. In *Structure and Cognition in Art*, edited by D.K. Washburn, pp. 38–165. Cambridge, MA: Cambridge University Press.

   1983b *Structure and Cognition in Art*. Cambridge: Cambridge University Press.

Whallon, Robert, 1968. Investigations of Late Prehistoric social organization in New York State In *New Perspectives in Archaeology*, edited by S.R. Binford and L. Binford, pp. 223–44. Chicago: Aldine.

1984. Unconstrained clustering for the analysis of spatial distributions in archaeology. In *Intrasite Spatial Analysis in Archaeology*, edited by H. Hietala, pp. 242–77. Cambridge: Cambridge University Press.

Whallon, Robert, and James A. Brown, eds., 1982. *Essays on Archaeological Typology*. Evanston, IL: Center for American Archaeology Press.

White, Leslie A. 1949. *The Evolution of Culture; the Development of Civilization to the Fall of Culture*. New York: McGraw–Hill.

1959. *The Evolution of Culture*. New York: Farrar Strauss.

Whittaker, Robert H. 1972. Evolution and measurement of species diversity. *Taxon* 21 (2/3): 213–51.

Whittlesey, S.M. 1974. Identification of imported ceramics through analysis of attributes. *The Kiva* 40 (1–2): 101–12.

Wiessner, Polly 1983. Style and social information in Kalahari San projectile points. *American Antiquity* 48 (2): 253–76.

1984. Reconsidering the behavioral basis of style. *Journal of Anthropological Archaeology* 3 (3): 190–234.

Williams, Carrington Bonsor 1964. *Patterns in the Balance of Nature and Related Problems in Quantitative Archaeology*. New York: Academic Press.

Williams, S. 1985. Turkana ornament and representation: a postmodern application of Mauss' *The Gift*. Unpublished Master's thesis, Department of Anthropology, State University of New York, Binghamton.

Williamson, M. 1973. Species diversity in ecological communities. In *The Mathematical Theory of the Dynamics of Biological Populations*, edited by M.S. Bartlett and R.W. Hiorns, pp. 325–35. New York: Academic Press.

Wing, Elizabeth S., and Antoinette Brown 1979. *Paleonutrition: Method and Theory in Prehistoric Foodways*. New York: Academic Press.

Wobst, H.M. 1977. Stylistic behavior and information exchange. In *For The Director: Research Essays in Honor of James B. Griffen*, edited by C.E. Cleland, pp. 317–42 Anthropology Papers No. 61. Museum of Anthropology, University of Michigan.

Wolda, Henk 1983. Diversity, diversity indices and tropical cockroaches [Blattarial]. *Oecologia* 58 (3): 290–8.

Wolff, J. 1981. *The Social Production of Art*. New York: St. Martin's Press.

Wright, R. 1983. Standardization as evidence for craft specialization: a case study. Paper presented at the annual meeting of the American Anthropological Association, Chicago.

Wuthnow, R., J.D. Hunter, A. Bergeson, and E. Kurzweil 1984. *Cultural Analysis. The Work of Peter Berger, Mary Douglas, Michel Foucault and J. Habermas*. London and Boston: Routledge and Kegan Paul.

Yellen, J.R. 1977. *Archaeological Approaches to the Present: Models for Reconstructing the Past*. New York: Academic Press.

Zar, J.H. 1974. *Biostatistical Analysis*. Englewood Cliffs, NJ: Prentice Hall.

INDEX

Peer Polity Interaction and Socio-political Change
Edited by Colin Renfrew and John Cherry

Thirteen leading archaeologists have contributed to this formative study of the socio-political processes – notably imitation, competition, warfare, and the exchange of material goods and information – that can be observed within early complex societies, particularly those just emerging into statehood. Their common aim is to explain the remarkable formal similarities that exist between institutions, ideologies and material remains in a variety of cultures characterized by independent political centres yet to be brought under the control of a single, unified jurisdiction.

A major statement of the conceptual approach is followed by en case-studies from a wide variety of times and places, including Minoan Crete, early historic Greece and Japan, the classic Maya, the American Mid-West in the Hopewellian period, early Bronze Age and early Iron Age Europe, and the British Isles in the late Neolithic.

Contributors: GINA L. BARNES; RICHARD BRADLEY; DAVID P. BRAUN; SARA CHAMPION; TIMOTHY CHAMPION; ROBERT CHAPMAN; JOHN CHERRY; DAVID A. FREIDEL; RICHARD HODGES; COLIN RENFREW; JEREMY A. SABLOFF; STEPHEN SHENNAN; ANTHONY SNODGRASS.

0 521 22914 6

Hunters in Transition
Edited by Marek Zvelebil

Hunters in Transition analyses one of the crucial events in human cultural evolution: the emergence of postglacial hunter-gatherer communities and the development of farming. Traditionally, the advantages of settled agriculture have been assumed, and the transition to farming has been viewed in terms of the simple dispersal of early farming communities northwards across Europe. The contributors to this volume, however, adopt a fresh, more subtle approach. From a hunter-gatherer perspective, settled farming implies both advantages and disadvantages, and certainly involves organizational disruption during the period of transition and far reaching social consequences for the existing way of life.

The hunter-gatherer economy and farming shared in fact a common objective: a guaranteed food supply in a changing natural and social environment. Drawing extensively on research in eastern Europe and temperate Asia, the book argues persuasively for the essential unity of all postglacial adaptations whether leading to the dispersal of farming or to the retention and elaboration of existing hunter-gatherer strategies.

Contributors: TAKERU AKAZAWA; PAUL DOLUKHANOV; CLIVE GAMBLE; STEFAN KAROL KOZLOWSKI; JANUSZ KOZLOWSKI; JAMES LEWTHWAITE; GERALD MATYUSHIN; PETER ROWLEY-CONWY; SLAVOMIL VENCL; MAREK ZVELEBIL.

0 521 26868 0

Island Societies
Archaeological Approaches to Evolution and Transformation
Edited by Patrick Kirch

Concentrating their attention on the Pacific Islands, the contributors to this book show how the tightly focused social and economic systems of islands offer archaeologists a series of unique opportunities for tracking and explaining prehistoric change. Over the last thirty years excavation has revolutionised Oceanic archaeology and, as the major problems of cultural origins and island sequences have been resolved, archaeologists have come increasingly to study social change and to integrate newly acquired data on material culture with older ethnographic and ethnohistorical materials. The fascinating results of this work, centring on the evolution of complex Oceanic chiefdoms into something very much like classic 'archaic states', are authoritatively surveyed here for the first time.

Contributors: R. C. GREEN; GEORGE J. GUMERMAN; ROBERT J. HOMMON; TERRY L. HUNT; PATRICK V. KIRCH; BARRY ROLETT; MATTHEW SPRIGGS; CHRISTOPHER M. STEVENSON.

0 521 30189 0

The Archaeology of Prehistoric Coastlines
Edited by Geoff Bailey and John Parkington

The Archaeology of Prehistoric Coastlines offers a conspectus of recent work on coastal archaeology, examining the various ways in which hunter-gatherers and farmers across the world exploited marine resources such as fish, shellfish and waterfowl in prehistory.

Changes in sea levels and the balance of marine ecosystems have altered coastal environments significantly in the last ten thousand years and the impact of these changes on the nature of human settlement and subsistence is assessed. General consideration is also given to the ways settlement may have been geared to seasonal movements of population and resource scheduling and altered over time in response to variations in resource abundance and climate. An overview of coastal archaeology as a developing discipline is followed by ten case studies from a wide variety of places, including Scandinavia, Japan, Tasmania and New Zealand, Peru, South Africa and the United States.

Contributors: TAKERU AKAZAWA; ATHOLL J. ANDERSON; GEOFF BAILEY; SANDRA BOWDLER; BILL BUCHANAN; MARGARET R. DEITH; JON M. ERLANSON; ROBERT A. FELDMAN; MICHAEL A. GLASSOW; TONY MANHIRE; MICHAEL E. MOSELEY; JOHN PARKINGTON; CEDRIC POGGENPOEL; PRISCILLA RENOUF; TIM ROBEY; JUDITH SEALY; JUDITH C. SHACKLETON; LARRY R. WILCOXON; DAVID R. YESNER.

0 521 25036 6

Documentary Archaeology in the New World
Edited by Mary Beaudry

Designed to appeal to a broad spectrum of archaeologists and historians, *Documentary Archaeology in the New World* outlines a fresh approach to the archaeological study of the historic cultures of North America which places history alongside anthropology, cultural geography, and a whole range of cognate disciplines.

The authors' common belief is that historical archaeologists must develop their own frameworks for interpretation through exhaustive documentary research rather than simply borrow models from colleagues working in the prehistoric past. Specific topics examined in individual papers include urban archaeology, historical ecology, consumerism, smuggling, folk classifications, gender relations, ethnicity, seasonality and ideology. The approach presented could readily be adapted to historical cultures outside North America and the volume as a whole will serve both as a guide to the techniques of documentary analysis available and as a source for the innovative interpretation of historical archaeological materials anywhere in the world.

Contributors: LAWRENCE BABITS; MARY C. BEAUDRY; JOANNE V. BOWEN; KATHLEEN J. BRAGDON; MARLEY R. BROWN III; JULIA B. CURTIS; HENRY LANGHORNE; JANET E. LONG; GEORGE L. MILLER; HENRY M. MILLER; STEPHEN A. MROZOWSKI; FRASER D. NEIMAN; ADRIAN PRAETZELLIS; MARY PRAETZELLIS; PETER R. SCHMIDT; NANCY S. SEASHOLES; GARRY W. STONE; ANNE E. YENTSCH.

0 521 30343 5

Centre and Periphery in the Ancient World
Edited by Michael Rowlands, Mogens Larsen and Kristian Kristiansen

This collaborative volume is concerned with long-term social change. Envisaging individual societies as interlinked and interdependent parts of a global social system, the aim of the contributors is to determine the extent to which ancient societies were shaped over time by their incorporation into – or resistance to – the larger system. Their particular concern is the dependent relationship between technically and socially more developed societies with a strong state ideology at the centre and the simpler societies that functioned principally as sources of raw materials and manpower on the periphery of the system.

The papers in the first part of the book are all concerned with political developments in the Ancient Near East and explore the concept of a regional system as a framework for analysis. Part 2 examines the problems of conceptualising local societies as discrete centres of development in the context of both the Near East and prehistoric Europe during the second millennium BC. Part 3 then presents a comprehensive analytical study of the Roman Empire as a single system showing how its component parts often relate to each other in uneven and contradictory ways.

Contributors: COLIN HASELGROVE; LOTTE HEDEAGER; PHILIP KOHL; KRISTIAN KRISTIANSEN; MOGENS LARSEN; MARIO LIVERANI; LEON MARFOE; ROGER MOOREY; DAPHNE NASH; MICHAEL ROWLANDS; CARLO ZACCAGNINI.

0 521 25103 6

The Archaeology of Contextual Meanings
Edited by Ian Hodder

This *New Directions* volume focuses on the symbolism of artefacts. It seeks at once to refine current theory and method relating to interpretation and show, with examples, how to conduct this sort of archaeological work. Some contributors work with the material culture of modern times or the historic period, areas in which the symbolism of mute artefacts has traditionally been thought most accessible. However, the book also contains a good number of applications in prehistory to demonstrate the feasibility of symbolic interpretation where good contextual data survive from the distant past.

In relation to wider debates within the social sciences, the volume is characterised by a concern to place abstract symbolic codes within their historical context and within the contexts of social actions. In this respect, it develops further some of the ideas presented in Dr Hodder's *Symbolic and Structural Archaeology*, an earlier volume in this series.

Contributors: SHEENA CRAWFORD: LIV GIBBS; IAN HODDER; ROBERT JAMESON; NICK MERRIMAN; KEITH RAY; TONY SINCLAIR; MARIE LOUISE SØRENSON; TIMOTHY TAYLOR; LINDA THERKORN; SARAH WILLIAMS.

0 521 32924 8

Archaeology as Long-term History
Edited by Ian Hodder

In marked contrast with the anthropological and cross-cultural approaches that have featured so prominently in the archaeological research of the last twenty-five years, this contributory volume emphasises the archaeological significance of historical method and philosophy. Drawing particularly on the work of R. G. Collingwood, the contributors show that the notion of 'history seen from within' is a viable approach that can be applied in ethnoarchaeology and in both historic and prehistoric archaeology. There is a discussion of short, medium and long-term historical structures in relation to social events generating observed material culture patterning. Examination of the relationship between structure and event within historical contexts leads to new insights into the interdependence of continuity and change, and into the nature of widely recognised processes such as acculturation, diffusion and migration.

Contributors: DAVID COLLETT; ALEXANDER VON GERNET; KEVIN GREENE; KNUT HELSKOG; IAN HODDER; PAUL LANE; HENRIETTA MOORE; JACQUELINE NOWAKOWSI; AJAY PRATAP; PETER TIMMINS; ELISABETH VESTERGAARD; JAMES WHITLEY.

0 521 32923 X

The Origins and Development of the Andean State

Edited by Jonathan Haas, Thomas Pozorski, and Sheila Pozorski

The work of sixteen leading scholars actively engaged in fieldwork in Peru, this volume brings together recent research on the evolution of civilization in the Andean region of South America. Beginning with early chiefdom societies living along the Peruvian coast 2000 years before Christ, the authors trace the growing complexity of Andean states and empires over the next 3000 years. They examine the accomplishments of the ancient Andeans in the rise of the magnificent monumental architecture and the construction of unparalleled prehistoric irrigation systems. They also look at the dominant role of warfare in Andean societies and at the collapse of empires in the millennia before the arrival of the Spanish in 1534. Together, the contributors provide the first systematic study of the evolution of polities along the dry coastal plains and high mountain valleys of the Peruvian Andes.

Contributors: RICHARD DAGGETT; ROBERT A. FELDMAN; JONATHAN HAAS; CHARLES M. HASTINGS; WILLIAM H. ISBELL; ALEXANDRA M. ULANA KLYMYSHYN; CAROL J. MACKEY; BETTY J. MEGGER; THOMAS POZORSKI; SHEILA POZORSKI; KATHARINA J SCHREIBER; ISUMI SHIMADA; JOHN TOPIC; THEREZA TOPIC; M.C. WEBB; DAVID J. WILSON

0 521 33102 1